Usage-Driven Database Design

From Logical Data Modeling through Physical Schema Definition

George Tillmann

Apress®

Usage-Driven Database Design: From Logical Data Modeling through Physical Schema Definition

George Tillmann
Ship Bottom, New Jersey, USA

ISBN-13 (pbk): 978-1-4842-2721-3   ISBN-13 (electronic): 978-1-4842-2722-0
DOI 10.1007/978-1-4842-2722-0

Library of Congress Control Number: 2017938116

Managing Director: Welmoed Spahr
Editorial Director: Todd Green
Acquisitions Editor: Jonathan Gennick
Development Editor: Laura Berendson
Coordinating Editor: Jill Balzano
Copy Editor: Kim Wimpsett
Compositor: SPi Global
Indexer: SPi Global
Artist: SPi Global
Cover image designed by Freepik

Distributed to the book trade worldwide by Springer Science+Business Media New York, 233 Spring Street, 6th Floor, New York, NY 10013. Phone 1-800-SPRINGER, fax (201) 348-4505, e-mail orders-ny@springer-sbm.com, or visit www.springeronline.com. Apress Media, LLC is a California LLC and the sole member (owner) is Springer Science + Business Media Finance Inc (SSBM Finance Inc). SSBM Finance Inc is a **Delaware** corporation.

For information on translations, please e-mail rights@apress.com, or visit www.apress.com/rights-permissions.

Apress titles may be purchased in bulk for academic, corporate, or promotional use. eBook versions and licenses are also available for most titles. For more information, reference our Print and eBook Bulk Sales web page at www.apress.com/bulk-sales.

Any source code or other supplementary material referenced by the author in this book is available to readers on GitHub via the book's product page, located at www.apress.com/9781484227213. For more detailed information, please visit www.apress.com/source-code.

Printed on acid-free paper

For

Eva Marie

and in memory of

Catherine.

Contents at a Glance

Contents

About the Author

George Tillmann is a retired Booz, Allen Hamilton partner, a former programmer, analyst, management consultant, and CIO who managed Booz Allen's global IT organization. He brings more than 30 years experience as a database administrator, database consultant, and database product designer. He has written two books, was a Computerworld columnist, and has had articles published in CIO, Infoworld, Techworld, Data Base, The Standard, Database Programming & Design, among others. He is a former member of the ANSI/X3/SPARC Data Base Systems Study Group.

Preface

The common knowledge of a profession often goes unrecorded in technical literature for two reasons: one need not preach commonplaces to the initiated, and one should not attempt to inform the uninitiated in publications they do not read.

—Stephen Jay Gould

Human beings, who are almost unique in having the ability to learn from the experience of others, are also remarkable for their apparent disinclination to do so.

—Douglas Adams

Every year Stack Overflow (a programmer Q&A site on the Stack Exchange Network) surveys readers about a number of issues. A 2015 survey of more than 26,000 system developers found that only 38 percent had a computer science degree and 33 percent had never taken even one college computer science course. An amazing 42 percent said that they were totally self-taught.[1]

These miserable statistics are for system developers as a whole. Although there are no numbers readily available, those who have spent decades in the database arena indicate that database designer training is even worse. Universities and companies spend more time and more education dollars on the process side of system development, leaving the data side the underserved orphan.

What Happened?

Many database designs are terrible because many database designers are undertrained. Don't blame the designers—they are working in a system in which all the cards are stacked against them. The problem is a poor system of educating database staff. Anecdotal information indicates that the average database designer or database programmer has about 10 percent of the training in information management that the average process-oriented system designer or programmer has in process management. The majority of database designers learned their trade from database management system (DBMS) vendor courses or from reading books and trade publications.

The training goals of the average DBMS vendor, understandably, do not focus on providing a balanced data management education but rather on teaching customer staff how to use its products. The student might come away schooled in the use of a particular DBMS, but any understanding of the fundamentals of what it is to be a database management system are serendipitous.

Most database books are no better. There are many titles on information management. Some purport to focus on logical data modeling, others on database design, and the majority on both. Some mention a specific data architecture (hierarchical, relational, object-oriented, NoSQL, etc.) or product (Oracle, DB2, Cassandra, etc.), while the covers of most of these books make no claim to an alignment or preference for a specific architecture or product. However, the contents of these books tell a different story. Almost all of the "generic" books are saturated with relational terms, relational concepts, and relational thinking. Any concession to generic or nonrelational information management is marginal. The reader is left with a tunnel-vision view of the field.

Worse, techniques, such as logical data modeling, which should have nothing to do with any particular DBMS architecture or any physical design issues, are jam-packed with DBMS-specific—usually relational—terminology and thinking. For example, logical data modeling relationships are represented using foreign keys, primary keys are arbitrarily selected from the pool of candidate keys, and many-to-may relationships are "resolved" with junction tables.

There is nothing wrong with the relational model. In fact, no database education would be complete without a good understanding of the relational model and relational database management systems. However, relational is not the only architecture, not the only DBMS, and not the only way to design a database. A myopic education might train the reader in how to use a specific DBMS but imparts little of what it is to be a DBMS. Learning about the relational model is essential; learning about it exclusively is harmful.

Another common characteristic of most database design books is that they are written by academics. Many of these books are excellent, and every database professional should have a bookshelf bristling with their titles. But a balanced education needs more than just a classroom view of the information management world. Formal instruction is good, but it just doesn't go far enough. Most database designers will not find themselves in the rarefied air of the ivory tower but rather deep down in the corporate trenches with, as Johnny Cash put it, "the mud and the blood and the beer." They need the practical as well as the academic, the team room as well as the classroom.

This book's approach to data management is far less theoretical and far less dogmatic than the books sitting on that bookshelf. Rather, it focuses on what works, what doesn't work, and what to avoid at all costs. It includes some of the knowledge, techniques, and tricks that can turn a disaster into a success. The major influences on this book certainly include numerous academic authors but also incorporate the experiences of database developers, designers, and users all over the world who did it right or, unfortunately, did it wrong.

Finally Resolving the Database Design Missing Link

There are many books on logical data modeling and many books on creating a database schema for a particular DBMS. There is also much that can be learned from listening to the tales of the experienced. However, this is not enough. There are certain critical topics where both books and experience come up short. What is missing in the database design process is an effective and efficient way to get from the logical data model to the physical database schema. The problem is that the logical data model is a static look at the definition of the data documented using techniques specific to data. Logical process models are a dynamic look at how data are used in an application or by an end user.

Process models have their own techniques geared to documenting business functions. What is needed is a way to merge process and data so that the database design represents the union of definition and use. This is the *database design missing link*—the critical component that marries these two distinct elements. When this link is missing, the database design focuses almost entirely on the definition of data without taking use into account. These databases tend to be poor performers and the cause of numerous end-user complaints. Alternatively, a database design can be based solely on use. These databases become prematurely old, requiring costly and constant maintenance and updates.

Usage-Driven Database Design (U3D) gives the database designer the necessary tools to resolve the missing link problem. Using U3D, database designs can have the resilience of the data model with the functional responsiveness of the process model. U3D can eliminate the database design missing link.

The goal of this book, therefore, is not so much education as inheritance—to pass on to the database designer, database administrator (DBA), or database programmer the technique and tricks uncovered and used by some of the best and some of the worst database people in the world.

A Solution

This book is divided into five parts. Part I consists of a single chapter; Chapter 1, "Introduction to Usage-Driven Database Design," introduces the four database design principles. Although these principles are geared toward database design, they are, in fact, a sound starting point for any system development activity. The chapter ends with the introduction of usage-driven database design, an end-to-end framework for developing a functioning database, starting with the logical data model and ending with a physical database schema.

Part II focuses on logical data modeling. Chapter 2, "The E-R Approach," introduces Peter Chen's entity-relationship (E-R) approach, while Chapter 3, "More About the E-R Approach," focuses on more advanced logical data modeling topics. Chapter 4, "Building the Logical Data Model," uses the Usage-Driven Database Design: Logical Data Modeling phase as a template to tackle the real-world tasks of actually building a logical data model for an enterprise.

Chapter 5, "LDM Best Practices," presents lessons learned from the database trenches. Chapter 6, "LDM Pitfalls," gives advice on what to avoid when data modeling. Chapter 7, "LDM Perils to Watch For," presents some logical data modeling cautionary tales.

In Part III, the logical data model becomes a functioning database schema. Chapter 8, "Introduction to Physical Database Design," presents a limited history of data management; however, the focus is gaining practical rather than historical insight. The concepts presented are used in later chapters for creating great databases.

Chapter 9, "Introduction to Physical Schema Definition," introduces the four steps in the Usage-Driven Database Design: Physical Schema Definition phase that will turn the logical data model into a physical database schema.

Chapter 10, "Transformation: Creating the Physical Data Model," converts the logical data model into a physical data model.

Chapter 11, "Utilization: Merging Data and Process," modifies the physical data model to reflect exactly how an application will use the database. This is an important chapter because many database design approaches do not adequately take data usage into account.

Chapter 12, "Formalization: Creating a Schema," converts the modified physical data model into a functioning physical database schema and subschemas.

Chapter 13, "Customization: Enhancing Performance," addresses those situations where a simple database design cannot handle the load that will be placed on it. This step introduces performance-enhancing techniques (software, hardware, NoSQL, etc.) that can be applied to almost any situation to accommodate almost any performance requirements.

Chapter 14, "The Data Warehouse," shows how U3D can be used to construct a data warehouse to support a decision support system.

Chapter 15, "The Big Data Decision Support System," shows how U3D can be used with nontraditional data management products, such as Hadoop, to accommodate unstructured Big Data.

Part IV contains a single chapter, Chapter 16, "A Look Ahead," which discusses where the DBMS community (teachers, vendors, and technical users) are or should be going.

Part V contains five appendixes that include a glossary, data management object definitions, formulas, and a list of U3D deliverables.

This book is aggressively practical and generic. For example, it vigorously keeps logical data modeling logical, while holding off on physical issues until physical database design—not to justify some philosophical or theoretical construct but for the practical reason that it greatly increases the chances of developing a successful database design.

It is DBMS generic or agnostic in that it does not tie the hands of the developer who is attempting to solve real-world information management problems. The right solution might involve a relational DBMS or it might require a NoSQL DBMS. Or, more likely, the DBMS choice was made some time ago, and now the database designer needs help in making the best of an imperfect DBMS situation.

In summary, this book is for the undervalued data management professional who has to transform a combination of glossy DBMS vendor brochures and dry textbook commentary into a functioning fundamental part of the enterprise.

George Tillmann

george_tillmann@gmx.com

georgetillmann@optonline.net

Note

1. The Stack Exchange, http://stackoverflow.com/research/
    developer-survey-2015#profile-education

PART I

■ ■ ■

Introduction

PART I

Introduction

CHAPTER 1

■ ■ ■

Introduction to Usage-Driven Database Design

As to methods, there may be a million and then some, but principles are few. The man who grasps principles can successfully select his own methods. The man who tries methods, ignoring principles, is sure to have trouble.

—Harrington Emerson
(American efficiency engineer and business theorist)

Those are my principles. If you don't like them, I have others.

—Groucho Marx

In 2015, the IT industry cost the world about $3.5 trillion according to Gartner, Inc., a research and advisory firm.[1] The Standish Group[2] reported that, in the United States alone, about $250 billion of that was spent on application development. Less than 30 percent (about $72 billion) was spent on successful undertakings, with almost $50 billion written off on failed projects. In the United States, another $130 billion was spent on projects that were completed but were over budget, late, or lacked promised functionality. A pretty dismal picture. Why?

In almost any area of endeavor, there are experts and there are neophytes. You can usually recognize the neophyte by his nose in the "how to" book. The expert? He is just standing there, comfortable that any needed knowledge is in his head. Let's call it the Confident Expert Syndrome.

However, in at least three professions there is no Confident Expert Syndrome. The first is airline pilot. Any senior airline captain will tell you that they meticulously go through both the takeoff and landing checklists. They will also tell you that they are wary of flying with a copilot who cuts checklist corners. That's the reason they have lived long enough to become a senior captain.

The second profession where the Confident Expert Syndrome does not apply is project management. The seasoned project manager is the one poring over the system development manuals and plumbing the depths of the project plan. They know that

© George Tillmann 2017
G. Tillmann, *Usage-Driven Database Design*, DOI 10.1007/978-1-4842-2722-0_1

success flows from following the system development life cycle (SDLC) methodology and the project plan *to the letter*. The neophyte project manager is the one who feels that steps can be left out or shortened or that time can be made up in future tasks. Successful project managers know that if you want to bring the project in on time, on budget, and fully functional, then you must complete every step.

The third profession where the Confident Expert Syndrome does not (or should not) exist is database designer. Experienced database designers are the ones who perform all the necessary design functions, in their proper sequence, leaving out nothing. It is the rookie designers who think that the single database design course they took, taught by their database management system (DBMS) vendor, is all they need to design quality databases.

However, there is one significant difference between poor project management or poor analysis or poor programming and poor database design. Poor project management results in failed projects, and poor analysis and poor programming result in programs that will not compile or run. Poor database design, on the other hand, results (far too often) in a database that seems to work just fine.

Database management systems, by their very nature, cover up a multitude of design errors. It might run slow—it might run very slow—but it will usually work. An IT shop might live with a poor database design for years, blaming the DBMS software, the hardware, the system software, or even the application programmers for performance that is the result of very poor up-front database design decisions.

How do you design good databases? Do what the pros do—follow the tried and true steps for creating a great design. However, while there are a few good database design techniques and guidelines, many if not most of them have not been incorporated into a full, end-to-end database design method. Application developers have great end-to-end methods; in fact, many system development life-cycle products, if followed, can lead to great applications. Project managers have a host of available project management methods, techniques, and tools to choose from. Database designers? Not so much...at least until now...sort of.

Doesn't such a process already exist? Well, yes and no. Snippets of a method are available and in use, but there is no end-to-end solution. However, that is not the only problem.

Looking to the best practices of the experienced is not always enough. Even premier development approaches, first-class training courses, and books by experts have a common failing. They all lack an effective approach to merge the definition of the data with the data's use.

There are, or should be, two major inputs to any database design approach—the logical data model and the logical process model (both are discussed in detail in later chapters). *Logical data modeling* uncovers the definition of data, their characteristics, and their relationship with other data. *Logical data models* are a static though longer-term picture of an organization's data. *Logical process modeling* documents how the data move through the enterprise. *Logical process models* paint a shorter-lived albeit dynamic picture of the information—the processes and procedures—an enterprise uses to go about its business.

Many traditional database design approaches focus exclusively on the logical data model, ignoring how the data will be used, resulting in poor performing systems. Other database design approaches focus on the use of the data, while giving short shrift to the definition of data, resulting in databases that are expensive to maintain. The absent component to effectively merge the dynamic process models with the static data models is the *database design missing link*.

This book solves the missing link problem, providing a technique that effectively and efficiently marries data and process. The result is a database design encapsulating the stability and longevity of the logical data model with the functionality and applicability of the logical process models.

The goal of this book is to provide the designer with the best thinking and best practices on database design, gleaned from decades of hands-on experience working with database designers in dozens of IT organizations. Where best practices are lacking or acceptable methods or approaches do not exist, this book provides them.

The approach presented here is a composite of how to use what has worked and how to avoid what hasn't worked at all costs. But is it a database design methodology?

It is not really a method because a method should bristle with excruciatingly detailed steps. This approach is better called a framework for developing databases—more than an unrelated string of techniques but less than ten binders of forms to fill out.

The pillars of this approach are four database design principles.

Database Design Principle 1: Separation Principle

The *Separation Principle* specifies the separation of logical design from physical design. This is a simple concept that has been ignored, neglected, and corrupted by some of the best minds in the IT industry. The principle is as follows: identify, analyze, and exhaust everything knowable about the logical definition of data before considering any physical design concepts.

Many years ago, a time-sharing service published a cartoon showing a number of programmers at their desks while one individual was walking out of the frame saying, "You guys start coding. I'm going up to ask the users what they want."

How could the programmers code an application without any idea of what the users wanted that application to do? Almost every analyst and programmer knows of such situations and how they invariably result in disaster.

There are few real laws in IT, but one of them surely is to figure out what the system is supposed to do before determining how it is going to do it. System development methodologies are all based on that law: *figure out the what before the how*. It is easy to see this in waterfall methodologies, where analysis or requirements definition (logical data modeling and logical process modeling) is completed before any design or development work (physical data modeling, physical process modeling, or schema definition) begins. It is less obvious in the various iterative methodologies and techniques, such as rapid application development, prototyping, continuous improvement, joint application development, agile development, and so on. However, even these methods and techniques involve figuring out what is wanted before determining how to do it (Figure 1-1). It might take a half-dozen cycles of sitting down with a user to figure out what is wanted and then coding the results before showing them to the user for additional information or changes, but the principle is always the same— put the parachute on before jumping out of the plane.

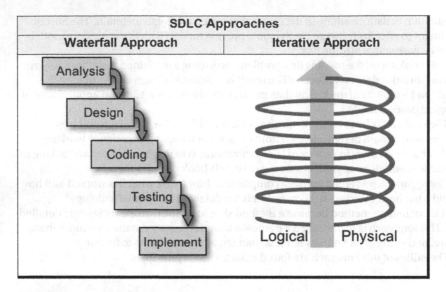

Figure 1-1. *Waterfall and iterative SDLC Approaches*

There are project management books that describe the disasters that await the system developer who ignores this best practice. Unfortunately, database design books often ignore this principle with similar disastrous consequences.

The hard reality is that data require the same insight and attention as processes do, which is why the first principle of this book is to always, even with iterative development, separate the *what* (logical design) from the *how* (physical design).

There is a corollary to Principle 1—call it the *Real World Corollary*. It states the purpose of logical design is to document the real world, which, in this context, is the business world. There are two parts to Corollary 1.

- *Corollary 1 (a)*: A logical design is valid if, and only if, it reflects the real (business) world.

- *Corollary 1 (b)*: A logical design is invalid if it contains nonreal (business) world objects or concepts. Invalid objects and concepts include elements belonging in physical design such as foreign keys, pointers, and disk drives.

Database Design Principle 2: Distinction Principle

The *Distinction Principle* distinguishes logical data modeling from logical process modeling. All data definitions, characteristics, and relationships need to be analyzed, designed, and documented separately from all process definitions, characteristics, and uses. There are five reasons to distinguish logical data modeling from logical process modeling.

- *The nature of the two is different.* Logical data modeling is concerned with the definition of data, not its use. In fact, designers strive to keep the use of data out of its definition.

- *The longevity of each is different.* Data tends to be far more static, stable, and unchangeable, while processes tend to be volatile, variable, and unstable. You can count on the description of processes changing ten times more often than the definition of data. The wise database designer keeps the two concepts apart to avoid confusion and the need to redo completed work.

- *The techniques and tools to document data differ from those to document processes.* There are a number of techniques to document processes, such as data flow diagrams, flow charts, and structure charts, and a number of software tools supporting these techniques. There are also techniques for database design, such as the entity-relationship approach and IDEF1X, and software tools that implement these and other database design techniques. However, the process side and data side are supported by different techniques, and even different tools, making a unified data-process approach difficult.

- *Data staff training, skills, and experience are different from process staff training, skills, and experience.* Attend any application project team meeting and ask everyone present to raise their hand if they have taken more than one course in process analysis or development (process modeling, process documentation, programming, etc.) provided by a school, outside vendor, or in-house training department. The majority of the people in the room will probably have their hand in the air. Then ask the same question about data. If your organization is like most, then less than 10 percent of the staff will have their hand up. The reason: IT has always been process focused. From the earliest days of IT history to today, data are considered properties or characteristics of a process and not, as it should be, the other way around.

  It would be ideal if all the members of the project team's technical staff were equally skilled in process and data, but that simply is not the case. Unfortunately, to ensure the proper analysis and development of data, a separate, data-trained team on the project is needed.

- *Process definition can overwhelm data definition.* The substantially greater number of process techniques, tools, and staff compared with data techniques, tools, and staff means that project data can be overwhelmed, and critical information and work lost or never completed, unless the study of project data is distinguished from the study of project processes.

These two categories of logical design—data and process—can be antithetical (Table 1-1). This is one of the reasons, among others, that project management often creates two separate teams for data and process.

Table 1-1. *Data-Process Distinction*

Logical Design	
Data	**Process**
• Static	• Dynamic
• Stable	• Unstable
• Long life	• Short life
• Based on definition	• Based on use

This is not to say that the two teams do not need to communicate and coordinate efforts. The deliverables of the two teams, while they need to reflect the work of the other, also need to be independent of each other.

The Difference Between Separation and Distinction

Note that the separation of logical and physical in the first principle is based on the well-studied and well-tested fundamentals of system development (the *what* before the *how*), while the distinction between data and process is strictly for practical reasons.

To underscore this difference, note that Principle 1 is about "separation" while Principle 2 is about "distinction." The two are very different. Think of the Separation Principle as an impenetrable wall between the logical and physical. The Distinction Principle, on the other hand, is not nearly as impenetrable because it is based on how we actually work and not on how we could, or should, work. While violating a "separation" might be a major error, violating a "distinction" can be a major error or just a *faux pas,* depending on the degree of the infraction.

Database Design Principle 3: Convergence Principle

The *Convergence Principle* governs the merging of physical process models with physical data models. During physical design, data and process should converge into a single usage-driven physical database design.

Visit a bookstore and look at the database design books on the shelves. Read the books or chapters that deal with logical data modeling and see how many of them—which are supposed to document the business definition of data—are festooned with talk of foreign keys and transitive dependencies. Then look at the books or chapters dealing with database schema creation and observe how many of them do not take a serious look at how the data will be used. *Many authors have it backwards.*

The right time to add usage to a database design is after the distinct physical data and the distinct physical process models are complete. Then, and only then, the physical process model can be *merged* with the physical data model to develop a hybrid data model that represents both definition and use of data. In simplest terms, you describe a database based on its definition, then you augment it based on its use.

The Separation, Distinction, and Convergence Principles

The first three principles can be summarized as follows: usage should not exist at all in the logical data model, but it should be deeply embedded in the physical database design (Table 1-2).

Table 1-2. *The Separation, Distinction, and Convergence Principles*

	Logical Design	Physical Design
Data	Stand alone	Combined
Process	Stand alone	

The central themes of this book are as follows: (1) logical and physical design are kept separate, and (2) during logical design, data and process are kept distinct, but (3) the two converge during physical design.

Database Design Principle 4: Minimal Regression Principle

The *Minimal Regression Principle* states that the database should be designed so that business and technology changes require the least amount of database redesign.

Database design consists of a number of steps from the first logical modeling activities through schema maintenance. Changes to any database design step should not require going back to the beginning and starting the design process over again. Rather, a good database design approach minimizes going back and revisiting previous steps.

For example, there is a flaw in the original design approach if migrating to a new DBMS version requires going back to the user to understand the implications. Minimal regression means that making a change to the deliverable of any database design step should not, ideally, require going back to previous steps. If reexamination of previous steps is required, then the regression should be minimal in terms of both frequency and how far back the designer needs to go.

Usage-Driven Database Design

Usage-Driven Database Design (U3D) is a database design principles–compliant, end-to-end approach to designing databases that encompasses the entire database development life cycle, from logical data modeling through database schema definition.

U3D is divided into two phases (Figure 1-2).

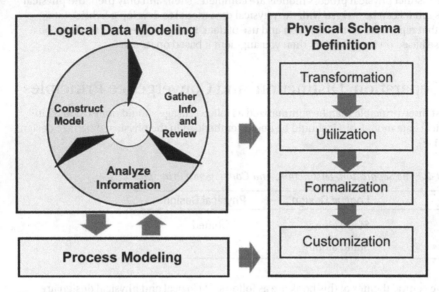

Figure 1-2. *U3D*

The first phase, *Usage-Driven Database Design: Logical Data Modeling* (U3D:LDM), follows the entity-relationship approach, as designed by Peter Chen and expanded over the years by many others, to understand and document the data the database will store and the applications will use.

The second phase, *Usage-Driven Database Design: Physical Schema Definition* (U3D:PSD), converts the logical data model into a fully functional database schema.

The *Process Modeling* step is not part of U3D, but it does interact with it. The logical data modeler and the logical process modeler should be in constant communication, sharing relevant information. The Process Modeling step is also a source of information for the Physical Schema Definition phase.

Logical Data Modeling

The *Logical Data Modeling* (LDM) phase consists of an iterative approach focused on identifying entities and then determining the attributes and relationships supporting those entities. In concert, the identified attributes drive the expansion or modification of entities and relationships. An examination of the relationships between entities involves the refinement of both entities and attributes. With LDM, examining any piece of the puzzle—entity, attribute, or relationship—improves the designer's understanding of all three. This phase consists of three steps.

- In the first step, *Gather Information and Review*, the data modeler assembles all available documentation about the subject area, interviews subject-matter experts, and then reviews the results with both experts and management.

- In the second step, *Analyze Information*, the logical data modeling principles and techniques are applied to the information gathered.

- In the third step, *Construct Model*, the logical data model is created using the collected and analyzed information.

This three-step cycle is repeated as many times as necessary until the LDM is complete to the satisfaction of all concerned parties.

Physical Schema Definition

The second Usage-Driven Database Design phase, *Physical Schema Definition* (PSD), takes a different approach. PSD is divided into four steps. The first step, *Transformation*, turns the logical data model into a physical data model by converting the logical objects (entity, attribute, and relationship) into the physical database objects (record, data field, and linkage).

The second step, *Utilization*, takes the processes defined in Logical Process Modeling and Physical Process Modeling and merges them with the physical data model. The result is a modified or *rationalized physical data model* that represents how the applications will use the database. This is the step where the database design missing link—the inability to adequately and efficiently merge data and process into a single effective database design—is eliminated.

The third step, *Formalization*, identifies the data architecture, database management system, and version that will be used and, combining them with the rationalized physical data model, creates a working database schema.

The fourth and last step, *Customization*, analyzes and improves the performance of the database schema using a number of hardware and software techniques.

U3D is data architecture independent (hierarchical, network, inverted, relational, object-oriented, NoSQL, etc.), system software independent (z/OS, UNIX, Windows, Linux, OS X, etc.), and hardware independent (mainframe, server, PC). It works with Oracle, SQL Server, Cassandra, IMS, DB2…and even flat files.

The Terminology Trap

There appears to be an unwritten law in IT that for every concept there needs to be at least three different words or phrases to describe it. What is the first phase of developing a system? Is it requirements definition? Analysis? Logical design? Conceptual design? User requirements? Sometimes the names change over time. IT was once IS, which was once DP. How many IT staff can differentiate among decision support, business intelligence, and predictive analysis? Is there a real difference?

The same problem exists in database design. This book has two terminology goals. The first is to communicate database concepts, and the second is to be term agnostic. Every attempt is made to inform you of the different labels used to describe a concept but to stick with the term or terms that seem to be most popular—unless that popularity conflicts with the first goal.

For example, most process-oriented system development methodologies, regardless of their specific terminology, are compatible with a logical/physical distinction, where logical steps deal with the understanding of business requirements, devoid of hardware or software, while physical steps deal with the computer-based implementation of those business requirements. But this is not always the case in database design, where the counterpart to logical process design might be something called database conceptual design. Logical database design is often a physical design step dealing with hardware and software issues. In this book logical is logical, and physical is physical—and the twain meet only in Principle 3.

Notes

1. Gartner, Inc., `www.gartner.com/technology/research/it-spending-forecast/`

2. The Standish Group International, Inc., `www.standishgroup.com/Reports2015`

Logical Data Modeling

PART II

Logical Data Modeling

CHAPTER 2

■ ■ ■

The E-R Approach

The sciences do not try to explain, they hardly even try to interpret, they mainly make models. By a model is meant a mathematical construct which, with the addition of certain verbal interpretations, describes observed phenomena.

—John von Neumann

What is the use of a book, thought Alice, without pictures?

—Lewis Carroll

In 1992, Dorothy Keenan, a social worker in Catawba County, North Carolina, had a problem. She was interviewing a boy named Douglas about his family history. As Douglas talked about his relatives, Dorothy took notes. After the interview, Douglas reviewed her notes and agreed with their content.

Here are her notes...

> Douglas was born in 1977. His parents were Gregory and Cathy. His maternal grandparents were Joseph and Marie, who were married in 1945. They had two daughters, Megan (born in 1946) and Cathy (born in 1950). Megan married Brian and adopted a daughter Jennifer before divorcing in 1980. Doug's paternal grandparents were Ryan and Alice, who married in 1942. They had two children, Gregory (born in 1950) and Ellen (born in 1944). Ellen gave birth to a daughter Karen in 1996 before she divorced in 1999. Gregory married Cathy in 1973. They had two sons, Douglas (born in 1977) and Randy (born in 1981). Joseph died in 2001, Marie in 2003, Brian in 1979, Ryan in 2001, and Ellen in 2012.

Social workers spend much of their time interviewing people, and often, those interviews involve recording family histories. Business and systems analysts also spend considerable time interviewing people, but they do it to understand how the business works or exactly what a new computer-based application needs to do. If the interview is about the database, then the notes center on data, the definition of that data, and how they are used in the business. Often the scenario works as follows. The database designer

© George Tillmann 2017

15

G. Tillmann, *Usage-Driven Database Design*, DOI 10.1007/978-1-4842-2722-0_2

or social worker questions the interviewee and records, as meticulously as possible, the interviewee's comments and answers. Then the interviewer goes back to the office and transcribes the interview notes into a more formal format, all the while looking for errors, missing information, or new questions that need to be asked and answered. Then back to the interviewee to review the transcribed notes, looking for errors and omissions, and to ask those new questions uncovered while transcribing the notes. Gaining feedback from the interviewee, the database designer returns to the office and adds the new information just gathered. Then back to the interviewee to confirm the changes...you get the idea. The problem for a social worker, as well as a database designer, is that a complete and accurate interview can require multiple iterations of questions, answers, notes, analysis, and then back with new questions, which might generate or uncover additional significant errors. Interviews are a necessary but error-prone way of gathering information.

Luckily, social worker Dorothy Keenan came across a 1985 book, *Genograms in Family Assessment* by Monica McGoldrick and Randy Gerson, which introduced a graphical method of recording family histories.[1] McGoldrick and Gerson used simple symbols to diagrammatically depict a family. For example, a square represents a male, while a circle a female. A horizontal line between them indicates a relationship. A vertical line shows progeny. An *X* through a square or circle indicates that the individual is dead.

Using a genogram, Dorothy Keenan produced a simple diagram of Douglas' family (Figure 2-1). Just creating the chart raised a few obvious questions.

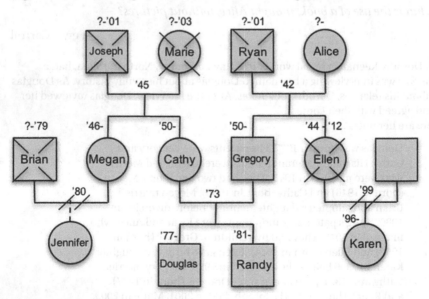

Figure 2-1. *A genogram*

Who did Ellen marry?

When was Brian born?

When was Jennifer born?

Is Alice still alive?

A closer look raised a few not so obvious questions including

> Did Ellen really have a child at age 52?

And it introduced a glaring error.

> Brian could not have died a year before his divorce.

The diagrammatic approach also saves time because the chart can be hand drawn during the interview and "read back" to the interviewee for comments and to fill in missing information—all in one meeting.

The amazing thing about genograms is that they are

- *Accurate*: They can increase the correctness of information transferred from interviewee to interviewer.

- *Efficient*: They can reduce the time required to complete an effective interview.

- *Teachable*: Virtually anyone can learn how to read or how to create them with just a few hours of (self) instruction.

- *Expandable*: You can easily add more complex concepts, such as family member behavior (abusive, manipulative, estranged, etc.), health (heart disease, Alzheimer's, diabetes, etc.), and relationships (divorced, foster child, twins, etc.).

The lesson of including diagrams in data gathering and communicating with users and colleagues is not lost on IT. Flowcharts were, in fact, developed long before the first working computer, going back to the early twentieth century. They were used to document manual workflow but were quickly adapted in the 1950s to represent computer-based algorithms. The first use of a diagram to represent data was probably by Charles Bachman in the 1960s. In all these cases, using diagrams to supplement data gathering increased model accuracy, understanding, and communication.

A Little Data Modeling History

Charles Bachman has an interesting IT history, wearing three separate, thought-related hats. He designed one of the first database management systems and the first network DBMS, an offshoot of which is still available today (IDMS from CA Technologies). Second, he was the driving force behind CODASYL's database standards work, and the standards later published by the Data Base Task Group (DBTG) were greatly influenced by Bachman's network model. DBTG developed a number of database concepts still used today, such as schema, subschema, Data Definition Language (DDL), and Data Manipulation Language (DML). Bachman's third contribution is the *data structure diagram* (DSD), also called the *Bachman diagram*.

In 1969, Bachman published a paper on a technique he and others had used for the previous five years to graphically document database concepts such as entities (called *entity classes*) and relationships (called *set classes*).[2] A rectangle represented an entity, while an arrow represented a relationship. The "owner" of the relationship was at the nonarrowhead end of the relationship line, and the "member" was at the arrowhead end (Figure 2-2).

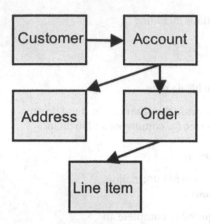

Figure 2-2. *A DSD, or Bachman diagram*

The set is not just the basic network model building block—its owner-member structure is the fundamental one-to-many relationship used throughout the entire database industry.

The Bachman diagram's graphic nature quickly moved beyond the network model to be used by designers of older hierarchical and newer inverted databases as well. It was a clear winner for representing database structure. What was less clear was whether the Bachman diagram was a logical or physical representation of the data, or both. Because the emphasis in the early 1970s was more on the physical side of computing than the logical, many Bachman diagrams were described as pictures of the physical database schemas. Bachman, however, always maintained that his creation was a conceptual picture of the logical structure of data and not its disk and software incarnation.[3]

The Bachman diagram, and the confusion surrounding its use, continued for a few years until, in 1976, Peter Chen published a paper that both expanded the concepts of Bachman and explicitly limited the scope to the logical definition of the data. Chen's work, called the *entity-relationship model* or the *entity-relationship approach*, was a big hit and today is still the gold standard for representing the logical definition of data.[4]

Subsequent years saw the expansion of the entity-relationship (E-R) approach as well as spin-offs such as the Integration Definition for Information Modeling (IDEF1X) and the Unified Modeling Language (UML). (UML is a synthesis of logical data and logical process modeling.) No offshoot has come close to the E-R approach in popularity, versatility, efficiency, or ease of use.

Some Important Definitions

Let's get a few definitions out of the way.

A *model* is an abstract representation of a subject that looks and/or behaves the same as all or part of the original. Although it is not real, the model can be physical, such as a mock-up of the International Space Station, a drawing, or a blueprint, or it can be conceptual, such as the mathematical formulas used for weather forecasting.

Modeling is the process of creating the abstract representation of a subject. A subject is modeled so that it can be (1) studied more cheaply (a scale model of an airplane in a wind tunnel), (2) examined at a particular moment in time (weather forecasting), or (3) manipulated, modified, and altered without disrupting the original (economic models).

A *data model* represents the definition, characterization, and relationships of data in a given environment.

A *logical data model* is a data model of the information used in an organization from an end-user perspective, without regard to its functional or physical aspects.

Although the phrase *logical data model* is more specific than the generic *data model*, the two terms are often used interchangeably.

The *entity-relationship approach* is the logical data modeling technique created by Peter Chen and expanded in subsequent years by a number of authors.

An *entity-relationship diagram* (ERD) is the logical data modeling diagram created using the E-R approach.

Regrettably, some people equate the "data model" with a diagram—the graphic or picture of the data. However, as the definition clearly states, a data model includes the definition, characterization, and relationship of the data in addition to any pretty pictures. The logical data model or E-R model consists of a logical data modeling diagram, or ERD, and the definition of any data in the model, also called a *data dictionary*.

Logical Data Modeling Objects

DNA, it is said, is made up of four basic building blocks—cytosine, guanine, adenine, and thymine—which can be arranged into millions of different and unique combinations. The basic building blocks of logical data modeling are entities, attributes, and relationships, and they too can be arranged into a nearly unlimited number of combinations representing the information a business or enterprise needs to function.

Entities

An *entity* is a person, place, or thing about which an organization wants to save information. Examples of entities would be people, employees, cars, invoices, students, diseases, and anything else important to an enterprise. Entities are graphically represented by a rectangle, one rectangle per entity, with the name of the entity inside. Figure 2-3 illustrates two entities: Customer and Car.

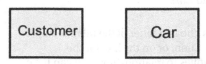

Figure 2-3. *A rectangle is used to diagram an entity*

There are a few grammatical rules surrounding entities. First, an entity name (almost) always is a noun. Second, as a convention, the first letter of an entity name is capitalized, for example, Employee, Boat, State. Third, entity names are often singular in number, but this rule is not hard and fast and, as you will be see later, sometimes discarded in the interest of communication.

Type-Instance Distinction

Before continuing, you need to take a short philosophical side trip. When talking about the entity Customer, one can mean a single customer, such as "Jones," or the group or set of all customers. If you remember your college philosophy class, you probably learned about the *type-token distinction*. A *type* is the name given to a group of things, such as turtles, balloons, and customers, while a *token* is a particular instance or occurrence of a type, such as the Bob the turtle. Database design talks about *types* and *instances* or *occurrences*. Customer is an *entity type*, while "William Canynge," the person who buys your wares, is an entity *instance* or *entity occurrence*. The *type-instance* distinction is used throughout database design.

Relationships

A relationship is a connection between two or more entities. Examples of relationships are buy, support, is a member of, owns, include, and so on. Chen used a diamond to graphically represent a relationship (Figure 2-4) although other authors have used a simple line. The diamond is more dramatic, but it also takes more real estate on a small piece of paper. A line is less impressive but more concise. Either is acceptable.

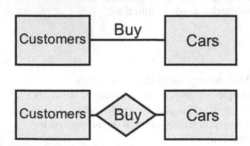

Figure 2-4. *The relationship Buy links Customers and Cars*

Relationships are usually verbs. As with entities, the first letter of the relationship name is capitalized and placed in the diamond, *à la* Chen, or on the line for the diamond-less. The type-instance distinction also applies to relationships. You can have a *relationship type* between entity types and a *relationship instance* between entity occurrences.

Relationships fit nicely between entities. Take the phrase "Customers Buy Cars." Customer and Car (the two nouns) are entities, and Buy (the verb) is the relationship. This is a common structure (entity-relationship-entity) and is called a *relationship-entity pair*. Relationship-entity pairs are bidirectional. To say "Customers Buy Cars" is the same as saying "Cars Are Bought by Customers." Figure 2-4 shows the relationship Buy between the entities Car and Customer.

Attributes

An *attribute* is a property or characteristic of an entity. The simplest way to explain an attribute is with an example. COLOR is an *attribute type*, while "red" is an *attribute occurrence*. Attributes do not stand by themselves. You would never have just COLOR or just "red." There must be something that has the color red for either color or red to exist. You can say that the entity type Car has the attribute type COLOR and that an instance of the entity type Car, the Sunbeam Tiger in the back lot, has the COLOR instance "red."

As a convention, attribute types are in all capital letters, and attribute instances are in double quotes. Some authors put attributes on the logical data modeling diagram, either in the entity rectangle or alongside it. Others use ovals connected to the entity rectangle containing the entity's attributes (Figure 2-5). All of these approaches are acceptable although, once again, size matters. Academic papers and textbooks, which usually show a data model of no more than a handful of entities and a dozen attributes, can use the "attributes on the page" convention. Real-world data models, with dozens of entities and 100 or more attributes, would require a piece of paper the size of a ping-pong table— unrealistic in most cases. The more practical solution is to leave the attributes off the diagram and in the data dictionary.

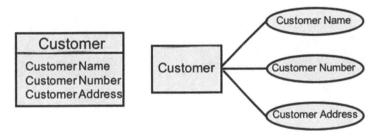

Figure 2-5. Diagramming attributes

A similarity among entity, relationship, and attribute names is that spaces are not only allowed but encouraged, and length is not an issue. The goal of logical data modeling is to communicate, and Customer Name or Registered Student does a better job of communicating than Cust_Nam or Reg-Stud.

The next chapter introduces more advanced topics for logical data modeling using the entity-relationship approach.

Notes

1. *Genograms in Family Assessment* is currently published as Monica McGoldrick, Randy Gerson, and Sueli Petry, *Genograms: Assessment and Intervention, Third Edition.* New York: WW Norton and Company, 2008.

2. Charles Bachman, "Data Structure Diagrams." *DataBase: A Quarterly Newsletter of SIGBDP.* Vol. 1, No. 2, Summer 1969, pages 4–10.

3. I was on a conceptual modeling committee with Mr. Bachman, when a committee member referred to the Bachman diagram as a physical representation of data. Bachman responded by saying that Bachman thought the Bachman diagram was a logical representation.

4. Peter Pin-Shan Chen, "The Entity-Relationship Model— Toward a Unified View of Data." *ACM Transactions on Database Systems (TODS).* ACM, New York, Vol. 1, No. 1, March 1976, pages 9–36.

CHAPTER 3

■ ■ ■

More About the E-R Approach

The relationship between the data is more important than the data.

—James Burke

Data matures like wine, applications like fish.

—James Governor

Chapter 2 introduced logical data modeling using the entity-relationship approach. This chapter expands the logical data model building blocks: relationships, entities, and attributes.

More About Relationships

Relationships, so far, seem rather pale and lifeless. However, relationships have three characteristics that give them the texture needed to express the richness of the real world, namely, membership class, degree, and relationship constraints.

Membership Class

Membership class indicates the number of instances of one entity type that can be related to the instances of another entity type. Knowing the exact number is helpful but not always possible. For example, in most parts of California, a husband can have only one wife, while a wife can have only one husband. A page has two sides, and a cat has only nine lives. A school might have a rule that a course must have at least 5 students but no more than 25. When the exact number is known, it should be documented at least in the data dictionary if not on the E-R diagram. However, usually all you know are three simple possibilities: zero, one, and many. A dog has zero wings, a citizen has one birthplace, and a politician has many positions. The maximum number of possible cases is called *cardinality*, while the minimum number of cases is called *modality*.

© George Tillmann 2017

G. Tillmann, *Usage-Driven Database Design*, DOI 10.1007/978-1-4842-2722-0_3

Cardinality

To understand the concept, start with two relationship-entity pairs. The first pair uses the relationship Sire (a male horse fathering a foal), as in "Stallions Sire Foals," or, from the other direction, "Foals Are Sired by a Stallion." The second pair uses the relationship Pull, as in "Stallions Pull Wagons."

In the first case, "Stallions Sire Foals," you know that a stallion can sire many foals, but a foal can be sired by only one stallion. However, in the second case, a stallion can pull many wagons, while a wagon can be pulled by many stallions (think beer wagon).

The first case demonstrates that a single occurrence of entity type A can be related to one or many occurrences of entity type B, but entity B can be related to, at most, only one occurrence of entity A. This is called a *one-to-many relationship*, and they are everywhere. A customer can have many accounts, but an account can be for only one customer. An order can have many line items, but a line item can be for only one order. A mother can have many children, but a child can have only one mother.

Not all relationships are one-to-many. As was mentioned earlier, a husband can have only one wife, and a wife can have only one husband. Here the relationship is one-to-one.

There is a third case. Take the example "Customers Buy Products." A customer can buy many products, while a product can be bought by many customers. This is an example of a many-to-many relationship.

Cardinality is the maximum number of occurrences of an entity type, usually expressed as one or many, that can be related to an occurrence of another entity type. There are four cardinality states.

- *One-to-one (1:1)*: An occurrence of entity A can relate, at most, to one occurrence of entity B, and an occurrence of entity B can relate, at most, to one occurrence of entity A. For example, a husband can have only one wife, and a wife only one husband.

- *One-to-many (1:N)*: One occurrence of entity A can relate to many occurrences of entity B, but an occurrence of B can relate to only one occurrence of A. For example, a mother can have many children, but a child can have only one mother.

- *Many-to-many (M:N)*: An occurrence of entity A can relate to multiple occurrences of entity B, while an occurrence of entity B can relate to many occurrences of entity A. For example, an uncle can have many nephews while a nephew can have many uncles.

- *Many-to-one (M:1)*: Because relationships are bidirectional, a many-to-one relationship is the inverse of a one-to-many relationship.

Note that the cardinality of a relationship is about the maximum number of occurrences allowed in the relationship, not the minimum. Note the word *can* in the definitions. Cardinality says A *can* relate to multiple Bs, but it does not have to. The cardinality of "Customers Own Cars" might be one-to-many, while an instance of a customer, say Jones, might own only one or even no cars.

Diagramming cardinality is easy. Chen placed the number 1 on the relationship line next to the diamond to represent one and an N or M to represent many (see Figure 3-1). Most modern modelers have dropped the Chen notation in favor of the bar to represent the one and the trident, or, more popularly, the "chicken foot" or "crow's foot," to represent the many.

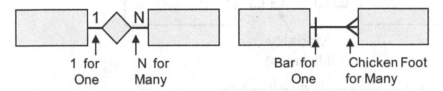

Figure 3-1. Cardinality using Chen and "chicken foot" notation

Modality

The other side of the membership class coin is modality, the minimum number of occurrences that can be in a relationship. Take, for example, the relationship-entity pairs Orders Contain Line Items and Artists Paint Pictures (Figure 3-2). We know that the cardinality of Orders Contain Line Items is one-to-many—an order can consist of many line items, but a line item can be part of only one order. We also know that the cardinality of Artists Paint Pictures is also one-to-many (no artist worth his salt ever gave credit to an assistant). However, there is a significant difference between the two. You cannot have an order without at least one line item, but there are many artists who have never painted a picture (just go to any singles bar near a women's college).

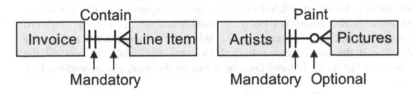

Figure 3-2. Modality showing both mandatory and optional relationships

Because you cannot have a line item without an order, then a Line Item occurrence *must* be linked to an Order occurrence; put another way, Line Item's role in the relationship Contain is *mandatory*. Can you have an order without a line item? If not, then Order's role in Contain is also *mandatory*. The same is true for Pictures and Artists. A Picture occurrence *must* be linked to an Artist occurrence, so the modality is *mandatory*. However, an Artist occurrence need not be linked to any Picture occurrence, so Artist's involvement in the relationship Paint is *optional*.

Modality specifies whether an entity's involvement or role in a relationship is mandatory or optional. By convention, a mandatory modality is diagrammatically represented by a bar on the relationship line, while an optional modality is depicted by an *O* on the line, as in Figure 3-2. In the notation, the modality symbols are placed on the relationship line within the cardinality symbols, as in Figure 3-3.

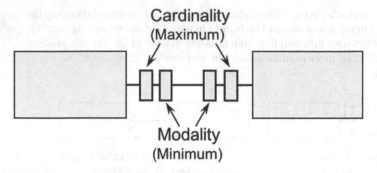

Figure 3-3. *Diagraming cardinality and modality*

When referring to cardinality, modelers often use the shorthand one-to-many or many-to-many to identify the cardinality at each end of the relationship between entity A and entity B. Similarly, for modality, modelers use the terms *mandatory-optional relationships* and *optional-optional relationships*. However, it is easy to confuse the order of the words. Take the expression "A Department Contains Employees." A Department can have zero to many Employees, while an Employee must be in one and only one Department. We say the cardinality is *one-to-many* because we read the expression left to right.

> Entity (Department) – Cardinality (one) – Relationship
> (Contain) – Cardinality (many) – Entity (Employee).

Some modelers have a problem with the order of the words. They point out that the word *one* is next to the entity Department and not next to the entity Employee. Doesn't it seem that the word *one* should be next to Employee and not Department? The answer is to remember that cardinality is a property of a relationship and not of an entity. The word order one-to-many and not many-to-one is used in this example because you are reading the relationship line. In the relationship-entity pair Department Contains Employees, the relationship line has a bar on the left and the crow's foot on the right, so you read the line as one-to-many.

The same is true for modality, although for some people, it is even less obvious than how you read cardinality. Following the "read the relationship line left to right (or top to bottom)" rule, we have four possible modality cases.

- *Mandatory-mandatory (M:M)*: Every occurrence of entity A must be related to at least one occurrence of entity B, and every occurrence of entity B must be related to at least one occurrence of entity A. For example, an Order must be related to at least one Line Item, and a Line Item must be related to an Order.

- *Mandatory-optional (M:O)*: Every occurrence of entity A must be related to at least one occurrence of entity B, but an occurrence of entity B need not be related to any occurrences of entity A. For example, an Account need not be related to any Orders (it might have been just set up), but an Order must be related to an Account.

- *Optional-optional (O:O)*: An occurrence of entity A need not be related to any occurrences of entity B, and an occurrence of entity B need not be related to any occurrences of entity A. For example, in Banks Finance Cars, a Bank might, but need not, finance any Cars, and a Car might not have been Financed by a Bank.

- *Optional-mandatory (O:M)*: Because relationships are bidirectional, an optional-mandatory relationship is the inverse of a mandatory-optional relationship.

WORD SOUP

Some authors call modality *optionality*; others call it *participation*. Optionality is an odd word to call modality because you can wind up with a relationship of mandatory optionality as in the phrase "its optionality is mandatory." If that is not a contradiction, then it should be. Participation is almost as odd because you can have a participation of no-participation. Both optionality and participation would be at home in a Lewis Carroll story.

The word *modality* comes from modal logic, which defines a proposition as either necessary or contingent—exactly what we want to express in membership class.

By now you have probably figured out that you do not need both the bar and the crow's foot or both the bar and the *O*. For cardinality, the absence of the crow's foot could indicate a one, and for modality, the absence of the *O* could indicate mandatory. However, the bar is not redundant—it communicates an important message. Having all three symbols (bar, crow's foot, and *O*) tells you when the modeler knows the cardinality or modality and when they do not. The bar distinguishes unknown from one or unknown from mandatory.

Degree

Degree is an indicator of the number of entity types that are allowed in a relationship. Relationships can be binary, n-ary, or unary (recursive).

Binary Relationship

The most common relationship, involving only two entity types, is called a *binary relationship*. Binary relationships are so fundamental to data management that most database management systems support only them, to the exclusion of other types of relationships.

N-ary Relationships

The phrase "Customers Buy Cars from a Dealer" illustrates an n-ary relationship. The relationship Buys binds together three entities (Customer, Car, and Dealer). It is called an *n-ary relationship*, where *n* can be any number greater than 2 (Figure 3-4a).

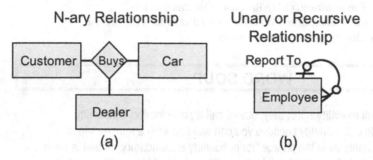

Figure 3-4. *N-ary and recursive relationships*

N-ary relationships are quite common in the business world; representing them on the logical data model is crucial to accurate database design.

Unary or Recursive Relationships

An entity can also be related to itself. Take the example of Employee and the relationship Report To. The Employee instance of "Smith" can report (on the organizational chart) to his supervisor, the Employee instance of "Jones." A relationship between two or more occurrences of the same entity type is called a *unary relationship* or *recursive relationship* (Figure 3-4b).

Recursive relationships are important because they help the data modeler (and later the database designer) with the *bill of materials* problem.

Assume that you work for an automotive repair company and you need to create a parts database. Mechanics access the database to find the parts they need, which can be as large as an entire engine or as small as a single bolt for the starter motor. The problem is an engine is made up of hundreds of parts, and most of those parts have subparts. That bolt can be a stand-alone part or a part of another part, such as a starter motor, which, in turn, is part of an engine. There is a hierarchy of parts, from the top, the car itself, down to the bolts and washers at the bottom (Figure 3-5a). In between are ignition systems, starter motors, fuel pumps, and radiators.

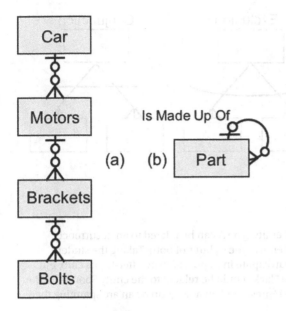

Figure 3-5. *A bill of materials hierarchy*

The problem for the data modeler is how to represent the hierarchy. How many Part entity types, stacked on top of each other, should be included in the data model? Four to accommodate the example? Maybe six, to leave some room for expansion? But remember, a car is made up of hundreds, if not thousands, of parts. Maybe 100 levels are needed?

Luckily, the recursive relationship solves the problem. Having a single entity type, Part, with the single unary relationship, Is Made Up Of, the model can handle any number of part levels from one to literally thousands (Figure 3-5b).

The data modeler will find the recursive bill of materials structure throughout the real world.

Relationship Constraints

A relationship *constraint* is a restriction on how entities can relate to each other. There are three classic relationship constraints: exclusion, inclusion, and conjunction.

Inclusion

Examine the three entity types and two relationship constructs in Figure 3-6. *Inclusion* states that an occurrence of entity type A can be related to an occurrence of entity type B or to occurrence entity occurrence C, or to both. This is your garden-variety case of occurrence: "Jack" of entity type Student, related to entity Class occurrence "History 101" or to entity Sport occurrence "Baseball," or to both. Inclusion is the most common type of relationship constraint. There are no diagramming features required for inclusion.

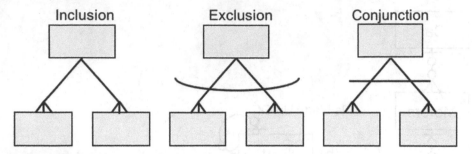

Figure 3-6. *Relationship constraints*

Exclusion

Exclusion states that an occurrence of entity type A can be related to an occurrence of entity type B or to an occurrence of entity type C, but not both. Taking the student example, assume that a student can participate in a sport or in an after-hours club, but not both. Therefore, entity occurrence "Jack" could be related to the entity Sport or to the entity Club, but not both. Exclusion is represented on a diagram by an arc spanning the excluded relationships.

Conjunction

Conjunction states that if entity occurrence A is related to entity occurrence B, then it must also be related to entity occurrence C. There are two types of conjunction: simple conjunction and conditional conjunction.

Simple Conjunction

Simple conjunction states that given three entities (A, B, and C) and two relationships (one between A and B, and one between A and C), every A occurrence must be related to an occurrence of B *and* related to an occurrence of C. An example would be the case where every Employee occurrence must be related to a Benefits occurrence *and* to a Security Clearance occurrence. This is easily diagrammable with two mandatory-mandatory relationships, as in Figure 3-7a. No special graphic symbols are needed.

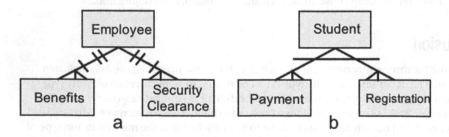

Figure 3-7. *Simple and conditional conjunction*

Conditional Conjunction

Conditional conjunction states that, given three entities (A, B, and C) and two relationships (one between A and B, and one between A and C), if an occurrence of A is related to an occurrence of B, then that occurrence of A must also be related to an occurrence of C. An example would be the case where a student can register only if the semester fee is paid, as in Figure 3-7b. Student occurrence Jones has a spring Registration occurrence only if he also has a spring Payment occurrence. Note the straight line used to show the conjunction.

Conjunction is not limited to three entities. The Student example can be expanded to four entities by including an Admission entity, where Registration is conditional on Payment and Payment is conditional on Admission.

The bar indicates that there is a conjunctive constraint among the relationships, but unfortunately it does not tell you which relationship is conditional on which other relationship. You can use arrows to show the condition (Figure 3-8), which works for the three-entity example.

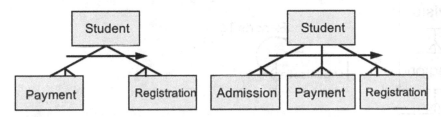

***Figure 3-8.** Directional conditional conjunction*

However, the arrow can become confusing as the number of entities increases. The simplest solution is to use the straight line as a flag for the developer to indicate conjunction and then document the constraint in the data dictionary.

WORD SOUP

Some authors call membership class and degree by other names or use no names at all.

Some authors refer to membership class as *structural constraint.* A second group calls membership class *degree*, which conflicts with the mathematical definition of degree used by most authors.

A third group avoids the membership class naming issue by not having a name for membership class at all, instead just referring to its constituents—the cardinality and modality (or optionality, or participation) of the relationship. Problem solved through obfuscation.

Membership class and degree are concerned with a single relationship between one or more entities. Relationship constraints are unique in that they are concerned with multiple relationships between multiple entities. It is the only time in data modeling when one relationship can directly affect another relationship.

Recursive Modality Constraints

Recursive relationships can be uniquely complex.

Take the five-level organization consisting of the entities: Headquarters, Division, Region, District, and Local offices (Figure 3-9).

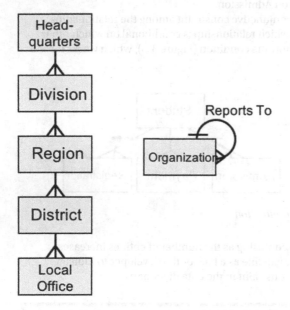

Figure 3-9. *A five-level organization and its recursive equivalent*

What if all locations do not have all the levels? Assume that the Cleveland Local office reports directly to the Midwest region and not to a District office. Suppose in France some local offices have six or seven organizations between them and the Division level. This example is a classic case for an n-level structure and can be represented by the entity Organization and the recursive relationship Report To.

Problems can arise, however, when you try to assign the modality of the relationship. There are four options: mandatory-mandatory, optional-optional, mandatory-optional, and optional-mandatory. Which is it?

Some could argue that any mandatory relationship is impossible, because it would require that every occurrence have at least one level above it and at least one level below it. This is an infinite regression, because no level could be the top or the bottom. For example, the Headquarters occurrence would have to report to some organization occurrence above it, and some organization occurrence would have to report to the Cleveland Local office.

Take another example—the Mayor entity for a city. The mayor can have a successor and/or be a successor (have a predecessor). Is the relationship Succeeds mandatory or optional? Answer: it must be optional because the first mayor had no predecessor and the very last mayor has no successor. (The same is at least temporarily true for the current mayor—at least until he has a successor.) To say that every mayor has a predecessor means that there must be an infinite number of mayors stretching back in time forever. Because this is impossible, the relationship must be optional (Figure 3-10).

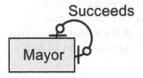

Figure 3-10. *An optional-optional relationship*

This argument suggests that recursive relationships cannot be mandatory. But wait...

Try a very different type of example. Suppose the police department has a rule stating every police officer must have a partner and only one partner. This is a one-to-one recursive relationship that is clearly mandatory-mandatory (Figure 3-11).

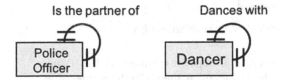

Figure 3-11. *Two mandatory-mandatory recursive relationships*

Here is another example. A dance contest requires that every dancer must have one and only one partner. Clearly, the relationship "Dances with" is also mandatory-mandatory.

You can also construct mandatory recursive many-to-many relationships. Figure 3-12 describes a relationship in which everybody (parent, sibling, cousin, uncle, etc.) relates to at least one other person and probably more (actually, at least two, because everyone has two parents). This relationship is clearly mandatory-mandatory.

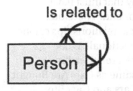

Figure 3-12. *A mandatory many-to-many recursive relationship*

What does all this mean? Why is it that in some cases it seems that mandatory relationships are impossible and in other cases possible? The answer is that there are actually two different types of recursive relationships.

Look at the relationships in the two different situations. The cases in which a mandatory relationship appears impossible are those with relationships such as Reports To or Succeeds. The cases in which a mandatory relationship appears possible are those with relationships such as "Is the partner of" or "Dances with."

The officer hierarchy and mayor examples define relationships that are asymmetrical. In other words, A is related in some way to B, but B is not related in the same way to A. Examples of asymmetrical relationships are Owns and Hits, because A Owns B does not automatically mean that B Owns A. Again, to say A Hit B does not mean that B Hit A. An asymmetrical relationship is represented on the logical data model by a dashed relationship line (Figure 3-13).

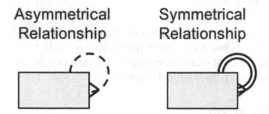

Asymmetrical Relationship   **Symmetrical Relationship**

Figure 3-13. *Asymmetrical and symmetrical recursive relationships*

The dance partner and police partner relationships are symmetrical. If A "Dances with" B, then B "Dances with" A; if A "Is the partner of" B, then B "Is the partner of" A. A symmetrical relationship is represented by a double relationship line.

Asymmetrical relationships are unidirectional implying a sequence or hierarchy that must have a beginning or end. Symmetrical relationships are bidirectional and have no beginning or end. Therefore, asymmetrical relationships cannot be mandatory, while symmetrical relationships can be.

This is called a *recursive modality constraint*. However, to understand this constraint you must first grapple with the concept of role. A *role* is the part an entity plays in a relationship. In a *symmetrical relationship* all entity occurrences play the same role. Examples would be Marries and Dances with. In an *asymmetrical relationship,* the entity occurrences play different roles. For example, take the relationship supervises. One role is "Supervisor," and the other role is "Is supervised" or "Supervisee."

An asymmetrical relationship involves a sequence or hierarchy that must have a beginning or end. Symmetrical relationships have no beginning or end. Therefore, asymmetrical relationships cannot be mandatory, while symmetrical relationships can be.

But wait...was it not said earlier that all relationships are bidirectional? What was said earlier was that there is no need to name each direction of a relationship. Relationship bidirectionality says that Customers Buy Cars is the same as Cars Are Bought by Customers. Relationship asymmetry says that Customers Buy Cars and Cars Buy Customers are not the same.

Recursive modality constraints can be summarized as follows:

- Symmetrical relationships can be mandatory-mandatory or optional-optional, but not mandatory-optional or optional-mandatory. The latter two categories are meaningless.

- Symmetrical relationships cannot be one-to-many. One-to-many symmetrical relationships are meaningless.

- Asymmetrical relationships cannot be mandatory. If they were, that would mean they fall into an infinite regression.

Recursive modality constraints are discussed in greater detail in Chapter 7.

More About Entities

So far, only one kind of entity was presented—a proper entity. A *proper entity*, also called a *fundamental entity*, is a person, place, or thing that is existentially independent of any other entity type or occurrence. However, this is not the only kind of entity. This section expands the notion of entities to attributive, associative, and S-type entities.

Attributive Entity

Not all entities are equal. Some entities can exist independently of other (proper) entities, while some entities can exist only if a companion exists. Take the two entities Customer and Customer Address. You can have an occurrence of Customer without a relationship to an occurrence of Customer Address, but you cannot have an occurrence of Customer Address that is not related to some occurrence of Customer. An entity that is dependent on another entity for its existence is called an *attributive entity* or *weak entity*.

Attributive entities are usually, although not always, on the many side of a one-to-many relationship with a proper entity, and that relationship with that proper entity is often, but not always, the only relationship the attributive entity has.

Do not confuse attributive entities with mandatory relationships—they are quite different. An entity in a mandatory relationship with one entity can be in an optional relationship with another. Some modelers have difficulty identifying attributive entities because they overthink the problem. You simply need to ask yourself this question: "Would this person, place, or thing exist if X did not exist?" If your answer is No, then the entity is an attributive entity.

An attributive entity is depicted on an E-R diagram as a double-bordered rectangle, as in Figure 3-14.

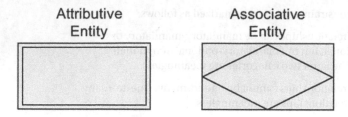

Figure 3-14. *Attributive and associative entities*

Associative Entities

Go back to the entity-relationship pair, Customer Buys Car. It should be obvious that MAKE and MODEL are attributes of Car and that CUSTOMER NAME and PHONE NUMBER are attributes of Customer, but what are DATE OF PURCHASE and SELLING PRICE attributes of? Not Customer, not Car, but of the relationship Buys. An *associative entity* is a relationship with its own attributes (Figure 3-15). Why is it called an entity and not a relationship? Good question. Because it is a cross between an entity and an attribute-less relationship, you would think it could be either one. Nonetheless, it is universally called an associative entity.

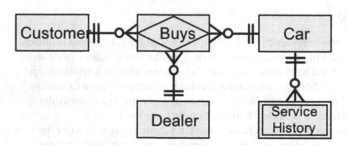

Figure 3-15. *Attributive and associative entities on the LDM*

Carrying forward its dual nature, the associative entity is diagrammatically represented as an amalgam of an entity and a relationship—a diamond in a rectangle.

Supertype and Subtype Entities (Generalization and Specialization)

Entities can sometimes play different roles in an organization. A business has customers, but not all customers are alike. There can be wholesale customers, retail customers, and customers that appear to be both. Whatever their role, both retail and wholesale customers have a lot in common. They both have properties such as name, address, telephone number, and customer number. However, their roles might also have different attributes and be treated differently because of them. A wholesale customer might have a credit status, a discount level, and an outstanding balance that the retail customer does not. The retail customer might have a frequent customer card tied to a bonus program, get coupons from a marketing campaign, and receive birthday cards on their birthday.

How do you model this? The data modeler has three options. The first is to have a single entity Customer containing the attributes for both wholesale and retail customers, leaving blank the unused attributes. That's not a very elegant solution. Empty attributes make many modelers fidget uncontrollably.

The second option is to have two different entities, Wholesale Customer and Retail Customer, but then the common information for each must be duplicated in the two entities. This option would have the dual disadvantages of duplication and spreading of customer information all over the data model. You can almost feel the fidgeting.

Luckily, there is a third option. A *supertype-subtype* (sometimes abbreviated *S-type*), also called *generalization* and *specialization*, is a single entity, with its own attributes and its own relationships, which also contains multiple entity *roles*, where each role can have its own attributes and relationships. The supertype contains all common data and relationships, which are *inherited* by the subtypes, while the subtypes house their own role-specific attributes and relationships. In the example, Customer is the supertype, while Retail and Wholesale are the subtypes.

The most descriptive way to represent S-types is with the box-in-a-box—place the subtypes in an entity rectangle within the supertype entity rectangle, as in Figure 3-16.

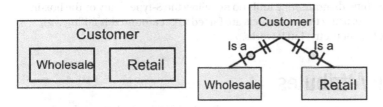

Figure 3-16. A supertype-subtype entity

An alternative to the box-in-a-box is the "is a" relationship, as in Customer "is a" Retail or Customer "is a" Wholesale. The "is a" representation requires three proper entities with the two subtypes linked to the supertype with two "is a" relationships (Figure 3-16). The two relationships are one-to-one mandatory-optional.

Relationships can be at the supertype or at the subtype level, as in Figure 3-17.

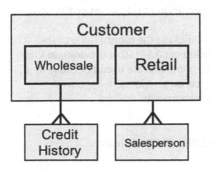

Figure 3-17. Supertype and subtype relationships

S-types are not limited to two levels; instead, they can be nested, one inside the other, as in Figure 3-18.

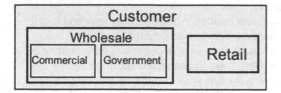

Figure 3-18. *Nested supertypes and subtypes*

There are three advantages to the box-in-a-box diagramming technique. First, it is easy to see which relationships are to the supertype and which are to the subtypes. Second, it does not require phantom relationships between the various entity roles. Third, S-type nesting does not need to stop at two levels. Some businesses require three, four, or more levels of supertypes and subtypes. N-level S-types are more obvious with the box-on-a-box construct than the "is a" construct.

Unfortunately, some diagramming tools do not allow the S-type entity or the box-in-a-box graphic. Modelers using these products are forced to get around this failing with the "is a" structure. It's not pretty, but it works.

More About Attributes

For shorthand, most data modelers refer to an attribute type as an attribute and an attribute occurrence as an *attribute value* or just *value*. This section takes a closer look at attributes and values.

Attribute Domain

An *attribute domain* is the set of possible values of an attribute type. Examples of domains include dates, foreign cars, integers, and gender. Domains can be quite broad, as in the domains of text and real numbers, or very specific, as in U.S. states or Fibonacci numbers.

Domains have rules, so the domain Dates cannot include the month Betty or the day of the month 36. Equally erroneous would be the integer 3.14159 or the domain Vice Presidents of the United States containing Sarah Palin. Domains are useful because they can flag data entry and calculation errors before they cause problems.

Take the following example of the computer code fragment:

If EMPLOYEE STATUS = "Full Time"

and CURRENT DATE minus DATE OF EMPLOYMENT greater than (25x365)

then RETIREMENT ELIGIBILITY = "YES"

This works only if CURRENT DATE and DATE OF EMPLOYMENT are in the same domain Date, the domain for EMPLOYEE STATUS includes the value "Full Time," and the domain for RETIREMENT ELIGIBILITY includes "Yes."

If the database allowed the value of DATE OF EMPLOYMENT to be "Thomas Chatterton," or the value of RETIREMENT ELIGIBILITY to be "May 3, 2018," then this employee would be in for a rough career.

Domains tend to be of three types.

- *Data types*: Broad categories of data values such as text, integers, dates, and so on, commonly found in programming languages

- *Ranges*: Values between two end points such as dates between December 7, 1941, and September 2, 1945; integers between 0 and 255; and last names between A and J

- *Acceptable values*: Specific values such as days of the week, U.S. state abbreviations, or the values Male or Female

Domains can be nested, so the subdomain of dates between December 7, 1941, and September 2, 1945, is also a member of the domain Dates. Subdomains inherit the properties and rules of their parent. Take the example of postal codes. In the United States, a ZIP code is either a five-digit integer or a nine-digit integer and can be a subdomain of the domain Integers. Canadian postal codes are alphanumeric. In Canada, the postal code follows a specific pattern of uppercase letter, integer, uppercase letter, space, integer, uppercase letter, integer (such as K1A 0A9). Both American and Canadian postal codes also follow an acceptable value list, which disallows certain combinations.

Attribute Source: Primitive and Derived

A *primitive attribute* is one that cannot be derived from other attributes.

A *derived attribute* is the result of a calculation or algorithm applied to one or more other attributes (primitive or derived). The attribute CURRENT AGE is the result of subtracting DATE OF BIRTH from CURRENT DATE. On an invoice, TOTAL AMOUNT is the sum of the individual AMOUNT attributes.

Derived data break both the Separation Principle and Distinction Principle of the database design principles presented in Chapter 1 and should be left to the process modelers to describe and document. Although such derived data are not part of a data model, there is nothing wrong with including them in the LDM documentation (data dictionary), if those data are part of the business users' "real world." But they must be identified as derived data. Derived data are never included on the E-R diagram.

Attribute Descriptor and Unique Identifier

A *descriptor attribute* is a not necessarily unique characteristic or property of an entity or relationship (associative entity). Examples are COLOR and NAME.

A *unique identifier attribute* is an attribute used by the enterprise to point out a specific entity occurrence. Examples are SOCIAL SECURITY NUMBER and CUSTOMER NUMBER.

WORD SOUP

Identifier or unique identifier? Some modelers use the two terms interchangeably; others make a distinction between attributes that uniquely identify an entity and attributes that nonuniquely identify an entity (where there can be duplicates). For example, EMPLOYEE NUMBER is a unique identifier of Employee, while EMPLOYEE NAME can identify an employee if you allow for duplicates.

Identifier or key? There is no hard and fast rule, but many designers make a distinction between identifier and key. Identifiers are reserved for logical data modeling, while keys are used for physical schema definition.

It's a useful distinction although not always possible. Even adherents to the rule sometimes have to use one word to describe the other, although only as an adjective.

Must all entities have a unique identifier? It would be nice, but it's not necessary. The goal of logical data modeling is to document the business (the real world), not the IT department's wish list. If the business uses an identifier, then it should be in the LDM. If it does not have an identifier, then the data modeler should not take on deciding how the business should be run. Deciding how other people should live their lives is, as always, left to systems programmers.

Compound or Concatenated Unique Identifiers

Sometimes an identifier is made up of multiple attributes. LICENSE PLATE NUMBER is a unique identifier within a state, but multiple states can issue the same plate number. Appending STATE to the attribute LICENSE PLATE NUMBER creates a unique identifier. A *compound* or *concatenated identifier* is two or more attributes used by the business to uniquely identify an entity occurrence.

If the business uses a compound unique identifier, then the modeler should model it. If it does not, then it is not the job of the logical data modeler to create one.

Attribute Complexity: Simple and Group

Attribute complexity is a term that refers to the intricacy of an attribute. There are two types of attribute complexity, simple and group. A *simple attribute,* also called an *atomic attribute,* does not contain any other attributes.

A *group attribute* contains a fixed number of other attributes. An example would be the group attribute CUSTOMER ADDRESS, which contains the five simple attributes CUSTOMER STREET NUMBER, CUSTOMER STREET NAME, CUSTOMER CITY, CUSTOMER STATE/PROVINCE, and CUSTOMER POSTAL CODE.

Some modelers try to ignore group attributes by modeling only the simple attributes it contains or modeling the group attribute and ignoring its constituent simple attributes. Either approach is a mistake. Groups are not only an integral part of the business but reflect how people talk. An employee might be told to "put the customer address on the label." They would never hear, "Put the customer street number, customer street name, customer town, customer state, and customer postal code on the label."

Attribute complexity has various other names such as group data item, aggregate group, compound attribute, aggregate, and, unfortunately, group.

Attribute Valuation: Single Value and Multivalue

Attribute valuation describes how many values the attribute can have at any one time. There are two types of valuation, single value and multivalue. A *single-value attribute* can have only one value at a time. An example would be COLOR = "blue." If COLOR is "blue," then it cannot be "red," at least not at the same time.

A *multivalue attribute* can have a number of values at the same time. As an example, take the Employee entity and its attribute EMPLOYEE DEGREES. Smith might have only one degree, a "BS," while Jones has three degrees, "BS," "MA," and "PhD."

This type of attribute has various other names such as repeating group and, unfortunately, group.

Attribute Complexity and Valuation

Where as a group attribute can contain only a fixed number of attributes of various domains, a multivalue attribute can contain a variable number of values, but all of the same domain.

Confusion sometimes surrounds group attributes and multivalue attributes because both are often called groups. However, they are different logical data modeling concepts (Table 3-1). Making data modeling even more interesting, group attributes and multivalue attributes can be nested; for example, a group attribute could have multiple values. For example, the group attribute EDUCATION could contain the group attributes UNDERGRADUATE and GRADUATE, each containing the multivalue attribute DEGREES EARNED.

Table 3-1. Attribute Aggregation and Valuation

Valuation Complexity	Single-Value	Multivalue
GROUP	DATE consists of MONTH, DAY, YEAR	EXAM DATES = "1/15/2018," "5/15/2018," "8/15/2018"
SIMPLE	COLOR = "blue"	EMPLOYEE DEGREES = "BS," "MS," PhD"

IS CUSTOMER ADDRESS AN ENTITY OR IS IT A PROPERTY/ATTRIBUTE OF CUSTOMER?

There are two near-universal elements in data modeling books. First, virtually every definition of entity involves the phrase "person, place, or thing." The second is that customer address (or employee address, student address, etc.) is treated as an entity. Why? Why is it not an attribute (group attribute) of Customer?

There are two reasons, neither of which is terribly satisfying. First, look at the almost universal definition of entity. Note that word, *place*. Because address is a place, many modelers automatically make every address an entity.

The second reason is even less satisfying. The customer/customer address, employee/employee address, and so on, conundrum existed long before data modeling, even before the first DBMS. It goes back to the punched-card era when any repeating group was placed on a separate punched card, as a child, following the parent card. When punched cards became disk files, address just fell into being a child record rather than a data item in a parent record. Then when the DBMS became available, it was natural to continue this distinction. (As you will see in a later chapter, this parent-child relationship is the basis for all data management systems.)

The fact is, sometimes customer address is an entity, and sometimes it is a (group) attribute. What should the discerning modeler to do? Do the same thing you do with the data object *shoe size*. Look at its definition and determine, on your own, if customer address is an entity or an attribute.

To demonstrate the different roles address can play, this book sometimes treats it as an entity and other times as a group attribute. It's not fence sitting—it's pedagogy.

Figure 3-19 is the family tree of logical data modeling, showing the various data modeling objects and their pedigree.

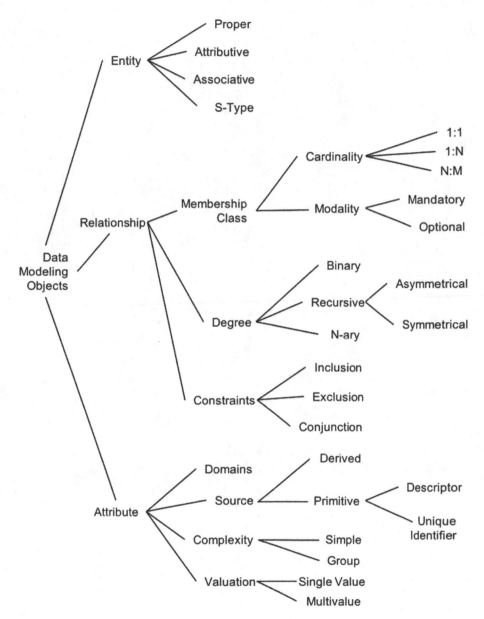

Figure 3-19. *Logical data modeling objects family tree*

CHAPTER 4

■ ■ ■

Building the Logical Data Model

When we mean to build, We first survey the plot, then draw the model.

—Shakespeare

We used to dream about this stuff. Now we get to build it. It's pretty great.

—Steve Jobs

Knowing the fundamentals of logical data modeling is important, but that is only half the equation. A successful designer also needs the skills to build the model. This chapter introduces a few techniques that can help ensure an efficient model.

The major difference between logical data modeling and physical data modeling is the same as the major difference between logical process modeling and physical process modeling—the skills needed to carry out the tasks. Logical data and logical process modeling staff need strong people skills for interviewing business staff, presenting results, and gathering feedback. Physical design staff interactions, if the logical design staff have done their job, are, for the most part, limited to other technical staff. The subjects in this chapter are designed to make the three logical data modeling steps (information gathering, analysis, and model construction) easier and more effective.

Perhaps the most important point to remember about building a logical data model is that it is an iterative process revolving around interviewing subject experts. As Figure 4-1 shows, there is no beginning and no end but rather a series of repetitive cycles—each pass corrects errors and adds detail to the previous pass.

© George Tillmann 2017

G. Tillmann, *Usage-Driven Database Design*, DOI 10.1007/978-1-4842-2722-0_4

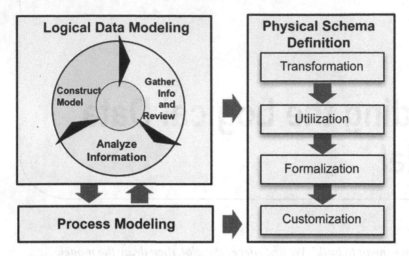

Figure 4-1. *Usage-Driven Database Design*

The Interview Process

Interviewing might seem like a simple task, but effective interviewing is an important and sometimes complicated skill. Unfortunately, like driving a car, it is a skill where 90 percent of the people say they are above average. For the 50 percent who are actually in that bottom 10 percent, this section explores a few interviewing tips.

Figure 4-2 shows the iterative interview and model building process needed to construct an accurate and detailed logical data model.

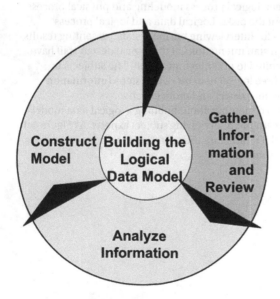

Figure 4-2. *The interview process*

Gather Information and Review

Just four tasks allow the designer to gather the information to build the LDM.

1. Identify the Users Who Are Authorities or Experts on the Subject

This might seem like an obvious task, but it is also fraught with danger. The problem is not the experts but the pseudo-experts. The first activity is to develop a list of subject-matter experts. To do that, you must interview business and technical staff. If you ask enough people, you should get a good feel for who knows the subject and who does not. However, in the process of figuring out who to talk to, you might encounter three impediments.

The first is the senior guy who really knows nothing about the subject, but you have to talk to him, if for no other reason than he demands it. Talk to him, ask a lot of questions, take a lot of notes, throw them away after the interview...well, you better keep them in case he asks for a follow-up interview sometime.

The second is the expert on how they did it in 1999. This guy is usually now a manager who worked in the subject area a decade or two ago. He thinks he knows the area cold but is unaware of the changes made since the Reagan administration. You have to interview him also, bobbing your head at all the appropriate places.

The third impediment is the manager who cannot let you interview the person who really knows what is going on, because she cannot be disturbed. (She might be the one doing all the work in the department, and productivity will plummet if she takes an interview break.) You might need to call on your boss to do some ice breaking.

Don't make enemies with the impediments. You need these people more than they need you.

2. Meet and Interview the Experts and Identify the Subject (Application) Entities

There are a few important points to follow.

Preparation

The purpose of the interview is to learn about the data used in the interviewee's area. However, considerable work can be completed before the interview. Gather forms used in the area, reports, and even computer screenshots. They give an initial picture of the subject's entities and attributes, and maybe even a few relationships, and allow you to create a first-draft E-R diagram. Use this information to kick off the first interview. The purpose of this preparation is not so much to gain knowledge of that area (although anything you learn is useful) but rather to craft the questions you want to ask the subject-matter experts.

The First Interview

Explain to the interviewee the purpose of the interview and of the system. They might know about it; they might not. They might be glad about the proposed system; they might not be—there could be fear of job replacement. Don't lie, but you are not required to tell them more than you have to.

Ask them questions about the existing process. What they do, what others do, what they like about it, and what they don't like about it. Get them talking. If you say more than 10 percent of the words during the interview, then something is wrong.

After a brief introduction, start by talking about data. What things are they involved with? Aim for ten things (entities) at the first meeting, but don't be surprised if they can't come up with a half-dozen. Talk about relationships between the things.

Show and/or walk the interviewee through the first-draft data model you created from the reports, forms, and screenshots. Find out what is right and what is wrong.

3. Identify Relationships Between the Entities

Most interviewees do a good job identifying entities and attributes. Relationships are a bit harder and require the interviewer to guide the discussion. While you can explain what an entity is to an interviewee and they deal with attributes every day, relationships are considerably more abstract. This is when those relationship-entity pairs become useful. "Analysts report to marketing managers" is much more meaningful than any technical jargon. Forget talking about cardinality and modality; rather, concentrate on how a customer relates to an account or an employee to a department. You can gain all the membership class information you need without mentioning technical terms at all.

Near the end of the model building phase, you might need only one meeting with a subject-matter expert. However, at the beginning of the process multiple meetings per interviewee might be required. This is because early interviews are laden with new information for the modeler while subsequent interviews tend to confirm what is already uncovered.

Follow-up interviews should start by confirming what you heard in the last session by showing or talking the interviewee through the emerging data model. Get confirmation, corrections, and expansions.

4. Identify the Properties or Attributes of the Entities and Relationships

This is a straightforward activity. However, do not be surprised if half the attributes you uncover are at your prodding. The interviewees might think they gave you all the data, but targeting questions to the entities often turns up a raft of new information.

Analyze Information

Go back to your office, cubicle, or warren, grab a cup of coffee, and think. Create as detailed a picture as possible of the entities, their relationships, and the attributes you uncovered. Remember, a logical data model is more than just a diagram. Explicit information is needed about each data modeling object. Rather than doing it all at the end, the seasoned data modeler starts building the gathered minutia into a data model right away. Appendix B gives a few examples of the information the model's data dictionary might require. Formalize the entity, relationship, and attribute definitions as best you can, looking for holes in the detail to become your new to-do list.

Construct Model

Create, expand, or modify the logical data model (diagram and documentation) to accommodate new information. The previous two chapters have given you sufficient information to build a construct of almost anything a user can throw at you.

Repeat as Necessary

Go back to the experts, walk them through the new and improved model, and get their buy-in or feedback. When, and only when, you are satisfied that you have all the information you need is the process complete.

FINDING INTERVIEWING SKILLS CHALLENGING?

There are a number of good books on developing effective interviewing skills. Raymond Gordon is the dean of the technique although more modern materials are available in any library or bookstore.[1]

Don't overlook sources inside your organization. If your company is of any size, then your training or HR department might offer a course in interviewing, although any such course is probably geared toward hiring new employees. But look at the bright side; if your logical data modeling skills are weak, then that hiring interview course might come in handy in another context.

Remember, this is an iterative process with no formal limits on how many times you should repeat the cycle. Keep at it until the model is correct.

The next sections present some aids for building an accurate and effective data model.

Making Sense of the Interview

Remember Dorothy Keenan the social worker? Her challenge was to take her interview notes and make sense of them, a task virtually identical to that of the logical data modelers, except whereas Dorothy was interviewing people with social or emotional problems, the data modeler is interviewing senior executives with social...you get the idea.

Simple interview statements can contain a lot of information. Take the following example:

> "Employees can report to either a supervisor or the Human Resources department."

This sentence can be decomposed into the following:

- "Employees" and "supervisor" are common nouns and, therefore, entities.

- "Human Resources" is a proper noun, not a common noun (such as "organization" or "department"). You should create an entity called Department with an occurrence containing the attribute data value "Human Resources."

- "Report" is a verb and, therefore, a relationship.

- Exclusion is implied by the words "either...or."

- "Can" indicates that the relationship is optional, but you already know that from the exclusion construct.

- The plural form of "employees" and the singular for "supervisor" and "department" tell you that the cardinality is one-to-many.

What the statement does not tell you, however, is the complete modality of the relationship (i.e., must a supervisor have at least one report?). Nor does it tell you if "supervisor" should be an entity or a role (subtype) of Employee (Figure 4-3). These issues have to be probed by the interviewer.

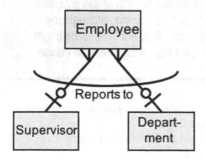

Figure 4-3. *"Employees can report to either a supervisor or the Human Resources department"*

Peter Chen, the man who created the entity-relationship approach, published a few papers to help data modelers unpack the interview, turning English into E-R objects.[2,3] Table 4-1 summarizes some of the concepts in two of these papers.

Table 4-1. *English to E-R Conversion*

English to E-R Conversion	
What to Look For	**E-R Component**
Common noun	Proper entity type
Proper noun	Proper entity instance
Transitive verb	Relationship
Intransitive verb	Attribute
Gerund	Associative entity
Adjective	Proper entity attribute
Adverb	Associative entity attribute
Words such as: many at least one only one at most	Cardinality
Words such as: must can may not	Modality
Words such as: and but	Conjunction
Words such as: or either...or nor neither...nor	Exclusion

Many organizations abound with inside jargon that the data modeler can add to Table 4-1, making it a more organization-relevant chart.

Modeling Rules

Unpack the following statement:

> "Orders are promptly shipped from the warehouse."

- "Orders" and "warehouse" are common nouns and, therefore, entities.

- "Shipped" is the verb and, therefore, the relationship.

- "Promptly" is an adverb, so it is a relationship attribute. (Actually, it represents two attributes, ORDER DATE and SHIPPING DATE, which means that "shipped" is really an associative entity.)

See Figure 4-4.

Figure 4-4. *"Orders are promptly shipped from the warehouse"*

Some statements are more difficult to model, and neither the English to E-R diagramming technique in particular, nor data modeling in general, can accurately represent them. Here's an example:

"An employee cannot report to his or her spouse."

"Employee" is an entity, and "report to" is a relationship. What might not be so obvious is the second relationship implied by "spouse." The diagram might look something like Figure 4-5.

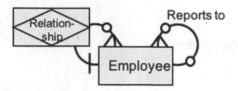

Figure 4-5. *"An employee cannot report to his or her spouse"*

What you cannot capture in the diagram is the fact that if the nature of the family relationship between two employees is "spouse," then one cannot report to the other. An exclusive relationship does not capture this situation because "spouse" is a data value and not an entity.

There is an important lesson in this example. If data modeling models data and process modeling models processes, which technique models rules? Actually, and unfortunately, the answer is neither and both. Rules such as "Every employee is assigned to one, and only one, department" are easily modeled by E-R techniques. However, the "rule" that an employee cannot report to his or her spouse cannot be modeled by current data modeling techniques alone. You must also use process modeling to represent rules.

The critical component in this example is not the diagram but rather the data dictionary—documentation that accompanies every diagram. The rules might be presented in English or in math or as computer pseudocode, but they must be recorded.

It would be nice if there was some rule-modeling technique that could be used to review all business rules. But for now, at least, to understand the rules of the business, you must examine both the data and process models.

Verifying What You Have Heard

"Do you want fries with that?" Hate that question? Presumably, if you wanted fries, you would have asked for them! Fast-food restaurants might be providing a fat-infused, artery-clogging, slow death, but they know how to market. They ask that annoying question because it sells fries. A monetarily significant number of customers say yes when posed with that irritating question. Asking seemingly obvious and repetitive questions can result in surprising answers containing valuable new information. Although the *burger-meister's* broken-record approach is annoying, it does point out the need for you to ensure you capture what the interviewee really knows. The first answer to an important question might not always be the right answer or the best answer or the complete answer.

The data modeler has two methods of model verification: immediate interview feedback and formal walk-throughs. Use both.

Immediate Interview Feedback

The best time to correct mistakes and omissions is during the interview process. Constantly read back to the interviewees what you were told by them or someone else in a previous interview. This not only ensures that you have heard what was said but also gives the interviewee an opportunity to correct any errors or omissions.

An important point to remember is that most nontechnical staff understate business rules and constraints. Interviewees tend to give the 80 percent answer and only discuss the other 20 percent when prodded. You may need to push them to gain the information you need to understand the boundaries of entity relationships. For example, if you are told that every account is owned by a customer, you should follow up and ask whether or not firm, transient, suspense, or general ledger accounts exist. If you are told that there is only one customer for an account, you might ask whether multiple family members can use the same account. You have to probe to test the limits of what you are being told. Remember the fries!

Formal Walk-Throughs

After you have added the input from other interviews and your own analysis to the data model, you will want to go back to some, or all, of those interviewed to show them a draft of the result, probing for any additional comments, corrections, or additions. In contrast to immediate feedback, these formal walk-throughs generally take place sometime after the initial interviews and can involve just one user or a dozen users at a time.

Because, to the interviewees, the data model probably looks more confusing and less informative than the Tokyo subway map (Figure 4-6), you will have to "walk" or guide them through the model (thus the term *walk-through*). You have three choices.

- Escort the interviewee through the data modeling diagram slowly, confirming each object.

- Convert the model back into English and read the model aloud in a narrative style.

- Do both.

"You users should review the data model
and get back to us tomorrow with any changes."

Figure 4-6. Verifying the data model can be overwhelming

Which method you choose depends on the receptivity of the interviewee to data modeling esoterica.

With some interviewees, you may be able to draw the model on paper or a white board during the initial interview or, alternatively, unveil the printed model during the walk-through. If you describe what you are doing line by line, many people can follow the analysis sufficiently to point out errors and omissions (remember the genogram). Other people are more comfortable being "read" to, in which case you should be prepared to interpret the data model to them in English.

Keep the conversation on an end-user level. There is no better way to stop a promising interview or walk-through than to get into techno-babble. Talk about end-user data, end-user activities, and end-user relationships—not about entities, recursion, or cardinality.

Increasing E-R Diagram Comprehension

For many organizations, the logical data model can become quite large and complex. It is not uncommon for a major enterprise system to involve dozens of entities and relationships and hundreds of attributes. Dealing with so complex a diagram can be confusing and time-consuming. It is often useful to divide or partition the ERD into more bite-size chunks (ideally containing ten entities or fewer) that facilitate understanding and use while minimizing the risk of hiding critical information. Subject areas, entity fragments, and neighborhood diagrams are three techniques for accomplishing this goal.

Subject Areas

For budgeting and statistical purposes, the U.S. government created metropolitan statistical areas (MSAs) consisting of large population centers and their surrounding support areas and bedroom communities. MSAs are identifiable not only by their high central populations densities but also by their lower-population boundaries. For example, both New York and Philadelphia are MSAs. Both include their respective cities of New York and Philadelphia, but they also incorporate the surrounding suburbs, including towns in New Jersey and Connecticut for the New York MSA and New Jersey and Delaware for the Philadelphia MSA. Furthermore, the boundary between the two MSAs is obvious by the lower population density of south-central New Jersey.

Now look at the ERD and think of it as a city and its surroundings. The town center is jammed with buildings and streets. Moving out of the center to the suburbs, the roads are fewer and farther apart. Finally, moving out into the country, the buildings and the roads are scarce, with the few existing roads often used to connect different cities. Think of relationships as roads. At the core of the ERD is a group of entities linked together with many relationships clustering around a single theme. Further away the number of relationships drops off until there are finally only a few relationships that tend to link separate clusters together. These clusters usually share a theme such as customer, supplier, or employee.

A *subject area* is a subset of a data model containing the entities, relationships, and attributes that share certain common business characteristics or uses and that facilitates the creation and development of, and communication about, the complete logical data model (Figure 4-7).

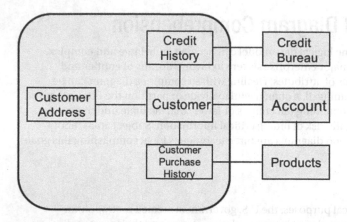

Figure 4-7. *Customer subject area*

Subject areas can serve a number of purposes. First, they can be the basis for dividing the data modeling workload among staff. If three teams are developing a data model, assigning a separate subject area to each team reduces the required interactions between teams.

Second, subject areas can be a useful communications tool for discussions with end users. Showing marketing staff a logical data model filled with manufacturing entities and relationships might not be the best use of their or your time, while presenting a marketing (only) subject area could be very productive. And do not forget the focus factor. Few things are more disturbing when trying to gain feedback from marketing staff about the marketing entities, relationships, and attributes than one guy in the back of the room who wants to offer a verbal dissertation on manufacturing relationships.

Entity Fragments

An *entity fragment* is a view or portion of the data model that deals with a specific process. Take the example of the "Update Customer Account" function. This process might need Customer, Account, and Credit data but might not be concerned with the Production Schedule, Raw Materials, or Distributors entities. Entity fragments are useful for logical process modelers who want to understand the data used in a particular function or to elicit process information from end users. They can also be useful for physical process designers.

Do not confuse entity fragments and subject areas. An entity fragment contains the entities, relationships, or attributes associated with a particular process or function (Figure 4-8). Subject areas are not concerned with functions, but only with the commonality of the data itself. Think of the subject area as an *uber*-entity.

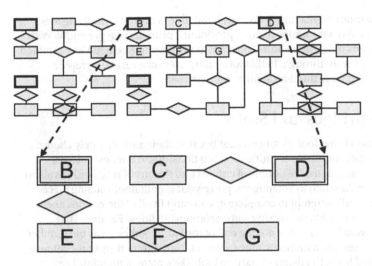

Figure 4-8. Entity fragment

Neighborhood Diagrams

For many projects, the data model can grow to 100 or more entities and the same number of relationships. That's an imposing diagram. The ultimate simplification of a logical data model is the neighborhood diagram. A *neighborhood diagram* highlights a single entity with only its relationships and the entities that are directly tied to those relationships (Figure 4-9). If there are 100 entities, then there are 100 neighborhood diagrams.

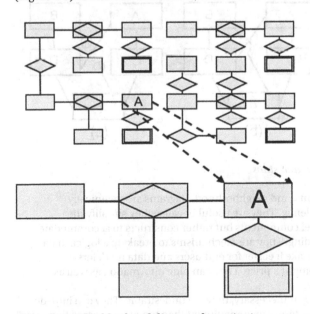

Figure 4-9. Neighborhood diagram for entity A

57

This would be a monumental task if done by hand, but many data modeling tools contain a neighborhood diagramming feature, providing a printed page per entity. With neighborhood diagrams only those entities relevant to the interviewee need be examined during the interview or walk-through. In this way, many users can review a graphic representation of their data without becoming overwhelmed.

Relationship Bridges and Stubs

E-R diagrams in books always look clean and neat because their authors rarely choose examples with real-world numbers of entities and relationships. A data model for a major business function can involve dozens of entities and dozens of relationships all on a single piece of paper. As much as you might try, like your grandfather rotating pieces of a jigsaw puzzle in a futile attempt to complete it, you can't fit all of the entities and relationships on the paper without crossing some relationship lines (Figure 4-10a).

Don't fret. A crossed line or two is not the end of the world, although as the number of crossed lines increases, the communications value of the diagram drops precipitously. With too many crossed lines, the diagram starts to look like a plate of linguini. The solution? There are two. The first solution is a relationship bridge—a graphic "bypass" or hill over the offending line (Figure 4-10b).

Sometimes the number of crossed lines is not only considerable but involves entities on opposite ends of the chart. For these, the second solution, the relationship stub, is the better answer. A relationship stub is a sort of data modeling dongle similar to a flow chart off-page connector. It consists of a small graphic, usually a circle with a letter in it (Figure 4-10c). Match the letter in one circle with the letter in another circle, and you have a complete relationship.

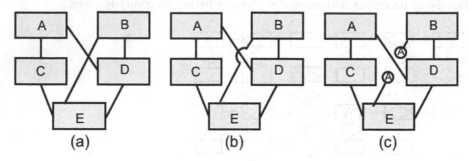

Figure 4-10. *Relationship bridges and stubs*

Subject areas, entity fragments, and neighborhood diagrams are technically unnecessary for logical data modeling. They are useful because they simplify the complex. They are not data model components but rather constructs to accommodate the frailties of human understanding. They are mechanisms to break up a logical data model into bite-size pieces that make it easier for end users and data modelers to understand the data. But they come at a price. They can hide information as well as emphasize it. Use them with care.

Bridges and stubs are not only unnecessary, they are undesirable. They can impede communication, although they are less of an impediment than too many crossed lines. Use them only when their absence would subtract from the diagram communication value.

Some Model Building Best Practices

Model building is a project, and like all projects, there are some painful lessons learned. The good news is that newer data modelers can learn from the unpleasant adventures of the experienced. A few are included in the following sections.

Getting Started

Consultants have a conundrum. Do you recommend the best solution to your client's problem, even if you know the client won't follow it, or do you recommend an acceptable, but not the best, solution that you believe the client will follow?

As a data modeler, unless you live in a perfect world, the first thing you must do is to decide whether you can live with the world you are given. This issue is determinative in three crucial areas: the plan, the team, and the users.

- *The plan: the data modeler needs to feel comfortable with the data modeling plan.* Any designer being held to a plan (budget, schedule, resources), no matter what the project, needs to feel confident that the work is doable. If you know that the budget is insufficient or the schedule unrealistic or the needed resources not available (staff, users etc.), then you need to decide whether you are on board the project or want to take a pass. This is the standard conundrum for any project team member, regardless of project type, and is an even bigger problem for the data modeler if the overall project manager does not sufficiently understand the data modeling process and its associated costs.

- *The team: the data modeler needs to feel comfortable with the data modeling team.* Experience shows that for any medium-to-large project, about half the data modeling team has never created, or worked on, a data model of any size. If you don't see experience, then look for enthusiasm with a willingness to learn.

- *The users: the data modeler needs to feel comfortable that the subject-matter experts are available to the team.* There is a story, which might even be true, of the Soviet-era, Russian manufacturing facility that had the new, faster, and cheaper machines that would double factory productivity sitting on the factory floor for years, uninstalled, because the Soviet bureaucracy would not allow the one-month disruption in production to install the new equipment. You might not believe this tale until you ask permission to interview the user department expert on how the current process works. More than one potentially spiffy new system has been postponed, if not derailed, because access to the people in the know was restricted. Getting buy-in from user management on access to user resources is critical to a successful project.

Don't Lose Control of the Project to Users

Having the "right" relationship with the user staff is of utmost importance. In data modeling, the user must be heard. However, one common cause of project failure is the loss of control of the assignment to the user, as in the following example:

> A securities firm was redesigning its account processing system. During the data modeling exercises, the issues of portfolios and positions came up. The business user wanted them on the data model, while the data modelers insisted that both were derived data and should not be part of the model. (Portfolios and positions are actually views of selected asset occurrences.) The user technical staff did not intervene and tactfully supported the business users, forcing the acceptance of the derived data on the data model.

> Because portfolio and position were on the data model, none of the process modeling teams felt it was important to develop the processes to create the derived data. The unfortunate outcome was disharmony on the development team, uncertainty about who was in control, disruption and disagreement over what process modeling tasks had to be completed, and eventually the collapse of the project.

The moral of this story is to maintain control of the project and do that by

- Knowing what you are doing.

- Advertising what you are doing and why.

- Sticking to the plan.

- Making others stick to the plan.

Don't Lose Control of the Project to Technical Staff

Losing control of data modeling to technical staff can be more disruptive and dangerous than losing control to a user. The problem is the "little knowledge" syndrome. Whereas end-user staff usually admit that they have no idea what data modeling is, technical staff often feel they either know more about it than anybody else or don't have to know about it because it's not important.

The remedy is up-front training on the advantages of data modeling and, perhaps more important, the dangers of not data modeling correctly.

Don't Become Dependent on Tools or Techniques

Too many organizations welcome new methodologies, techniques, and tools without fully understanding the consequences. Here's an example:

> The development team at Rossetti & Siddall Publishing decided that a computer-aided system engineering (CASE) tool was needed. After acquiring the tool, the team charged into a major application and in no time at all was up a creek. The team quickly discovered that having a tool is no substitute for knowledge and experience with the underlying techniques.

As Chris Gane, the systems development guru and co-author of *Structured Systems Analysis: Tools and Techniques*, once said, "A fool with a tool is just a faster fool."[4]

The moral of the story is to understand the technique before picking a tool.

Techniques follow an approach, framework, or method, so the approach the project follows should be established before any discussion of techniques (Figure 4-11). For example, this book focuses on the entity-relationship approach to data modeling and contains a number of techniques for creating a good E-R design.

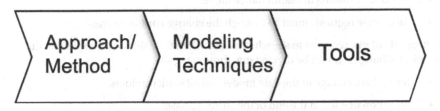

Figure 4-11. *Confirm the approach, then the technique, then the tool*

Likewise, the techniques the project uses should be understood before making any tool decisions. Altering the sequence can invite excessive learning-curve pain and poor system workmanship.

Don't Get Bogged Down in Endless Analysis

Modeling is difficult. The logical data modeler must juggle hundreds of data objects. Moreover, data modeling is only a small part of the systems development process that requires the examination and reexamination of data, and subsequent LDM modification, over and over again. However, because incomplete or inaccurate logical data models can be linked to disastrous application development efforts, the prudent analyst would be wise to ensure that the data model is as correct as possible. While an inaccurate object in a process model might cause the incorrect execution of a business function, an incorrect data object can cause the failure of many different functions.

Some project staff, however, go to the other extreme and get bogged down in endless analysis. In their quest for perfection, some designers never finish the model, potentially causing the ultimate failure of the project.

Data modelers get bogged down for a number of reasons. They:

- Don't recognize modeling diminishing returns.

- Fear moving ahead and/or lack confidence in the model.

- Have a poor understanding of how the model is used.

Complete analysis is essential, but knowing when enough is enough requires judgment. Analysis should be called to a halt when

- New information provides little additional value.

- Users and analysts are quibbling over unimportant items.

- There is sufficient information to move on to the next phase.

Then freeze the data model, with the following rules:

- Establish a data model change control process.

- Declare the model in maintenance mode.

- All change requests must go through the change control process.

Evaluate all change requests to see whether and when they should be applied to the model/project. Changes should be divided into three categories.

- Immediate change to the data model and all work products.

- Attention needed at the end of the current phase.

- Attention required at some future release of the application.

When all is said and done, data modeling is a systems development task of a systems development project and shares the vast majority of problems as well as best practices with other system development tasks.

The Players…and the Rules of Engagement

Putting together a constructive team to collect and properly analyze an organization's data is a difficult task. Surprisingly or not, many system professionals do not look forward to the data modeling process. Why?

Data modeling is highly abstract, and not all systems professionals understand the problem, much less the solution. Clearly, if individuals cannot sufficiently conceptualize the problem and the solution, then all the techniques and tools in the world will not help them. Also, data modeling is nondeterministic. There is no single right answer because a business can be modeled in a number of different ways. However, there certainly are wrong answers. Some system professionals have trouble with the subjective nature of the technique in a profession they see as stressing objectivity.

What can the data modeler do to eliminate this problem? The answers are the same as for every other area within IT.

- *First, data modeling needs a champion.* A champion is an individual who is (1) an IT professional or non-IT senior executive who either is an expert in the subject area (telecommunications, government regulation, employment law, data modeling, etc.) or is willing to acquire and support the expertise from elsewhere, (2) is willing to unequivocally and publicly promote the area (tout its benefits, justify its costs, and communicate its need), and (3) has sufficient status in the organization that they are listened to at the highest levels.

- *Second, an agreed-upon set of rules is required.* A set of guidelines or rules is critical to the success of any data modeling project, and the ground rules should be established before the project starts to avoid unnecessary battles.

First, the logical data model is a communications tool. Its purpose is to convey to system designers, programmers, and database designers the real world of the business—both what they currently have and what they want. To converse intelligently, they need a common language that all parties know and use. The data model is that primary means of communication. Rules, both of data modeling syntax and semantics, are essential to successfully accomplish this mission.

There is another reason for preapproved rules. Arguments become less intense and less detrimental to progress when they are covered by previously approved abstract rules. For example, the statement "Do not model derived data" is abstract—without emotional ties to a real-life situation. On the other hand, "Portfolio is derived data and, therefore, not to be modeled" is grounded in reality, and arguments about whether to observe this rule can evoke an emotional response.

The successful data modeler prepares for these eventualities before drawing the first rectangle.

Deliverables

Logical data modeling is not finished until all documentation is complete and turned over to project management as input to the Physical Schema Definition phase of U3D.

The primary deliverables are

- *LDM.1 logical data model (E-R diagram)*: The diagram showing all entities and relationships (Figure 4-12).

- *LDM.2 logical data model object definitions (data dictionary)*: Detailed documentation for each entity, attribute, relationship, and domain (Figures 4-13 through 4-16 in the "Example of Deliverables" later in this chapter). Any automated CASE or system development tools might dictate what can be stored and how it should look. However, information that physical designers need but is not required by your particular data dictionary can always be included as comments or notes. Appendix B gives an example of the data that should be in a data dictionary.

63

- *LDM.3 logical data modeling notes*: Any comments, advice, difficulties, questions, suggestions, warnings, or other information the logical data modeler wants to communicate to physical designers.

Physical data base designers use these three deliverables along with the business requirements (process model business requirements, i.e., processes, procedures, and all volume information) uncovered by the logical process modelers and physical process modelers to create the physical database design.

Examples of Deliverables

The E-R diagram might be quite large. If so, the single-page diagram should be supplemented with a number of subordinate, perhaps subject area, diagrams.

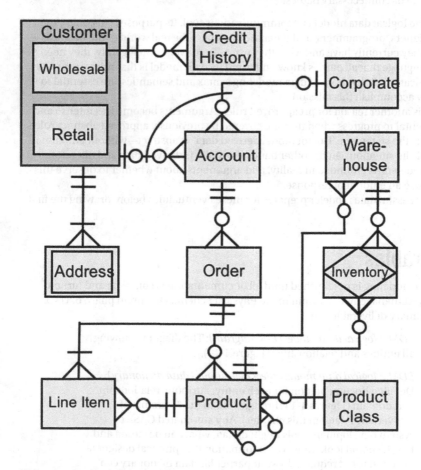

Figure 4-12. Sample logical data modeling deliverable: E-R diagram

The purpose of the E-R diagram is communication, not being a wall covering. The diagram should be understandable by most end users and all physical database designers.

Sample Data Dictionary, Data Object Definitions

Logical Data Object Definition Entity	Explanation
Name: _____ Type: _____ Description: _____ _____ Synonyms: _____ Relationship _____ Attributes: _____ _____ Est. No. Occur:_____ Annual Growth: _____ Notes and Comments: _____ _____ _____ Update Date:_____ By: _____	*Type*—Proper, associative, attributive, or S-type. *Relationships*—All relationships to which the entity is a party. *Estimated Number of Occurrences*—Total number of record instances. *Annual Growth*—Percentage annual growth rate.

Figure 4-13. *Entity type definition*

Some information, such as annual growth rate, might be a bit sketchy. It doesn't matter. Enter it anyway. You can always qualify with uncertainties in the Notes field.

Logical Data Object Definition Relationship	Explanation
Name: _____ Description: _____ _____ Relationship Type (Unary, binary, N-ary): _____ Between entities: Entities Cardinality Modality _____ _____ _____ Other Constraints: _____ Notes and Comments: _____ _____ Update Date: _____ By: _____	**Explanation** *Notes*—The relationship definitions typically contain the largest notes field as the modeler tries to describe the complexities of some relationships. *Other Constraints*—Explain in English, any constraints that are not diagrammable or the logical data modeler feels need additional explanation.

Figure 4-14. *Relationship definition*

Relationship constraints become the bulk of the information regarding how entities relate to each other. Feel free to write as much as necessary.

Logical Data Object Definition Attribute	Explanation
Name: _____ Description: _____ _____ Synonyms: _____ In Entity: _____ Attribute Type: __ Source: __ Primitive or __Derived If Derived what Algorithm?:_____ _____ Complexity: _ Simple or _ Group If Group Contains?:_____ Valuation: ___ Single or _ Multivalue Size: _____ Data Type: _____ Domain(s): _____ Notes and Comments: _____ _____ _____ Update Date:_____ By: _____	*In Entity*—Usually an attribute exists in only one entity type. If there are (intentional) duplicates, then list all the entity types and which contains the original or master copy. *Attribute Type*—Descriptor or unique identifier. If it is a compound identifier the other attributes and their order should be in the Notes field. *If Derived what Algorithm?*—The data items and formula used to calculate the data value. *If Group Contains?*—The data items that make up the group. *Data Type*—Such as integer, text, picture, movie, etc. *Domain*—If the attribute participates in a formally defined domain.

Figure 4-15. Attribute definition

Logical data model designers are often uncertain about some of the characteristics of some attributes, such as derived data. That's OK. Just make sure that your document indicates what you do know, what you don't know, and what you are not sure of. Anything less places the database designer at a considerable disadvantage.

Logical Data Object Definition Domain	Explanation
Name: _____ Description: _____ Type: Data Type: _____ Range: _____ Acceptable Values: _____ _____ Notes and Comments: _____ _____ Update Date:_____ By: _____	*Description*—Type of domain (data type, range of values, acceptable values, etc.). *Data Type*—The broad category of values that are acceptable such as integer, text, and real numbers. *Range*—Continuous values with a specific start and stop. For example, dates between January 1, 1950, and December 31, 1990. *Acceptable Values*—Specific itemized values, such as male and female.

Figure 4-16. Domain definition

Domains are the most forgotten part of logical data modeling. Worse, they are also the most forgotten part of physical database design. Document domains early and often, even if all the information about them is uncertain.

Notes

1. Raymond L. Gordon, *Basic Interviewing Skills.* Long Grove IL: Waveland Press, Inc., 1998.

2. Peter Pin-Shan Chen, "English Sentence Structure and Entity-Relationship Diagrams." *Information Sciences.* 29.2-3, 1983, pages 127–149.

3. Peter Pin-Shan Chen, "English, Chinese, and ER Diagrams." *Data & Knowledge Engineering.* Vol. 23, No. 1, June 1997, pages 5–16.

4. Chris Gane and Trish Sarson, *Structured Systems Analysis: Tools and Techniques.* Englewood Cliffs, NJ: Prentice Hall, 1985.

CHAPTER 5

■ ■ ■

LDM Best Practices

Do not let what you cannot do interfere with what you can do.

—John Wooden

Do well and right, and let the world sink.

—George Herbert (Welsh poet)

Did you ever add a column of figures and the total did not agree with someone else's total? Accountants have a quick test for such an accounting error. Subtract one column total from the other column total. If the difference between them is evenly divisible by nine, then two digits were probably reversed (129 instead of 192) or a zero is left off the end of one of the numbers.

Little tricks like this can easily catch simple mistakes before they can grow into humongous disasters. Logical data modeling does not have any *divide by 9* equivalents; however, there are a number of lessons learned that can help detect small errors and anomalies while they are still in the disaster incubation stage.

This chapter presents some things experienced data modelers think all data modelers should allow or do. Other chapters look at some don'ts and a few things to watch out for.

Chapter Subjects

- Abbreviations
- Almost unique identifiers
- Clarity
- Compound unique identifiers
- Conceptual integrity
- Conjunctive relationships

- Duplicate super-subtypes "type" data
- Exclusive relationships
- Group attributes
- Level of abstraction
- Many-to-many relationships

- N-ary relationships
- Naming objects
- Null attributes
- Optional relationships
- Subject areas
- Supertypes and subtypes
- Unique identifiers

Abbreviations

Abbreviations should be kept to a minimum, and when used, they should be meaningful to the end user.

Computer-based abbreviations should not be confused with business abbreviations used in data modeling. Computer-based abbreviations were created for use with operating systems, computer languages, file managers, and DBMSs, which limit the length of, and put restrictions on, field, record, file, and program names. The conventions permit text to physically fit into computer-managed directories. It was not uncommon in years past to have an operating system or programming language with a five-character limit on data field and file names. Spaces were not allowed and many special characters forbidden. Luckily, the logical data modeler does not live in this world, but rather in the real world of the business. Names in this world should reflect this world.

There is a significant difference between computer-based abbreviations and legitimate end-user abbreviations. For example, in retailing, a product sold in a store is identified by a number called a stock keeping unit, although everyone in the business calls the number a SKU (pronounced as one word rhyming with *few*). SKU would be an acceptable name even though it is an abbreviation. However, if you've identified CUSTOMER FINAL PRE-PAYMENT DATE as an attribute, it should be written as CUSTOMER FINAL PRE-PAYMENT DATE (meaningful to the end user) and not CUS_FIN_PREPMT_DTE (required to satisfy a name length restriction).

The developer should be sensitive to the unfortunate fact that CASE and system development tools usually have name length limits that can sometimes force the use of nonbusiness abbreviations. If you must use abbreviations, keep them in English. Avoid schemes such as stripping out vowels to shorten words, which usually results in unrecognizable and unpronounceable gobbledygook. For example, a vowel-dropping scheme would turn VENDOR ASSIGNED USER CODE into the horribly mashed VNDR ASGND USR CD. Stick with simple English abbreviations and standard initials such in Table 5-1.

Table 5-1. *Abbreviations*

Words	Abbreviations/Initials
Customer	Cust
Account	Acct
Lysergic Acid Diethylamide	LSD
Pennsylvania	PA

If the offending development tool name length restriction is too short, such that a meaningful abbreviation is not possible, then the modeler should use both the preferred logical data modeling name *and* the shorter tool-compliant version. Many tools have an alias function that allows different names to be entered for the same object, or the data modeler can place the real object name in a comment field. Make sure the tool enhances the process, not detracts from it.

A good set of approved abbreviations for the logical data model makes the transition from the logical to physical design easier. Publishing a list of acceptable abbreviations is particularly useful. However, recognize that the list will not be exhaustive and will have to be constantly updated.

Almost Unique Identifiers

Identify *almost unique identifiers* when known because they can be useful for application development.

Ideally, there are unique and nonunique attributes. However, the world is not as clean and simple as that. Sometimes there are attributes that might not be mathematically unique but are sufficiently unique to be useful. Examples include people's names, employee or student numbers that are reissued after a period of time, and even Social Security numbers (occasionally a Social Security number is mistakenly issued to more than one person).

Almost unique attributes have varying levels of uniqueness. Names might be much less unique than reissued employee numbers. While a not completely unique employee number might be acceptable as a record key in a database, a name probably would not. However, a person's name is sufficiently unique to serve as an adequate secondary index.

Many magazine publishers use a "match code" (Table 5-2) consisting of a string of nonunique attributes, which, when put together, form a key that is close to being unique for even large populations.

Table 5-2. *Magazine Match Code Example*

Characters	Description
1–5	First five characters of postal code
6–10	First five characters of last name
11–11	First name initial
12–14	First three digits of street number
15–18	First four characters of street name
19–20	Tie breaker

A second type of almost unique identifier is an attribute that is unique for only part of its life. Imagine an organization that reuses document numbers after a maximum number is reached, but never before 2 years has passed. For example, assume the maximum document number is 99,999, which will take, on average, 4 years to reach. After that period, caution is needed.

Almost unique identifier information is useful for physical designers and should be communicated to them.

Clarity

Remove confusing objects from the data model.

Examples of extraneous objects are unnecessary super-subtypes, extraneous relationships, and unnecessary entities.

This is a "judgment call" rule. However, if you remember that the dual purpose of a data model is to

- Provide feedback information to end users.

- Communicate end-user information to physical designers.

then you can better judge whether objects added to the model, or left out, contribute to communication or subtract from it. Look at the example in Figure 5-1.

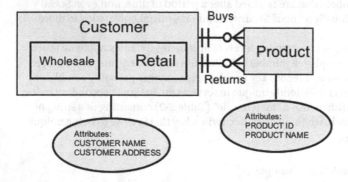

Figure 5-1. *Data model containing extraneous objects*

The data model contains extraneous data objects.

- Because the participating entities and connectivity for the relationships Buy and Return are identical, they should be represented by the single relationship Buy and Return.

- Because the subtypes Retail and Wholesale have identical attributes and relationships, they are superfluous and should be eliminated.

Clarity is an important underlying principle of logical data modeling right behind communication.

Compound Unique Identifiers

Compound unique identifiers are acceptable, and the position of the attributes within the unique identifier might, or might not, be important.

Sometimes the business uses more than one attribute to uniquely identify an entity occurrence. For example, a course a student took might require the COURSE NUMBER (Chemistry 101), the YEAR (2017), and the SEMESTER (Fall) to uniquely identify it.

No single attribute, or any two, uniquely identifies the student's course. These three attributes together form a *compound unique identifier* or simply *compound identifier*. If you talk to the school administrators and teachers, you might discover that the order is unimportant to them—they might talk of the fall 2107 chemistry course or the 2017 chemistry course taught that fall, and so on.

Other compound unique identifiers involve a specific business order. Personnel assignments for chain-store employees could involve the compound unique identifier STORE NUMBER and DEPARTMENT NUMBER, always in that order. The ERD cannot capture this distinction although the accompanying documentation in the data dictionary can and should.

The reason? Logical data modeling unique identifiers might very well become physical design keys. The sequence of fields in a compound key can be the major determinant in index and data storage clustering. The physical designers need to know how much latitude they have regarding key field sequence. Is the business dictating the acceptable field sequence in the compound key, or do the physical designers have free rein to determine the best ordering? The logical data modeler needs to communicate this to the physical designers. (See the "Unique Identifiers" entry in this chapter.)

Conceptual Integrity

Maintain the integrity of logical data modeling concepts, even if the tool you are using makes it difficult.

Data modeling and system development tools can often confuse or corrupt logical data modeling concepts. While it is necessary to observe the data modeling conventions followed, or required, by the development tool you are using, do not lose sight of the correct logical data modeling concepts and why they are important.

An example can best illustrate this point. Is the entity-relationship pair Customers Buy Cars, one relationship or two? The answer, of course, is one. To confirm this, just examine how people speak. You hear that a husband and wife share a relationship, not that the husband has one relationship and the wife another. People also speak about the relationship between the United States and Japan knowing that it encompasses both directions.

Unfortunately, that is not the way all CASE tools work. Some tools would treat the automobile example as two separate relationships (Customers Buy Cars *and* Cars Are Bought By Customers) and require completion of two dictionary entries (i.e., two names, two definitions). See Figure 5-2.

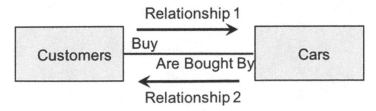

Figure 5-2. *A binary relationship treated as two separate relationships*

This problem is more persistent in tools that consider all relationships binary or in tools using a line as the graphic convention for a relationship. The problem is less likely to occur in tools that permit n-ary relationships or the use of a diamond as a relationship symbol.

As an example, take the n-ary relationship Customers Buy Cars From Dealers (Figure 5-3). Is this one relationship, two, three, or six? The correct answer is, of course, one; however, various tools require anywhere from one to six separate relationships (Figure 5-4).

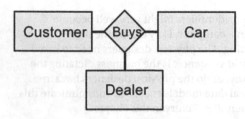

Figure 5-3. *N-ary relationship linking three entities*

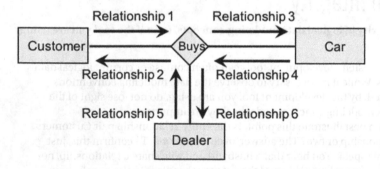

Figure 5-4. *N-ary relationship treated as six binary relationships*

You might have to bend your principles to use available tools. If you have to compromise the implementation of the logical data model, remember to keep the conceptual integrity of your model strong and document (even if only in a comments field) all tool-induced compromises in the data dictionary.

Conjunctive Relationships

Allow conjunctive (*and*) relationships because they are a legitimate end-user concept.

Conjunctive relationships stipulate that if entity occurrence "A" is related to entity occurrence "B," then occurrence "A" must also be related to entity occurrence "C." Unfortunately, few data modelers include conjunctions in their model for any of four reasons.

- Few data modeling tools support them.

- Conjunctive relationships are not common in businesses.

- Few DBMSs directly allow their implementation.

- Most modelers don't know that the concept of conjunction exists.

The first and second reasons might be true. The fourth reason is all too true. The third reason is the misplaced physical design issue again. True as it might be that most DBMSs do not allow easy implementation of conjunction, the argument is, nonetheless, misplaced in logical design. If conjunction is a real end-user concept, model it. If it is important to the business and the DBMS does not support it, it can always be implemented through triggers, stored procedures, or application code.

Duplicate Super-Subtypes "Type" Data

A duplicate "type" attribute is appropriate in super-subtype entities.

Common attributes should exist in the supertype. Only subtype-specific attributes should be in the subtype—with one exception.

Many modelers use a special attribute to distinguish the different subtypes. Look at the following example:

> Quik-Drop Parachutes Inc. is developing a data model for its new human resource system. The model must reflect the special attributes and relationships for the four roles of employee: active, retired, terminated, and leave of absence (Figure 5-5).

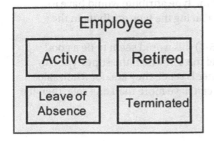

Figure 5-5. *Duplicate attribute data can exist in the subtype*

To distinguish the roles, Quik-Drop modelers created the EMPLOYEE TYPE attribute with the acceptable values of "Active," "Retired," "Leave of Absence," and "Terminated." To work properly, the modelers must duplicate the attribute EMPLOYEE TYPE in all four subtypes.

This duplication of EMPLOYEE TYPE in all the subtypes is acceptable.

Exclusive and Nonexclusive Generalization

Many modelers like to use a type or role attribute to differentiate the roles that subtypes play in the supertype. For example, Figure 5-6 is the entity Customer, which has two subtypes: Retail and Wholesale. To communicate this information, the modeler created the attribute CUSTOMER TYPE with the acceptable values of "Retail" and "Wholesale."

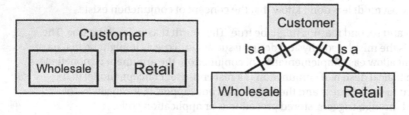

Figure 5-6. *Supertype box and "isa" constructs*

The important question is whether the role for a subtype in a generalization is best described by an attribute or by a relationship.

Those who use the "is a" construct, in which the subtype is shown in a one-to-one relationship with the supertype, tend to prefer describing the role as a relationship. They would define the role options of retail or wholesale in the relationship definition.

A more popular and probably better approach is to define the subtype role using a type or role attribute such as CUSTOMER TYPE with the acceptable values of "Wholesale" and "Retail." Advocates of this approach prefer it because most subtype roles have a domain of acceptable values, and domains are a property of an attribute, not a relationship. However, this raises another question. Should the type attribute be in the supertype or the subtype? The answer is not always obvious.

Most modelers place the type attribute in the supertype. Their argument is simple: if you placed the type attribute in the subtype, then the type attribute would have to be duplicated as many times as there are subtypes. Placing the type attribute in the supertype avoids this duplication.

Certainly with the Customer example (Figure 5-7) this would seem to be a good idea. Unfortunately, this answer assumes that all the roles in which the supertype can participate are exclusive. In other words, if a customer is retail, they are not wholesale, and vice versa. However, if a supertype occurrence can have more than one role, then the type attribute in the supertype runs into trouble.

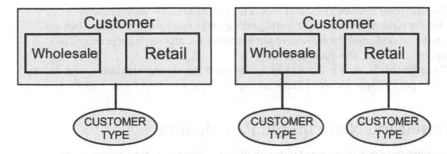

Figure 5-7. *Supertype/subtype attributes*

Imagine the supertype Soldier with Officer and Enlisted as the two subtypes, MILITARY STATUS as the type attribute, and "Officer" and "Enlisted" as the acceptable values (Figure 5-8a). Although in most cases a soldier is either an officer or enlisted but not both, this is not always the case. There are examples where a soldier is an officer in the reserves but an enlisted person on active duty. For this individual, the supertype occurrence would have both roles and would have to be linked to both subtypes (Figure 5-8b).

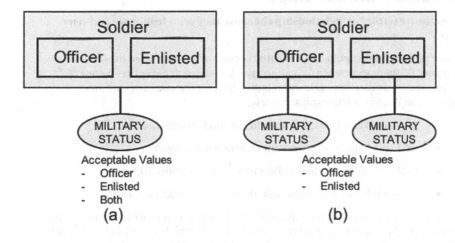

Figure 5-8. *Nonexclusive generalization*

If the type attribute MILITARY STATUS is in the supertype, then the acceptable values of the attribute would have to be "Officer," "Enlisted," and "Both." On the other hand, if MILITARY STATUS were in the subtype, then the acceptable values could be limited to just "Officer" and "Enlisted."

The military example has only two subtypes. Imagine a case where there are four, five, and ten subtypes. The combinations or nonexclusive supertype participation would be quite large and unwieldy. Certainly in these cases, the type attribute works better in the subtype.

The difference between the two cases is that in the first, the subtypes were exclusive—a supertype occurrence could participate in one role, or the other, but not both. In the second case, the roles were not exclusive—a supertype occurrence could participate in one role, the other, or both.

The moral of the story is that unless you are sure that the generalization is exclusive, it is best to put the type attributes in the subtype.

Required and Nonrequired Participation

Some supertype occurrences must participate in a subtype as in the Customer and Soldier examples. In other cases, supertype participation in a subtype might be optional. Take the case of the supertype Boat with subtypes Sailing and Power Plant used to describe the type of sails it has (if it has any) and/or its engine or engines (also if it has any). A rowboat has neither sails nor a power plant, so it would not participate in either of these subtypes. Boat would be a supertype that is not required to have a subtype. If the type attribute BOAT TYPE were in the supertype, it would have a value of null or blank.

Exclusive Relationships

Allow *exclusive* (*either or*) relationships because they are a legitimate end-user concept.

Exclusive relationships stipulate that if entity occurrence "A" is related to entity occurrence "B," then occurrence "A" cannot also be related to entity occurrence "C."

Some modelers disallow exclusive relationships for the same reasons they disallowed conjunctive relationships, namely:

- Most tools and DBMSs simply do not support *exclusive or*.

- Exclusive relationships are not common in businesses.

- Exclusion can sometimes allow null values in primary keys.

- Most modelers don't know that the concept of exclusion exists.

It is certainly true that few data modeling tools support *exclusive or* relationships, and even fewer database management systems do so, although some level of support is available through the use of processes embedded in the DBMS. Nevertheless:

- Physical design issues should be kept out of logical design and remain in physical design where they belong (revisit Principle 1 of the database design principles, Separate Logical Design from Physical Design, in Chapter 1).

- Data modeling should not be limited to what is supported by a particular DBMS or tool. For example, if the need for exclusion is sufficient, the physical designers could decide to implement it through triggers, stored procedures, or application code.

This last argument raises an important point. If a particular DBMS or file management system does not support a certain feature, the developers still have the option to include the feature with triggers, stored procedures, or application code. However, they can do this only if they know that the feature is desired and the desired feature is communicated to them through the logical data and process models.

As for nulls, contrary to what some relational database advocates believe, exclusive relationships do not require nulls in primary keys; however, they are possible if the primary key is also the foreign key (see entries on "Null Attributes" in this chapter and "Primary Keys" and "Foreign Keys" in Chapter 6). Do not concern yourself with this argument because it is misplaced. Issues such as null values and keys (primary or foreign) are physical design issues (the *how* from Chapter 1) and not relevant to a discussion of logical data modeling (the *what*) (Principle 1 again).

Group Attributes

Group attributes are allowed, but be careful because they can hide information about data objects.

In many IT circles, the term *group* can be applied to either attribute complexity's group attribute, which is an attribute that contains other attributes (as in DATE containing the attributes MONTH, DAY and YEAR), or attribute valuation's multivalue attribute, which can contain multiple values (as in the attribute CHILDREN with the three values "Peter," "Paul," and "Mary.") (See Chapter 3.)

Both are an acceptable part of logical data modeling if (1) they are a legitimate part of the business and (2) they do not hide from the physical designers their true nature and all the attributes or values they contain.

Level of Abstraction

Make the data model as abstract as possible while making sure it still fully and adequately describes the business.

The "Data Values" entry in the next chapter illustrates how some modelers model the values of data rather than the attribute types. This could result in the data model representing only a subset of the total possible occurrences of the attribute type, leaving a prematurely aging data model requiring possibly frequent changes and updates.

Models are more accurate and stay current longer when their structure is abstract. For example, using the more abstract attribute POSTAL CODE (and its more abstract domain) rather than the less abstract attribute ZIP CODE can extend the life of the model beyond the first time an international address is stored. Likewise, the more abstract entity Employee can accommodate more and varied attributes and relationships than the more concrete entity Hourly Worker. Abstraction allows a data model to express more diverse data and do so with fewer data objects.

However, taken too far, abstraction could be just as damaging, if not more so, than being too concrete. Abstracting the entities Employees, Customers, and Regulators to the single entity People is excessive because it hides the basic and different roles of the three groups within the organization. Likewise, combining the high-school grade system attributes GRADE, EFFORT, and ABILITY into COMMENTS causes loss of meaning and potential utility.

The challenge is to forgo premature aging of a data model by making sure the data objects are sufficiently abstract, while ensuring that anyone reading the data model knows what the subject is about. When the name and/or description of the object starts to become meaningless, then abstraction has gone too far.

Taken to its extreme, excessive abstraction could collapse an entire data model into what some call a TUAKASUDM (commonly pronounced "too-ack-a-sue-dum") or The Universal All Knowing All Seeing Ultimate Data Model (Figure 5-9).

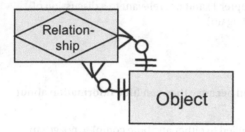

Figure 5-9. *Excessive abstraction*

A TUAKASUDM (not to be confused with an Egyptian pharaoh) can represent any complex and less abstract data model as two generic entities in a recursive relationship. In fact, a TUAKASUDM is the logical conclusion of allowing either data value–differentiated data objects (see "Data Value–Differentiated Entities and Attributes" in Chapter 6) or excessive abstraction. It says that anything might be related to anything given some relationship. Who can argue with that? The problem is that it's not very expressive or specific, and readers of the data model know nothing more about the subject after reviewing the data model than they did before they started.

Sound farfetched? Not at all. Some system directories, data dictionaries, and even some interpretative programming environments use this approach for their data management. It works—it just doesn't work fast.

As always, when trying to decide how abstract or concrete to be, apply the logical data modeling principles. Increasing the level of abstraction of a model until the next level would decrease the ability of the model to communicate relevant information to a reader.

Many-to-Many Relationships

Allow many-to-many (M:N) relationships.

Although an M:N relationship is a legitimate end-user concept, some modelers insist on "resolving" it during logical data modeling because no major database management system currently directly supports the concept.

During database design, the M:N relationships are usually converted to two one-to-many relationships with the introduction of a *junction* or *intersection* record or table (Figure 5-10). Because it must be done eventually, the obvious question becomes, why not convert M:N relationships during logical data modeling? The answer: because a junction record is an artificial construct that hides the fact that many-to-many relationships exist in the real world—as any end user will tell you.

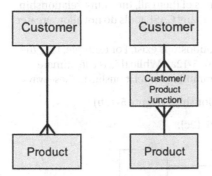

Figure 5-10. *A junction or intersection record resolving a many-to-many relationship*

In addition, resolving M:N relationships is a physical design issue that might (or might not) have to be addressed during database design. After all, who knows what DBMS the database administrators will use or what DBMS will be available ten years from now? The logical model should be immune to all physical issues so that the physical designers can separate what is end-user-related information from what is relevant to physical design.

Some modelers create "phantom" associative entities to resolve many-to-many relationships. This is a mistake and a misuse of logical data modeling.

An associative entity is a relationship that has its own attributes. For example, an automobile has a list price but often sells for a totally different amount. The exact price of a car depends on who is buying the car and when (Figure 5-11). However, an attribute-less phantom associative entity should not be created simply to resolve an M:N relationship.

Figure 5-11. *An associative entity should not be used to resolve a many-to-many relationship*

N-ary Relationships

Relationships can legitimately exist between two, three, or more entities.

Many data modeling techniques and the most famous of them all, the entity-relationship approach, support n-ary relationships. Regrettably, many CASE tools do not allow greater than binary relationships.

In the real world, three-way and more-way relationships exist. For example, take the case of a customer buying a car from a dealer (Figure 5-12a). While this is a legitimate three-way relationship, most CASE tools require diagramming the relationship in these ways:

- With two or three separate binary relationships (Figure 5-12b).

- As an empty associative entity (Figure 5-12c).

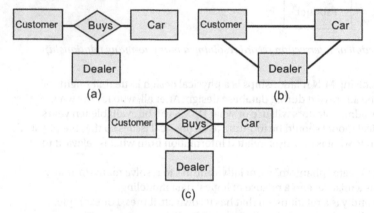

Figure 5-12. *Diagramming n-ary relationships*

Neither accurately reflects the business. (See the "Empty Entities" entry in Chapter 7.)

While it is true that most CASE tools simply do not support exotic relationships such as exclusion, conjunction, and n-ary relationships, that is no good excuse for ignoring robust relationships. These relationships are legitimate and valuable end-user concepts that should be documented if they exist. How they are documented could be tool specific. In some tools, the exclusive or the n-ary nature of a relationship might have to exist only as comments in the data dictionary definition of relationships.

Another excuse frequently cited for excluding n-ary relationships is that none of the major DBMSs directly supports them. This ignores the possibility of future systems supporting these relationships. If their occurrence is not documented, the information will not be accessible when more sophisticated data management products become available. Moreover, physical designers could implement n-ary relationships through computer code if the need were sufficient.

N-ary Relationships and Membership Class

Some designers encounter problems with membership class (cardinality and modality) when diagramming n-ary relationships. Take the n-ary relationship Customers Buy Cars from a Dealer. Looking at the relationship Buy as a series of relationship-entity pairs, you get the following:

- A Customer can Buy zero to many Cars.

- A Dealer can sell (Buy in the other direction) to zero to many Customers.

- A Car can be bought by zero to many Customers.

- A Customer can Buy from zero to many Dealers.

- A Dealer can sell (Buy in the other direction) zero to many Cars.

- A Car can be bought from zero to many Dealers.

The membership class of the relationship can be easily diagrammed, as in Figure 5-13.

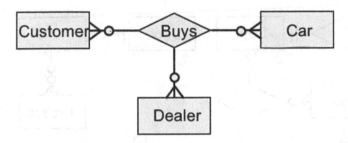

Figure 5-13. *N-ary cardinality and modality*

Take a second case, Many Employees from many Departments can be assigned to a Project. The relationship-entity pair is as follows:

- An Employee can be in one and only one Department.

- A Department can have zero to many Employees.

- A Project can have zero to many Employees.

- An Employee can be assigned to zero to many Projects.

- A Department can have zero to many Projects.

- A Project can be associated with zero to many Departments.

If you try to diagram the relationship, there is a problem (Figure 5-14). Do you place two bars next to Department to reflect "An Employee can be in *one and only one* Department," or do you use a zero and crow's foot to reflect "A Project can be associated with *zero to many* Departments"?

What should the designer do?

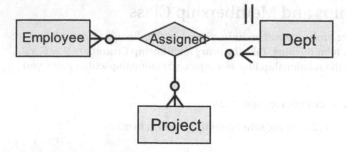

Figure 5-14. *N-ary cardinality confusion*

The first reaction might be to make the n-ary relationship either three binary relationships (Figure 5-15a) or two binary relationships (Figure 5-15b). The problem with either of these solutions is that too much information is lost, namely, that there is one business relationship dealing with three entities.

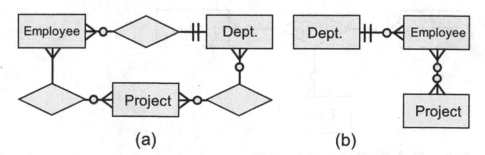

Figure 5-15. *Incorrect N-ary resolution*

There are a couple of things the designer can do to resolve this problem.

1. *Change the diagrammatic conventions.* This is a case where the diamond, as a diagrammatic convention, is superior to just using a line to represent a relationship. A line can cause the designer to see the relationship as multiple binary relationships rather than as a single n-ary relationship. Focus on the relationship diamond rather than the entity rectangles when assigning cardinality and modality. The problem should go away.

2. *Confirm that the relationship is not an associative entity (a relationship with its own attributes).* A relationship involving three or more entities is not that common, and often when it does appear, the relationship is transactional, meaning that the relationship describes a specific event that is the glue that binds the three, or more, entities together. Events often have their own attributes. In the Customer Buys Car from a Dealer example, in what entity should you find the attributes DATE OF SALE and SALE PRICE? They are properties of the relationship Buys not of Car, or Dealer, or Customer. Buys is actually an associative entity.

Look at the relationship Assigned in the Employee, Department, Project example. Is Assigned a relationship or an associative entity? If it contains attributes such as START DATE and END DATE, then it is an associative entity, as in Figure 5-16.

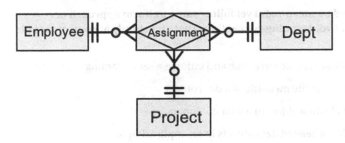

Figure 5-16. *N-ary event entity*

3. *Make sure that the relationship is a single relationship.* Sometimes a poorly defined relationship hides multiple relationships. For example, that an Employee can be in one and only one Department sounds more like an organizational structure rule rather than a project staffing one. The problem might be with the word *assignment*. There is assignment, call it *assignment-1*, which relates to the structure of a company, and *assignment-2*, which describes the temporary staffing of an employee to a project, as in Figure 5-17.

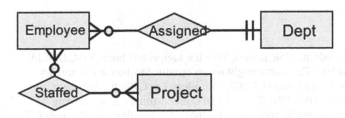

Figure 5-17. *Two separate relationships masquerading as a single N-ary relationship*

4. *Rely on the documentation.* The previous three approaches should solve more than 99 percent of any n-ary membership class problems. If not—if the relationship is so (legitimately) convoluted—then this is a case where graphic techniques need to take a backseat to natural language explanations. The data object definition in the data dictionary can be used to adequately explain the complexities of the most convoluted relationship.

Is this a case of the entity-relationship approach not being able to handle real-world relationships? Not at all. The entity-relationship model handles them fine. It's the artwork that needs improvement.

Naming Objects

Data object names should be meaningful yet follow some uniform approach or standard when possible. Avoid naming conventions that aim simply at control yet fail to communicate.

There are only three legitimate reasons to create and enforce a set of naming conventions.

- Help communicate the meaning of a data object.

- Locate a specific data object in a data dictionary.

- Identify similar or related data objects in an application or organization.

Achieving these objectives is often difficult because of these reasons:

- Data objects usually need multiple names to reflect various tool and/or computer language requirements.

- Most naming conventions in use predate, and often are out of touch with, current requirements.

- Uniqueness requirements vary by data object user.

- Naming convention goals vary within an organization.

Each is examined in turn.

Multiple Names

In many cases, an object needs multiple names. Take the logical attribute COMMERCIAL CUSTOMER PRE-TAX CREDIT. This name might be acceptable for the data dictionary and CASE tool, but it is too long for most COBOL compilers. For COBOL, you might have to shorten it to COMM_CUST_PRE_TAX_CREDIT, substituting the underscore for the spaces. Even this would not be acceptable for many C compilers, which cannot accept more than an eight-character name and do not accept an underscore. For such languages, the name might have to be shortened to TAXCRDT. And even this name may be too long for some assemblers, which do not allow names of more than five characters.

The reality is that names are context dependent. What an object is called might need to vary based on the context in which it exists, such as in data dictionaries, CASE tools, and computer languages. A name acceptable for the data dictionary might be unacceptable for an APL program.

Naming Conventions

Naming conventions are not new. Their use goes back almost to the inception of computer languages. What is new is the explosion of the number of objects that need to be named and the restrictions imposed by the places in which these new objects are stored.

Originally, names were limited to identifying physical objects such as files, records, and fields within records. To live within the confines of computer languages, system directories, and job cards, a set of rules was established that focused on name restrictions, reserved words, character length, and the use of delimiters and abbreviations.

Now these same conventions are used to gauge the appropriateness of names for objects, e.g., entities, attributes, relationships, external entities, and much more, which may be stored in a data dictionary or CASE tool. Unfortunately, the old ways of naming objects do not always work well with modern objects or tools. Conventions designed to uniquely define the 20 to 100 data objects in the files of yesteryear are inadequate for defining the potentially thousands of data objects in a data dictionary of today. Consequently, names, and their conventions, often need replacement or modification to make sense in the modern systems organizations.

Name Uniqueness

All data objects need to be unique within a specific context. However, not all tools and languages have the same context. Here's an example:

> Maitland Trust Company and Rossetti Marriage Counseling are two separate and unrelated companies. Both have the logical attribute CUSTOMER NAME, but with two different definitions. However, Maitland need not be concerned about Rossetti's CUSTOMER NAME, because the context of the two attributes is very different. Both companies can consider their definition of the attribute CUSTOMER NAME unique.

> In the same vein, one of Maitland's assembler programs might use the variable CUSTN for "customer name," while another Maitland program uses CUSTN for "custody number." Both are acceptable uses of CUSTN because the context (the program) of the two objects is different.

While the name must be unique within its context, in this case the computer program, the name need not be unique outside its context. In the previous Maitland example, there is no confusion even though the programs use the same object names because the context in which the names are used is different.

Contexts can vary by object. Whereas logical entity names might have to be unique across the enterprise, relationships need only be unique together with their entities. For example, it is acceptable to have the relationship-entity pair Customers Buy Products and Divisions Buy Raw Materials because the entities that tie together the relationship Buy are unique (Table 5-3).

Table 5-3. *The Context of Uniqueness Can Vary by Object*

Object Type	Uniqueness Context
Attribute	Enterprise
Entity	Enterprise
Relationship	Between entities
Record	File or database
Field	Record
File	Database or system
Database	Enterprise

Naming Convention Goals

Everyone within an organization does not have the same goals for a set of naming conventions. Two groups often at loggerheads are data administration and application development. Projects sometimes suffer because the data administration group sees naming conventions as a means to control and regulate the collective data asset, while the application developers are concerned with ease of use, productivity, and building applications in the quickest and cheapest way possible (Table 5-4). Conflict is often unavoidable.

Table 5-4. *Comparison of Data Administration and Application Development Naming Convention Goals*

Data Administration Naming Convention Goals	Application Development Naming Convention Goals
• Unique names across enterprise	• Unique names within programs, application, database, etc.
• Central control of names and all changes	• Application development freedom to customize and shorten names as needed
• Dictionary-oriented names	• Tool-oriented or programming language–oriented names

The clash can often be avoided, or at least minimized, with some preproject understanding of the contexts of the different data objects.

Naming conventions should reflect the needs of both groups.

- Facilitate the use of the data objects.

- Provide a modicum of control.

In some organizations there is little room for negotiation—with the application developers having to "knuckle under" to the prevailing standards. On the other hand, if these two groups are viewed as two separate contexts, compromise is possible.

While naming conventions vary, a good context-sensitive naming convention for attributes might look something like Table 5-5.

***Table 5-5.** Context-Sensitive Logical Attribute Naming Convention Example*

- Use full words—no abbreviations unless necessary. Length should be as long as necessary—60 characters is not excessive.

- Do not use abbreviations unless they are

    - Routinely used by a business (see the "Abbreviations" entry in this chapter).

    - Absolutely necessary for the data object name to fit in the data dictionary.

- Use a blank as a delimiter, i.e., CUSTOMER NAME, not CUSTOMER_NAME or CUSTOMER-NAME.

- Use names that are unique within context...

- ...and in English.

- Follow a consistent naming framework or rule set (see the following).

- Do not use special characters, codes, prefixes, or suffixes to specify the source, location, organization, entities, technology, or use of the object.

- Follow a naming rule set consistent with tool and data dictionary restrictions.

When creating object names, a set of rules should be applied. A popular rule set is the Prime-Modifier-Class approach (Table 5-6).

Table 5-6. *Attribute Naming Rule Set Example*

- All attribute names should be constructed of words in a specified order, for example:

  Prime Word [+ Modifier] + Class Word

  - Prime Word is a noun used to identify a basic data object, such as Customer, Account, and Employee.

  - Modifier is an adjective that further describes the prime word, such as Current and Last.

  - Class Word describes the object classification. Examples would be Address, Amount, Name.

- There should be only one Prime Word and only one Class Word per name.

- A name could have zero to many Modifiers.

An example of a correctly named attribute, using the previous framework, would be CUSTOMER LAST NAME.

Physical objects need a different set of conventions and rule set, as in Table 5-7.

Table 5-7. *Context-Sensitive Physical Naming Convention Example*

- The maximum length of the name is determined by the tool or computer language used. For example, the length would vary for C, DB2, and Assembler.

- Abbreviations are used where needed to conform to length restrictions.

- Names need not be unique across the entire enterprise, only within context.

- Delimiter is language/tool dependent.

Names should follow the naming rule set as much as possible given the computer language length restrictions. For example, an eight-character Assembler language name cannot support the Prime-Modifier-Class construct.

Naming conventions for other data objects, such as entities, relationships, or programs, can be similarly constructed. If the result of using a naming convention is a series of unintelligible phrases, then there is something wrong with the convention, and the phrases should be either changed or replaced.

Rule sets such as the Prime-Modifier-Class set mentioned earlier can be particularly problematic. Keep rule sets in perspective. Remember:

- Most rule sets produce junk from time to time.

- Always let reason prevail over form (*form follows reason?*). If the output of a rule set is unintelligible, change the name to something that is reasonable and makes sense—regardless of what the rules say.

Which naming approach you use is less important than achieving some level of agreement on its purpose and structure. For example, a satisfactory approach is usually found if the data administration and application development team discussions focus on why and where naming conventions are needed, rather than on how they are to be enforced.

This is actually good news for the data modeler. Many modelers are under pressure to use a naming convention that is not ideal for communication. Having different conventions means that there can be one for the logical data modeling process that does not have length or delimiter restrictions while keeping system programmers happy (or as happy as system programmers ever are). (See the "Abbreviations" entry in this chapter.)

Null Attributes

Null attributes are perfectly acceptable, but the more appropriate question is, why do you care? Nonetheless, make sure they are not the result of combining multiple entities or subtypes into one.

There really should be no reason to talk about null attributes because there is no place in logical data modeling for the concept of a null attribute. Null-talk comes from the relational model where the null attribute is either a clever innovation or a bugaboo— relational theorists are not sure which.

Here's a little background. IT, for the first three decades of its long and glorious history, lived in the world of two-value logic. A proposition is either true or false. A thing existed or it didn't. There is no in-between. Ted Codd, as part of his relational model work, proposed a three-value logic for true, false, and beats me (although Codd preferred "don't know" or "undetermined").[1] The relational community spent the next three-plus decades of IT's long and glorious history trying to figure out what that meant. (Actually, if you discount the option "ignore it," they are still working on it.) Relational database people, as opposed to relational theorists (same religion, different sect), have three basic responses to nulls: (1) treat them as blanks, (2) recognize they exist but avoid them at all costs, and (3) what nulls?

Nulls are a relational issue and not a logical data modeling one. If a relational DBMS is to be used for the modeled application, then physical designers in the Physical Schema Definition phase can wrestle with nulls. For now, put that battle aside and focus on something more important.

There Be Blanks in Them Thar Nulls

Of more importance to the logical data modeler is the question of too many blanks. If you take the advice of some more grounded relational theorists and treat nulls as blanks, then you can look at the potential problem a bit more rationally in the "Too Many Blanks or Nulls" entry in Chapter 7.

Optional Relationships (Optional-Optional Relationships)

Allow optional relationships.

The argument against optional relationships (Figure 5-18) is usually voiced by relational database theorists who are upset at the possibility of having a null value as part of a key.

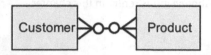

Figure 5-18. *Optional-optional relationship*

Contrary to what some relational database advocates believe, optional relationships do not require nulls in primary keys; however, nulls are possible if the primary key is also a foreign key (see the entries "Null Attributes" in this chapter and "Primary Keys" and "Foreign Keys" in Chapter 6). The good news is that because null values and keys are physical design questions, they are not relevant to a discussion of logical data modeling.

Subject Areas

Allow subject areas.

Subject areas partition the data model into smaller parts. However, the model should be segmented in a way that minimizes cross-subject-area relationships. For example, a banking data model might be partitioned into two subject areas for customer-related entities and account-related entities. This segmentation recognizes the reduced number of relationships required to span the partition.

Subject areas are also a good way to partition a data model for tasking purposes (dividing a data modeling exercise into separate smaller pieces so that multiple individuals or teams can work simultaneously without stepping on each other's toes).

They are also used, although with less success, as a means of breaking a big data model down into multiple physical databases. The reason subject areas are a poor method of database design is that they do not take into account how the data are to be used. For example, to say that there should be a customer database and an invoice database is acceptable if an application has no need to access both customer and invoice information. If, on the other hand, you regularly need customer and invoice information together, you might want to store them in the same database. However, you obtain this information from the process model, not from the data model. The data model only gives information on the relationship between data, not how data should be physically stored. To develop a physical database design based solely on logical data is a serious mistake.

There is a second danger to guard against when using subject areas. The subject area can become a self-fulfilling prophecy. The subject areas at the beginning of the data modeling process might not be the ones you should have at the end. Unless the modeler is careful, early subject areas could become permanent unless the modelers constantly review and correct the structure.

Another word of caution. Do not confuse subject databases with subject areas (Table 5-8). The former is a physical design issue involving physical constraints based on how data is accessed, while the latter is a logical data modeling construct based on entity relationships and the issues of clarity or tasking. The reason to have multiple databases instead of one is usually driven by the physical size of the database, transaction volume, and/or location.

Table 5-8. Subject Areas vs. Subject Databases

Concept	Segmentation Criteria
Subject area	Relationships between entities
Subject database	Data access

Supertypes and Subtypes

The use of supertypes and subtypes is acceptable.

Super and subtypes (S-types to the *in* crowd) show how an entity can fulfill multiple roles involving different attribute types. They are particularly useful for avoiding blank filled attributes without having to duplicate relationships (Figure 5-19).

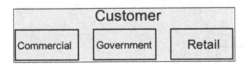

Figure 5-19. A nested supertype

The point to remember about an S-type is that it does not represent multiple entities with multiple relationships, but rather it is a single entity that plays multiple roles. A subtype represents each role that has its own attributes. The attributes common across all roles are part of the supertype. Subtypes inherit the attributes of the supertype.

Some modelers prefer to have all relationships to the S-types linked through the supertype (Figure 5-20); however, this is only appropriate for relationships that are common for all roles. As with attributes, subtypes inherit the relationships of the supertype.

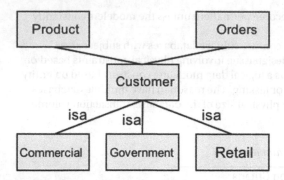

Figure 5-20. *Subtype relationships through the supertypes*

Some relationships apply to only one or a few roles. These relationships should be represented through the subtype. Linking these relationships through the supertype would hide important information about how the role relates to other entities.

In Figure 5-21, Products and Orders relate to Customers, while Salesman only relates to the Commercial role of a Customer. The Federal Systems Division entity is only linked to Government Customers.

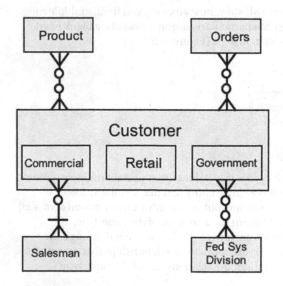

Figure 5-21. *Common and role relationships through supertypes and subtypes*

■ **Note**   S-types sometimes go under the name of *generalization* or *specialization*.

Unique Identifiers

The designation of one or more attributes as an entity unique identifier is encouraged and should be specified if the unique identifier is a legitimate end-user concept. However, "assigning" a unique identifier or arbitrarily making one unique identifier "primary" for systems purposes is wrong for logical data modeling and should be discouraged.

A unique identifier is an attribute or group of attributes that uniquely determines a single entity occurrence. Some system development techniques and tools require that all entities have unique identifiers, and some go further to require that one unique identifier be designated "prime." They use terms such as *key* and *primary key*. Keys and primary keys are an important part of physical database design and are required by some database management systems. However, these physical issues are inappropriate here.

If there is more than one unique identifier in an entity, some authors recommend arbitrarily identifying one as the prime unique identifier and the others as alternative unique identifiers. However, it is absurd (even for physical design—and by definition an arbitrary decision) to pick one unique identifier over another as the prime identifier. Modelers should not build arbitrariness into a model (revisit the Real World Corollary to Principle 1 in Chapter 1).

More important, unique identifiers are not needed for all entities. Take the example of an accounts payable system (Figure 5-22).

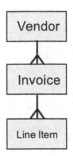

Figure 5-22. *Accounts payable data model*

What is the unique identifier of Line Item (Table 5-9)?

Table 5-9. *Identifying the Identifier*

Identifier	Description
LINE NUMBER?	No, it is not unique.
INVOICE NUMBER and LINE NUMBER?	It is unique but requires the duplication of INVOICE NUMBER in two entities.
PRODUCT ORDERED, LINE NUMBER, and DATE?	Not necessarily unique.

To create a unique Line Item unique identifier, some analysts designate a system-generated key, also called a *surrogate key*, such as a sequential number (a physical design issue), or use a unique identifier from another entity and duplicate it in the subject entity. For example, INVOICE NUMBER could be the unique identifier of Invoice and, concatenated with LINE NUMBER, the unique identifier of Line Item. Neither the system-generated key nor the borrowed unique identifier is a good idea because they are artificial, fictitious, and certainly not real world. If there is no legitimate unique identifier for an entity, leave it "identifier-less."

Table 5-10 illustrates two examples where nonidentified data might exist.

Table 5-10. Nonidentified Data

Example 1	Example 2
Good Health Insurance Co. wants to create new weight-height tables for its actuarial department. To do this, it sends to each resident of several randomly selected towns an information package and a postcard to fill out and return. Anonymity is guaranteed. The postcard information contains fields for the following:	Fair Play Inc. provides a service that looks at other companies' personnel records and reports whether they show any indication of racial, gender, or age discrimination. The program works as follows:
Height Sex	Clients send to Fair Play their personnel records of all employees minus any identifying information. For example, data would include the following:
Weight Race	Race Years with firm
Date of Birth	Sex Education
The cards are entered in Good Health's database with no end-user unique identifier.	Date of Birth Position in firm
	Weight Years in position
	Height Salary
	Information not included:
	Name Employee number
	Address Phone number
	Social Security number

A word of caution: some modelers use the phrase *unique identifier* and the word *identifier* interchangeably. Other modelers reserve *identifier* for attributes that can pick out an entity though not necessarily uniquely. For example, CUSTOMER NAME could be used to find a customer occurrence even though there is no guarantee of uniqueness. In physical database design, nonunique identifiers are commonly used as secondary indices.

Unique identifiers that are a legitimate part of the business should be modeled. Some system development tools insist that a nonbusiness unique identifier be assigned, which requires data and/or processes that are not part of the business. To alter the business, or the representation of the business, to satisfy a development tool is misleading, unnecessary, and simply wrong.

Note

1. E. F. Codd, "A Relational Model of Data for Large Shared Data Banks." *Communications of the ACM,* Volume 13, Issue 6 (June 1970), p. 384.

CHAPTER 6

■ ■ ■

LDM Pitfalls

I think knowing what you cannot do is more important than knowing what you can.

—Lucille Ball

But then it dawned on me that the opinion of someone who is always wrong has its own special utility to decision-makers.

—Warren Buffett

Chapter 5, the "do's," should help with some thorny logical data modeling situations by presenting best practices from some of the best data modelers in the business. There is also an almost equal number of best-practice don'ts. Sometimes the don'ts are more useful than the do's.

Chapter Subjects

- Circular relationships
- Data values
- Data value–differentiated entities and attributes
- Derived data
- Discrete attributes

- Embedded attributes
- Entity fragmentation
- Foreign keys
- Junction entities
- Normalization
- Presentation Data
- Primary keys

- Process data
- Repeating groups
- Single-attribute entities
- Substitution data
- Substitution tables
- Transient data

Circular Relationships

Do not model circular relationships; they should not exist.

A circular relationship is the data modeling equivalent of a cat chasing its tail and is usually identifiable as three or more entities, all one-to-many, with the crow's feet all pointing in the same circular direction (Figure 6-1). If you have a circular relationship, then at least one relationship and/or one entity is incorrect. To prove this to yourself, try to construct one. You will quickly see that the task leads to a meaningless model.

© George Tillmann 2017

G. Tillmann, *Usage-Driven Database Design*, DOI 10.1007/978-1-4842-2722-0_6

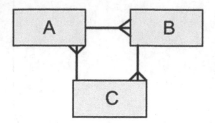

Figure 6-1. *(Meaningless) circular relationships*

The circular relationship problem might be that at least one one-to-many relationship is actually a one-to-one or many-to-many relationship or that one of the entities should be two entities or part of another entity.

Data Values

Do not model the values of data.

Data models model data objects, not the values of data objects. Even experienced modelers have trouble with this simple concept. End users often confuse data values with entities or attributes and conclude that the data model is in error if data values are not included on the E-R diagram. Take the following case, for example.

During the creation of the data model, the end users made a distinction between commercial and government clients. If the client is the government, the 30 days net payment rule does not apply. However, if a commercial account is not paid within 30 days, a second notice is sent.

The modelers decided to create two entities: Commercial Client and Government Client.

The error is letting the data value of an attribute, CLIENT TYPE, differentiate entity types. In the previous example, the modelers have uncovered no distinct *data definitions* to differentiate the entities Commercial and Government. Rather, all they had discovered was that the model needed the attribute CLIENT TYPE to contain the value "Commercial" or "Government" so that a process could distinguish the two.

A quick test to determine whether values are being modeled is to examine the entity and attribute names. If the entity or attribute name is a proper noun, then it is a good bet that what is modeled is the value of an attribute (Table 6-1). To avoid this problem, you may have to replace one attribute with two or more.

Table 6-1. *Examples of Invalid and Valid Attribute Types*

Invalid Attribute Type	Valid Attribute Type
IBM MODEL	VENDOR, COMPUTER MODEL
US TAX	COUNTRY, COUNTRY TAX
S&P RATING	RATING SERVICE, RATING
ZIP CODE	POSTAL CODE

Take the Yes/No-type attribute US CITIZEN, which limits the acceptable data values to "Yes" and "No." A better approach is to model a CITIZENSHIP attribute for which the acceptable values are the names of countries.

Data Value–Differentiated Entities and Attributes

Do not allow data values to differentiate or define entity or other attribute types.

This issue is the reciprocal of modeling data values (see "Data Values" in this chapter). Data value–differentiated entities and attributes occur when the value of an attribute is used to define an entity type or another attribute type. For example, imagine the following:

> The order entry data model for Wittgenstein & Tarski Inc., a consumer products firm, includes the entity Product with the attributes PRODUCT SOURCE and MANUFACTURER. If the value of PRODUCT SOURCE is "Internal," then the attribute MANUFACTURER contains the location (New York, Chicago, Ship Bottom, NJ) of the Wittgenstein & Tarski Inc. plant that created the product. However, if the value of PRODUCT SOURCE is "Purchased," then the attribute MANUFACTURER contains the name of the company that made the item.

In Table 6-2 the definition of MANUFACTURER depends on the value of PRODUCT SOURCE.

Table 6-2. *Differentiated Entities*

Product Name	Product Source	Manufacturer
Elbow-Master	Internal	Ship Bottom, NJ
Veg-atomic	Purchased	Oncor Manufacturing

Another example of a data value–differentiated entity would be when the entity Customer contains the name of a customer when the value of the attribute CUSTOMER TYPE is "Commercial" or when it contains the name of the salesperson assigned to the account when the value of CUSTOMER TYPE is "Confidential."

In both cases, the definition of an attribute or entity is determined by the value of an attribute. This is an error because it does the following:

- Eliminates or hides from the data model the definitions of real business entities, attributes, and relationships and replaces them with attribute values.

- Makes an entity or attribute into a property or characteristic of a data value when, by definition, data values are characteristics or properties of attributes, and attributes are characteristics or properties of entities.

In one case, this rule appears to be broken, but in fact, it is not. A subtype often has a type or role attribute that defines the subtype and thus determines the properties of the subtype (see "Duplicate Sub-Supertype 'Type' Data" in Chapter 5). But closer examination reveals that the "Type" attribute in a subtype is actually a role determinant and should, for the purposes of this guideline, be considered a characteristic of an entity.

Some readers might note that this is similar to the restrictions imposed by normalization's second normal form. (See "Level of Abstraction" in Chapter 5.)

Derived Data

Avoid placing derived data on the E-R diagram, although it should be in the data dictionary.

Derived data items are data objects that can be calculated from primitive data or from other derived data. For example, if an accounts payable system stores data on each purchase, then the data item, TOTAL AMOUNT ORDERED, can be derived by adding the amount ordered for each of the individual orders. TOTAL AMOUNT ORDERED is the sum of the values of all the occurrences of the INVOICE AMOUNT data element.

Three Poor Arguments Against Modeling Derived Data

Some modelers feel that derived data should not be part of the logical data model at all.

They have three traditional arguments against modeling derived data. They believe that derived data

- Are redundant, which can cause synchronization problems.

- Take up database storage space.

- Limit the choices of physical designers.

Many modelers would say that TOTAL AMOUNT ORDERED is redundant because it can be calculated from the individual orders. This redundancy is undesirable because it can lead to inconsistencies if the value of TOTAL AMOUNT ORDERED does not equal the sum of the INVOICE AMOUNT values. Put simply, the argument is that if data are stored only once, you do not have inconsistencies.

The second argument is that because derived data are redundant, they unnecessarily take up storage space (e.g., on disk or tape) and increase storage costs.

The third argument is that deciding whether a data object should be stored or calculated is a physical design issue. The relevant questions deal with the cost/benefit trade-offs between the storage space to house the redundant data and the input/output (I/O) and CPU cycles necessary to calculate them every time they are needed. If the derived data are left out of the data model, the physical designer, it is argued, can always turn them into stored data if desirable. However, if derived data are part of the data model, the physical designer might not know they are derived and, therefore, not know that there is a store or calculate option. Thus, placing derived data on the data model limits the options open to the designer.

These arguments are not very compelling. The redundancy argument ignores the fact that redundant data can be inconsistent only when some or all of them are wrong. But if they are wrong, they are wrong, whether they are in the model once or multiple times. Redundancy, in fact, might point out incorrect data that would otherwise go undetected.

It is true that storing derived data in the database increases storage costs. However, the argument is misplaced. Issues such as database storage should not be part of logical design but should be left to physical design.

The third argument would be correct if there were no other way to communicate the derived nature of the data object to the physical designers. However, there are numerous alternative methods of conveying that data are derived without dropping them from the data model.

The notion that those who argue against derived data also believe they should not exist is a common misconception. Enlightened derived data opponents are merely against placing derived data on the E-R diagram. They would say that derived data are really the restatement of data that already exist on the model. To include them in the diagram would be to corrupt the fundamental nature of the model.

Derived Data as Process

Derived data do not really behave like data. For example, you can completely understand primitive data with its definition, but to understand derived data, you need a formula or algorithm. Look at the following example:

> TOTAL AMOUNT ORDERED for ACCOUNT NUMBER = "1234"
> is the sum of the values of INVOICE AMOUNT for that Account.

To understand TOTAL AMOUNT ORDERED, you need a formula or action diagram. However, formulas and action diagrams are properties of process modeling, not data modeling. So, the real issue with including derived data on a data model is that they are not data at all. They are, instead, a process for applying a set of rules to data values to calculate other data values.

In Table 6-3, the value of TOTAL AMOUNT ORDERED depends on applying a process to the individual values of INVOICE AMOUNT. If one of the latter changes, then TOTAL AMOUNT ORDERED must change.

Table 6-3. Derived Data as a Process

Primitive Data Can Be Understood by Looking at Their Definition	Derived Data Need a Formula or Algorithm
Attribute Definition	**Action Diagram**
Attribute name: ACCOUNT NUMBER	Calculate TOTAL AMOUNT ORDERED
Definition: A unique identifier of an approved account of any status. The Accounts Payable Dept. assigns account numbers.	For each ACCOUNT NUMBER Tally INVOICE AMOUNT giving TOTAL AMOUNT ORDERED End
	End

Recognizing that derived data look more like a process than data is important to systems developers. Just giving a definition when a formula is required will not do. An action diagram or some similar process modeling construct is required to properly communicate the nature of the derived data object to the physical designers.

Derived Data and Physical Database Design

From a physical database design perspective, whether derived data are stored in the database or calculated every time they are needed is a mathematical question. The physical database designer can calculate the resource costs to store the derived data, compare them with the resource costs to calculate the data every time they are needed, and choose the less expensive option. The only real question is how does the physical database designer know the data are derived?

If derived data are not in the data model, then how are they communicated to the physical database designers? This can be a problem. Many data modelers make the mistake of so efficiently excluding derived data from development documentation that physical designers do not even know they exist.

The solution to this problem is relatively simple: derived data should exist as a process with data flows and data stores and be represented in the data dictionary. The dictionary should explicitly state that the attribute is derived and give the name of the process (action diagram) that defines that attribute (Figure 6-2).

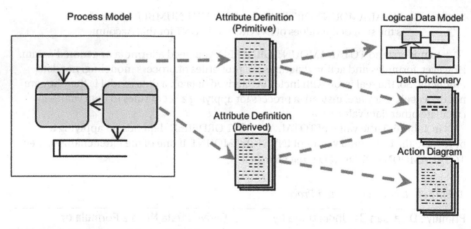

Figure 6-2. Location of derived data

If derived data are properly documented, then the physical database designers know that derived data exist, where they are used, and how they are defined. They are then in a position to intelligently introduce derived data into the physical database design process.

If your only data dictionary is tied to a data modeling tool and because some data modeling tools require that all attributes be associated with an entity, the data modeler might have to create one or more dummy data objects to house derived data.

Who should define the derived data's process or algorithm is more a question of complexity than of organizational structure. If the process to calculate the derived data is simple, as in the previous examples, then the data modeler can certainly document it. If, on the other hand, the process is complex, then the task is better turned over to the process modelers who have more appropriate tools and a better understanding of the context in which the derived data live.

In summary, derived data should not be included on the E-R diagram, but they should exist in the data dictionary along with their describing process.

Discrete Attributes

Do not include an attribute in the model more than once.

Placing an attribute in the model more than once is usually a sign of confusion about the name and/or definition of the attribute or a misunderstanding about logical data modeling. Nevertheless, despite the rule, modelers must be mindful of some exceptional situations.

- If your data modeling tool requires foreign keys, then an attribute might appear in your model more than once. Following its first occurrence, however, an attribute should appear only as a foreign key. (See the "Foreign Keys" entry in this chapter.)

- Certain attributes might seem to appear more than once, but this is usually because an attribute name is less specific than it should be and/or there is an issue of context. For example, generic names, such as DATE, AMOUNT, or TOTAL AMOUNT, which may appear in several places in the model, are acceptable if everyone understands that DATE in the Customer Billing entity is a different attribute from DATE in the Product Price Schedule entity. (In this example, everyone has agreed—implicitly or explicitly—to call the attribute not by its name but by its domain.) To be more accurate, the attributes should be named CUSTOMER BILLING DATE and PRODUCT PRICE SCHEDULE DATE.

- A variation of the previous situation can occur with codes and indicators. For example, a number of entities might have the attribute STATUS CODE. This is acceptable, although perhaps not in the best form, if the domains (all the acceptable values, such as "Active," "Inactive," and "Closed") are all identical. If the domains are different, then the attributes need different names.

- A differentiator attribute might appear in each subtype of a supertype-subtype entity defining the separate role each subtype plays (see "Super-Subtypes" and "Duplicate Super-Subtype 'Type' Data" in Chapter 5). This is acceptable because the attribute type still appears only in a single entity type.

Be careful. An attribute appearing more than once could signal a number of other problems, such as modeling data values, improper use of supertypes and subtypes, or an attempt to get around a (misguided) restriction on repeating groups.

Concatenating the entity name to the attribute name (such as using "dot" notation in Entity Name.Attribute Name as in CUSTOMER.ADDRESS) is not an acceptable method of making an attribute name unique. Attribute names must stand on their own, independent of the entity with which they are associated.

Embedded Attributes

Do not allow embedded attributes.

Embedded attributes are attributes with other attributes hidden inside them. This is usually done to (1) make the assembled attribute unique or (2) combine two or more attributes into an undeclared and covert *group attribute*.

Uniqueness

The attribute ACCOUNT NUMBER for a bank is sometimes made up of a branch code and a sequence number within the branch. The sequence number can be repeated from branch to branch, so combining it with branch code uniquely identifies an account within the overall bank.

Making identifiers unique is an important physical design task. *Identifying* unique attributes is an important logical data modeling function, but *making* attributes unique is not. Do not hide attributes in other attributes to create uniqueness.

Group Attributes

Some modelers use embedded attributes to hide a group attribute. Using the bank account number example, the real-world situation is that there is a group attribute, ACCOUNT NUMBER, which consists of two simple attributes, BRANCH CODE and SEQUENCE NUMBER. However, many modelers fear group attributes because they are not supported by some, mostly relational, database management systems. Put your fear aside. This is logical data modeling, not physical database design. Group attributes are not only allowed but encouraged because they enhance communication (information is not hidden) and reflect the real world.

The Problem with Embedded Attributes

The problem with embedded attributes is that they hide information from other data modelers, physical database designers, database administrators (DBAs), and application developers.

In the bank example, if a branch code is embedded in an account number, then where would the application programmer find the branch code? Will the programmer know to look inside the account number? Where will the programmer get that information? Should the branch code be duplicated (once in the account number and once as a stand-alone attribute)? If so, then how does the designer ensure that when the branch code is modified, it is updated in two places?

Embedded attributes put an unfair burden on the application programmer. If both the account number and branch code are needed for the application, then the programmer must dissect ACCOUNT NUMBER to extract the branch information. This is an inelegant and error-prone process.

The Solution

An acceptable solution is to create a compound unique identifier consisting of the attributes BRANCH CODE and SEQUENCE NUMBER. A better solution is to make the unique group attribute ACCOUNT NUMBER containing the simple attributes BRANCH CODE and SEQUENCE NUMBER.

The Moral of the Story

Logical data modeling should uncover information, not hide it. Avoid embedded attributes.

Entity Fragmentation

Avoid unnecessarily fragmenting entities.

Some modelers fragment entities into multiple entity types to avoid unnecessary duplication of empty (blank, null) attributes. For example, because most employees do not have a TERMINATION DATE attribute, the modeler for the diagram in Figure 6-3 removed TERMINATION DATE from the Employee entity and created a new Termination Date entity.

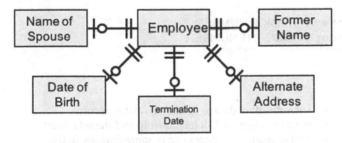

Figure 6-3. Entity fragmentation

The fragmented data can and should be bundled in the subject entity so that TERMINATION DATE along with DATE OF BIRTH and FORMER NAME are all part of Employee. Fragmenting entities just to avoid empty attributes should be discouraged.

Multiple entities, however, are often needed to express information about major business concepts. For example, a logical data model might have a number of entities dealing with a customer or a product. This is one of the reasons for subject areas. However, the designer must guard against indiscriminately splitting entities, especially for physical reasons, such as to avoid unnecessary empty, blank, or null attributes.

Do not confuse entity fragmentation with an entity fragment (see "Entity Fragments" in Chapter 4). Entity fragments are often used by system designers to build process models.

Foreign Keys

Do not define relationships using foreign keys.

A foreign key is not a legitimate logical data modeling concept. It is a physical design issue, tied to the relational model, and even then not required or even supported by every relational database management system. Unfortunately, some modelers and tools use foreign keys as a way to define relationships between entities.

Relational fans cover your ears. OK? Well, for the rest of you, a foreign key is a type of pointer (actually a symbolic key) to another tuple (relational record). By using pointers, relational systems perform "joins" and—dare I say it—navigate. This is how these systems work. If an Account occurrence is related to one or more Invoice occurrences in a one-to-many relationship, then a "linking" data element must exist in both records (Figure 6-4). The value of the data element ACCOUNT NUMBER in Invoice must be the same as the value of ACCOUNT NUMBER in the Account record. Thus, when you want both account information and all invoices for account 1234, the system can find the appropriate occurrences of Account and Invoice using the specified value "1234" for attribute ACCOUNT NUMBER. (The linking data elements need not have the same name.)

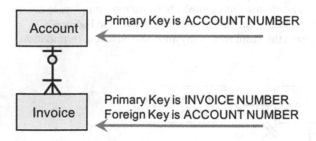

Figure 6-4. *Foreign keys*

Simple. It just requires a bit of redundant data to "point" to related records.

There is a theoretical difference between the E-R relationship and the relational relationship. In the E-R model, a relationship associates two or more entities. In the relational model, a relationship associates two or more attribute values.

On the practical side, foreign keys simply have no relevance to logical data modeling—except in one awkward situation. Some data modeling tools are designed to primarily, or exclusively, work with relational systems. The only way to relate entity "A" with entity "B" using these products is to specify a foreign key. If you are using one of these tools, hold your nose and make the best of a bad situation.

Interestingly enough, after all this relational talk, many relational systems do not require foreign keys declarations. (See "Unique Identifiers" in Chapter 5.)

Junction Entities

Do not use junction entities to eliminate many-to-many relationships. The use of junction entities should not be confused with the role of legitimate associative entities.

Most physical database management systems do not explicitly support many-to-many relationships. For those products, the M:N relationships must be "resolved" into two one-to-many physical record–type links separated by an additional record type, sometimes called a *junction* or *intersection* record (Figure 6-5). This is appropriate for physical database design but inappropriate for logical data modeling.

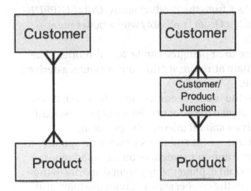

Figure 6-5. *Resolving many-to-many relationships*

Associative entities should be viewed as attributed relationships. Unfortunately, many modelers incorrectly believe that at least one of the roles of an associative entity is to "resolve" many-to-many relationships. If the business supports many-to-many relationships, then the data model should model them.

Normalization

Do not normalize the logical data model. Normalization is a physical database design activity and should be left until then.

Normalization is the application of a set of mathematical rules to a database design to eliminate or reduce insertion, update, and deletion (IUD) anomalies. It does this by ensuring that all fields are completely dependent on the record key for their existence and not on any other field. Properly applied, normalization can go a long way toward solving the problem of deleting a record that contains one type of data and, in the process, inadvertently deleting other information. (See Chapter 10.)

The problem with normalization is that it requires each relation (entity) to have a unique primary key. Normalization is a decomposition process. It breaks down or decomposes existing "compound" records (entities) into simpler ones that might, or might not, be recognizable by end users.

All database designs should be normalized; all logical data models need to wait until physical data modeling to undergo the process.

109

Presentation Data

Do not place data on the E-R diagram simply because they are in a presentation, on a report, on a computer screen, or part of a transaction.

Presentation data are not legitimate attributes but rather the replication of legitimate attributes. An example illustrates this point.

The Church, Frege & Quine Inc. database contains the attribute AMOUNT DUE in the Order entity. The same attribute is called DUE on the order entry screen and ITEM AMOUNT in the daily sales report. On the customer order confirmation form, AMOUNT DUE is AMOUNT DUE from the Order entity plus any SHIPPING CHARGE from the Shipping entity minus any DISCOUNT from the Product entity. Only SHIPPING CHARGE, DISCOUNT, and AMOUNT DUE from Order (probably with a better name) should be on the data model.

Presentation data are dangerous because their pedigree can be totally hidden. The data might be a simple synonym for a legitimate attribute, a duplicate attribute, a derived attribute, or even a totally unrelated attribute.

The exclusion of presentation data from the model seems obvious; however, it can be problematic when using one set of data object names for presentation purposes and another internally. Some digging by the analysts should uncover the problem.

Some modelers have encountered difficulties with end users who are disappointed when they do not see data that appear on the computer screen, or on a printed report, reflected in the E-R diagram. The designer should explain the apparent disparity to the user and take this as an opportunity to confirm the correct status of both modeled and unmodeled data.

Although presentation data should never be on the E-R diagram, placing them in the data dictionary as aliases or derived attributes does no harm as long as the data's pedigree is obvious and well understood. It might be useful to physical designers if inclusion of such data in the data dictionary clears up uncertainties, and it might ease end-user angst.

Presentation data are really an odd combination of redundant data, derived data, nondiscrete attributes, and simple synonyms. Careful attention to the derivation of data should uncover their true nature. (See "Transient Data" in this chapter.)

Primary Keys

Do not be concerned with keys, primary or otherwise. The uncovering and documentation of one or more unique business identifiers for an entity is a fundamental part of logical data modeling. The assignment of one of the unique identifiers as the "primary key" is a physical data modeling issue and not a component of logical data modeling.

The specification of identifiers for an entity is a good piece of end-user information. If an identifier is known, convey it to the physical designers. However, the notion of a "primary key," or arbitrarily picking a unique identifier and specifying it as a primary key, is a physical design concern and not relevant to logical data modeling. The insistence on identifying primary keys is a sure sign that the modeler has trouble distinguishing logical from physical data modeling and calls for a review of Chapter 1.

What is important is the identification of unique identifiers. That an attribute or group of attributes can uniquely identify an entity occurrence is important business information that should be communicated back to the end user for verification and to physical designers for possible use as a key. If an entity type has multiple unique identifiers, which one to pick as the primary key is unimportant, arbitrary, and irrelevant to logical data modeling. (See "Unique Identifiers" in Chapter 5.)

Process Data

Do not model process data, data flows, triggers, formulas, policy, rules, or the passing of control.

Process data are not legitimate end-user data but rather interim or transformation data, program codes, internal flags, etc., used by an application to tally interim results, control process flow, and the like. They should not be modeled. When process data are modeled, they usually reflect one of two problems.

- Regardless of training or warnings, some people read a data model as a process model, which prompts them to introduce some temporal notions (e.g., how data might look at different times during their life) into the model. In short order, what evolves is a mini data flow diagram masquerading as a logical data model.

- Some analysts and designers interpret data-driven development to mean that things such as business policy or business rules should be placed in the logical data model. Or they are simply puzzled as to where they should store documented business rules and policy and, lacking an alternative, store them in the data dictionary.

The data model, however, is only for data objects that fit the definition of logical data. Things that should be excluded from the logical data model include the following:

- Rules and policies, which do not fit into the data modeling definition of an attribute, entity, or relationship, should not be included as part of a logical data model.

- Although simple single attribute rules such as a credit limit can be modeled (e.g., "if...then, else" rules), complex rules belong in the logical process model.

- Textual material, such as a business policy statements, should also be excluded. Clearly, the CEO's annual report policy statement is important, but it does not belong on the data model.

- Lastly, just because something belongs in the physical database does not mean it should be part of the logical data model. An application development organization might decide to build table-driven systems (applications that use tables to direct computer processing) and to store the tables in the database. This is perfectly acceptable; however, these system tables are not part of the logical data model. They are processes that developers have decided should be performed interpretatively. Simply because they are stored in the database does not mean they are not intended for processing code.

PUB TRIVIA

Some relevant history might be of interest. Data modeling, or at least modern data modeling, was first done by Charles Bachman. Bachman diagrams used boxes for records (entities) and arrows for sets (relationships). Two problems quickly became apparent. First, how do you tell the difference between a process model and data model at first blush? Answer: It is not always easy. Second, the Bachman diagram was also used by some to represent a database schema (many network system designers still do). This confusion with process models and database schemata led some to seek a distinct diagramming technique for logical data modeling. The results have been good; however, as this entry implies, confusion sometimes still reigns.

(See the "Transient Data" entry in this chapter.)

Repeating Groups

Do not delete an attribute because it is a repeating group. Do not make it a separate entity.

The language surrounding repeating groups can be confusing. For some, a repeating group is more correctly called a *multivalue attribute*, while others are actually referring to a *group attribute* (see Chapter 3 for detailed explanations of both). Both multivalue attributes and group attributes are acceptable logical data modeling concepts and should be part of the model if they are part of the business.

Multivalue Attribute

Multivalue attributes are attributes that contain more than a single data value. Take the entity Project, which has the attribute TEAM containing the values "Bob," "Carol," "Ted," and "Alice." Some modelers want to remove TEAM from Project and make it an entity in a one-to-many relationship with Project. The new entity Team would contain four entity occurrences, each with the single attribute TEAM MEMBER containing a single value.

Group Attribute

A group attribute contains a fixed number of other attributes. An example would be the group attribute CUSTOMER ADDRESS, which contains the five simple attributes CUSTOMER STREET NUMBER, CUSTOMER STREET NAME, CUSTOMER CITY, CUSTOMER STATE/PROVINCE, and CUSTOMER POSTAL CODE. Some modelers believe that no attribute should contain other attributes. They would delete the group attribute leaving only the simple attributes or delete the simple attributes leaving a single attribute of the entire address.

Some modelers feel the need to "resolve" multivalue and group attributes out of existence. There are four reasons their approach is wrong. First, both multivalue attributes and group attributes are acceptable logical data modeling concepts. Second, if a multivalue or group attribute is part of the business, then it should be part of the model that represents that business. Third, if the multivalue or group attribute is an attribute (meaning it meets the definition of *attribute* in Chapter 2), then it should not be arbitrarily transformed into an entity or deleted. Fourth, removing multivalue attributes could result in a single attribute entity, a sure sign that there is something wrong with the model (see the next entry).

Single-Attribute Entities

Do not allow single-attribute entities. An entity should have more than one attribute in it.

Single-attribute entities are usually a sign of one of the following:

- The single attribute in the entity is a code.

- The single attribute in the entity is there to "resolve" a multivalue (or repeating group) attribute.

Imagine a system that allows each customer to have multiple phone numbers and assigns to each customer a credit status of "OK" or "No Good." The overworked or undereducated logical data modelers created the E-R diagram in Figure 6-6.

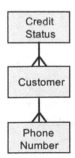

Figure 6-6. *Incorrectly modeling single-attribute entities*

The entity Credit Status in Figure 6-6 contains the single attribute CREDIT STATUS, and the entity Customer Phone Number contains the single attribute PHONE NUMBER.

Code

Credit status is an attribute and not an entity because it is a property of Customer. Interestingly, you could place a second attribute in Credit Status and call it EXPLANATION, which is a text field defining the credit status codes (e.g., "OK = the customer has a good credit rating with at least one credit rating agency"). However, the two-attribute entity should still not be modeled because Credit Status is now a lookup table—a physical design programming technique.

Multivalue Attribute (Repeating Group)

Because customers can have more than one phone number, the modeler removed it from the Customer entity and created the new entity Customer Phone Number. Many database management systems do not allow repeating groups. The relational model sees them as heresy and calls for the creation of a new table housing the offending attributes. However, in Chapter 2, it says that an entity is a person, place, or thing about which an organization wants to save information and that an attribute is a characteristic or property of an entity. A phone number is not a person, place, or thing, but rather a characteristic or property of a person, place, or thing, in this case Customer. Characteristics or properties are attributes, not entities.

It might be the case that Customer's PHONE NUMBER needs to be "resolved"; however, that is a job for the physical database designers, not the logical data modelers.

Note that (erroneously modeled) codes are always at the "one" end of a one-to-many relationship with the legitimate entity, while (erroneously modeled) multivalue attributes are always at the "many" end.

Associative Entities

There is one case when single-attribute entities *might* be acceptable, and that is when the entity is associative. Take the case of a library that wants to know who checked out a book and when. Who and the book are in the entities Borrower and Book. When is the only attribute in the associative entity Borrows (Figure 6-7).

Figure 6-7. *Acceptable single-attribute entity*

However, even with associatives, single-attribute entities are rare and should be examined closely.

Substitution Data

Do not model substitution data unless they are part of the business or necessary for understanding the business.

Substitution data often involve codes, abbreviations, or shortcuts that allow the smaller data values to stand in for larger ones. Such data can include items such as common knowledge codes (NJ = New Jersey), abbreviations (A = Active, I = Inactive), or transaction codes (07 = Add Customer). When to use substitution data is a physical performance issue best left to physical database designers.

There is one exception, and that is when the code or abbreviation is a recognized business data value. For example, in the securities processing business, DK stands for "Don't Know" and is used when part of a securities transaction is unintelligible. It is a business-recognized abbreviation routinely used in writing and conversation instead of using the entire phrase. The wise data modeler includes both DK and its definition in the data dictionary.

Substitution Tables

Avoid substitution tables if at all possible, and if not, then avoid linking substitution tables to other entities.

A substitution table is an abbreviation table listing what is stored in the database along with what is displayed when accessed. For example, the database might store in the Customer record type the data field POSTAL CODE but not the data fields CITY and STATE. Rather, the application goes to a Postal Code-City table to look up the city and state name. If POSTAL CODE is "08008," then that value is used to find the CITY and STATE values "Ship Bottom" and "NJ" in the Postal Code-City entity.

Substitution tables are how a database stores substitution data. They are an important physical database design tool but not a logical data modeling concern. They should not be modeled, with one exception.

Sometimes substitution tables are needed for end users. Insurance company staff often use codes for actions the insurer takes (or doesn't take). For example, staff might deny a claim for reason "807," which, when the claim denial letter is printed, translates into "Claim denied for no real reason other than the CEO needs a bigger boat."

Even if there is a legitimate business reason to model a substitution table, it should not be in a relationship with any other entities. Note that this is one of the few instances when disassociated entities (islands) are acceptable. (See "Disassociated Entities" in Chapter 7.)

Transient Data

Do not model transient data because they are usually temporary, duplicate, or process-related data.

This concept is best introduced through an example. Imagine an application that uses a memo post approach to update a database; in other words, changes are taken online during the day and written to a transaction file. At night, a batch program reads the transaction file and updates the database. The question is, should the transaction file be modeled? The answer is, in most cases, "no," for two reasons. First, the data in the transaction file are duplicate data. To model them would mean that attributes, such as CUSTOMER NAME, would appear in both the Customer and Transaction entities. Second, the transaction file has a limited life and therefore should be looked upon, in process modeling terms, as a slow data flow (Figure 6-8b) rather than as a data store (Figure 6-8a).

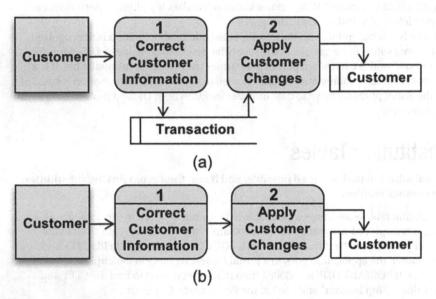

Figure 6-8. Transaction files

The single possible exception is when the exclusion of transaction data would cause considerable business data loss or misinterpretation. For example, if the entities in the transaction file have attributes or relationships that are different from those already defined, then, in this rare case, transient objects can be included in the model.

Location-Dependent Data

Location-dependent data are an interesting variation of the transient data problem. Years ago, when information was stored on ledger cards, data were separated into batches by their status. Active accounts might be located in one "tub" (special cabinets to handle large numbers of ledger cards) and inactive accounts in another. The status of an account was determined by the tub in which the card was located.

Early electronic systems continued this practice. First, punch cards came in various colors corresponding to the tub file in which they were located. Active accounts might be in the blue tub (and have blue punch cards), inactive accounts in the green tub, and accounts containing some error in the red suspense tub.

Tubs eventually became disk files, and the rest, as they say, is history—unfortunately. There are still systems being built that use the location of the record, whether it is in the master, suspense, or transaction file (whether the notion of location is physical or logical), to determine the status of the record.

For modeling purposes, the location of an entity (physical or logical) is not a property of the entity. Status, such as active, inactive, or suspense, is a value of one or more attributes, not a location on disks, in tubs, or whatever. In logical data modeling, an account is not moved to an inactive file—it is declared "inactive."

Transient data can also appear as presentation data, transaction data, suspense data, location-dependent data, temporary data, in-process data, transformation data, or what have you. If the data are transient, do not model them.

CHAPTER 7

■ ■ ■

LDM Perils to Watch For

Fools you are...who say you like to learn from your mistakes...I prefer to learn from the mistakes of others, and avoid the cost of my own.

—Otto von Bismarck

I learned an awful lot from him by doing the opposite.

—Howard Hawkes (American film director)

The last two chapters dealt with logical data modeling do's, and don'ts. This chapter addresses characteristics that aren't do's and aren't don'ts but rather somewhere in the middle. These are not wrong but, nonetheless, things to watch for.

Chapter Subjects

- Associatives related to other associatives
- Diagrammable objects
- Disassociated entity clusters ("islands")

- Duplicate unique identifiers
- Multiple relationships
- One-of-a-kind (OOAK) entities
- One-to-one relationships
- Rare entity relationships

- Recursive modality constraints
- Spiderwebs
- Too many blanks or nulls
- Too many recursives

Associatives Related to Other Associatives

Be wary of associatives related to other associatives because, in a correct model, they are somewhat rare.

An event related to another event is one of the few situations where an associative entity is correctly related to another associative entity. Take the following case:

> Typically, Chatterton Enterprises' purchasing department employees have a job title that they hold for a number of years. At the same time, some of these employees might also have a temporary assignment as a purchasing agent for a particular vendor.

On the data model, the associative entity Job stores the time-dependent information about the employee's official title, while the associative entity Purchasing Role stores the time-dependent information about the purchasing agent temporary role (Figure 7-1).

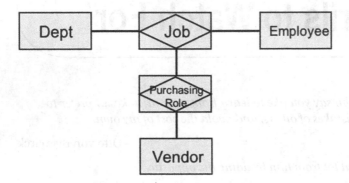

Figure 7-1. *Associative related to another associative*

Although this example is legitimate, the use of associatives related to other associatives is not that common. Therefore, when you see these relationships on a logical data model, review them closely. They might be incorrect.

Diagrammable Objects

Not all data objects should be represented in part, or at all, in the logical data model. Carefully review all data objects to determine (1) which should be part of the E-R diagram and the data dictionary, (2) which should be only in the data dictionary, and (3) which should be excluded from both.

When modelers talk about data objects, they mean three different types of data.

- Data objects that are candidates for an E-R diagram

    - Entities
    - Relationships
    - Attributes (for space reasons, attributes are usually not on the diagram but are represented by the entity in which they participate)

- Valid data objects that *might* be in the data dictionary but should not be on the E-R diagram

    - Global data
    - Derived data
    - Transient data
    - Presentation data (screen or report data)

- Data objects that are not part of logical data modeling
  - Records and fields
  - Keys and indices
  - Storage (disk, tape, etc.)

At the beginning of every project, the entire development team should reach a clear understanding about which objects are diagrammed (the easy part), which are only documented and exactly how they are documented (the harder part), and which are not part of logical data modeling at all (an experience up there with a tax audit). The Data Administration group should handle global data, such as CURRENT DATE. Application-specific attributes, such as NEXT ACCOUNT NUMBER and NEXT BILLING DATE, should be documented by the process modeling or application development team, and the data should be stored in the data dictionary. However, these attributes are not usually placed on the E-R diagram.

Derived data are actually the product of a process and should be documented in the process model. (See "Derived Data" in Chapter 6.)

Do not model presentation data. Rather, presentation data should exist in the data dictionary if they are different from their source (the diagrammed data they represent). (See "Presentation Data" in Chapter 6.)

Transient data are process-specific data and should be documented in the process model. (See "Transient Data" in Chapter 6.)

Disassociated Entity Clusters ("Islands")

Legitimate disassociated entities and entity clusters are rare; their occurrence on the model most often reflects incorrectly modeled data.

Data models have entities that are related to other entities. A few data models, however, may have entities that are not related to any other entities. These entities generally are referred to as *disassociated entities* and sometimes as *islands*. A small group of entities can also function as an island if they are not related to the main body of entities (Figure 7-2).

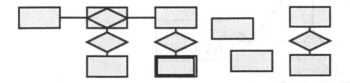

Figure 7-2. *Disassociated entity clusters*

The legitimate cases of such islands are more common in strongly diversified organizations or found on a data model for an organization whose parts are weakly related. For example, the data model for a conglomerate that sells services to the government and commercial products to consumers might have a disjointed data model. Also, a data model that is limited to raw materials management and stock holder services would also be legitimately disjointed (although one wonders about the application that this data model is intended to support).

Other than in the previous situations, entity islands are rare. When they do show up, they are often incorrectly modeled transient or substitution data. (See "Substitution Data," "Substitution Tables," and "Transient Data" in Chapter 6.)

Duplicate Unique Identifiers

Although it is not uncommon or wrong for an entity to have two unique identifiers or for two entities to share an attribute as their unique identifier, the occurrence should be investigated.

One Entity, Two or More Identifiers

Occasionally, modelers have an entity with multiple unique identifiers. However, not all identifiers have the same importance. Often one identifier is the official unique identifier or is more universally used than the others. If so, this fact (which might be important to physical designers) should be documented in the data dictionary.

If there are multiple identifiers for an entity, then the modelers should re-interview business users to determine whether all the unique identifiers are of equal importance.

One Identifier, Two or More Entities

Ideally, every entity has its own unique identifier. However, the unique identifier of some entities could be (in whole or in part) the unique identifier of another entity. Take the Employee example in Figure 7-3, where the unique identifier of Employee is EMPLOYEE NUMBER.

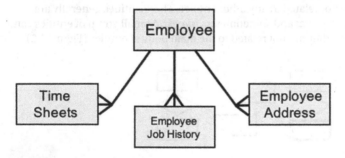

Figure 7-3. *Duplicate identifiers*

Each of the entities in Figure 7-3 could have an identifier that is, in whole or in part, the attribute EMPLOYEE NUMBER. However, the better solution is to make the three entities attributive entities (to show their dependence on Employee) and eliminate the duplicate data. Alternatively, the attributes could become part of a group or multivalue attribute.

Multiple Relationships

If two or more relationships exist between two entities—particularly if their membership class (cardinality and modality) is the same—examine them closely to ensure that the relationships are indeed distinct.

One Relationship, Multiple Views

Sometimes, modelers uncover "different" relationships when interviewing different end-user staff. The modeler needs to ensure that these relationships are indeed distinct and not just different names for the same relationship. Figure 7-4 shows a relationship between Contactor and Product that was mistakenly documented as three different relationships.

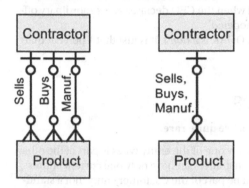

Figure 7-4. *Simplifying multiple relationships*

Multiple Different but Similar Relationships

Sometimes the relationships are different but similar. Different but similar relationships are not uncommon because end users and business departments often legitimately see relationships from their individual perspectives. Such multiple relationships can raise a presentation issue. In some diagrams, displaying excessive relationships between the same two entities can be confusing (Figure 7-4). If that is the case, the modeler can consider showing only one or some of the relationships on the E-R diagram, although all must be documented in the data dictionary.

The two cases of multiple relationships can be summarized as follows:

- *One relationship, multiple views*: Ensure that only one relationship is modeled.

- *Multiple different but similar relationships*: Ensure that all the relationships are documented in the data dictionary, but be conservative in placing them on the E-R diagram.

Examine multiple relationships between the same entities with care.

One-of-a-Kind (OOAK) Entities

Try to avoid modeling OOAKs.

A "One-of-a-Kind" entity, sometimes called an OOAK (rhymes with "nuke"), is an entity with a single occurrence. An example of an OOAK would be an entity occurrence that stores the current date, the next account number to assign, or the next billing date. These data have various names, such as *system data* or *global variable*, but they are all the same thing—physical implementation data.

The name OOAK comes from CODASYL database management system (DBMS) users who used this construct to support global data before the DBMS took over the task. By having a single occurrence record type, the necessary data are stored once and available to all application programs. Because this entity specifically relates to a physical construct, it should normally be left out of logical data modeling.

Only in the rare case, where single occurrence data is needed to understand the business, such as storing the date-of-record when the CEO declares an extraordinary off-cycle stock dividend, should an OOAK be modeled.

In 99 percent of the cases, modeling an OOAK is a *don't*. It is just that 1 percent that places it in the "to watch for" category.

One-to-One Relationships

One-to-one relationships, while legitimate, are quite rare.

When a one-to-one relationship occurs, usually one of the entity types is part of the other or is a role of the other (super-subtype). If a customer can have only one current address, then the current address information should be part of the Customer entity, not a stand-alone entity (Figure 7-5).

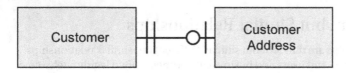

Figure 7-5. *One-to-one relationship*

Sometimes modelers create an entity to avoid blanks or null attributes. Take the example of a financial institution that has a Customer entity consisting of standard attributes such as name and address. However, imagine that 2 percent of its customers are foreign nationals living abroad. For those customers, the firm must store information about their U.S. tax status, both foreign and U.S. addresses, their nationality, and so on. To accomplish this, the modelers created a second entity called Foreign Customer Information (Figure 7-6).

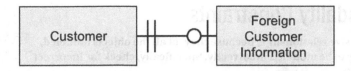

Figure 7-6. *Creating a second entity to avoid null values*

The following are the reasons for creating the second entity:

- If foreign customer information is in the Customer entity, then 98 percent of the Customer occurrences would have blank, empty, or null attributes.

- Storing foreign customer information in the Customer entity would waste a considerable amount of space.

Both reasons are, of course, inappropriate. Blank, empty, or null attributes are not improper. If the attributes in question are properties of the Customer entity, then they should be in Customer, not somewhere else. Second, computer storage considerations are a physical design issue and not part of logical data modeling. (See "Entity Fragmentation" in Chapter 6.)

Rare Entity Relationships

Certain entity-relationships simply do not occur that often. When they appear on the model, they should be investigated.

Rare relationships are sometimes a sign of poor modeling techniques. Examples are mandatory one-to-one relationships and mandatory many-to-many relationships. Mandatory one-to-one relationships are usually two fragmented entities (see "Entity Fragmentation" in Chapter 6) that should be a single entity.

Mandatory many-to-many relationships are less rare than one-to-one relationships but still not that common (Figure 7-7). They can indicate a poor understanding of modality and are worth a second look by an observant data modeler.

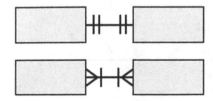

Figure 7-7. *Mandatory many-to-many relationships*

125

Recursive Modality Constraints

Double-check all recursive relationships because they, of all the objects modeled, are the ones most likely to be modeled incorrectly. Specifically, check for incorrect modality and cardinality.

Recursive modality constraints are presented in Chapter 3. This entry focuses on how these constraints can be used to double-check the validity of a relationship.

Recursive modality constraints are listed in Table 7-1 and can be summarized as follows:

- Symmetrical relationships can be mandatory-mandatory or optional-optional but not mandatory-optional or optional-mandatory. The latter two categories are meaningless.

- Symmetrical relationships cannot be one-to-many. One-to-many symmetrical relationships are meaningless.

- Asymmetrical relationships cannot be mandatory. If they were, that would mean they fall into an infinite regression. (See "Updating the Constraints.")

Table 7-1. Evaluating Possible Relationships

Cardinality	Modality	Asymmetrical Relationship	Symmetrical Relationship
One-to-one	Mandatory-mandatory	X ???	OK
	Optional-optional	OK	OK
	Mandatory-optional	X	X
One-to-many	Mandatory-mandatory	X	X
	Optional-optional	OK	X
	Mandatory-optional	X	X
	Optional-mandatory	X	X
Many-to-many	Mandatory-mandatory	X	OK
	Optional-optional	OK	OK
	Mandatory-optional	X	X

Note: X = Impossible, OK = Possible, ? = An exception

You can test this by trying a few cases on your own. Try converting a case that works to one that should not work, and look at the results. For example, convert "Is the partner of" to include a police officer's former partners. A police officer must have one and only one partner at a time; however, they can change partners as they like. Is this represented in Figure 7-8?

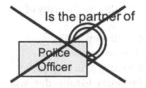

Figure 7-8. *A one-to-many symmetrical relationship is impossible*

The answer is "no."

Look at a police officer occurrence (call him Officer Molloy). Molloy can have only one partner at a time, but over his career he might have many partners. Is this one-to-many? No, many officers could have had Molloy as a partner. Actually, the relationship is many-to-many. In reality, a one-to-many symmetrical relationship does not exist.

Updating the Constraints

Since the author introduced the concept of recursive modality constraints in the early 1990s, a number of other authors have expanded the definition of an asymmetrical relationship.[1,2,3,4] One case is presented here.

Imagine a lake where three lifeguards are posted around the entire shoreline. Each lifeguard is required to back up the lifeguard to his right. The data model would include the entity Lifeguard and the recursive relationship Backs Up. The relationship is mandatory-mandatory because each lifeguard must back up the guy to his right. However, the relationship is also asymmetrical because while A backs up B, B does not back up A; in fact, B would back up C. An asymmetrical mandatory-mandatory relationship breaks the rule stated earlier—at least that is the argument of some authors. Their solution is to expand the notion of asymmetrical to include a number of special cases.

These critics are partially right; however, their conclusion might be misguided. A more accurate conclusion might be that "backs up" is a hybrid, where the recursive modality constraint is determined by the number of instances in the relationship.

Take the case of the entity Employee and the relationship Supervises. It is an asymmetrical hierarchy where Abbott supervises Burns, who supervises Chatsworth. It is asymmetrical because while Abbott supervises Burns, Burns does not supervise Abbott. It is also optional-optional because Chatsworth supervises no one, and no one supervises Abbott.

Now return to the lifeguard example and make Abbott, Burns, and Chatsworth lifeguards where Abbott backs up Burns, who backs up Chatsworth. This is asymmetrical and mandatory-mandatory, so the critics are right.

However, go back to the Supervises example and fire Chatsworth. Now Abbott supervises Burns, but Burns still does not supervise Abbott. Nothing is changed; the relationship Supervises is still asymmetrical optional-optional. Go back to the lifeguard example and, once again, fire poor Chatsworth. As before, Abbott backs up Burns, but now Burns backs up Abbott. This case is now symmetrical mandatory-mandatory.

What happened? There seems to be a special case where, if the number of occurrences is three or greater, then the relationship is asymmetrical; however, if the number of occurrences is two, then the relationship is symmetrical.

127

How often does this special case arise? Not often, but it is intriguing and worthy of further discussion.

The critics present some additional distinctions that are not at all convincing (for example, saying that a manager can manage himself). Most involve convoluted relationships that seem implausible. However, further investigation might turn up some interesting cases that could affect data model development for the better. Ideally, they will continue their work.

What should a data modeler do? First, look carefully at all relationships and ensure that they make sense. Apply the smell test to see whether they are credible. Second, take what everyone else says, including this author, with a grain of salt. All are trying to give you the best information possible, but data modeling, as with everything else in IT, is a moving target with new ideas (some better, some worse) coming out all the time. *Caveat emptor.*

Spiderwebs

Spiderwebs are usually the sign of an immature data model or incorrectly defined relationships.

Also called *porcupines* or *pincushions*, spiderwebs are entities that are directly related to most other entities on the diagram (Figure 7-9).

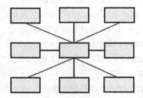

Figure 7-9. *A spiderweb data model*

Many models have one or more crucial entities, sometimes called *anchor entities*, that form the center of major portions of the diagram (Figure 7-10). Customer, Account, Product, and Project are excellent candidates for anchor entities.

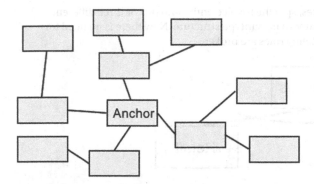

Figure 7-10. *An anchor entity forms the core of the data model*

A data model for a bank could conceivably have a dozen relationships involving Account. That is not wrong. What might be wrong is linking all or most entities directly to the anchor because anchors are usually linked only indirectly (through other entities) to the rest of the model.

Spiderwebs are sometimes the basis for a data warehouse schema, which often have more pleasant names such as star schema or snowflakes. (Star schemas and data warehouses are examined in Chapter 14.) Look closely. The spiderweb might just be the product of a data warehouser jumping the gun and applying a physical database design concept to a logical data model.

If you find a spiderweb on a diagram, it might be any of the following:

- Incorrectly modeled data.

- A simplistic representation of the business.

- A physical data design technique applied to a logical data model.

Too Many Blanks or Nulls

Be careful of too many blanks or nulls in an entity. They might indicate incorrectly defined entities.

Blanks and nulls are a cause of concern for many users of some (particularly relational) database management systems. The reason for the concern is that nulls can play havoc with DBMS key requirements. However, in logical data modeling, unique identifiers, while encouraged, are not required.

A few blank attributes are OK—there are always fields for which the desired information is missing. However, if there are a considerable number of blanks, it might signal that the designer is combining multiple different entity types into one.

For example, imagine an Invoice entity that contains the attributes DISCOUNT, MINIMUM ORDER, SALESMAN, and CONTRACT NUMBER for commercial accounts and the attributes CREDIT CARD NUMBER and ORDER SOURCE (i.e., whether the order is from the Web, by phone, or over the counter) for retail customers. For a given occurrence, the first four attributes are blank if the customer is retail, while the latter two are blank if the customer is commercial.

To avoid the blank attributes, split the Invoice entity into two or three different entities (Figure 7-11) or into a supertype-subtype structure. Now there is no need for blanks and no logical data modeling rules are broken.

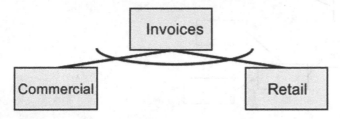

Figure 7-11. *Entities can be split to avoid blanks*

Note that in this example, the relationship between Commercial and Retail and Invoice is an *exclusive or*. In other words, one occurrence of Invoice can associate with one occurrence of Commercial or with one occurrence of Retail, but not both.

Remember that you are modeling the business, not creating a database schema. The task is to correct an error made when the single entity was created, not concoct new entities to solve a minor concern.

Do not create entities if they do not (1) conform to the definition of an entity and (2) do not reflect the business.

Too Many Recursives

Be careful of too many recursive relationships, which often reflect the efforts of an inexperienced data modeler.

In a complete data model, rarely are more than 2 percent of the relationships recursive. If 10 percent or more of the relationships are recursive, there may be a problem. Because this problem is not common, there is little information describing how it comes about, although the most likely cause is "students' disease." Students' disease is a phenomenon predominantly suffered by medical and psychology students. It works this way: after hearing about a new disease in class, a number of students are convinced that they suffer from the recently discovered malady.

If you find, or have developed, a data model where 10 or more percent of the relationships are recursive, you should

- Review the definition and uses of recursives.

- Revisit the data and discuss them with end users to resolve any misconceptions.

When too many recursive relationships occur, odds are high that the data modelers are new and trying out all the neat stuff they learned in class or from some recently read book.

* * * * *

This completes the Logical Data Modeling phase of Usage-Driven Database Design (U3D).

Next U3D Phase: Physical Schema Definition

In the next phase of U3D (Figure 7-12), the logical data model is merged with the logical process model to create a physical data model, which represents not only the definition of the data but how the new application will use the data.

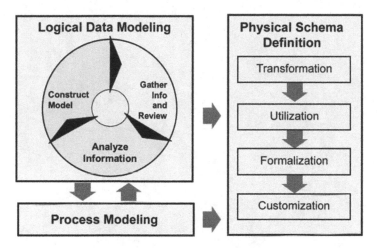

Figure 7-12. *U3D framework*

The physical data model, in turn, drives the creation of the Physical Schema Definition phase that determines the database structure, how the database is ultimately used, and its overall performance.

Notes

1. George Tillmann, *A Practical Guide to Logical Data Modeling.* New York: McGraw-Hill, Inc., 1993.

2. James Dullea and Il-Yeol Song, "An Analysis of Structural Validity in Unary and Binary Relationships in Entity Relationship Modeling." *Proceedings of the 4th International Conference on Computer Science and Informatics, Research Triangle Park, NC, USA.* 1998.

3. James Dullea and Il-Yeol Song. "A Taxonomy of Recursive Relationships and Their Structural Validity in ER Modeling." *Conceptual Modeling—ER'99.* Springer Berlin Heidelberg, 1999, pp. 384–399.

4. James Dullea, Il-Yeol Song, and Ioanna Lamprou, "An Analysis of Structural Validity in Entity-Relationship Modeling." *Data & Knowledge Engineering* 47.2 (2003), pp. 167–205.

PART III

Physical Schema Definition

CHAPTER 8

■ ■ ■

Introduction to Physical Database Design

Though this be madness, yet there be method in it.

—Shakespeare

You appeal to a small, select group of very confused people.

—Message in a fortune cookie

In the early 1980s, a Honeywell customer was having problems with DBMS batch jobs. A Honeywell field-service engineer was visiting that company for a number of management meetings. During her lunch break, she wandered into the DBA's area where she found the customer's staff stymied by the processing problem. Their most important application, the one that processed customer orders each night, was taking longer and longer to complete its task. It now took almost 5.5 hours to run, pushing the envelope of the nightly batch window. The Honeywell engineer looked at the database design and the application and, after less than 20 minutes, recommended changes to about 20 lines of code. She then returned to her meeting.

The DBA team made the recommended changes, tested the results in the test environment, and had the changes approved and installed by that evening. The 5.5-hour job ran that night for 1 hour and 10 minutes. No other jobs, batch or online, were adversely affected.

This example illustrates a peculiarity with databases. Computer programs either compile or don't. Compilers are very fussy. If you don't have everything right, the compile fails. DBMS compilers (precompilers, translators, interpreters, etc.) are not so picky. They allow atrocious database designs to compile and be placed in production. And they work, albeit not well. Database management systems have a resilience and ability to tolerate some really poor designs. They just run slow. It might be a simple task, but if the database design is poor, that simple task might take hours, even days, to run. DBAs might blame other jobs or complain that the machine is too small, but it is not uncommon that a few small changes in the design can make all the difference in the world. The application programmer knows when his code is bad; the compiler tells him. Too often, the DBMS compiler is silent, and that can really hurt.

© George Tillmann 2017
G. Tillmann, *Usage-Driven Database Design*, DOI 10.1007/978-1-4842-2722-0_8

Often the cause of the poor performance is relying only on the static definition of data and not paying sufficient attention to how the data are used. Logical data modeling correctly defines the data without reference to their use. The physical database design's purpose is to explain how the users and applications want to use the data.

Before converting entities, attributes, and relationships to records, data items, and links, the designer should look at how the current crop of database management systems came about.

Now, you say, why should I care about the history of the DBMS? Well, as they say, "The more things change, the more they stay the same." As you traipse through the history of data management, you see the same concepts used, forgotten, and then rediscovered. Like NoSQL? Then you will probably love the DBMS of the 1970s and 1980s. Want to know what your DBMS vendor will come up with next? It just might be in that 30-year old manual you use to prop up your wobbling desk. Read and see.

A Short Incondite History of Automated Information Management (or, a Sequential Look at Random Access)

The mid-twentieth century rise of the computer created a need to manage not only the machine hardware and software but also the data that changed its parlor-trick abilities into something meaningful. Getting information in and out of a computer is still an expensive and slow task; however, it was much more expensive and slower in the beginning.

Information Management Era 1: Sequential Processing

The punched card was invented in the eighteenth century, reinvented in the late nineteenth century (for the 1890 census), and saw its first automated use with tabulating machines in the early twentieth century, all before meeting up with the computer in the 1950s. Although it had many shapes and sizes, the 80-column card was certainly the most well-known information repository of the era—allowing the storage of 80 characters, or 960 bits, of information. The cards had three significant features. First, they were easily storable, if space was not an issue—stack 'em, rack 'em, or put them in long, low cabinet drawers. If treated properly, cards could last centuries and were easily stored remotely for security purposes. Second, they came in colors, which functioned as a file attribute telling the operator what they were part of—green, new customer; yellow, existing customer; red, customer in arrears. Third, a new card could be inserted into a deck, and an unwanted card could be removed, quickly and easily. No automation required.

A significant disadvantage of punched cards, other than size and weight, was that they had to be read sequentially. Combine this with computer memory being small—the amount of data it could hold in its buffer was often little more than a card's worth—the system could read only a card or two and complete its processing task before memory had to be flushed and reused. Sequential processing and limited memory meant that all the data the computer needed to do its job had to be in its buffers at roughly the same time. If an account had multiple orders, the Account and its Order records had to be sufficiently close together that the machine could grab them as a single transaction.

The solution to the problem was to integrate the card files—to physically place all the Order cards after their related Account card (Figure 8-1). The machine would read the Account card and then read each Order card, one at a time, adding up the amount of money the account owed. When the last Order card was read, the totals would be tallied, a bill printed, and perhaps a new Account card punched. The machine then went on to read the next Account card, and the process repeated.

The punched cards could be sequenced in a parent-child relationship order.

This approach would be mimicked by virtually all future database management systems.

Figure 8-1. *Punched cards*

For a monthly payroll system, the Employee card might be followed by four or five weekly Time cards. This parent-child relationship of account-order, employee-time card, student-grades, product-parts, and so on, became the basis for most sequential processing. The introduction of tape, paper or magnetic, made little difference; although faster, the files were still processed sequentially and used this parent-child model.

Tape did provide one advantage, although it was hardly a breakthrough. It allowed the segregation of data by type. Accounts could be in one physical file, while Orders were in another. Two tape drives could be used, one containing a tape of Accounts, sorted by ACCOUNT NUMBER, and a second tape drive containing an Order file also sorted by ACCOUNT NUMBER. The application would read one ACCOUNT NUMBER from Drive 0, and then, using Drive 1, see whether there were any Orders with the same ACCOUNT NUMBER; if there were, it would process the lot until it ran out of Orders and then read the next Account from Drive 0.

Information Management Era 2: The First Random Access DBMS

Disks, with random access memory, changed the game. Now data could be accessed nonsequentially. The Account record might still be read sequentially; however, its associated Orders could be read from a totally different file stored in ORDER NUMBER or some other sequence. You just had to find it among the myriad orders.

Random access was a great advance but a messy one. How do you find one record in a pile of a few thousand records? A simple and efficient way to retrieve a record was to use the record's disk address. Every record on disk has an address telling the system where it lives. It might be something like disk 5, cylinder 3, platter 4, sector 6. Jump to that location and your record should be there. You just had to know 5, 3, 4, 6.

How do you remember 5, 3, 4, 6? Two record retrieval approaches were, and still are, popular. The first approach is to store the disk address of the Order record in the Account record, and then every time you read the Account record the disk address of its Order record is right there.

What do you do if there is more than one Order record and they are not stored in ACCOUNT NUMBER sequence but rather are scattered all over the disk (there are always a few unfortunate data points that challenge a good theory)? A good solution is to store the disk address of the first Order record in the Account record, store the disk address of the second Order record in the first Order record, store the disk address of the third Order record in the second Order record, and so on, and so on. This is known as a *linked list*.

The first popular database management systems stored each record type in its own file, and then it allowed the designer to specify parent-child relationships across the files. The parent-child relationships were carried out using pointers. It was a good system to find Order records, but it had just one problem: how do you find the Account record if it's stored randomly?

The second record retrieval approach used a different tactic. If you had a randomly stored Account record (suppose all new Account records were stored at the end of the file), then create another smaller file, sorted by ACCOUNT NUMBER, that stores only the ACCOUNT NUMBER and the disk location of the Account record and, to top it all off, give this new sequential file a spiffy name such as *index*—because, after all, it does seem to mimic a library card catalog index. *Voilà*.

Two of the remaining champions of era 2 are IBM's Information Management System (IMS) and CA Technologies' IDMS. (A little trivia: the father of IDMS is Charles Bachman, who is also the father of data modeling.)

WORD SOUP

In the word soup that is the database arena, the term *data model* is applied to two very different concepts. Back in the salad days of data processing, *data model* referred to the architectural approach behind the file or database management system. Using this definition, the main types of data models were the hierarchical data model, used by IBM's IMS; the network data model, *à la* CA Technologies' IDMS; and the relational model as with Oracle Corporation's Oracle. There were, of course, others.

More recently, the term *data model* is used to describe the abstract representation of the definition, characterization, and relationships of data in a given environment.

In this book, *data model* refers to the abstract representation of data, while the broad approach used by a DBMS to go about its business is referred to as its *data architecture* or *architectural approach* or, more simply, just *architecture*. Using this terminology, IMS uses a hierarchical *architectural approach*, while SQL Server uses a relational *architectural approach.*

Don't like either *data model* or *architectural approach*? You can still successfully straddle the fence by simply using the word *model* as in network model or relational model.

IMS is a hierarchical DBMS; in other words, data are stored in an inverted tree (parent-child). You enter the database at the top, the root, and then progress down. Account might be the top (parent), while Order is below it (the child). The tree might have many levels, so below Order you might find the Line Item segment (*segment* is IMS for record), a sort of grandchild. Everything was done with embedded pointers—the root points to the first Account occurrence, the Account occurrence points to the first Order occurrence, and so on.

Databases can grow quite large in terms of both record types and record occurrences. As the functionality of a database grows, the number of record types can blossom, resulting in multiple trees of multiple levels of quite complex structures. IMS had a way of making it easier for the programmer by supporting application-specific subsets of the database. Rather than seeing the entire database structure, IMS supported a *logical database description,* which is a *view* or *subschema* to provide the application with a subset of all the records and data items it required. The database objects not needed could be left out of the view.

The hierarchical DBMS had a few advantages. First, it was fast. As long as you could start at the root, you could find all associated records under it quite quickly. This made it ideal for online transaction processing (OLTP). Second, relying on a single system to manage all data (adding new data, retrieving existing data, or deleting unwanted data) made database integrity and recovery relatively easy. Third, the *logical database description* allowed applications to deal only with the data they needed and not the entire, potentially complex, database.

However, the hierarchal model had two annoying drawbacks. First, you had to enter at the top of the tree and then go down. You could never go up. You could enter the data at the Order record (if you could find it), but there was no way to go up to its associated Account record. The second problem was that it was strictly one-to-many. If your data was many-to-many, you were out of luck.

The network architectural approach solved both of these problems with pointers that pointed up as well as down. Want to go to the related Account record from an Order record? No problem. Want to go from Account to Product and then to any other Accounts that ordered the same Product (many-to-many)? No problem. Want to go horizontally from Account to Account or Order to Order? No problem, because the network DBMS used *linked lists.*

PUB TRIVIA

The network architecture was codified into a standard by the Conference/Committee on Data Systems Languages (CODASYL). CODASYL was a volunteer standards group that gave the world, among other things, standardized COBOL. CODASYL's data management group became the Data Base Task Group (DBTG), which spearheaded numerous database standards. Some books refer to the network DBMS as the CODASYL model, others as the DBTG model; however, they all refer to the same thing.

DBTG gave us a number of DBMS concepts and terms that still exist today, such as *schema*, the specification of the database structure and how data in it is organized; *subschema*, the subset of the schema that is the programmer's or end-user's view of the database; *Data Manipulation Language (DML)*, a sublanguage that defines how database information is accessed, created, and destroyed by the programmer or end user; and the *Data Definition Language (DDL)*, the commands used by the database administrator to create, modify, and delete database schemas and subschemas.

Although not a direct line, there is a link between DBTG and the American National Standards Institute X3/SPARC committees, which carried on its work. ANSI introduced a three-level database model replacing schema with *internal schema* and subschema with *external schema* and added a new layer called the *conceptual schema*, which is the enterprise-wide view of the data.

The key to the network model was the *set*, a defined owner-member (parent-child) relationship. Sets were limited to two levels, but the member (child) in one set could be the owner (parent) of another set, providing a tree structure of any number of levels. The set had another trick. The member of one set could be a member in a second set, allowing the system to support many-to-many relationships (Figure 8-2). Invisible pointers, buried in records, allowed the programmer to *navigate* from set to set, record to record.

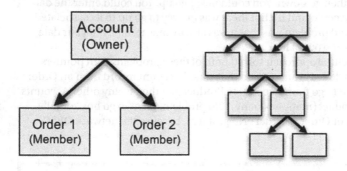

Figure 8-2. Network sets

Navigation required that at any given time the programmer had to be aware of where they were in the database. The current position (record, data item, or relationship) was known as *currency*. Knowing the *current record* allowed the programmer to *navigate* anywhere else in the database. CODASYL systems also supported a robust *subschema* architecture minimizing the need for extensive navigation.

CURRENCY

If you have ever used a word processor, then you are familiar with currency. If you look at a document on a computer screen and start typing, the characters you type do not necessarily go where you are looking. Rather, the keystrokes entered go where the cursor is located, which might be in a part of the document not even displayed on the screen.

Database currency is similar to the word processing cursor. It is the place in the database where the next function performed happens.

Network systems had another neat feature. When inserting a new record, you could specify that you wanted it stored near another record occurrence. For example, when inserting a new Order, you could specify that you wanted it stored on disk near its Account occurrence parent, ideally on the same database page. This meant that when you accessed an Account occurrence, there was a good chance that its associated Order occurrences were on the same physical page.

Era 2—the first true DBMSs (from the late 1960s to today)—had a number of kudos to its credit. First, the DBMSs were fast. You can't beat pointers for speed, which is still true today. The emergence of online transaction processing (OLTP) became their strong suit. No DBMS approach got data to a computer screen faster. Second, they were reliable. They oversaw the entire transaction, no matter how many places on disk it touched. They guaranteed that the database always faithfully represented what was entered (which is something many of the newest DBMSs today cannot say).

They also had some drawbacks. First, the hierarchal model was inflexible. Its one-directional nature and its one-to-many requirement made it sometimes difficult to fit into the real world. The network architecture solved these problems, but the database programmer required an additional ten IQ points to keep track of currency (i.e., where they were in the database). Navigating, following pointers up, down, and sideways, was confusing to many of our more challenged colleagues.

Modern-day versions of both IMS and IDMS are quite different, although they have managed to maintain their best qualities. IMS can now "look up" and handle many-to-many relationships, although some would say its solution is a bit klugey. Indices allow entry into the database at any level in the tree. IDMS had a rebirth with a number of relational features that reduced or, in some cases, eliminated navigation.

Hierarchical and network systems became the database workhorses of the 1970s and early 1980s and are still used today in transaction-heavy environments such as banking and airline reservation systems.

A Small Digression: A Couple of Words About Database Access

One of the reasons hierarchical and network systems were fast was their methods of fetching data. Both used *hashing* techniques and, later in their life, *indices*.

As with everything else in life, database access is all about costs. In computer terms, there are two information management cost drivers: storage and speed. Storage costs dollars for disk space. The more data you store, the more it costs. It's rather straightforward. If you want to cut down of storage costs, get rid of some data.

Speed is more interesting. The faster processing occurs the sooner the machine can do something else, so fast batch processing means that more jobs can be run in a unit of time. Online processing is a little trickier. If an online application runs from 9 to 5, it runs 8 hours whether it's fast or slow. However, slow online transaction speeds can cost a business in reduced sales (because customers get fed up waiting) or require more call center staff, pushing up personnel costs.

Information cost structures have changed significantly over the years. When the DBMS was a teenager, storage costs were high, and processing costs were relatively low (compared to storage costs). For example, the disk to store 1 megabyte of data in 1955 cost about $10,000, while that same megabyte costs less than 1/100 of a cent today to store. That's a million times cheaper!

The DBMS of the 1970s worked hard to keep storage costs down; however, with storage costs so low today, the cost focus has shifted to processing time. The effort now is to process as much as possible as soon as possible, which brings us to disk speed.

What is the simplest accurate way to measure database processing speed? The answer: disk I/O. The relative difference in speed of fetching information from main memory and fetching it from disk varies based on the speed of the processor and the speed of the disk, but as a useful round number, think 1,000 to 1. Fetching something from main memory is arguably about 1,000 times faster than getting it from disk. So, the important question for this millennium is how many disk I/Os does it take to fetch the data you require and how can you reduce that number?

How many disk I/Os are needed to fetch a specific customer record from disk? If there are 10,000 customer names on disk (and you assume each read of a customer record requires one I/O, an assumption discussed later), then the average number of reads to find your customer is 5,000 (number of records/2).

Hashing

Go back to the database file where each record had a physical address on disk (disk ID, cylinder number, platter number, sector number). Imagine a file to store customer information by CUSTOMER NAME. Also, imagine that you have a file consisting of 26 database pages. One way to store customer information is by allocating each letter of the alphabet its own database page. Names are *hashed* by their first letter. Those starting with an A are stored in page 1, all names starting with a B are stored in page 2, and so on. When you want to fetch "Smith," you know to go directly to database page 19. One I/O and you have "Smith."

Hashing consists of performing a function on the *search key* that always results in the same number in the desired range. The previous example used the first letter of the name, which is translated (hashed) into a disk location (A=1, B=2, etc.).

More complex schemes are both possible and the norm. Imagine a database with 950 pages storing information on an ACCOUNT NUMBER that can range from 1,000 to 9,999. A simple hash is to divide the account number by 950 (the number of pages) and use the remainder as the location to store the record. In this example, ACCOUNT NUMBER is the *search key*, the *hash algorithm* divides the search key by the number of database pages, and the *hash key* is the remainder of the division.

To find the storage location for ACCOUNT NUMBER = 4560 (the *search key*), divide 4650 by 950 (the *hash algorithm*), and you get 4 and a remainder of 760. The record should then be stored in page 761 (1 is added to the remainder to account for a remainder of 0). It's fast...using only a single I/O. Both IMS and IDMS used hashing techniques to store and retrieve data.

PUB TRIVIA

It's an interesting question whether hashing would have been invented today if it had not been discovered in the 1960s. Files today are easily expandable. Create a file and the operating system allocates the space as the file requires it. It was not always the case. Early mainframes and minicomputer operating systems required that the size of the file be declared when it was created. The operating system then allocated the entire declared space for the file. Need more space? You were out of luck until newer operating system versions allowed dynamic allocation of space. This was good for hashing because the number of database pages would be a constant, allowing the hash algorithm to always return the same hash key for the same search key.

Today, the number of database pages may be increased to accommodate new records. However, when the number of pages changes, the hashing algorithm no longer returns the same hash key for the same search key. To make hashing work, the DBMS must, somehow, maintain the same number of pages (logically or physically) regardless of file size.

There are probably as many different hash algorithms as there are databases, all with the goal of producing a rather even distribution. Because even the most complex hash algorithm rarely requires more than a knowledge of simple arithmetic, even the less mathematically eloquent can get into the game.

When hashing works, it is great. When it doesn't work, then things get complicated and efficiency degrades. Take the example of storing the record "Smith" in a 26-page database. The DBMS looks at the key "Smith," says it should be stored on database page 19, goes to page 19, and discovers that the page is full. What does the DBMS do now? Systems that use hashing have sometimes elaborate schemes for expanding pages or storing information in overflow areas. Whatever overflow technique is employed, the speed expected from hashing is compromised. Every time "Smith" is accessed, the DBMS will go to the wrong page and, not finding "Smith," start searching other locations.

Reorganizing the database also becomes difficult. Adding pages to the database can require removing every record from the database, rehashing using a different algorithm variable, and then restoring the records on their new page.

While hashing is great in certain situations, it is no access panacea. Luckily, other access approaches are available. Enter the *inverted index*.

Inverted Indices

An *inverted file* or an *inverted index* is a sequential file of keys and file or database pointers sorted in a different order than the file they support.

The concept dates to a time before the computer age. Take your average library. The books are stored on the shelves using some classification system such as the Library of Congress or Dewey Decimal system. Because few people know the classification number or code of the book they want, they require a method to find the right shelf containing the book. Enter the card catalog, which usually stored three index cards for each book—one for the book title, one for the author's name, and one for the subject. The title index card was placed in a file of similar title cards sorted by title name, the author card was placed in a file of authors sorted by author name, and the subject card was stored in a subject file sorted by subject. If the reader knew only the title, they could find the desired card in the title file. The card would then tell the reader where to find the book in the stacks.

The card catalog was three separate lists of all the books in the library, each sorted in a different order than the books on the shelves. That is why it is called an inverted file or inverted index, because the order of the cards was inverted from the order of the books.

This approach works for computer files as well. Take a customer. The actual Customer file might be sorted on CUSTOMER NUMBER, but it could have inverted indices on CUSTOMER NAME and CUSTOMER PHONE NUMBER. Look up a name in the Customer Name index and find a pointer to the correct record in the Customer file.

One problem with inverted files is that adding new entries or modifying old entries requires re-sorting the entire file, which could be a long and nasty process depending on the size of the file.

How good is an inverted file? Well, it finds the desired record, but it is not very efficient. An inverted file is still a sequential file with its records in sort-key order. Finding a record still requires, on average, reading half the file. Using the previous example of the Customer file of 10,000 entries, finding the correct index entry, assuming one disk I/O per entry (an assumption discussed later), requires, on average, 5,001 I/Os (5,000 I/Os are spent in the index alone, with one I/O to fetch the Customer record). Regardless of the speed of your computer, this is "go get a cup of coffee, your data will be showing up about the time you get back" speed.

One solution is the *binary search*. The binary search is also a technique used long before automation. Go back to the library card catalog. Suppose you want a book written by Herman Melville. You go to the author catalog and see 100 drawers containing index cards of author names. Where do you start? Drawer 1 with Abbott? No. Because Melville is in the middle of the alphabet, it would be smart to start in the middle with drawer 50. However, suppose drawer 50 ends with the letter *J*. Now you know that Melville is not in the first 50 drawers. Congratulations, you just eliminated half the author file. Next, go to the middle of the Js to the Zs, drawer 75. At drawer 75, you find the first author name starts with an *S*, so you have gone too far. You now know that the Melville card is between drawers 51 and 74. Halving the distance again, you reach for drawer 62, and bingo, you find the desired entry. This search is called a *binary search* because with each probe, you eliminate half of the remaining drawers. A sequential search or scan would have required 50 reads or probes, but using a binary search, you did it in three.

Three probes seem too good? Actually, we were lucky. According to the math... where:

N = Number of entries to search

C = Average number of compares to find desired entry

W = Worst-case number of compares

$$C = \log 2\ (N) - 1 \tag{1}$$

or in Microsoft Excel format...

$$= (\text{LOG}\ (N,2)) - 1 \tag{2}$$

...with the worst case being...

$$W = \log 2\ (N) + 1 \tag{3}$$

or in Microsoft Excel format...

$$= \text{FLOOR}\big(\text{LOG}\ (N,2),1\big) + 1 \tag{4}$$

...a binary search of 100 drawers should take an average of 5.6 compares or probes. A binary search of the 10,000 record file should find a hit after 12.3 probes on average, which is much better than the scan of 5,000 ($N/2$) probes.

Database Pages

Luckily, DBMS vendors identified the I/O bottleneck early on. The typical operating system (and a few programming languages), as well as disk drive manufacturers, see the magnetic disk as a series of rather small *sectors*. Sector size, often hard-coded into the disk by hardware or software, allowed only a limited number of bytes written or retrieved per disk I/O, some as small as 128 bytes. DBMS vendors worked around this limitation by creating a *database page*, an allotment of disk real estate consisting of multiple contiguous sectors read or written as one block. If you assume a sector of 128 bytes and a database page of 32 sectors, then each database page can store 4,096 bytes. If the Customer record is 800 bytes, then each database I/O can access five Customer records (a *blocking factor* of 5). Finding a single customer in a 10,000-record file would then not require on average 5,000 I/Os, but only 1,000 I/Os. That's a significant improvement.

LOGICAL VS. PHYSICAL I/O

There was a time when each I/O meant a trip to the I/O device. The physical record was then read into the main memory's buffer. The size of the allocated space in main memory (the data buffer) was the same size as the physical record.

As main memory size increased, buffers expanded. The operating system could now read multiple records into the buffer at a time. Buffer content was transparent to the application, which still merrily issued an I/O request for each record. However, now the operating system just might have the desired record in its buffer, saving considerable resources. This led to the distinction between logical I/O (a request for a record from secondary storage) and physical I/O (the actual fetching of data from the storage device).

The gain for the inverted indices is even greater because each index record is smaller, consisting of only CUSTOMER NAME and its database location. If we assume CUSTOMER NAME is 12 bytes and the database key is 4 bytes, then 250 index entries can be stored on a single database page (a *blocking factor* of 250), requiring fewer than two physical I/Os to find an index entry.

However, there are even better ways to find a record than a binary search. Read on.

B-Trees

In the early 1970s, a few people, working independently, developed the B-tree index. A B-tree stores index entries in a tree structure, allowing not only fast retrieval but also fast insertion and deletion (Figure 8-3).

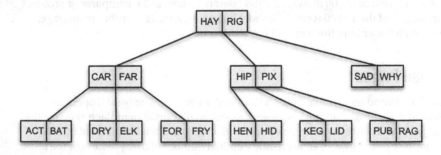

Figure 8-3. A simple B-tree

B-trees consist of *nodes*. A node is a record containing a specified number of index entries (search key and location ID). When the index node becomes full, it is split into three or more nodes with a parent node linking to two or more child nodes. As the index grows and the number of nodes expands, new levels are added to the *height* of the tree. The top node is called the *root node*, the bottom-level nodes are the *leaf nodes*, and the levels in between store the *branch nodes*.

There are many variations of B-trees. There are binary search trees, B+-trees, balanced trees, unbalanced trees, and many more. They differ in how they work. Some work better with very large amounts of data, while some work better with smaller amounts. Some B-trees specialize in highly volatile data (many inserts, updates, and deletes); others specialize in highly skewed data (uneven distribution). Some are useful for retrieving a single record, while others are best for fetching whole groups of records. Some promise fast sequential searching, while other favor fast random retrieval. Regardless, they all follow the same basic root, branch, leaf structure.

How fast are B-trees?

The answer is easily calculated:

where:

N = Number of index entries to search

C = Average number of compares to find desired entry

m = Blocking factor of index

$$C = \log N / \log m \hspace{4cm} (5)$$

in Microsoft Excel...

$$= LOG(N)/LOG(m) \hspace{3cm} (6)$$

For the 10,000-record customer file and a blocking factor of 250, that's fewer than 2 physical I/Os.

A main advantage of the B-tree over the binary search of an inverted file is not in fetching data but in index maintenance. For the inverted file, every time a record is entered or a search key modified, the entire file must be re-sorted. That's not the case for the B-tree. Usually, the new entry is just entered. If there is no more space in the node, then, in most cases, three or fewer I/Os are required to add the new nodes and index entry.

where:

Percent Split = Probability that the index node will need to split.

$$Percent\ Split = 1/(m/2-1) \hspace{3cm} (7)$$

or in Microsoft Excel...

$$= 1/((CEILING(m,1)/2)-1 \hspace{3cm} (8)$$

Using the previous example, less than 1 percent of the time an insertion requires a node split, so B-trees are very efficient.

B-trees were also retrofitted to hierarchical and network database systems, allowing them to access even nonroot data easily and quickly.

Every major DBMS implementation today, regardless of architecture, uses some type of B-tree, and other than minor variations, they are almost identical to those available 30 years ago.

Bitmaps

While bitmaps are usually found in the index section of every database book, their similarity to other indices is tenuous. Bitmaps work well when the possible values of an attribute are known and limited. Imagine an Employee record with the data item GENDER. Short of discovering life on Mars, GENDER can have only two values, "Female" and "Male."

There are a few assumptions about the following example. First, all Employee records are the same fixed length (assume 1 KB). Second, assume the database is a flat sequential file so that any record can be found if its position in the file is known. If there are 1,000 employees at 1 KB per employee, then the database file is 1 MB long. The first Employee record has a displacement (distance from the start of the file) of zero (it's in the first position). The second employee has a displacement of 1 KB and the third of 2 KB. The 501th employee would have a displacement of 500 KB, and so on.

For a bitmap, the system creates a file of, not 1 MB, but 1 Mb (not 1 million bytes, but 1 million bits). If the first employee in the file is a male, then the first bit is set to 1; if the first employee is a female, then the bit is set to 0. The same is done for each of the 1,000 employees.

For the query, "How many 'females' work for the company," the system adds the total number of 0 bits in the bitmap file and you have your answer. For the query "Display the NAME and SALARY of every 'Female'," the system can go to the bitmap and search each bit for a 0. When it finds one, it then goes to the Employee file and fetches the record with the displacement equal to the displacement of the bit times the length of the record minus 1 (because the first position is 0). If bit 125 is a 0, then the system should multiply 124 times 1,000 and go to the record with a displacement of 124 KB.

Bitmaps are great for systems where the query results (the *result set*) are usually a large number of records.

The example can be expanded to bring it closer to how bitmaps are actually used. Assume an Automobile database of 100 10 KB pages with a maximum of 10 Automobile records per database page, and assume that the data item COLOR can have the values "red" or "blue" or "green" or "black."

Because the database can store 1,000 Automobile records (100 pages at 10 per page), the bitmap needs to be 1,000 bits long. However, because there are four colors, four bitmap indices are required, one for each color. (Note: Actually only two bitmaps are needed if "No color" is excluded.)

With the four bitmaps, not only can a user find every car that is red, but, using Boolean logic, the user can easily find every car that is both red and black by "And-ing" the red and black bit maps.

Bitmaps are best where

- The database is used primarily for queries.

- The query outcome is a rather large result set.

- The queries are on attributes with a relatively small number of known values.

Bitmaps are amazingly fast, and the query can often be successfully completed without every going into the database file.

Associative Arrays

The associative array has been a data management mainstay almost from the creation of the disk drive. In a traditional array or vector (a vector is a one-dimensional array), the array contains only values. For example, in most programming languages, an array is defined as a collection (series) of elements or values. A particular value is found using its displacement (the first array value such as a bit, byte, string, etc., is placed in the first vector location, the second value in the second vector location, etc.). Assume the vector Employee with four locations or slots are numbered 1 through 4 and contain the values "Abrams," "Bailey," "Collins," and "Davis." Fetching Employee [slot 1] would yield "Abrams," while fetching Employee [slot 4] would return "Davis."

While the traditional array stores only values, the associative array stores key-value pairs. For example, the associative array Employee could store the key-value pair EMPLOYEE NUMBER:EMPLOYEE NAME (the key is separated from the value with a colon). The associative vector would now store ("101:Abrams," "107:Bailey," "231:Collins," and "103:Davis"). Fetching Employee[231] returns "Collins."

In this example, the keys are integers, but they need not be. The array could have been reversed with the key "Collins" and the value "231." Hashed associative arrays are often called *hash tables*.

An associative DBMS is a data management system whose architecture is based on the associative array. Many consider the associative database the ultimate in flexibility. It might offer variable-length records, consisting of a variable number of fields, each field of variable length. For example, imagine a record occurrence consisting of the following:

Key	Value
FIRST NAME	William
LAST NAME	Smith
EMPLOYEE NUMBER	34577
DEPENDENTS	Mary, Thomas, Roger

The associative system stores the field name with the value. On disk, the previous data might look like the following:

FIRST NAME:William;LAST NAME:Smith;EMPLOYEE NUMB
ER:34577;DEPENDENTS:Mary,Thomas,Roger;;

In this example, a colon separates key from value, a semicolon indicates the end of the variable-length field, a comma separates the multiple values in a single field, and the double semicolon indicates end of record. If the database contains 1 million employees, then the label FIRST NAME is on disk 1 million times. Some space could be saved by substituting a shorter label for each field name, such as $1 for FIRST NAME.

Associative systems are excellent for variable-length data and are popular for query-based systems.

Few associative database systems are referred to as associative database management systems. In practice, they are often referred to as hierarchal (such as DRS) or inverted file (Model 204) systems, reflecting the trend to classify database systems by how they link records together rather than how they store data fields.

Information Management Era 3: Inverted File Systems

Overlapping with the era 2 DBMSs was another whole DBMS animal—the inverted file systems. Products such as Adabas (now owned by Software AG), Model 204 (now called M204 and marketed by Rocket Software), and Datacom/DB (now marketed by CA Technologies) followed a different approach than their era 2 cousins. These systems removed all the pointers from the database and placed them in external indices. One entered the system and even "navigated" around it within the indices. Only when all the records wanted were identified did the DBMS delve into the database content to retrieve the records.

Inverted file database management systems were feasible only because of the advances made in indexing technology. B-tree indices, and their myriad spin-offs, made it possible to find a record on disk with just a few more I/Os than the pointer approach. Although not as good as era 2 hierarchical and network systems for transaction processing, inverted file system shined in query applications where the target was not just one or a few records but entire groups of records. Today, most query systems, 4GLs, document management systems, and many data warehouses use some form of inverted DBMS technology.

Information Management Era 4: The Age of Relational

The relational model does not leave IT people bored or apathetic. It is either the most loved or most hated DBMS model ever created. It is sanctified or vilified by academics, theorists, practitioners, and users, making it the most difficult model to discuss without upsetting someone. Talking to IT staff, one comes away with the belief that the relational model is a mixture of mathematics, computer science, and religion. Era 2 and era 3 products—and there were dozens and dozens of them—were designed by software engineers to solve software engineering problems. Their solutions, however, even the ones that worked well, were not always elegant. That bothered Edgar (Ted) Codd, an IBM researcher, who decided to develop an information management system that was both mathematically elegant and useful. He used set theory and predicate logic as his foundation. Although the relational model is technically as old as or older than many era 2 and era 3 systems, it took more than a decade for anyone to develop a viable product. That, and the radical change inherent in relational technology, gives it its own era.

Codd looked at the database landscape and didn't like what he saw. He thought the then-current database systems were too complex, requiring navigating multiple levels, dealing with pointers, handling indices, etc. He also disliked that the programs that accessed the database had to change if the underlying structure of the database changed. Adding new indices, pointers, or even database pages could require significant changes to the applications using the database.

He had a few major goals for his relational model. First, he wanted to simplify the database. He envisioned a system where data were represented in two-dimensional tables. Elaborate structures, which looked like a Jackson Pollock painting, were to be avoided. Artifacts that made the database lumpy (greater than two-dimensional), such as repeating groups and group items, should be eliminated. Keep it simple.

Second, he wanted *data independence*. The programmer (or end user because the new relational model was envisioned to not require programmers) should not have to know the innards of the database. Pointers were verboten, and even indices should be transparent to the user. In addition, how the data were used, by end user or program, should be unaffected by any structural changes to the database. Adding an index, modifying a relationship, etc., should all be possible without having to change how the data were used. (Changes to the DDL should not affect the DML.)

Third, Codd wanted a solid formal foundation for the model. Then-current DBMSs were like contemporary programming languages. They started as a simple concept, but then were expanded, modified, and jury-rigged until they are large, complex, and unwieldy, sometimes not resembling at all what they looked like in the beginning. His solution would have a mathematical background centered on set theory and predicate logic that would require little or no expansion.

Fourth, the model was to be *declarative*. Contemporary DBMSs were *procedural* in nature, requiring the programmer to tell the system, step by step, what to do. Declarative models have the user tell the system what is wanted and then leave it to the DBMS to decide how to obtain the desired result.

Fifth, the new system should eliminate redundancy and data inconsistency.

The mathematical nature of the new model required new terminology not familiar to many in IT. There were no longer files; there were now *relations*. Records were now *tuples* (rhymes with couples). Data items were *columns* or *attributes*. Perhaps most important, at least in hindsight, Codd separated theory from implementation. There was the relational model, and there were vendor (IBM, Oracle, Microsoft) implementations (DB2, Oracle, SQL Server), and as you will see, rarely the twain shall meet.

In the beginning, relational DBMSs (RDBMSs) suffered from poor performance. The emphasis on declarative syntax and data independence, and a de-emphasis of storage techniques, left the RDBMS relegated to use by small query applications.

However, time, and a mild shift of emphasis from the theoretical to the implementable, moved the RDBMS into the mainstream. Today, the RDBMS has had a long run, with more products out there than all the products from all the other DBMS architectures combined.

You can't talk about the relational model without talking about SQL. The relational fathers did not create a user interface (DML or DDL), but others did. An early implementation for a relational front end was SEQUEL, developed at IBM. It was followed by SEQUEL2 and then, after discovering SEQUEL was trademarked by someone else, SQL. (Old-timers still pronounce SQL as "sequel.") SQL became the most popular RDBMS language despite relational purists hating it. Adding insult to injury, many RDBMS products have SQL in their name and omit relational (SQL Server, MySQL, SQLBase, NonStop SQL, to name a few).

SQL's popularity extends beyond relational systems. Many nonrelational DBMSs, such as object-oriented DBMSs and NoSQL products (which are really "no relational"), use a SQL-like interface.

The RDBMS, without question, is the most popular DBMS model in the world today. It is the standard from which all others deviate. Look up Data Definition Language (DDL) or Data Manipulation Language (DML), and the explanation is likely to focus on relational DDL and relational DML without even a reference to its network origins.

It is the workhorse for many companies. If they have only one DBMS, it is likely to be relational. If they have two or more data management products, one of them is probably relational. It is the DBMS of choice for applications with relatively flat files, which use simple, well-defined data types, and are query based, such as data warehouses.

Problems with Relational

The RDBMS also has some shortcomings, particularly in moving from formal model to DBMS implementation.

First—Performance Issues

For many, the relational database management system is still not the DBMS of choice for high-volume, short-response-time transaction processing. Even some early relational advocates admitted it might be necessary to sacrifice performance for other relational features, and to at least some extent, that remains true today. Those vendors that have focused on performance have had to make some interesting theory versus implementation trade-offs if not totally abandon the soul of the model.

Second—Not So Simple Simplicity

The simplicity aspects of the relational model have proved surprisingly complex for some.

Data Types

Vendors had to modify the relational model to accommodate nontraditional data types (large text, audio, video, etc.) with very mixed results. Vendor-specific workarounds made moving between relational products, or even between versions within the same product line, problematic. In some cases, relational systems' unfriendly attitude toward new data types sparked whole new nonrelational database models.

Procedural Code

For some, the RDBMS is used for query processing, with SQL as a stand-alone language. For others, the RDBMS is used for transaction processing, with a SQL sublanguage embedded in a host programming language. In most of these cases, that host language is a procedural one using, of all things, a procedural SQL cursor to maintain currency. Many of these procedural addenda became industry standards.

Groups

Relational theory does not allow group attributes or multivalue attributes (repeating groups or group data items). Implementers of the relational model are not so fussy.

Unfortunately, as seen in logical data modeling, the real world is full of group and multivalue attributes. Price lists, tax tables, and other vectors and arrays abound in the real world, yet they are illegal in the relational world. The same is true for group data items such as DATE and ADDRESS.

This is at odds with most procedural languages, which provide, as a significant feature, the ability to process arrays and group data items. And for good reason. It is naïve to say that DATE is not an aggregate of MONTH, DAY, and YEAR. Or that EMPLOYEE NAME does not include the data items FIRST NAME, MIDDLE INITIAL, and LAST NAME. Programmers know this.

The argument against group attributes or multivalue attributes is that their exclusion makes the database easier to use. This might be true, but it also makes it less powerful and that much further away from representing the real world. And in truth, if programmers can learn to use these features with considerable success in their programming work, then they should be able to use them in their database access code.

Rather than benefiting from the "simplicity" of the relational model, database programmers are forced to replicate, on their own, features (such as arrays and groups) that were once readily available to them. Some IT shops purchase utility packages so programmers do not have to re-create missing functionality, while others write their own library routines. The relational model has not eliminated these real-world concepts; it just turned automated solutions into manual ones. In any case, a database feature that was designed to make the programmer's life simpler actually complicated it.

In fairness, many relational model purists, even the most pure of the pure, believe that some group data items are needed, with *date* being a prime example. And most vendors support groups even if they don't call them that. However, their accommodations, as welcome as they are, often involve two unpleasantries. First, the implementation is often a kluge, centering on vendor or user-defined domains or data types. The second inconvenient awkwardness involves intellectual honesty. If you are not allowing group data items, then don't allow group data items; if you are going to allow group data items, then do it straightforwardly, even if with a wink and a nod. The way it is now, each database designer and programmer must look closely to discover how their RDBMS vendor implements groups, if at all.

In short, the relational model simplifies the DBMS at the expense of the programmer.

Third—Communication and Language

For Codd, a major advantage of the relational model was its formal foundation. However, the simplicity of the mathematical foundation of the model was itself problematic. It might be clear to mathematicians but is much less so to the average programmer. Look at this sentence from his 1970 paper:

> The relations R, S, T must possess points of ambiguity with respect to joining R with S (say point x), S with T (say y), and T with R (say a), and, furthermore, y must be a relative of x under S, z a relative of y under T, and x a relative of z under R.[1]

153

This is not the most complex sentence in the paper. It was chosen because it does not require special symbols. For most programmers, it is incomprehensible. The relational model is considerably more difficult to understand for the average database programmer than any other database model. Many database administrators are left to dust off their college version of Gödel's incompleteness theorem or surrender to never understanding why the relational model does what it does. Codd seemed to recognize this. Twenty years after introducing the model, he wrote the following:

> One reason for discussing relations in such detail is that there appears to be a serious misunderstanding in the computer field concerning relations.[2]

The ugly truth is that although programmers had difficulty understanding the relational model, Codd had just as much difficulty understanding how nonmathematicians in general, and programmers in particular, comprehend math.

THEY LOOK BUT THEY CANNOT SEE…WELL, SOME CAN

Peter Chen, the founder of the entity-relationship model, published a paper in 2002 illuminating the problem. In it Chen states the following:

> It is correct to say that in the early 70s, most people in the academic world worked on the relational model instead of other models. One of the main reasons is that many professors had a difficult time understanding the long and dry manuals of commercial database management systems, and Codd's relational model paper[1] was written in a much more concise and scientific style.[3]

He goes on to say this:

> A lot of academic people worked on normalization of relations because only mathematical skills were needed to work on this subject.[3]

So why are there no better translations of Codd? What have the ocean of authors, writing hundreds of books and papers on the relational model, done to improve the situation? Very little. Read almost any instructions on normalization, and it's obvious that nonmathematical descriptions are rare. The authors seem either afraid to present the material in a nonmathematical way or simply do not understand their audience. And that is the fundamental issue. The intended audience for the relational model is (or should be) not mathematicians, not end users, but IT people. If you want to communicate with IT people, then you must speak their language. IMS, IDMS, and Adabas authors understand their audiences. Relational authors…not so much.

WHERE ARE YOU, CARL SAGAN?

It is not impossible to make the incomprehensible somewhat fathomable. It just takes understanding a complex subject and how people learn. A number of very smart people have done it. Theoretical physicist Stephen Hawking, who held the Isaac Newton chair of physics at Cambridge University, was able to write a book for the everyday person describing black holes.[4] His book was on the best-seller list for more than four years. Theoretical physicist George Gamow, the first to give us a mechanism for the Big Bang, wrote a number of popular books, two of which focused on quantum theory and mathematics.[5,6] Gamow, it is said, targeted his books at the middle-school reader.

So why is it so difficult to get a simple explanation of the relational model?

Is this Codd's fault? Not entirely. Chen's early work on the entity-relationship approach is quite mathematical and esoteric. However, Chen and even more so his followers wrote material more understandable for people who wouldn't know a Turing from a Tarski. Relational followers have been more reluctant to translate Codd into English. It is a shame because their reticence hides some of the beauty of the model from its users.

Fourth—Relational: Theory or DBMS?

Codd felt that the relational model was superior to its competitors, not just because it made a good database management system but because it did a better job of describing the real world, including doing a better job than the entity-relationship approach. Look at this passage from his 1990 book:

> With the relational approach, an executive can have a
> terminal on his or her desk from which answers to questions
> can be readily obtained. He or she can readily communicate
> with colleagues about the information stored in the database
> because that information is perceived by users in such a
> simple way. The simplicity of the relational model is intended
> to end the company's dependency on the small, narrowly
> trained, and highly paid group of employees.[7]

If programmers have trouble understanding the fundamentals of the relational model, then business executives will be totally lost, yet Codd could not see this. In fact, Codd saw the entity-relationship approach not as an analysis technique but as a relational model competitor.

> No data model has yet been published for the entity-
> relationship approach. To be comprehensive, it must support
> all of the well-known requirements of database management.
> Until this occurs, companies intending to acquire a DBMS
> product should be concerned about the risk of investing in the
> entity-relationship approach.[8]

155

The logical-physical distinction, as well as all the other database design principles discussed in Chapter 1, are totally ignored. It's as though Codd could not see the difference. He saw foreign keys and functional dependencies as a way of describing the business world to an executive.

Fifth—Where Are You Relational Model?

Lastly, the relational model Codd envisioned still does not exist. Unhappy with vendor implementations that did not meet the standards of his relational model, Codd, in 1985, came up with 12 rules that all RDBMS products should follow. By 1990, no vendors had implemented all 12 rules; however, that did not stop Codd from introducing 321 more rules. To date, almost half a century after its introduction, no RDBMS implementation incorporates more than a handful of the final total of 333 rules (see Table 8-1).

Table 8-1. *The Effectiveness of the Relational Model*

Relational Goals	
Goal	**Effectiveness**
Simplify	Questionable. In theory, yes; in practice, the features that had to be added to make the DBMS practical, such as nonstandard data types (large text, video, etc.), cursors, and triggers, added to the complexity and difficulty using the model.
Data independence	Effective.
Solid formal foundation	Mixed. The formal foundation is there but in a language understood by few in IT.
Declarative	Partially. The requirement to make the model work in the real world necessitated adding a number of procedural features.
Eliminate redundancy and data inconsistency	Mixed. The tool for eliminating redundancy (normalization) is a technique that can be applied to any DBMS. The need for foreign keys undercuts reducing redundancy.

Just Because It Has Failings Doesn't Mean It's a Failure

How successful is the relational model? Ask yourself this question: since the relational model was introduced, how many other theoretically based database management systems are there? Yet, despite all its failings, it is impossible to consider the relational model a failure. It fails to live up to its inventor's expectations, yet it endures as no other DBMS has ever endured. Even failure can't argue with success.

Information Management Era 5: Object Technology

Relational technology was king. Then in the 1990s, there appeared a new pretender to the throne—object technology. An *object* is a structure that includes both data and the *operations* (procedures) to manipulate those data. With the traditional database, an *object* (for example, the record Order) only contains data (the attributes of Order). However, the object-technology object Order contains not only the attributes of Order but also the operations (computer code) that manipulate Order, such as Create New Order and Fulfill Order. All the code associated with Order is in the Order object.

Object technology is, in part, a reaction against the traditional way of developing systems—separating into two groups the tasks and even the teams that work on data and process. Object technology says you can't separate the two. Rather, think of a system as a network of communicating objects that pass information or instructions to each other.

Object technology has a number of unique and defining features.

Association is the natural relationship between objects. For example, customers place orders, so there is a natural association between Customer and Order. Associations can have cardinality and modality and can exist between two, three, or *n* objects.

A child object can *inherit* properties from its parent object. Imagine objects organized into multilevel inverted trees. Objects at the top are the most general, such as Customer, while those lower down are more specific, such as Wholesale Customer. The lower objects can *inherit* properties (attributes and operations) from higher-level objects. In this example, the object Wholesale Customer inherits from Customer all of Customer's attributes and operations.

Although they routinely communicate with each other, the internal workings of each object are independent of any other objects. This is called *encapsulation*—what goes on inside an object stays inside the object. For example, the object Customer could contain the operation Add New Customer, and the Customer object knows exactly what to do when the operation is invoked, while the object Order knows nothing of, and is oblivious to, that operation.

Object-Oriented Programming Led to Object-Oriented Analysis and Design, Which Eventually Led to the Object-Oriented Database Management Systems (OODBMSs)

The OODBMS is, in many ways, a throwback to the era 2 DBMS. The 1990s were a time when computer usage was expanding into areas of nontraditional data types. The hierarchical structure of objects is more compatible with era 2 DBMSs than relational ones. Objects fit easily into multilevel trees stored in pointer-based systems. The database could no longer stay in the flat tables of relational systems but had to adjust to the distinct islands of multilevel data and code contained in the object.

Information management was no longer limited to numbers and small strings of text such as names and addresses. Now the DBMS was called upon to store complete documents, pictures, movies, music, graphics, X-rays, and any other type of exotic data, including computer code. The RDBMS choked on these data types (imagine performing a relational join on an artist name and a music video).

The OODBMS had everything in its favor (such as academic blessings and vendor investments) except customers. For whatever reasons, although usually attributed to massive corporate investments in relational technology, sales were weak. The solution? Join the enemy. Underfunded OO vendors died off, and their place was taken by RDBMS vendors adding OO features to their RDBMS offerings. The result was some strange bedfellows (particularly if you ignore the RDBMS vendors criticizing, a decade earlier, era 2 and 3 vendors when they added relational features to their hierarchical, network, and inverted file DBMS offerings to boost their weakening sales).

The OO-RDBMS, the multipurpose tool of the information management world, offered two, sometimes distinct, views of the data, one relational and one object oriented. SQL, never liked by the relational purists and becoming increasingly procedural, was modified to accommodate object technology. And it worked. The OO components were bolted onto the RDBMS without much loss in relational-ness.

How effective is this strategy? Well, the real question is how much real object-oriented system building is going on out there. Anecdotal information would indicate that OO technology use is strong in vendor development shops but has been largely abandoned (except in name) in end-user organizations.

A Small Digression (Again): The ACID Test

If you ask the question which DBMS is best, the right answer should be: for what? They all have their strengths, and they all have their weaknesses. One fundamental way to evaluate a DBMS is with the ACID test.

In 1981, Jim Gray, of Tandem Computers, published a paper in which he applied a formalized definition of transaction to DBMS activity.[9] In 1983, Gray's concept was expanded and given the acronym ACID by Haerder and Reuter.[10] ACID stood for the following:

- *Atomicity*: Every part of a transaction must be executed before the transaction can be considered complete.

- *Consistency*: Any change to the database must be consistent with all validation rules.

- *Isolation*: Every transaction must be completed as though it were the only transaction, regardless of how many transactions there are and in what sequence they are executed. Isolation deals with the notion of currency control.

- *Durability*: Once a transaction is committed, it stays committed. Failures from a loss of power to a computer, communications disruptions, or crashes of any type do not affect a completed transaction.

ACID is for transactions that insert, update, or delete database records. It guarantees the integrity of data. Unfortunately, integrity does not come cheap. To work, ACID databases require considerable support in the form of journals that store the image of the record occurrence before the change (the before image), another image of the record occurrence after the change (after image), and log files documenting each step of the transaction. All of this protection is expensive in terms of space and processing time.

The odd thing is that when the ACID paper was published in 1983, virtually every major DBMS conformed to the ACID criteria, which relegated the entire concept to an interesting academic sideline. As you will see, it was not until the advent of NoSQL, a decade later, that ACID compliance became an important DBMS selection criterion because many NoSQL systems do not meet ACID standards.

Information Management Era 6: NoSQL

NoSQL is an inaccurate name. It should really be called NoRelational because it is a revolt against the constraints of the relational model, not against SQL. It is also a catchall phrase that encompasses very different technologies targeted at very different problems.

Although NoSQL databases existed decades before the term was invented, they became popular around the millennium when IT organizations were faced with not only a growing number of relational-resistant data types but also big data. How big is big data? Nobody knows, but nobody admits it. It's just more and more of what IT has been dealing with—lots more. Gilding the lily, big data requires doing sometimes detailed, statistical analysis on large data sets.

Key-Value

There is no common NoSQL architecture, although one of the more interesting ones is the *key-value* approach. Imagine a file cabinet full of file folders. Each file folder has a tab stating what is in the folder. Although the contents of a single folder have something in common, the same cannot be said for any two folders. One folder might be labeled "bank statements," while a second might be labeled "dog vaccination papers," and a third "Doonesbury cartoons." Although a traditional file's contents are related to the file label, the contents of one folder might be totally different from the contents of any another folder. NoSQL key-value systems link, in a tree structure, related contents vertically but disparate contents horizontally.

NoSQL key-value database management systems are often an amalgam of hashing techniques and associative arrays of key-value pairs, providing a powerful mechanism for storage and retrieval. However, key-value databases have expanded the concept of the associative array. The key is still the key, but the value might be an entire folder consisting of many different data items of many different domains. Some key-value systems contain a hierarchy of keys, with the first relating to the highest-level content and subsequent keys to lower-level content (similar to the bank statement example).

Redis from Redis Labs and Oracle's Oracle NoSQL are good examples of key-value DBMSs.

Graph

Graph NoSQL databases are modern versions of the network architecture with two major differences. First, they are tuned for high performance using techniques regularly found in other NoSQL products. Second, they have a DML that makes it easier to navigate the database.

Graph is a mathematical term for a structure consisting of a number of nodes. Nodes are connected to each other by edges. Unlike trees, there is no up or down. The nodes are, of course, records, and the edges are lines or links. Graph systems are often hybrids combining other architectures into a single implementation, with key-value being a favorite. Graph systems get their speed from embedded pointers linking the various notes.

Neo4j, from Neo Technology, Inc., is an example of an ACID-compliant graph database management system.

Document Management

The *document management* system, usually listed as a separate NoSQL model, is often a subset of the key-value approach. The key is the document name or description, and the value is the underlying document. Each value occurrence contains not only the document but the description (metadata, data type) of the document.

MongoDB from MongoDB Inc. is a good example of a document DBMS.

Multimodal

Multimodal systems are the strangest NoSQL animal. Multimodal systems provide a layer on top of other database architectures. The user or program interacts with the top layer. If the data to be stored are documents, the MMDBMS stores them using a document manager. If the data to be stored are in tabular form, the MMDBMS stores them in a relational format. The multimodal system is surely the *turducken* of the data management world. Whatever data you have, the MMDBMS finds an appropriate way to store them.

MarkLogic from the MarkLogic Corporation and OrientDB developed and marketed by Orient Technologies Ltd. are multimodal DBMSs.

Is That an ACID or a BASE?

You should know whether your DBMS complies with ACID even if all of its components are not important to you. For example, ACID deals with inserting, updating, and deleting records in a database. If you have a read-only data warehouse, then you might not care about ACID compliance. Table 8-2 shows a simple comparison of DBMS types against the ACID model.

Table 8-2. Database Architecture and ACID Compliance

| Illustrative | | | | | | | <---- NoSQL ----> | | |
Characteristic	Hierarchical	Network	Relational	Inverted File	Object	Multimodal	Key-Value	Document	Graph
Atomicity	XXX	XXX	XXX	XXX	XXX	XX	X	XX	XX
Consistency	XXX	XXX	XXX	XXX	XX	XX	XX	XX	XX
Isolation	XXX	XXX	XXX	XXX	XX	XX	XX	XX	XX
Durability	XXX	XXX	XXX	XXX	XXX	XX	X	XX	XX

Note: XXX high, X low

161

The takeaway from Table 8-2 is that the older database architectures, shown on the left, are all ACID compliant. These were, and still are, the basic information manager workhorses that keep the enterprise going. As you move to the right, ACID compliance drops off. These information managers tend to be special-purpose tools designed to do one or two things well at the expense of other features, notably ACID.

A word of warning about Table 8-2. The products represented by some of the columns are so different in their implementation that it is hard to categorize all the products covered by a column. Look at the key-value column. Some key-value products are ACID compliant, such as upscaledb; others are not, such as Redis; while still others are partially compliant, such as Cassandra. Worse, because so many NoSQL products are relatively new, their ACID compliance could be significantly different by the time you read this.

Many NoSQL database management systems have given up the ACID guarantees for exceptional performance in one or another area. However, because so many developers and DBMS purchasers know about the benefits of ACID, the NoSQL community came up with its own acronym: BASE. (Apparently, this community likes chemistry puns.) Yes, those super-fast or super-big DBMSs that fall short on the ACID standard can now possibly claim that they support the BASE model. What does BASE stand for? Why **b**asic **a**vailability, **s**oft state, and **e**ventual consistency!

- *Basic availability*: Data requests are not guaranteed for completeness or consistency.

- *Soft state*: The state of the system and its data are unknown, although it will probably be determinable in some future time.

- *Eventual consistency*: The system is, or will be, consistent but cannot be guaranteed to be consistent at any specific time.

Want to ensure that your data are valid? BASE systems will eventually figure it out, if you can wait. For all others, stick with ACID.

And the Winner Is…

It is difficult to identify winners and losers in the database management sweepstakes. For every serious DBMS, there is some application somewhere for which that DBMS shines like no other. And if there is no sufficiently important application to keep some old DBMS or DBMS technology alive today, then it just might show up tomorrow. Just look at NoSQL as an example. Almost every academic, vendor, and practitioner in the late 1980s thought the relational model would reign, unopposed, forever. However, new applications using new data types that did not work well with the relational model were mainstreamed, and the DBMS landscape changed forever.

So, which of the current crop has the fortitude to last for the next few decades? Well, it just might be the one thing that everyone can agree on, the one thing that everybody hates: SQL.

The most hated data management language in the world is the language of choice for many different vendors, supporting many different products, using many different data architectures. Its resilience eclipses its ugly duckling persona. It reigns over the relational world like a diamond in a plastic tiara. In a twist of language worthy of Monty Python, it is the only commonality among NoSQL products.

SQL just might outlast them all.

What's to Come

Processes are notoriously more volatile than data, which is one of the reasons for separating any examination of the two. Many organizations update their business processes every year or so, but they revise their data definitions far less frequently, often going a decade without a major change. Likewise, while application code requires frequent changes to accommodate procedural updates, the database structure can more likely forgo frequent process-driven revisions. The database design steps introduced in this book were created to capitalize on this reality.

The following chapters introduce the second phase of the U3D framework for adding how that data will be used by end users and applications (defined during logical process modeling) to the definition of the data (defined during logical data modeling). The result is a data-definition/usage-driven database design.

References

Charles A. Bachman, 1973 ACM Turing Award Lecture "The Programmer as Navigator," *Communications of the ACM*. Volume 16, Number 11, November 1973, pp. 653–657.

E. F. Codd, "A Relational Model of Data for Large Shared Data Banks." *Communications of the ACM*. Volume 13, Issue 6. June 1970, pp. 377–387.

E. F. Codd, *The Relational Model for Database Management Version 2*. Reading, MA: Addison-Wesley Publishing Company, Inc.,1990.

Donald E. Knuth, *The Art of Computer Programming, Volume 3: Searching and Sorting*. Reading MA: Addison-Wesley Publishing Company, 1973.

Notes

1. E. F. Codd, "A Relational Model of Data for Large Shared Data Banks." *Communications of the ACM*. Volume 13, Issue 6, June 1970, p. 384.

2. E. F. Codd, *The Relational Model for Database Management Version 2*. Reading MA: Addison-Wesley Publishing Company, Inc. 1990. p. 3.

3. Peter Chen, "Entity-Relationship Modeling: Historical Events, Future Trends, and Lessons Learned," in Manfred Broy and Ernst Denert (Editors). *Software Pioneers: Contributions to Software Engineering*. Springer Science & Business Media, 2002, pp. 296–310.

4. Stephen W. Hawking, *A Brief History of Time: From the Big Bang to Black Holes*. New York: Bantam Books, 1988.

5. George Gamow, *Thirty Years that Shook Physics: The Story of Quantum Theory*. Doubleday & Co. Inc., 1966.

6. George Gamow, *One Two Three... Infinity: Facts and Speculations of Science*. Dover Publications, 1974.

7. E. F. Codd, *The Relational Model for Database Management Version 2*. Reading MA: Addison-Wesley Publishing Company, Inc., 1990, p. 3, p. 434.

8. Ibid., p. 478.

9. J. Gray, "The Transaction Concept: Virtues and Limitations." *Proceeding of the 7th International Conference on Very Large Database Systems* (Cannes, France), September 9–11, 1981, ACM, New York, pp. 144–154.

10. Theo Haerder and Andreas Reuter, "Principles of Transaction-Oriented Database Recovery." *Computing Surveys*. Volume 15, Number 4, December 1983, pp. 287–317.

CHAPTER 9

■ ■ ■

Introduction to Physical Schema Definition

There will come a time when you believe everything is finished. That will be the beginning.

—Louis L'Amour

In theory there's no difference between theory and practice. In practice there is.

—Jan L. A. van de Snepscheut (among others)

The challenge for physical database designers is to convert the logical specifications created during requirements definition into something that is usable by the organization. This can be a trying task because, unlike the logical data modeler, the physical database designer must adjudicate competing requests for resources. For example, do you tune the database to rapidly access online customer information and in the process penalize batch order processing, or do you favor order processing and, as a result, decrease the performance of customer service? For some, this dilemma is a no-win proposition—no matter what you do, you will displease someone. However, if you recognize that, beyond applying the fundamentals of physical database design, database designers spend most of their time juggling the trade-offs of aiding one user's data access at the cost of another's, you realize that the methods of measuring resource usage and arriving at the right balance for the organization is what physical database design is all about.

There are three main sources of input to the physical database design process: (1) the information requirements uncovered during analysis and documented in the logical data model, (2) how the applications will use that data, and (3) the rules of the information manager that will store the data (Figure 9-1). The job of the database designer is to create a database design that adequately reflects these three separate inputs.

© George Tillmann 2017

G. Tillmann, *Usage-Driven Database Design*, DOI 10.1007/978-1-4842-2722-0_9

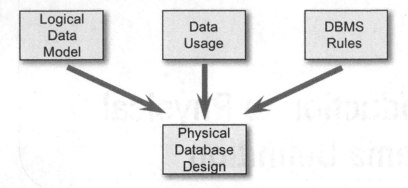

Figure 9-1. *The three inputs to the physical database design*

This approach is a departure from traditional database design. Some database designers do not rely on logical data models or process models. Although they may examine and review these documents before beginning the database design process, these documents are rarely an integral part of that process. Rather, too many designers jump right into physical database design by focusing on the tables and linkages dictated by a particular database management system (DBMS) or requested by those writing design specifications or computer code. This process is reactive and disappointingly superficial.

Other database designers simply take the logical data modeling and "physicalize" it, making it conform to their DBMS, without regard to how the data will be used by application programs or user queries.

In contrast with these two traditional approaches, this chapter lays out a framework for database design involving three elements: the logical definition of the data (logical data model), the business processing requirements (process model), and finally the features and restrictions of the information manager (DBMS, file manager, etc.). See Figure 9-2.

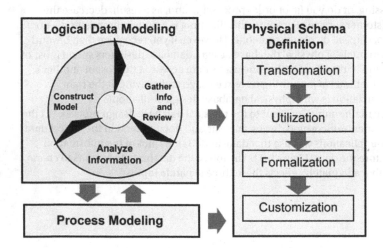

Figure 9-2. *Usage-Driven Database Design*

A fitting name for this Usage-Driven Database Design phase is *Physical Schema Definition*.

Usage-Driven Database Design: Physical Schema Definition

Usage-Driven Database Design: Physical Schema Definition (U3D:PSD) involves the evolution of the logical models into a working physical database design. U3D:PSD consists of four steps (Table 9-1). The first step, *Transformation*, converts the logical data model into a physical data model by substituting physical database objects for logical data modeling ones. The second step, *Utilization*, rationalizes the physical data model by addressing how the data will be used (read, insert, delete, update). The third step, *Formalization*, modifies the rationalized physical data model to comply with the rules/features of the DBMS (or file manager) being used—creating a functional physical database design. The fourth and last step, *Customization*, focuses on improving the performance and enhancing the usability of the database, resulting in an enhanced physical database design.

Table 9-1. *Usage-Driven Database Design*

Usage-Driven Database Design: Physical Schema Definition		
Step	**Purpose**	**Primary Deliverabe**
Transformation	• Translation • Expansion	Physical data model
Utilization	• Usage analysis • Path rationalization	Rationalized (application-specific) physical data model
Formalization	• Environment designation • Constraint compliance	Functional physical database design (schema and subschemas)
Customization	• Resource analysis • Performance enhancement	Enhanced physical database design (schema and subschemas)

The best way to understand how U3D:PSD works is to show how a designer would create a physical database design. The examples in this chapter are based on an order management system's logical data model similar to the one in Figure 9-3.

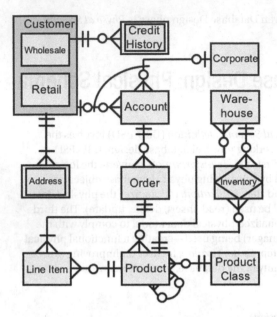

Figure 9-3. *Order processing system's logical data model*

The remainder of this chapter gives a quick synopsis of the overall approach using all four steps. The examples focus on a database to support an order management system that takes orders, bills clients, reports on sales, and sends stock replenishment notices to the manufacturers.

Step 1: Transformation

The first step in physical database design is to transform the logical data model into a physical data model.

Transformation (Table 9-2) consists of two tasks. The first is to translate the logical data objects into physical data objects; the second adds physical features to those objects. The output of the step, the physical data model, is similar to the logical data model except that while the logical data model's components are viewed as conceptual constructs, the physical data model's objects represent information potentially stored in a computer-based information system. However, it is not a database design yet—the physical data model is still an abstract representation of a database.

Table 9-2. *Step 1: Transformation*

Step 1: Transformation		
Sources	Procedures	Deliverables

• E-R diagram
• Logical data model object definitions (data dictionary)
• Business requirements (processes, procedures, and all volumes)
	• Task 1.1: Translation
	  • Activity 1.1.1: Transform logical data model objects to physical data model objects
	  • Activity 1.1.2: Diagram the objects
	• Task 1.2: Expansion
	  • Activity 1.2.1: Assign keys
	  • Activity 1.2.2: Normalize model
		• Physical data model (diagram)
		• Physical data model object definitions (data dictionary)
		• Transformation notes

The physical data model is not DBMS architecture specific (relational, network, hierarchical, object, inverted, etc.), product specific (Oracle, IMS, SQL Server, Model 204, Cassandra, etc.), or release specific (Oracle 12, SQL Server 2014, DB2 10.5, etc.). In truth, a physical data model is a rather skimpy view of stored data. While it does deal with records and data fields, there is no capability to express such concepts as access methods or physical storage components. These must wait until later in the phase.

Task 1.1: Translation

The first Transformation task, *Translation*, is relatively easy. It involves a one-for-one substitution of a physical database design construct for its corresponding logical data modeling one. Start with the entities and turn each into a record type. Next move on to the attributes and turn them into data fields. Lastly, relationships become database links. A logical data model with 6 entities, 24 attributes, and 3 relationships will, in most cases, be translated into a physical data model with 6 record types, 24 fields, and 3 links.

Each object must be uniquely named. A record type must have a unique name, such as Employee, to distinguish it from all other record types. Ideally, the names of the physical objects are the same as the names of their corresponding logical data modeling objects.

Figure 9-4 shows the translation of a simple logical data model into a physical data model. The entities Customer and Account become the record types Customer and Account (as a convention, record types are represented graphically by a rectangle, and record type names start with a capital letter), while the relationship Owns becomes the link Owns. As a convention, links are represented by a line. Linkage names start with a capital letter. Membership class (cardinality and modality) is similarly handled. Physical model modality is still represented by a bar or a zero. A cardinality of "one" is still represented by a bar, but the "many" crow's foot is replaced with an arrowhead.

Logical Data Model   Physical Data Model

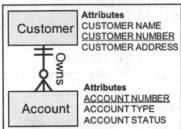
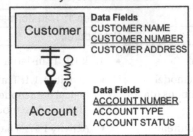

Figure 9-4. Transforming the logical data model into the physical data model

---

TERMINOLOGY

A cornerstone of this book is that to avoid prejudicing future decisions, it is critical to discriminate between logical concepts and physical constructs. To emphasize this point, a sharp distinction is made between the names used to identify logical objects and those used to identify physical objects. Logical objects include entities, attributes, and relationships, so different words are needed to express their physical model counterparts.

However, the file manager/DBMS is not identified/confirmed until step 3, Formalization. Until then, physical object names need to be file manager/DBMS independent. Using words such as *table*, *segment*, *tuple*, or *set* is DBMS prejudicial, so such terms are avoided whenever possible.

To remain file manager independent, this book uses the terms *data field*, *record*, and *link* to represent the physical equivalent of attribute, entity, and relationship. Other terms used later in the book follow suit. Only after the file manager is chosen, and in some cases even after the vendor and version of that manager is selected, will model-, product-, or version-specific terminology be used.

The attributes CUSTOMER NAME, CUSTOMER NUMBER, and CUSTOMER ADDRESS become the data fields CUSTOMER NAME, CUSTOMER NUMBER, and CUSTOMER ADDRESS. (Note: As a convention, field names are all uppercase.)

Task 1.2: Expansion

Translation is followed by *Expansion*, in which the structure of each record type is examined in further detail. The first order of business is to assign keys.

Each record type should have a unique identifier, often called a *primary key*, that unambiguously identifies any occurrence of that record type. The key is usually one field such as EMPLOYEE NUMBER but can be a concatenated key (multiple data fields) if necessary, as in SITE ID, BUILDING NUMBER. The logical data modeler might have uncovered a unique identifier that is used by the business for a particular entity. If at all possible, this business-designated identifier should be used. The convention is to underline the unique identifiers in diagrams, as in Figure 9-4.

Databases can experience synchronization anomalies when inserting new data, updating existing data, or deleting old data. For example, if, after deleting an employee's time cards, accurate information about the effort applied to a particular project is no longer present, then the database suffers from a deletion anomaly. The way to reduce, if not eliminate, this problem is through a technique called normalization. *Normalization* is a process of reducing the structure of the model to a state such that data in any given record occurrence is totally dependent on the key of that record occurrence. Normalization is examined in more detail in Chapter 10.

Step 2: Utilization

The second step, *Utilization* (Table 9-3), adds information to the physical data model about how the database will be used.

Table 9-3. *Step 2: Utilization*

Step 2: Utilization		
Sources	**Procedures**	**Deliverables**
• Physical data model (diagram)	• Task 2.1: Usage Analysis • Activity 2.1.1: Create usage scenarios	• Rationalized physical data model (diagram)
• Physical data model object definitions (data dictionary)	• Activity 2.1.2: Map scenarios to the physical data model	• Updated physical data model definitions (data dictionary)
• Business requirements (processes, procedures, and all volumes)	• Task 2.2: Path Rationalization	• Usage scenarios
		• Usage maps
• Transformation notes	• Activity 2.2.1: Reduce to simplest paths	• Combined usage map
		• Utilization notes
	• Activity 2.2.2: Simplify (rationalize) model	

Utilization maps the process models for the applications that will use the database to the physical data model.

Task 2.1: Usage Analysis

The first Utilization task, *Usage Analysis*, creates *Usage scenarios* from the application process models. Process models (logical or physical) can be long, involved descriptions of many actions and functions that have nothing to do with a database. Imagine a process model describing the algorithms to calculate taxes or missile trajectories. They could go on for pages without a single database activity. About 80 to 90 percent of a process model is information extraneous to the database design process. To reduce confusion, not to mention paperwork, the designer creates usage scenarios, which are shorter and sweeter, textual or graphic, depictions of how an application will use the data. Process models come in many forms. They could be process model fragments, such as data flow diagrams, logical transactions, use case scenarios, or any other means for documenting how the system will work.

A simple usage scenario might look something like the following:

Usage Scenario: Create an Order

1. *Enter* the database at the Account record occurrence for Account X.

2. *Insert* an Order record occurrence for Account X.

3. *Read* the Product occurrence for Product Y.

4. *Insert* record occurrence Line Item linked to the Product and Order occurrences.

A *Usage map* is a graphic representation of a usage scenario. It is created by drawing, or mapping, the scenario onto the physical data model.

Because there are always multiple scenarios for an application, the simplest way to create a comprehensive usage map is to first make a number of photocopies of the physical data model. Then draw one scenario on one photocopy showing how, if the physical data model was the final database design, the application would access the database. Use arrows to show database entry and navigation, and use the initials E, R, I, U, and D for the database actions of Entry, Read, Insert, Update, and Delete.

HEY! THIS LOOKS LIKE NAVIGATION—WE ARE A RELATIONAL SHOP

Calm down. The "navigation" you see is just conceptual—to help you understand how the data will be used given the logical data model. It does not contradict the relational model, preclude a relational DBMS, or eliminate joins between tables. In fact, it shows exactly what joins are needed and how they will work.

When you have completed one map for each scenario, you can then combine them into a *Combined usage map* (Figure 9-5) by taking the individual usage maps and combining them onto a single photocopy of the physical data model.

Usage Scenario 1: Create Order for Account x and Product y
Usage Scenario 2: List all Orders for each Product

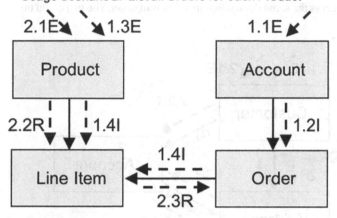

Usage Scenario 1
1.1 <u>Enter</u> database at Account using ACCOUNT NUMBER
1.2 <u>Insert</u> Order occurrence
1.3 <u>Enter</u> database at Product using PRODUCT NUMBER
1.4 <u>Insert</u> Line Item occurrence related to Account and Product

Usage Scenario 2
2.1 <u>Enter</u> database at first Product
    For each product occurrence
    2.2 <u>Read</u> related Line Item
    2.3 <u>Read</u> related Order

Figure 9-5. *Mapping usage to the physical data model*

Figure 9-5 shows a combined usage map for two usage scenarios. The first scenario involves searching the database for the appropriate Account and Product occurrences and then creating an Order occurrence and a Line Item occurrence. The second scenario involves entering the database at Product and then for each Product reading its Line Item and then its Order record.

The arrow with a dashed line indicates the route of access, and the number—for example, 2.3R—tells us that scenario number 2, step 3, is a Read.

Task 2.2: Path Rationalization

In practice, the finished diagram can look a bit like a bird's nest of lines and arrows. At first, this can seem a daunting task, but with a little effort and some time spent examining it (and maybe finding a bigger piece of paper), a few trends should start to emerge, the most important of which is that not all the paths on the diagram are needed. *Path Rationalization* is the task of reducing the complexity of the model to only what is needed to perform its assigned functions. Take the two usage scenarios in Figure 9-6. The first reads the Customer record and then moves to the Order record and finally to the Address record. The second also starts at Customer and then moves to Address followed by Order. These scenarios are redundant because they access the same data, albeit in a different order. The two could be combined into one.

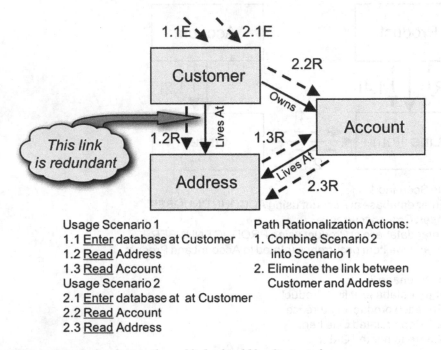

Usage Scenario 1
1.1 <u>Enter</u> database at Customer
1.2 <u>Read</u> Address
1.3 <u>Read</u> Account
Usage Scenario 2
2.1 <u>Enter</u> database at at Customer
2.2 <u>Read</u> Account
2.3 <u>Read</u> Address

Path Rationalization Actions:
1. Combine Scenario 2
   into Scenario 1
2. Eliminate the link between
   Customer and Address

Figure 9-6. *Redundant paths and links should be eliminated*

Note that if you combine the two scenarios, it becomes obvious that the link between Customer and Address and the link between Account and Address are not both needed. It would be possible to eliminate the redundant link.

The Step 2 deliverable is a Rationalized physical data model showing the application-relevant record types and linkages. Deliverables also include the Usage scenario and Usage maps. Both of these will be useful when creating database views and subschemas.

Step 3: Formalization

In the third step, *Formalization*, the rationalized physical data model is made to conform—first to the underlying file manager or DBMS architecture that will be used to store the data (i.e., hierarchical, network, relational, object, etc.), and second to the particular implementation of that model (product/version) such as Oracle 12 or SQL Server 2014. (See Table 9-4.)

Table 9-4. *Step 3: Formalization*

Step 3: Formalization		
Sources	**Procedures**	**Deliverables**

• Rationalized physical data model (diagram)
 • Updated physical data model definitions (data dictionary)
 • Usage scenarios
 • Usage maps
 • Combined usage map
 • Transformation notes
 • Utilization notes
 • DBMS features and constraints
	• Task 3.1: Environment Designation—Identify/confirm the target information manager (architecture, product, version)
	 • Task 3.2: Constraint Compliance
	   • Activity 3.2.1: Map rationalized physical data model to the data architecture
	   • Activity 3.2.2: Create a DBMS product/version-specific functional physical database design
		• Functional physical database design (diagram)
		 • Functional Data Definition Language (schema and subschema)
		 • Updated physical data model definitions (data dictionary)
		 • Formalization notes

This is the first time the file manager or DBMS is introduced into the U3D framework.

Task 3.1: Environment Designation

Before focusing on a particular product, the database designer needs to make the Rationalized physical data model reflect the architecture type of the DBMS that will be used. DBMSs can be grouped into a few basic architecture categories—the products in these categories share a large number of features. For example, relational database products use foreign keys to link different tables together, hierarchical systems use pointers, and some inverted file products rely on external multikey multirecord type indices. Which features to build into the database design (foreign keys, pointers, or indices) depends on the type of DBMS being used (relational, hierarchical, inverted, object, NoSQL, multidimensional, etc.).

Assume the application will use a relational DBMS. This assumption dictates the physical design because there are a number of potential database features the relational model does not support. Figure 9-7 shows a Rationalized physical data model and the Functional physical database design as it might look if a relational DBMS were used.

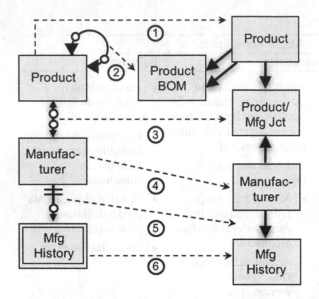

Figure 9-7. *A DBMS model-specific functional physical database design fragment*

The dotted arrows and numbered circles show how the Rationalized physical data model was transformed into a Functional physical database design.

The following are architecture-specific changes to the model in Figure 9-7:

1. The Rationalized physical data model's record type Product becomes the Functional physical database design's Product table.

2. Relational systems do not directly support recursive relationships. However, a many-to-many recursive relationship can be simulated with a bill-of-material structure consisting of a new table storing two foreign keys for the many-to-many links to the Product table.

3. Relational systems do not support many-to-many relationships. To simulate M:N relationships, a new table, often called a junction table, is inserted between the Product and Manufacturer tables.

4. The Manufacturer record type becomes the Manufacturer table.

5. The cardinality and modality of the record types becomes a simple relational one-to-many link (the only kind relational systems support).

6. The attributive record type Manufacturer History becomes the simple Manufacturer History table. Relational systems do not directly support attributive record types.

DBMS-specific language can now be used to describe data objects. For a relational system, data fields become attributes or columns, record occurrences become rows or tuples, and record types become tables.

Task 3.2: Constraint Compliance

Constraint Compliance is the task in which the Functional physical database design becomes product and version specific. For the first time, the database designer can apply the rules of the particular vendor's offering. This is also the first time the designer has a usable database design.

The SQL Data Definition Language (DDL) is needed to generate a relational database schema. However, before coding for SQL Server 16 or Oracle 12, the designer needs to remember Principle 4 of the database design principles (presented in Chapter 1), the Minimal Regression Principle—design a database so that business and technology changes minimize database redesign. To minimize unnecessary future changes, the first draft of the DDL needs to be DBMS version agnostic—relational to be sure—but using a generic SQL that does not tie the design to a specific vendor or product. Table 9-5 shows a fragment of the SQL code for an order management system using a generic form of SQL loosely based on the ISO/IEC standard. However, the designer could just as easily have used this step to create a Functional physical database design for a hierarchical, network, or object-oriented database system.

Table 9-5. *Functional Design DDL Using Generic SQL*

Order Management System
Data Definition Language (DDL) Code Fragment
Using Generic SQL

```
CREATE TABLE PRODUCT (
        PRODUCT_NAME            CHAR(30) NOT NULL,
        PRODUCT_NUMBER          CHAR(8) NOT NULL PRIMARY KEY UNIQUE,
        --  primary key assumes unique but both make the message plain
        --  even if not a primary key, keep this field unique
        PRODUCT_DESCRIPTION     VARCHAR(512),
        COST_BASIS              DECIMAL(8,2) NOT NULL,
        LIST_PRICE              DECIMAL(8,2) NOT NULL
        CREATE INDEX PROD_NO_IDX ON PRODUCT (PRODUCT_NUMBER)
);

CREATE TABLE MANUFACTURER (
        MFG_NAME                CHAR(30) NOT NULL,
        MFG_ID                  CHAR(6) NOT NULL PRIMARY KEY UNIQUE,
        MFG_CATEGORY            INTEGER DEFAULT 1 CHECK (MFG_CATEGORY IN
                                (1, 2, 3)),
        MFG_NOTES               VARCHAR(512),
        ORDER_INSTRUCTIONS      VARCHAR(512)
        CREATE INDEX MFG_ID_IDX ON MANUFACTURER (MFG_ID)
);
```

(continued)

Table 9-5. (*continued*)

Order Management System
Data Definition Language (DDL) Code Fragment
Using Generic SQL

```
CREATE TABLE PROD_MFG_JCT (
        PRODUCT_NUMBER          CHAR(8),
        MFG_ID                  CHAR(6),
        PRIMARY KEY (PRODUCT_NUMBER, MFG_ID),
        FOREIGN KEY (PRODUCT_NUMBER) REFERENCES PRODUCT ON UPDATE CASCADE
        ON DELETE CASCADE,
        FOREIGN KEY (MFG_ID) REFERENCES MANUFACTURER ON UPDATE CASCADE ON
        DELETE CASCADE
);
```

Keeping the DDL generic improves the communication value of the code and allows the reader to focus on the structure of the database and not release idiosyncrasies. It also gives designers and database administrators (DBAs) a source document to use when updating the database schema to a new release or entirely new product. For example, specifying that PRODUCT_NUMBER is both the primary key and unique is redundant in virtually all implementations of a relational DBMS, yet it does have communicative value. It tells those involved with the next phase of the design process that if, for some reason, a different primary key is chosen, then this field must be keep unique.

THE LANGUAGE OF DATABASE MANAGEMENT SYSTEMS

Occasionally, the database community gets it right. Too often, academics and vendors come up with their own proprietary words to describe commonsense objects. But not this time. It has become almost universal to describe database functionality using two sublanguages. The first is called the Data Definition Language (DDL), which includes the syntax and rules used to create database schemas and subschemas. The second is the Data Manipulation Language (DML) used in applications to process database data, such as reading, adding, or deleting data items. These concepts predate relational systems and originate with the Conference/Committee on Data Systems Languages (CODASYL) or network model. Luckily, DBMS vendors have chosen to use what has worked so well in the past rather than continuously inventing new and often confusing terminology.

There are two types of constraint compliance: structural and syntactical. Structural compliance oversees the addition, deletion, or modification of the database's architectural components (record type, links, etc.) to create and maintain a valid schema. Syntactical compliance oversees the grammar or communication value of the DDL to ensure that the system understands what is wanted. For example, if you cannot create a single table for Customer because there are too many fields in it, then the necessary change is structural. However, if the problem is that your DDL compiler will not accept table names longer than eight characters and yours is 15, that change is syntactical.

The order management system will require syntactical changes to run with the selected DBMS—for this example Oracle is assumed. The syntactical changes are needed to accommodate Oracle syntax rules and reserved words. For example, Oracle uses the NUMBER data type and not the SQL standard DECIMAL type used in the example. In addition, the chosen DBMS supports some referential integrity update constraints using triggers or application code, not DDL declarations. Table 9-6 illustrates the changes needed to make the schema code Oracle compliant.

Table 9-6. *Functional Design DDL Generic SQL Converted to Oracle*

Generic SQL	Changes Needed for ORACLE
CREATE TABLE PRODUCT (PRODUCT_NAME CHAR(30) NOT NULL, PRODUCT_NUMBER CHAR(8) NOT NULL PRIMARY KEY UNIQUE, -- primary key assumes unique but both make the message plain even if not a primary key, keep this field unique PRODUCT_DESCRIPTION VARCHAR(512), PRODUCT_HISTORY VARCHAR(512), COST_BASIS DECIMAL(8,2) NOT NULL, LIST_PRICE DECIMAL(8,2) NOT NULL, CREATE INDEX PROD_NO_IDX ON PRODUCT (PRODUCT_NUMBER));	PRODUCT_NUMBER CHAR(8) NOT NULL PRIMARY KEY, /*can't use UNIQUE in PK statement*/ PRODUCT_DESCRIPTION VARCHAR2(512), PRODUCT_HISTORY VARCHAR(512), /*LONG was the standard but was dropped. VARCHAR being dropped in favor of VARCHAR2 */ COST_BASIS NUMBER(8,2) NOT NULL, /* substitute NUMBER for DECIMAL*/ LIST_PRICE NUMBER(8,2) NOT NULL /* substitute NUMBER for DECIMAL */ /* Oracle automatically creates index on PRIMARY KEY columns */

Modifications are needed to support not only a particular vendor's product but the particular version of that product as well. For example, earlier versions of Oracle did not support more than one column per table that was longer than 255 characters in length, and it required use of the LONG data type. To support both the PRODUCT_DESCRIPTION and PRODUCT_HISTORY fields, the designer would need to shorten one of them to 255 characters or place it in a separate table.

The result of this step is a working database. How well it performs depends on a number of factors, including the data it stores and the design of the database.

Step 4: Customization

The database design created in step 3, Formalization, should be able to support all the tasks it is assigned. How efficiently it completes those tasks was not a concern until now. During *Customization*, the performance of the database is examined and any needed changes identified.

This sequence (Formalization then Customization) was created for two reasons. First, it is important to *confirm the design is right* before *making it fast*. Speeding up a database that does the wrong things is useless. Second, performance enhancement is one of the most common post-implementation activities. There are always usage surprises after the database is in operation as well as vendor enhancements and improvements to implement. The majority of these fall into the performance category. The goal is to limit functional "oops" when implementing performance improvements. Keeping the functionalization of the database (step 3, Formalization) separate from enhancement of its efficiency (step 4, Customization) is the best way to do that.

If the database is small, it's not very complex, usage is low, or performance is not a major issue, then pack up your toolkit because your work is done. The design created in Formalization should be sufficient. However, if more is needed, then Customization is where it happens. In step 4 (Table 9-7), the designer can apply all the tricks of the trade from a toolkit (hardware and software) provided by the DBMS vendor, third parties, or the in-house database management team.

Table 9-7. *Step 4: Customization*

Step 4: Customization		
Sources	**Procedures**	**Deliverables**
<ul><li>Functional physical database design (diagram)</li><li>Functional Data Definition Language (schema and subschema)</li><li>Updated physical data model definitions (data dictionary)</li><li>Usage scenarios</li><li>Usage maps</li><li>Combined usage map</li><li>Transformation notes</li><li>Utilization notes</li><li>Formalization notes</li><li>DBMS features and constraints</li></ul>	<ul><li>Task 4.1: Resource Analysis</li><li>Task 4.2: Performance Enhancement<ul><li>Activity 4.2.1: Customize hardware</li><li>Activity 4.2.2: Customize software</li></ul></li></ul>	<ul><li>Enhanced physical database design (diagram)</li><li>Enhanced Data Definition Language (schema and subschema)</li><li>Updated physical data model definitions (data dictionary)</li><li>Customization notes</li></ul>

Task 4.1: Resource Analysis

Before you can fix it, you have to know what is wrong. *Resource Analysis* examines the database to understand the demands placed on it and the impediments to meeting that demand.

The DBMS has an oddity built into it. Language compilers are willing to tell you when you made a mistake—they crash. Operating systems are intolerant of programs they do not like—they stall. DBMSs, on the other hand, often work even when major (particularly performance-related) mistakes have been made. The database dog that takes hours and hours to perform a particular update completes its job in minutes after an index is added or changed. Conversely, a decently performing database can grind to a halt if an ill-conceived index is added. The trick is knowing what and where to make improvements.

To illustrate this point, consider a simple database design of three record types (Figure 9-8) consisting of 200 Product occurrences and 1,000 Order occurrences, each linked to an average of 10 Line Items occurrences per Order. Also, assume that the DBMS allows two methods of improving performance: (1) *indices* placed on certain fields and (2) *clustering* of multiple occurrences of linked, but different, record types on the same physical database page. In this case, that would mean a Line Item occurrence could be stored either on the same physical page as its related Order occurrence or on the same physical page as its related Product occurrence, but not both. The questions to answered are: (1) which fields should be indexed and (2) next to which record occurrence, Order or Product, should the related Line Items be stored?

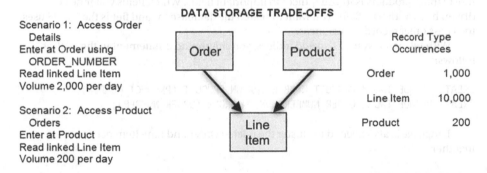

Figure 9-8. Physical database design trade-offs

Look at Scenario 1. The first task is to find a particular Order occurrence. Because there are 1,000 Order occurrences, it will take, on average, 500 logical inputs/outputs (I/Os) to find the right record occurrence. If you assume there are 10 Order occurrences on a physical database page, then finding the right Order will require, on average, 50 physical I/Os. However, if you create an index on the ORDER_NUMBER field, the average number of physical I/Os can be reduced to about four.

The second method of improving performance is clustering. Without design intervention, fetching one Order occurrence and its related 10 Line Items will require 11 physical I/Os—one for the Order occurrence and 10 for the 10 related Line Item occurrences (index I/O is ignored until Chapter 13, which covers step 4, Customization). Fetching each Product occurrence and its associated Line Items will require an average of 51 physical I/Os. (All calculations assume that the DBMS did not put more than one occurrence on an individual page.)

However, if each Line Item occurrence is stored on the same page as its related Order occurrence, then only one physical I/O is required. Storing Line Item with its associated Product reduces the 51 physical I/Os to only one physical I/O (assuming that all the Line Items could fit on one database page). Physical I/Os can be reduced more than 90 percent for the Access Order Details scenario.

The performance of Usage Scenario 2, Access Product Orders, could be improved by more than 90 percent by clustering Line Items around Product (rather than Order). But remember, you cannot have both. Which of the two storage options should you choose? Adjudicating this trade-off is the crux of Customization.

Of course, this example analyzed only two simple scenarios concerning three record types. A more realistic example would involve modeling dozens of scenarios, many requiring data from a half-dozen record types or more, against a much larger design. But the idea is the same.

Task 4.2: Performance Enhancement

In Task 4.2, the database design code was modified to reflect the performance improvements identified in Task 4.1. The simplest way to enhance performance with most DBMS products is to add indices to important fields. Which fields you index is driven by two criteria, fields you want to search the database for and fields the DBMS uses to access other record occurrences.

With relational systems, to add indices, you simply add a statement to the DDL as follows:

```
CREATE UNIQUE INDEX PRODUCT_NUMBER_IDX ON PRODUCT (PRODUCT_NUMBER);
CREATE UNIQUE INDEX ORDER_NUMBER_IDX ON ORDER (ORDER_NUMBER);
```

Language is also needed to cluster the related Order and Line Item occurrences together.

```
CREATE TABLE ORDER (
    •
    •
    CLUSTER LINE_ITEM_CLUSTER (ORDER_NUMBER);
CREATE TABLE LINE_ITEM (
    •
    •
    CLUSTER LINE_ITEM_CLUSTER (ORDER_NUMBER);
CREATE CLUSTER LINE_ITEM_CLUSTER (ORDER_NUMBER CHAR(8));
    •
    •
```

The designer can indicate clustering on the database diagram by placing the clustering record type name at the bottom of the record type box.

Figure 9-9 puts the small database fragment together, including the tables to accommodate Oracle's constraints and the clustering information, at the bottom of each record type box.

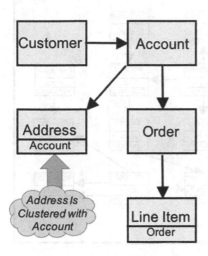

Figure 9-9. *Order management system physical database design*

Summary

Many a well-designed system is brought to its knees during maintenance. The reasons are many but particularly problematic is poor documentation. Correctly and efficiently modifying an application is difficult if the maintenance staff does not have an accurate picture of what the application does and how, exactly, it does it.

Equally important is not traveling over ground that had been trod before. It does not make sense to redesign a car simply because it needs new tires. Likewise, adding an index to a table or moving data from one file to another should not require going back to the business users to, once again, understand how those data are used.

When complete, Usage-Driven Database Design: Physical Schema Definition transforms a logical data model, based on the definition of the data from the enterprise, into a database design tuned to how the organization will use the application (Figure 9-10).

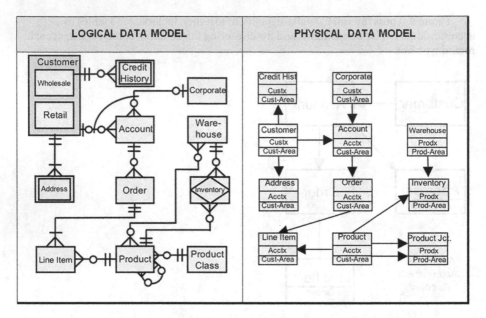

Figure 9-10. *Logical data model to physical database design*

The information presented in this chapter, as well as the examples, are an oversimplification of how U3D works, although they do present a realistic overview of the basic components. The following chapters look at each of the four U3D:PSD steps in greater detail, expanding on the points presented here.

CHAPTER 10

■ ■ ■

Transformation: Creating the Physical Data Model

*The time is a critical one, for it marks the beginning of the second half...
when a transformation occurs.*

—C.G. Jung

*Methods have to change. Focus has to change. Values have to change.
The sum total of those changes is transformation.*

—Andy Grove (founder and CEO of Intel Corporation)

One of the more emotionally satisfying, although less technically significant, components of the database design process is Transformation (see Table 10-1). During Transformation, the designer takes the first real, although small, step toward creating a physical database design. Its significance as a psychological milestone is that, from here on, the language of requirements analysis and logical data modeling is left behind in favor of the terminology of physical design, database management, and storage devices.

© George Tillmann 2017
G. Tillmann, *Usage-Driven Database Design*, DOI 10.1007/978-1-4842-2722-0_10

Table 10-1. *Step 1: Transformation*

Step 1: Transformation

Source	Procedures	Deliverables

LDM.1: E-R diagram
LDM.2: Logical data model object definitions (data dictionary)
LDM.3: Logical data modeling notes
PM business requirements (processes, procedures, and all volumes)
	• Task 1.1: Translation
	 • Activity 1.1.1:
	   Transform LDM objects to PDM objects
	   • Entity to record type
	   • Attribute to data item
	   • Relationship to link, etc.
	 • Activity: 1.1.2
	   Diagram the objects
	• Task 1.2: Expansion
	 • Activity 1.2.1: Assign keys
	 • Activity 1.2.2:
	   Normalize model
		1.1: Physical data model (diagram)
		1.2: Physical data model object definitions (data dictionary)
		1.3: Transformation notes

Step 1, Transformation, is where the objects identified during logical data modeling are transformed into physical database design objects. The result is the physical data model.

Task 1.1: Translation

Translation consists of two activities. The first activity, *Transform logical data modeling objects to physical design modeling objects,* involves a one-for-one substitution. For example, the entity becomes a record type. The second activity, *Diagram the objects,* creates the physical data model diagram.

Activity 1.1.1: Transform LDM Objects to PDM Objects

The first Transformation activity is a rather simple and mechanical step of substituting physical design objects for logical design objects. The logical data modeling entity becomes the physical data modeling *record*, the logical data modeling relationship becomes the become physical data modeling *linkage* or *link*, and the logical data modeling attribute becomes the physical data modeling *data item*. Simple. However, some situations can prove challenging.

Entities to Record Types

For decades, the basic unit of stored data has been the record. As with logical data modeling objects, the type/occurrence distinction is still useful and should be employed when discussing physical database design objects. Therefore, record type is the name given to the collections of all related record occurrences, such as Employee or Customer. A record occurrence or instance is the data that are stored as a discrete contiguous piece of information in an information system, such as Smith's Employee record or Thompson's Customer record.

In logical data modeling, there are four types of entities: proper, associative, attributive, and S-type. At its simplest, proper entities become *proper record types*, associative entities become *associative record types*, attributive entities become *attributive record types,* and S-type entities become *S-type record types*. The definitions of the four record types are almost the same as for their entity cousins (Table 10-2).

Table 10-2. *Record Type Definitions*

Object	Entity Type	Record Type
Proper	A simple or fundamental entity type	A simple or fundamental record type
Associative	A relationship that has its own relationships or attributes	A link that has its own relationships or data items
Attributive	An entity whose existence depends on another entity	A record type whose existence depends on another record type
S-type	An entity (the supertype) that contains more than one role (the subtypes)	A record (the supertype) that contains more than one role (the subtypes)

Diagramming conventions are the same for record types as for logical entities (Figure 10-1). The proper record type is represented by a rectangle. Associative record types are represented by a rectangle with a diamond in them. Attributive record types are rectangles drawn using double lines, and S-types are drawn either with the *is a* construct or with the box-within-a-box graphic.

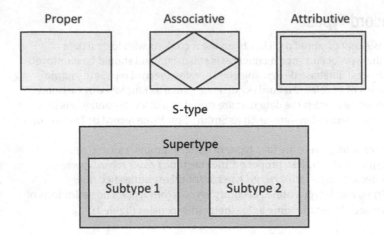

Figure 10-1. *Record types*

The naming convention for record types is the same as for entity types. A question often asked is, "Why are we keeping logical data modeling names when I know that the DBMS only allows a maximum of 18 characters, with no blank spaces and all uppercase?"

This is a fair question because DBMS restrictions can severely limit logical data modeling conventions. For example, many information systems do not allow unlimited name length, others restrict case use to uppercase or lowercase, and most do not allow spaces in a name, rather requiring underscores or other special characteristics. The answer to the question is that it is important to maintain a generic non-product-specific approach as long as possible. This allows the designer to hold off restricting *what we want* by *what we can have*. It is important to document what you would like to have, even if your current DBMS does not support your desires, because your current DBMS might not be your future DBMS. Without proper documentation, if you change DBMS products or if a new version of your current DBMS includes new functionality, there will be no evidentiary basis to support exploiting the new features.

WORD CAVIAR FORMALIZED FUNCTIONAL OSSIFICATION AND HOW TO COMBAT IT

Creating first-generation applications (automating manual processes) was easy. The designer figured out what the users wanted and coded away. Second-generation applications (creating new systems to replace first-generation systems) ran into a totally unanticipated problem: formalized functional ossification (a term made up for this sidebar).

The technology, as well as system development know-how, was limited when the first-generation systems were built. Users wanted a number of features that IT could not deliver. The solution was a series of workarounds and alternatives. It was not what the user wanted, but nonetheless, it got the job done.

The technology was more advanced, and systems staff were better versed in application development by the time the organization was ready for a second-generation application. Many of those workarounds could now be removed, and the original user requirements built into the new system. But then a miracle happened. The users no longer wanted that new-fangled stuff; they wanted the system to do it "the way it always did it" (i.e., how it did it after the first-generation system was implemented without their desired features). The old klugey workarounds had become fossilized—a formalized functional ossification (FFO?). The challenge for the second-gen team was to figure out what the new application should include and exclude, all without the constraints of FFO.

Formalized functional ossification (or fossilization if you prefer) can happen in IT as well. The then current version of the IT shop's DBMS, operating system, or project-management application could not do what was wanted, so workarounds were constructed. Now, a few years later, the vendor includes exactly what IT originally wanted. Do IT staff jump up and down with joy at the new features? Maybe not. The klugey workaround—that software dongle so to speak—is now encapsulated so deeply in the organization that no one knows what was originally wanted. Unless…

…unless they have the documentation detailing exactly what was wanted years ago and why. *U3D is a framework to keep that functional memory alive and ready to implement once the moment is right.*

This is an important point. Experienced database designers might be perplexed about why they should perpetuate something that does not exist in most database management systems, such as associative, attributive, and S-type concepts. Although popular in logical data modeling, they rarely exist as vendor-specified constructs in most DBMS products.

There are two answers to this question. First, it is important to understand what the logical data modeler is trying to tell the database designer, such as there is a difference between Address as a proper record type and Address as an attributive record type. This becomes more obvious in later U3D steps when the physical designer can treat the two differently, even if the DBMS doesn't. For example, an attributive record type might tell the database designer to use a *cascading delete* between the Customer and Account record types, a DBMS constraint that might not be employed if Address is seen as a proper record type.

Second, the designer should not want to give up information (here the distinction between the different kinds of record types) until absolutely necessary, where "absolutely necessary" is determined either by the DBMS selected or by the designer finding some other way to represent the construct. Therefore, the designer should hold onto this and other important information as long as possible.

Relationships to Linkages

The logical data modeling relationship becomes the physical database design *link* or *linkage*. A link is a way of associating two or more records together for the purposes of retrieval or maintenance. As in logical data modeling, physical database design links have *membership class, degree,* and *constraint* characteristics. Linkage naming conventions should be the same as for logical relationship names although, unfortunately, many designers do not name links at all.

Linkage Membership Class

As in logical data modeling, there are two types of membership class: cardinality and modality. Cardinality indicates the maximum number of occurrences of one record type that can be linked to another record type occurrence. The three types of cardinality are *one-to-one, one-to-many,* and *many-to-many.* Modality indicates the minimum number of record occurrences that must be linked to another record occurrence. Modality is either mandatory or optional.

Diagramming conventions are similar but slightly different for relationships and linkages (Table 10-3). As with logical data modeling, modality is still represented by a bar or a zero; however, the logical data modeling crow's foot gives way to the physical data modeling arrowhead.

Table 10-3. *Membership Class*

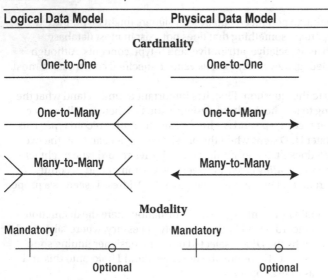

Logical Data Model	Physical Data Model
Cardinality	
One-to-One	One-to-One
One-to-Many	One-to-Many
Many-to-Many	Many-to-Many
Modality	
Mandatory	Mandatory
Optional	Optional

Cardinality is, so far, the only diagrammatic difference between logical and physical data modeling.

Linkage Degree

Degree relates to the number of different record types allowed to be linked to each other. There are three types of degree: *unary, binary,* and *n-ary* (Figure 10-2).

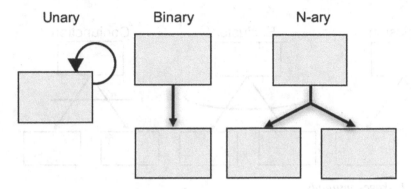

Figure 10-2. *Linkage degree*

Unary or recursive links are one or more occurrences of a record type related to one or more other occurrences of the same record type. An example of a unary linkage type is "Reports to," which links one or more occurrences of Employee to one or more other occurrences of Employee.

Binary links are one or more occurrences of record type A linked to one or more occurrences of record type B. This is the garden-variety link that associates occurrences from two distinct record types. For example, Employee is related to Department.

N-ary links are one or more occurrences of record type A linked to one or more occurrences of two or more other record types. An example would be Car, Dealer, and Customer sharing a linkage.

Note that, so far, the rules are the same for both logical and physical objects.

Linkage Constraints

There are three types of *linkage constraints*: *inclusion, exclusion,* and *conjunction.* Inclusion states that an occurrence of record type A can be linked to one or more occurrences of record type B and/or one of more occurrences of record type C. For example, an occurrence of record type Student can be linked to an occurrence of record type Class and/or an occurrence of record type Major.

Exclusion states that an occurrence of record type A is linked either to one or more occurrences of record type B or to one or more occurrences of record type C, but not both at the same time. For example, for the link "Owns," an occurrence of the record type Automobile might be linked to an occurrence of the record type Dealer or to an occurrence of the record type Customer, but not both.

Conjunction states that if an occurrence of record type A is linked to one or more occurrences of record type B, then it must also be linked to one or more occurrences of record type C. For example, a company might have a rule that if a Customer record occurrence is related to a Credit Balance record occurrence, then it must also be related to a Credit Check occurrence (Figure 10-3).

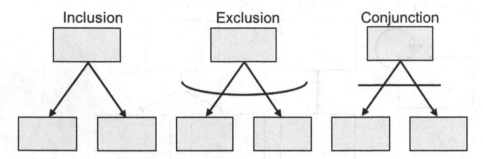

Figure 10-3. *Linkage constraints*

The diagrammatic conventions for linkage constraints are the same as those for logical data modeling relationship constraints.

There is a tendency not to carry forward relationship names from the logical data model to the physical data model. This is unfortunate, but it's because few database management systems let you name a link much less require it. However, linkage names help inform/remind the physical database designer why the link was created in the first place. Therefore, the use of linkage names, and associated documentation, is encouraged even if your information manager does not support them.

Attributes to Data Items

The physical database design equivalent of the attribute is the *data item* or *data field*. Just as the logical data modeling attribute is a descriptor or characteristic of an entity, a data item is a characteristic or descriptor of a record. If the record type is Employee, then typical data items are EMPLOYEE NAME, EMPLOYEE START DATE, and EMPLOYEE SALARY. A data item occurrence is called a *data value* or just *value*. For example, the data item DETECTIVE NAME could have the data item values "Sherlock Holmes," "Hercule Poirot," and "Ellery Queen." Developers often abbreviate *data item type* to *data item* and *data item occurrence* to *data value* or just *value*. Note: Do not call a data item type a *data type* because *data type* is frequently used to mean *data domain*.

Data Item Domain

A *data item domain* is the set of possible values a data item type can have. Examples of domains include dates, text, integers, years between 1900 and 2020, real numbers with three decimal places, abbreviations (USA, EU, UK), and so on. Domains are used to test for acceptable values for data items. For example, if the domain of INCOME is real values with two decimal places, then the value "Donald Trump" is unacceptable. Of course, domains cut both ways. Many a U.S. database designer was humbled after defining the domain of POSTAL CODE as integer and then encountering the Canadian postal code K1A 0A9.

Domains are one of the more important components of database design, yet few information managers support or require them. The relational model—the theology behind the relational database management system—centers on the concepts of domains and sets, yet both are underrepresented in many vendor products. That's truly unfortunate.

Data Item Source: Primitive and Derived

A *data item source* indicates how original or fundamental a data value is. A *primitive data item* cannot be broken down into other data items or derived from them. A *derived data item* is one whose value can be calculated from other data items. For example, the data items UNIT PRICE and QUANTITY can be used to calculate the COST data item by multiplying UNIT PRICE by QUANTITY. If you cannot derive a value from other data items, then the data item is probably *primitive*. In this example, UNIT PRICE and QUANTITY are probably primitive data items.

Primitive Data Item: Unique Identifiers and Descriptors

Primitive data items can be of two types: *unique identifiers* or *descriptors*. A unique identifier is a data item that can point to or choose a single record occurrence. Examples are EMPLOYEE NUMBER, SOCIAL SECURITY NUMBER, and PART NUMBER. Descriptors describe or give the characteristics of the record type. Examples of descriptors are COLOR, HEIGHT, LENGTH, WEIGHT, and LOCATION.

Be careful about calling a unique identifier a key. For many if not most DBMS products, a key need not be unique. The interest here is uniqueness, not keyness.

Data Item Complexity: Simple and Group

Data item complexity looks at whether a data item contains any other data items. A *group data item* is made up of two or more other distinct data items. For example, the data item ADDRESS could be made up of the data items STREET NUMBER, STREET NAME, CITY NAME, and POSTAL CODE. Data items that are not made up of other data items are called *simple* or *atomic*.

Data Item Valuation: Single Value and Multivalue

Data item valuation indicates how many different values a data item can have at one time. A *single-value data item* contains only one value at any given time. *Multivalue data items* can have more than one value simultaneously. For example, the data item GENDER contains only a single value at a time, while MONTHLY REVENUE could have 12 values, one for each month of the year ("$1000, $1330, $2056, $1820, $9368, $1343, $1588, $1190, $1030, $1110, $2110, $2100").

Multivalue data items are supported by most programming languages, which call them *repeating items* or *repeating groups*. Examples would be the OCCURS clause in COBOL and the *struct* function in C (Table 10-4).

Table 10-4. Examples of Multivalue Data Items

A Multivalue Data Item in:	
COBOL	**C**

01 MONTHLY-SALES-NUMB
        OCCURS 12 TIMES.
    05 UNITS-SOLD   PIC 999.
    05 VALUE-OF-SALES PIC S9(5)V99.
	struct monthly-sales-numb {
	    int units-sold;
	    float value-of-sales;
	};

Although data item sources, complexity, and quantity play only small roles in Transformation, they can take center stage later in the physical database design process, depending on requirements and the technology environment.

Other Data Item Information

The activity *Transform LDM objects to PDM objects* doesn't necessarily stop here. Other information that needs to be converted includes data item *size* or *length* (number of characters, bits or bytes), *edit rules* or *masks*, and any other information collected during the logical data modeling process.

Appendix C contains examples of information that should be gathered for all record types, links, and data items.

Activity 1.1.2: Diagram the Objects

As with logical data modeling, physical objects can be diagrammed, in most cases, on a single page. Figure 10-4 shows the draft physical data model for an order management system.

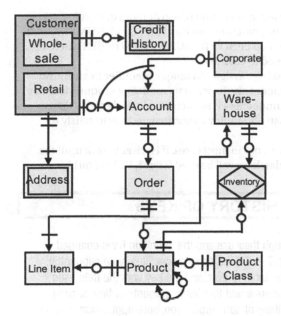

Figure 10-4. *Draft physical data model for the order management system*

The diagram is Figure 10-4 is not the task deliverable but simply a work-in-progress, actually just the start, toward that deliverable. That is why the word *draft* is used.

Task 1.2: Expansion

Expansion, the second Transformation task, is concerned with augmenting the most important, and most challenging, physical database design component, the record type. After creating the draft physical data model, the designer needs to look at the structure of each record type. The first order of business is to assign keys.

Activity 1.2.1: Assign Keys

In logical data modeling, unique identifiers were assigned to all entities for which business staff indicated they were used. In physical design, unique identifiers become keys. A *key* is one or more data items used to identify or pick out one or more record occurrences.

By its traditional definition, keys are of two types: *primary* and *secondary*. Primary keys uniquely identify a record occurrence (the logical data model's unique identifier). Some authors and systems restrict a record type to having only one primary key, while, less commonly, others allow a record type to have multiple primary keys, if by primary key you limit your definition to unique identifier. Secondary keys are rarely ever burdened with a uniqueness requirement. They are generally used to find record occurrences when duplicates are allowed. A traditional record type might have a primary key of the unique data item EMPLOYEE NUMBER but nonunique secondary keys for EMPLOYEE NAME and EMPLOYEE TITLE.

195

A key can be a single data item or a concatenation of two or more data items. A key consisting of a single data item would be something such as EMPLOYEE NUMBER, while a *concatenated key* or *compound key* would be SITE ID, BUILDING NUMBER where the uniqueness of building number is limited to each site.

In many cases, the logical data modeler assigned a unique identifier to an entity. Unless there are extenuating circumstances, the logical data modeling unique identifier should be used as the primary key. If uniqueness is not achievable using the LDM identifier, the database designer can usually employ a concatenated key to satisfy the uniqueness requirement.

Secondary keys can be defined now, but in most cases, it is wiser to wait until the designer better understands how the database will be used (step 2, Utilization).

A SHORT HISTORY OF KEYS

Keys have a long history in IT although their use and the definition have changed over time. Back in the early days of IT, call it the *first key era*, files were sequential, existing on punched cards, magnetic tape, or disk, and the key was the field used to sort the file. In those days, computers spent inordinate amounts of time sorting files, with the typical job stream a litany of sort, application, sort, application, and so on. The customer files might be sorted on account number for one application, then re-sorted on customer name for another, and later sorted a third time on billing date. *Sort keys* had no significance beyond their relevance in ordering the file.

The *second key era* came with the advent of random access technology. Now the application could fetch any piece of data in a file if it knew its location within the file. The key now took on a new role—that of an *access key*, *search key*, *search argument*, or *search criterion*. This is when the database management system really took off. The programmer simply passed the key of the desired record to the DBMS, and the system would deliver it to the application. The DBMS associated the key with a pointer to the record's physical location on disk (displacement from the beginning of the file, sector location, database page, etc.).

The relational model stood keys on their heads with the introduction of the key as a structural database component. This is the *third key era*. No longer were keys used simply for defining how you order a file (a sort key) or how you locate data in the file (an access key); the relational model made the key part of the architecture of the data. The *foreign key* linked a relational parent to its relational children. Keys were now fundamental to the structure of the database.

As a convention, many modelers underline the primary key in their diagrams. Unfortunately, the position of the data items in a compound key (which data item is first, which second, etc.) is important. The concatenated key ACCOUNT NUMBER, ORDER NUMBER is very different from the key ORDER NUMBER, ACCOUNT NUMBER.

Underlining does not always show this distinction unless the designer aligns the data items in the correct order, but there is no way to tell whether this has been done. Regardless, the data dictionary should contain this important information even if the diagram does not.

Activity 1.2.2: Normalize the Model

Normalization is a process of reducing the structure of the model to a state such that data in any given record is totally dependent on the primary key of that record. This restriction ensures that if, for example, some data items are deleted, then all associated data items are also deleted, while all nonassociated data items are not.

Database designers can get themselves in a rather nasty pickle if they are not careful about how they assign data items to record types. Improper assignment can cause grave errors or anomalies.

ANOMALY…ISN'T THAT A KIND OF FISH?

In the good old days, before data processing became information technology, programmers worked very hard never to have more than one input file and one output file open for any application. Rarely did a computer have more than one card reader, and even tape drives were few and had to be shared. Therefore, if a new data item suddenly appeared, the programmer would do almost anything to avoid creating another file. The new data item was often shoved somewhere in some existing file. After the application was a few years old, its file structure could look like the bottom of a dorm room closet.

One of the consequences of this throw-it-and-see-where-it-sticks approach is that updating a file often resulted in what early programmers described as "unanticipated results." Deleting one record might remove data that were needed elsewhere; modifying a record might mean that needed information was no longer findable. It could be a mess, so some great IT minds sat down, put their collective brains together, and, although they didn't solve the problem, came up with a new name for the mess that sounded a lot better than "mess." They called them *anomalies*.

By the way, the "fish" is a sea anemone.

An *anomaly* results when an action produces an unintended consequence. Imagine a database that contains information about employees and the projects they work on (Table 10-5), where the record type Employee contains the data items EMPLOYEE NAME (the primary key), DEPARTMENT, PROJECT, and HOURS WORKED THIS MONTH.

Table 10-5. *IUD Anomalies*

Employee Name	Department	Project	Hours Worked This Month
Andrews	Manufacturing	RumpMaster 2000	80
Bradley	Customer Service	Disposable Fry Pan	75
Casey	Product Design	RumpMaster 2000	20
Davidson	Customer Service	RumpMaster 2000	40
		Disposable Fry Pan	60

By adding up the hours worked this month by project, the user sees that a total of 140 hours were worked on the RumpMaster 2000 and 135 hours on the Disposable Fry Pan. However, this information would be lost or incorrect if employee Davidson were deleted from the Employee file or if Davidson moved to other projects.

An *anomaly* is a data integrity problem that occurs in a database when an object that is inserted, updated, or deleted causes an unintended change in another object or objects. For example, you cannot add a new project to this database until an employee (the source of the primary key) is assigned to the project. This is an insertion anomaly. Second, if you discover that Casey spells his name "Casie," you must change every Casey record instance. If you miss one, that is an update anomaly. Lastly, if employee Andrews quits the project and you delete her record occurrences, you lose information on how many hours were worked on her project. This is a deletion anomaly.

There is a solution. It is called normalization.

Normalization is the application of a set of mathematical rules to a database to eliminate or reduce insertion, update, and deletion (IUD) anomalies. It does this by ensuring that all data items are completely dependent on the primary key for their existence and not on any other data item. The various levels of normalization are called *normal forms*. The higher the level, the more likely any potential IUD anomalies have been eliminated. The forms are progressive, meaning the model must be in first normal form (1NF) before it can be in second normal form (2NF), which is a prerequisite for the third normal form (3NF), and so on.

Normalization is closely tied to the relational model. In fact, they were created and first presented together with the existence of one used, at least partially, to justify the existence of the other. Although normalization is tied to the relational model, it has a much broader use; in fact, with some adjustments, it can be used, and benefit, any database design for any available DBMS product, relational or not. Unfortunately, the adjustments can sometimes be confusing and painful to make.

Adjustments Needed for Normalization: Keys—Foreign and Domestic?

To normalize a model, every record type must have a unique key—no exceptions. U3D and virtually every DBMS on the planet do not require every record to have a unique key, including almost every relational DBMS. However, keys, specifically relational primary keys (the single simple or compound unique identifier selected as the record's sole primary key), are the soul of normalization.

Identifying unique identifiers where they do not exist can be a challenge, but the relational model offers a simple solution that should work in 95 percent of the key-less cases. The designer can use the relational notion of a foreign key to create unique record identifiers; it just takes thinking like a relational DBA. That raises the question, what exactly is a foreign key?

One of the benefits of a DBMS is that it provides the programmer with a way of linking together data that might physically live in different parts of the database. For example, in an order management system, the DBMS can make it easy for the programmer to move from any given account occurrence to the details for any product associated with that account. How the DBMS does this is the "special sauce" that separates one DBMS architecture or product from another. Network systems use pointers in records, inverted systems use external indices, and relational systems use embedded foreign keys.

That network or inverted file DBMS does not need every record to be unique because its pointers are unique. While Order might have a unique key (say, ORDER NUMBER), the Line Item record can get by with a LINE ITEM NUMBER that is just unique within a given Order. (Remember the discussion of "uniqueness within context" in logical data modeling?) If 500 Orders are all linked to two or more Line Item occurrences, then 500 Line Item occurrences have a LINE ITEM NUMBER = "1," 500 have a LINE ITEM NUMBER = "2," and so on.

The relational model does not use pointers; rather, it buries in the child record the primary key of its parent. Take the previous example of the Order and Line Item record types. Every Line Item record occurrence associated with a particular Order occurrence would have a special data item, a *foreign key*, that contained the same data value as the Order record's *primary key*. No pointers required. In practice, well, it depends on the implementation of the RDBMS. The pointers kept hidden in hierarchal, network, and inverted models are visible to application programmers and even end-user interfaces with the relational model. Doesn't this primary key-foreign key concept require the duplication of data? Is not the elimination of duplicate data one of the hallmarks of the relational model? Yes, and yes; however, this is rationalized away by saying that foreign keys are not data items at all but, well, foreign keys, which are a totally different beast.

If keys, particularly foreign keys, are not needed for all DBMSs, then why deal with them here rather than in step 3, Formalization, where the DBMS that will be used is identified? And if keys are just access methods, then why introduce them here and not where you deal with how efficiently you want to access the data, which is step 4, Customization? Why do this now?

The answer is that if you want to normalize your database, then you have to pretend that your DBMS conforms to the relational model, which means placing keys in all record types. Normalization does not say you need foreign keys, just that every record must have a primary key. Foreign keys are just a way of creating primary keys where they might not normally exist. In the example, the DBA could simply append ORDER NUMBER to LINE ITEM NUMBER, giving Line Item a unique compound primary key.

Will foreign keys work for all record types? No, foreign keys work only for record types at the many end of a one-to-many link. For other keyless record types, the designer should find some other solution. However, in most models, the only record types without a unique identifier are those at the many end of a one-to-many link.

The good news is that you can always remove the keys after normalization.

However, because the data architecture of the eventual database is still undecided, the designer must do a little prenormalization work to make the physical data model normalization friendly. In this book (and more than likely, only in this book), the preliminary work goes under the lofty name of zero normal form (0NF). As with other normal forms, 0NF must be completed before 1NF can begin.

Zero Normal Form

To be in zero normal form (0NF):

1. Every record must have a relational model–defined primary key.

When 0NF is complete, more traditional normalization can begin.

First Normal Form

To be in first normal form (1NF):

1. The record must be in zero normal form.

2. All multivalue data items (Codd calls them *repeating groups*) must be removed from the record.

The remedy for a first normal form violation is to remove the repeating group (multivalue data items) and create a new record type to house the offending data items.

For example, given the Customer record containing CUSTOMER NAME and the repeating group CUSTOMER PHONE NUMBER, remove CUSTOMER PHONE NUMBER. Place it in a new record type, and call it Customer Phone, with a one-to-many link between Customer and Customer Phone.

Note that 1NF does nothing toward achieving normalization's primary goal of reducing IUD anomalies. Rather, its purpose is to ensure conformity with the relational model's two-dimensionality requirement. However, because the normal forms are progressive (you complete one before completing two, etc.), 1NF technically needs to be adhered to in order to progress. (You'll learn more about this later in the chapter.)

Before Getting to Second Normal Form, a Slight Digression

The key to normalization is understanding *functional dependency*, a curious term for a confusing concept. Here goes.

Take the Employee record containing two data items, EMPLOYEE NUMBER and EMPLOYEE NAME, where EMPLOYEE NUMBER is the unique identifier (primary key). If you know EMPLOYEE NUMBER, then you can look up EMPLOYEE NAME, so EMPLOYEE NAME is determined by EMPLOYEE NUMBER or, in relational-ese, EMPLOYEE NAME is *functionally dependent* on EMPLOYEE NUMBER.

Assume there are two employees named Smith. One Smith is getting fired, and the other one promoted. If you know the EMPLOYEE NUMBER of the person to be fired, then you can be assured that you canned the correct Smith. However, if you only know that the employee to be fired is Smith, then you cannot guarantee that you will fetch the correct Smith from your database. Therefore, EMPLOYEE NUMBER is not functionally dependent on EMPLOYEE NAME because knowing EMPLOYEE NAME does not give you the record containing the correct EMPLOYEE NUMBER.

Functional dependency also works with compound keys. Take the record Line Item with the data items ORDER NUMBER, LINE ITEM NUMBER, ORDER DATE, PRODUCT, and PRICE. The primary key is the concatenation of (the foreign key) ORDER NUMBER and LINE ITEM NUMBER. PRODUCT is functionally dependent on the concatenated key ORDER NUMBER-LINE ITEM NUMBER. ORDER DATE is only functionally dependent on the ORDER NUMBER, part of the concatenated key. PRICE is not dependent on either but rather on the non-key PRODUCT. PRODUCT is *fully functionally dependent* on the primary key, while ORDER DATE is only *partially functionally dependent* on the primary key.

One more piece of information is needed before you can continue normalizing. Remember your college logic class when you learned about transitivity? An example might jar your memory. Transitivity says that if A=B and B=C, then A=C. *Transitive dependency* says that if A is functionally dependent on B and B is functionally dependent on C, then A is functionally dependent on C.

In the example, PRICE is functionally dependent on PRODUCT, which is functionally dependent on ORDER NUMBER-LINE ITEM NUMBER; therefore, PRICE is transitively functionally dependent on ORDER NUMBER-LINE ITEM NUMBER.

If you have grasped this, you can move on to 2NF.

Second Normal Form

To be in second normal form (2NF):

1. The record must be in first normal form.

2. Every nonkey data item must be fully functionally dependent on the primary key (no partial functional dependencies).

The remedy for a second normal form violation is to remove the data items not fully functionally dependent on the primary key and either create a new record type to house the offending data items or place them in another existing record type.

Using the Line Item example, to make the model 2NF compliant, remove ORDER NUMBER and ORDER DATE from Line Item and place them in the new record type Order.

Third Normal Form

To be in third normal form (3NF):

1.   The record must be in second normal form.

2.   There can be no transitive functional dependencies.

The remedy for a third normal form violation is to remove the data items transitively dependent on the primary key and either create a new record type to house the offending data items or place them in another existing record type.

To make Line Item 3NF compliant, create a new record type Product containing the data items PRODUCT and PRICE.

Figure 10-5 shows the changes that were made to Line Item as a result of normalization.

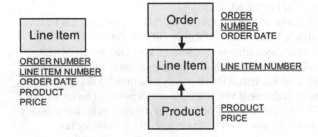

Figure 10-5. *Normalization (before and after)*

How many normal forms are there? Many. At least seven, although every now and then someone comes up with a new one. However, most practitioners and researchers agree that getting to third normal form is usually good enough. More can be just *gilding the lily*.

WHAT'S THE BIG DEAL? VERY LITTLE CHANGED.

If the E-R model is properly constructed, then normalization should add little. Remember, normalization was envisioned without the benefit of the E-R approach. This is why some E-R database design authors do not require, or even recommend, normalization.

Normalization can be a challenging subject that requires considerable more study than presented here. This entire book could easily focus on just normalization; however, that is unnecessary because there are many books dedicated to the subject. You are encouraged to investigate further.

Post-Normalization—Retreat of Sally Forth?

Once normalization is completed, the database designer faces a decision—what to do with all the relational-based changes made to the physical data model so it could be normalized. Does the database designer restore the model to its prenormalization pristine state or leave in all of the relational detritus?

To normalize a model, all record types must have a primary key. Some primary keys are quite natural, such as CUSTOMER NUMBER, while others require vivid imaginations to concoct. Foreign keys are not required for normalization because normalization is concerned with only one record at a time and its key and nonkey data items. Relationships are irrelevant to the Big N, so foreign keys, technically, play no role.

More troubling is the removal of multivalue data items, which were ejected for relational model reasons rather than normalization reasons. They could have been left in the record, and normalization would have been just as effective (although there is a decent argument that if you are going to normalize the model, then you should follow its steps).

Restore or not restore? It's up to the database designer, who can restore the model now or wait until step 3, Formalization, and either restore or not restore then based on the DBMS selected.

Issues with Normalization

As good as normalization is, and it is useful, it would be remiss not to mention some of its issues, problems, and misuses.

- *Normalization is a review process, not a design process.* It works *in media res.* It assumes that record types already exist, and the question to be answered is, "Are the data items living in this record type correct for this record type?" The database designer must already have a physical data model and then use normalization to improve/modify it.

- *Normalization is a decomposition process.* Normalization breaks down or decomposes existing "compound" record types into simpler ones. However, it does not provide a method for going in the reverse direction. For example, if the abstraction of the data is too granular, there is no way, using normalization, to build up to a more appropriate level. While normalization tells you to remove a data item from a record type, it does not tell you where to put it. It provides no information on where a data item belongs, only where it does not belong.

- *Normalization says little about key suitability.* Normalization is concerned with the primary key and its relationship with the record's nonkey fields. Nothing is said about whether the record type has the proper primary key. For example, normalization would not flag as an error PART NUMBER being the primary key of Employee. In fact, it would reject EMPLOYEE NAME from Employee because it is not functionally dependent on PART NUMBER. This is consistent with normalization's relational model roots. According to the relational model, if a table contains two unique identifiers (*candidate keys* in relational parlance), which one you choose as the primary key is totally arbitrary. Interestingly, this underscores the need for normalization to follow a logical data modeling process, such as the entity-relationship approach, to appropriately populate entities with relevant attributes, and any potential unique identifiers related to that entity, before undertaking normalization.

- *When do you stop?* There is no agreement among the gurus about how far you need to go when normalizing a database. Third normal form? Boyce-Codd normal form? Fourth? Fifth? Sixth? Domain-key normal form? Where does it end?

- *Normalization does not provide a viable end-game strategy.* The performance of a normalized database is often very poor compared with non-normalized databases, and thus fully normalized databases are rarely implemented. A common post-normalization exercise for many physical database design approaches is to denormalize the model to improve performance. Unfortunately, there are no accepted rules for denormalization that ensure IUD anomalies are not reintroduced.

- *Gobbledygook.* A major selling point for normalization is its formal mathematical roots. It's right out of formal logic and set theory, so it includes a strong mathematical pedigree. The problem with a mathematically based database design technique is that it is a mathematically based technique. It is a mathematical concept steeped in mathematical jargon, which is anathema to many IT staff. Unless you are a mathematician, it can be less understandable than an EBCDIC version of the *Bhagavad Gita*. If normalization gurus really want to spread the word, then they need to take a closer look at their audience and understand how those people think, how they talk, and the language that is meaningful for them.

HOW PREVALENT IS NORMALIZATION?

I received a very unscientific and inchoate answer to this question. In dealing with dozens of database designers on five continents over the past few decades, I found that about 90 percent said that they were familiar with normalization. Fifty percent said that they normalized their databases. Fewer than 15 percent actually did it, and fewer than 2 percent did it properly.

Normalization is confusing, annoying, and frustrating. It is also very useful. Wise database designers will roll up their sleeves, wear their thinking caps, put on the coffee, get out the college textbooks, and normalize the hell out of their database design.

Tranformation Notes

There is one very important task remaining. The database designer must document all the issues and all the decisions made during step 1, Transformation, in one or more documents called *Transformation notes*. The reason is not to record history—it is difficult to imagine a 23rd-century archaeologist rejoicing at finding some DBA's scribblings—but for the future of the database. Sometime in the days or years to come, some other database designer or DBA will need to make changes to the database. Ideally, before mucking about in the DDL, they will do some research to understand the intentions of the original users and database designers and the reasoning behind the decisions they made. If all the new designer has to work with is the current DDL or a few diagrams, your clever original thinking might be misunderstood or totally ignored.

Transformation notes should include answers to these four questions:

- *Why*? Why was something done? Knowing why a decision was needed and how was it made can prove very useful for future designers.

- *Where*? Some decisions cover the entire model, while others apply to only a portion of it. "Where" tells future database users and supporters the context or scope of a decision.

- *When*? Some decisions are time dependent. Identifying the temporal scope of a decision makes it easier to link it to other designer work products such as diagrams and procedures.

- *Results*? There is a tendency for designers to document only successes. Sometimes documenting what didn't work or what was rejected is more important than successes.

This is your chance to ensure that your legacy survives the ravages of some young undereducated upstart or just yourself three years from now when you are trying to figure out why you did what you did. In either case, write it down. It can only help.

Deliverables

Step 1, Transformation, produces three major deliverables.

1.1. *Physical Data Model*: The physical representation of the logical data model (Figure 10-6 in the next section).

1.2. *Physical Data Model Object Definitions (data dictionary)*: Record types, data elements, linkages, keys, formats, and so on (Figures 10-7 through 10-10 in the next section). Each should include a description and relevant information on all data objects. (Appendix C contains a glossary of physical data object definitions.)

1.3. *Transformation Notes*: The database designer's notes on relevant issues and decisions made during step 1, Transformation.

Examples of Deliverables

The first deliverable is a Physical data model diagram giving a graphic representation of the physical record types and how they are related to each other (Figure 10-6).

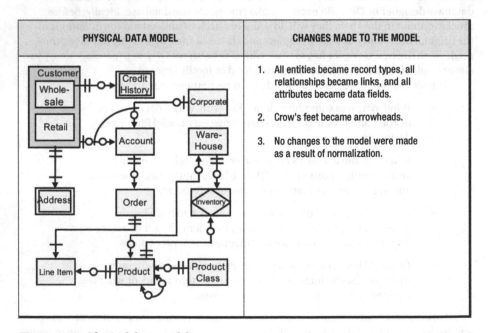

Figure 10-6. *Physical data model*

The second set of deliverables is the Physical data model object definitions that are part of the data dictionary. Below are a set of sample Physical Data Model Object Definition forms.

Physical Data Object Definition Record Type	Explanation
Name: _____ Type: _____ Description: _____ _____ Synonyms: _____ Links: _____ Data Items: _____ Storage: Cluster: _____ Partition: _____ Location (database or file name): _____ Constraints: _____ Logical data model name: _____ Key(s) and Type: _____ Est. No. Occur: _____ Annual Growth: _____ Notes and Comments: _____ Update Date: _____ By: _____	*Type*–Proper, associative, attributive or S-type *Links*–Linkages in which the record type participates *Key Types*–Primary, secondary, foreign, etc. *Estimated Number of Occurrences*–The total number of record type instances *Annual Growth*–Percentage annual growth rate

Figure 10-7. *Record type definition*

Not all physical data object information can be entered at this point. Some information will have to wait until further steps. For example, keys will not be finalized until Chapter 12, and storage issues, such as clusters and partitions, will be decided in Chapter 13. Other information might change as you delve further into database design, such as data items in the record type.

Physical Data Object Definition Data Item	Explanation
Name: _____ Description _____ _____ Synonyms: _____ Length: _____ Edit Mask: _____ In Record Type(s): _____ In Index(s): _____ Key Type (if any): _____ Source: ___ Primitive or ___ Derived If Derived,what Algorithm?: _____ Complexity: __ Simple or _Group If Group, Contains?: _____ Valuation : __ Single or _Multivalue Type: _____ Domain: _____ Logical data model name: _____ Notes and Comments: _____ _____ Update Date: _____ By: _____	*In Record Type(s)*—Usually a data item existsin only one record type. If there are (intentional) duplicates,then list all the record types and which contains the original or master copy. *Key Type*—primary, secondary, foreign, etc. *If Derived what Algorithm?*—The data items and formula used to calculate the data value. *If Group Contains?*—The data items that make up the group. *Type*—The data type such as integer, text, picture, movie, etc. *Domain*—If the data item participatesina formally defined domain.

Figure 10-8. Data item definition

One of the most important items in the record type definition is the "Notes and Comments" section. This is an opportunity for the database designer to convey to future designers and DBAs important information they will need but that might not be adequately explained elsewhere. A prudent designer will make liberal use of this opportunity.

Physical Data Object Definition Domain	Explanation
Name: _____ Description: _____ Type: _____ Range_____ Discrete Values _____ _____ Notes and Comments: _____ _____ Update Date: _____ By: _____	*Description*—Type of domain (data type, range of values, acceptable values, etc.) *Range*—Continuous values with a specific start and stop.For example, dates between January 1, 1950,and December 31, 1990. *Discrete Values*—Specific itemized values, such as male and female.

Figure 10-9. Domain definition

Most database management systems do not require the use of domains, although many do allow them. This is unfortunate because domains are an effective tool for maintaining database veracity. If the DBMS does not support them, then DBA or applications staff should develop the necessary functions to support them.

| **Physical Data Object Definition**
Link

Name: _____
Description: _____
_____
Participants and constraints:
Record Type   Constraint
_____   _____
_____   _____
_____   _____
Logical data model name: _____
Notes and Comments: _____
Update Date: _____ By: _____ | **Explanation**

Constraint–The cardinalities and modalities. |

Figure 10-10. *Linkage definition*

These documents are only a suggestion. How you document the model might be quite different. Many CASE and system development tool packages include robust data dictionaries that can store this and similar information. They are a good place to keep such documentation and should be used when possible.

This concludes the Transformation process. Next, step 2, Utilization, examines exactly how the database will be used and the modifications to be made to the physical data model to accommodate that use.

CHAPTER 11

▪▪▪

Utilization: Merging Data and Process

Our biggest cost is not power, or servers, or people. It's lack of utilization. It dominates all other costs.

—Jeff Bezos

Data is a precious thing and will last longer than the systems themselves.

—Tim Berners-Lee

Both the logical data and physical data models are static, only representing the definition of the data they contain. Many database designers stop here, never—or only inconsistently—taking into account how the data and the database will be used. See Table 11-1.

Table 11-1. *Step 2: Utilization*

Step 2: Utilization		
Sources	**Procedures**	**Deliverables**
• 1.1: Physical data model (diagram)	• Task 2.1: Usage Analysis	• 2.1: Rationalized physical model (diagram)
• 1.2: Physical data model object definitions (data dictionary)	• Activity 2.1.1: Create usage scenarios	• 2.2: Updated physical data model object definitions (data dictionary)
• PM: Business requirements (processes, procedures, and all volumes)	• Activity 2.1.2: Map scenarios to the PDM	
	• Task 2.2: Path Rationalization	• 2.3: Usage scenarios
	• Activity 2.2.1: Reduce to simplest paths	• 2.4: Usage maps
• 1.3: Transformation notes		• 2.5: Combined usage map
	• Activity 2.2.2: Simplify (rationalize) model	• 2.6: Utilization notes

© George Tillmann 2017
G. Tillmann, *Usage-Driven Database Design*, DOI 10.1007/978-1-4842-2722-0_11

Step 2, Utilization, adds to the physical data model how the procedures defined in the process models will store and access data. Utilization is where the formally separate data and process models meet to form the first hybrid definition/use model.

In this step, the *database design missing link* problem is finally resolved—designers can create a database that integrates the static definition of data (the data models, both logical and physical) with the more dynamic use of that data (the process models, both logical and physical). Utilization is the key, resulting in a structurally resilient, functionally rich, effective, and efficient database design.

Task 2.1: Usage Analysis

The first Utilization task is to gain an understanding of the functionality the database will support. The database designer must examine all data usage in the process documentation created by the application designers. In most cases, to do this effectively involves understanding at least some forms of process modeling. Because there are plenty of books on documenting processes, there is no need to go into depth here, although a cursory look is useful.

Process Modeling

A process model serves a purpose similar to a data model—to document existing or planned applications. Whereas data models represent information at rest, process models record information as it is created, used, modified, and deleted by an application.

As with data models, there are different types of process modeling techniques, and they can vary greatly. Some techniques stress a business-focused process requirements analysis, while others take on a more technical bent. Logical process requirements documentation can involve a narrative form using natural language, graphical techniques, or a combination of both.

As is the case with data, the process side of a system can be divided into logical process models and physical process models. *Logical process models* record the existing or planned functional capabilities of an application—the *what is wanted. Physical process models* focus on how the system (its hardware and software) does or should function—the *how it will work*. This processing modeling *what* versus *how* contrast is the complement to that presented in Chapter 1 for data modeling. The most popular documenting techniques for logical process modeling are structured English, data flow analysis, and, unfortunately, plain English. Physical process models are usually described using flow charts, structure charts, pseudocode, and, interestingly, plain English.

Logical Process Modeling

When most developers think of documentation techniques, they usually think of logical process models representing, in narrative or graphical form, the functionality of the existing or proposed application.

Natural-Language Logical Process Modeling Techniques

Natural language is the speech used every day. It is also, for better or worse, how most applications are described and documented. Natural languages, such as English, Russian, and Italian, have the advantage of being understood by large numbers of people, particularly the people who will be using the application. Unfortunately, natural languages, such as plain English, can be verbose and error prone, leading some designers to look for more formal approaches to give the model added structure and less bulk.

Plain English

Spend a fortune on college, go to training classes provided by your employer, read books and journals describing the latest analysis techniques, and then receive a requirements document written like a Lewis Carroll novel. It's not fair, but it's reality. The only thing the database designer can do is to try to translate the application prose into something more practical, as illustrated in the next section.

Oy Vey, There Has Got to Be a Better English Translation

At the opposite end of the spectrum from plain English is a formal language process modeling technique called *pseudocode*, which is a version of natural language that looks somewhat like computer code. Pseudocode rates high on the discipline scale but can appear robotic and mechanical to users and, for that reason, is not the approach of choice for logical process modeling. Between plain English and pseudocode are a number of attempts at giving plain language some discipline while not giving up its ease of understanding. The most popular language-based compromise techniques go by names such as *structured English* or *tight English* (or Portuguese, etc.).

Structured English

Every system ever developed had at least part of its inner workings documented using plain language. It might be in French or Japanese, but every application has been described somewhere in the plain language of its users. Because this book is written in English, plain language here is English.

There is probably not an analyst or designer on Earth who has not been given development instructions something like the following:

> *The teacher accesses the student's record using his or her student number. The student's grade for the course is entered next to the appropriate course and section.*

The problem with plain language is that it is easy to overlook important details. For example, what should the teacher do if the system responds with a matching student number but a different student name from the person attending his class? What if the actual section number does not appear?

An insidious problem with plain language is that requirements that look complete can be grossly inadequate.

Structured English is a concept introduced in the late 1970s by the proponents of structured analysis and structured design. It consists of English language concepts used with a little more exactness, simplicity, and rigor than found in everyday life.

Structured English consists of a set of rules, precisely defined words, and specified sentence structures that reduce ambiguity while increasing reader comprehension. Think of it as a system described by Mr. Spock contrasted with one dramatized by Richard Simmons. While one is emotional and inexact, the other is more detailed and precise. Creating structured English is relatively easy; you just have to remember that its purpose is to unambiguously document how a system is to work.

Because there is no standard for structured English, implementations vary and are often highly personalized. A simple structured English approach is to decompose the plain English requirements into separate simple declarative statements. These declarative statements are then treated to a few rules, such as statements formatted as sequential logic or drop-through statements, decision logic or trees, or decision loops.

Sequential logic is a list of events with one following another. Here's an example:

```
Read Customer record where Customer Number = "xxx"
Then Read Product record where Product Code = "yyy"
Then Insert Order record for Customer Number = "xxx" and
Product code = "yyy"
```

The logic is simple; start at the first statement and go down the list, one statement at a time.

Decision logic involves testing a condition and then taking an action based on that decision. The simplest decisions are branches and represented by the ubiquitous IF-THEN statement.

```
If Customer Status = "Active" then go to Active Customer
```

If the condition is true, branch to Active Customer; if not, go on to the next statement.

A more complex structure would be If-Then-Else.

```
If Customer Status = "Active" then go to Active Customer
Else Go to Inactive Active Customer
```

A variation of decision logic is appropriate when there are three or more options that are better represented by a decision table.

IF	THEN
Customer = "Active"	Go to Active Customer
Customer = "Inactive"	Go to Inactive Customer
Customer = "Credit Hold"	Go to Credit Problem
Customer = "National"	Go to National Accounts

Decision loops repeat a sequence of steps until a condition is met. For example, an order can consist of many products.

```
Enter Product
Insert Line Item record for Product Code = "yyy"
Repeat Enter Product until Product Code = "000"
```

A list of agreed-upon keywords, such as If, Then, Until, Repeat, etc., can improve comprehension, particularly if there are common (industry, organization, or even just team) definitions. Some designers like to require that keywords be in all capital letters.

Graphical Logical Process Modeling Techniques

The problem with all natural-language documentation techniques is that they tend to be verbose and sequential and, ironically, can miss both the detail as well as the big picture. As with logical data modeling, logical process modeling gains from the use of some graphical techniques.

The most popular graphical logical process modeling technique is the *data flow diagram* (DFD). A major advantage of the DFD, and the main reason for its popularity, is its simplicity and universality.

DFDs consist of four objects (Figure 11-1). An *external entity*, represented by a square, is an object external to the application, such as a person, department, or another application. A *process*, represented by a rounded rectangle, is a procedure that acts on data. A *data flow*, represented by an arrow, shows the movement of data, such as data passed between processes or to or from an external entity. A *data store*, represented by an open rectangle, is data at rest, such as a computer file, a file cabinet, a file folder, a Rolodex, or a card catalog.

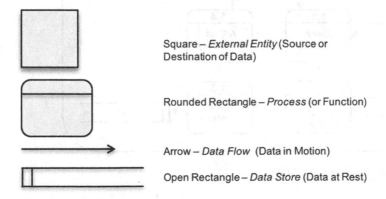

Square – *External Entity* (Source or Destination of Data)

Rounded Rectangle – *Process* (or Function)

Arrow – *Data Flow* (Data in Motion)

Open Rectangle – *Data Store* (Data at Rest)

Figure 11-1. *Data flow diagram symbols*

215

The highest level of a DFD is called Level 0 (Figure 11-2), and it represents the entire system or application. Level 0 can be decomposed into multiple Level 1 diagrams (Figure 11-3), one for each Level 0 process, each with its own subprocesses showing greater application detail. Level 1 can be decomposed into Level 2, and so forth, until the entire system is documented.

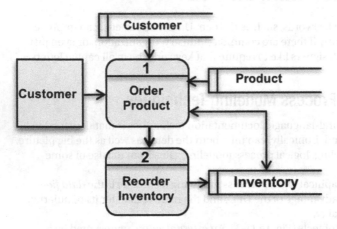

Figure 11-2. *Customer Orders Product Level 0 DFD*

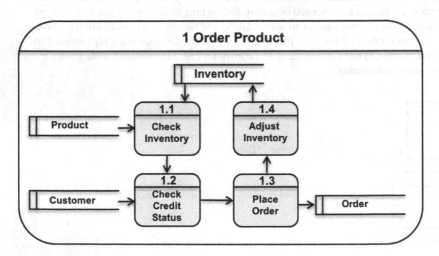

Figure 11-3. *Order Product Level 1 DFD*

DFDs also contain a narrative component. Each object requires a definition, and each process, particularly those at the lowest level, requires a narrative describing the operations it performs on the data. The difference between these process narratives and natural language techniques is scope. A DFD process narrative describes only a small single process, not an entire system. DFDs and structured English merge well, with the latter being used to describe DFD processes.

Physical Process Modeling

So far, only logical process modeling techniques have been described; however, the modeler must also be familiar with physical process modeling techniques. As with the data side, physical process modeling techniques instruct the designers and coders on how the internals of the application should work.

Natural-Language Physical Process Modeling Techniques

Some natural-language physical modeling techniques are holdovers from logical processing modeling, such as plain English (again), structured English (again), and pseudocode.

Plain English

No, this is not a mistake. The plain-language techniques used for logical process modeling are often, unfortunately, the same techniques used for physical process modeling. However, how they are used does often differ.

While the DFD is the most popular graphical logical process modeling technique and the flow chart is the most popular graphical process design technique, they are both, regrettably, eclipsed by the all-time winning documentation technique: English. Sad to say, simply writing down what the system is to do is, by far, the most common (if least practical) way to document both the logical and physical requirements of an application.

Why is plain English still around? In most cases, it can be boiled down to one of two reasons. First, the analyst/designer does not know any better technique. An amazing number of analyst/designers have little more than a passing knowledge of modern modeling techniques. Second, the analyst/designer is too lazy to use a more precise documentation approach.

Structured English

The structured English of physical process modeling differs little from the structured English of logical process modeling. The only difference might be the semantics of the narrative. Expect physical process structured English to delve more into process control and components internal to the application, such as data flags, branches, and loops.

Pseudocode

The philosophy behind *pseudocode* is to give the reader all of the specificity of computer code without referencing a particular computer language and without unneeded linguistic details. As with structured English, there is no pseudocode standard. Each practitioner can create their own, or agree on some local or team-wide standard set of rules. The following pseudocode example uses only three rules. The three simple rules are as follows:

1. State instructions as simple declarative or imperative sentences using well understood and documented data object names where possible.

2. Convert conditionals to IF THEN, ELSE, or decision table form.

3. Allow iteration using DO UNTIL or similar constructs.

The result turns convoluted constructs, such as the following:

Customers are of two types. Those with annual sales averaging more than $10,000 are given a 10 percent discount. Others are given a 10 percent discount only if the order is greater than $1,000.

into this more understandable pseudocode:

```
If LAST YEAR SALES > 10,000,
              or YEAR TO DATE SALES > 10,000,
              or ORDER AMOUNT >1,000,
 then CUSTOMER DISCOUNT = 0.10,
 else CUSTOMER DISCOUNT = 0.0.
```

Some designers like to customize their pseudocode around a particular programming language such as C, COBOL, or Java. Others believe in a more programming language–free pseudocode. Which is chosen is less important than consistency.

Graphic Physical Process Modeling Techniques

Graphical physical process modeling techniques predate the computer age and are considerably more popular than graphical logical processing modeling techniques. This section looks at the two most popular graphical process modeling techniques: flow charts and structure charts.

Flow Charts

By far the most popular graphical physical process modeling technique is the flow chart (Figure 11-4). Both revered and reviled, the flow chart predates the digital computer. Invented in the 1920s, the flowchart is a general-purpose tool for graphically representing processes as a system rather than a sequence of steps. John Von Neumann is thought to have been the first to apply them to computer programs in the 1940s. Their popularity exploded in the 1950s and continued right up to the early 1970s when batch systems began to be replaced with online applications. Although they still work well for documenting logic flow, newer techniques, such as structure charts, do a better job of documenting many kinds of processing. However, flow charts persist to this day because of their ease of use and their ubiquity in classroom instruction.

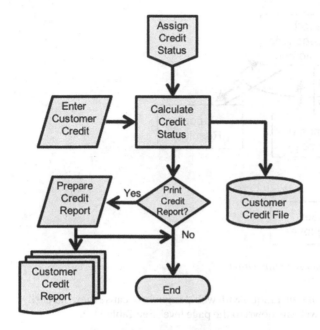

Figure 11-4. *Customer credit status flow chart*

While most everyone agrees that the flow chart has outlived its usefulness, they are still pervasive throughout the industry. Although your college professor might threaten to revoke your degree if you use the technique, flow charts are artifacts found in virtually every IT shop.

Structure Charts

A *structure chart* is a diagrammatic physical process modeling technique that represents the process as an inverted tree. The top of the tree is the root application or program level. Subsequent levels are modules representing greater process granularity. The very bottom levels usually represent program modules performing a single task. Structure charts date back to the structured design and programming era. Each box on the chart, called a *module*, represents a process with a single input and a single output. Modules are made up of submodules, which are in turn made up of even "subbier" modules...you get the idea. Arrows show the flow of data or control. An arrow with an empty (white) circle shows the movement of data (up or down), while an arrow with a filled-in (black) circle shows the passing of control such as decisions and flags (Figure 11-5).

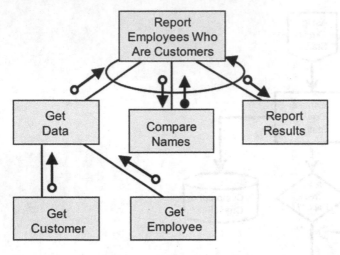

Figure 11-5. *Employee-customer structure chart*

Structure charts are a popular technique with web designers because they can easily represent the architecture of a web site down to the page level. See Table 11-2.

Table 11-2. *Logical and Physical Process Modeling Techniques*

Summary of Process Modeling Techniques	
Logical Process Modeling	**Physical Process Modeling**
• Structured English: Application of a regimen to natural-language English to diminish its ambiguities while adequately communication with users • Data flow diagramming: A simple yet robust graphical representation of the movement of data in a system	• Pseudocode: English language structured to mimic computer code • Flow chart: A diagrammatic technique to represent a computer algorithm • Structure chart: A tree structure to show the hierarchical breakdown of computer modules

At the end of this chapter is a list of sources where you can find materials on these and other popular processing modeling techniques.

Activity 2.1.1: Create Usage Scenarios

Usage scenarios document how an application uses a database. A usage scenario can be as simple as "Fetch Customer record where CUSTOMER NUMBER is 1234" or as complex as a subset of an application involving a significant portion of the database.

The purpose of a usage scenario is to make it easier for the database designer to understand how the database will be used. It gives the database designer a clear and simple document, devoid of confusing and extraneous process specifications, stating exactly how the application will create, read, modify, or delete the information stored in the database.

Logical process modeling can create a mountain of information, much of which is unrelated to the database design process. The usage scenario process boils down all of the logical process information into what is relevant to database design. To build a usage scenario, the database designer reviews the application's various process components, such as requirements definitions, functional specifications, flow charts, and so on, and culls from them all the relevant data fetching and storing information. This information forms the basis of the usage scenario.

Clearing the Decks for Action

One thing all process modeling techniques have in common (if they have the appropriate level of detail) is that they provide far too much information to the database designer. Even a moderately sized system can involve hundreds of pages of text and diagrams that explain what the system should do. These specifications, created during analysis or design, contain considerable information beyond how the application accesses, or uses, data. They also include detailed algorithms, user interaction, control, branching instructions, report or screen layouts, and so on. The database designer needs only about 10 percent of this information. A good idea is to strip these components out, leaving just the interaction between the process and the database. A *usage scenario* boils down the hundreds of pages of requirements analysis to the few that are relevant to the database design process.

The following is an example of a plain English specification.

Activity: Create a New Customer Account

The clerk enters the caller's phone number into the system. If the caller has an account, then the account information is displayed, and the clerk informs the customer that an account already exists. If an account does not exist, then the credit status of the caller is checked with the outside credit bureau. If the caller's credit is OK, a new account is created and the new customer informed. If the caller's credit is Not-OK, the new account is denied and the caller informed.

This plain English specification can be converted into a more structured format as follows:

Activity: Add New Customer Account

1. *The clerk enters the caller's phone number into the system.*

2. *If there is a customer account in the system, the system displays all customer and account information.*

3. *The clerk informs the customer that he already has an account and asks whether he wants a new account. If the customer does not want a new account, terminate the call; else go to 5.*

4. *If the caller is not in the system, the clerk enters the caller's information.*

5. *The system checks the credit status of the caller with the outside credit bureau.*

6. *If the credit status is OK, the system creates a customer account and informs the clerk.*

7. *The clerk informs the customer that a customer account was created, gives the customer all the account information, and then terminates the call.*

8. *If the credit status is Not-OK, the system informs the clerk, who informs the caller and terminates the call.*

However, this specification contains substantial activity extraneous to any database activity, which the designer can ignore with impunity.

Using the data model in Figure 11-6, look at the following:

1. The clerk enters the caller's phone number into the system.

   There is no database activity here. The process is between an agent external to the application, the clerk, and the application itself.

2. If there is a customer account in the system, the system displays all customer and account information.

   This is the first interaction between the application and the database:

   (Database Action 1) Fetch Customer and Account occurrences where PHONE NUMBER matches the search argument.

3. The clerk informs the customer that he already has an account and asks whether he wants a new account. If the customer does not want a new account, terminate the call; else go to 5.

   There is no database activity here.

4. If the caller is not in the system, the clerk enters the caller's information.

   There is no database activity here.

5. The system checks the credit status of the caller with the outside credit bureau.

   There is no database activity here.

6. If the credit status is OK, the system creates a customer account and informs the clerk.

   (Database Action 2) Add/Update Customer and Add Account occurrences for new Customer

7. The clerk informs the customer that a customer account was created, gives the customer all the account information, and then terminates the call.

   There is no database activity here.

8. If the credit status is Not-OK, the system informs the clerk who informs the caller and terminates the call.

   There is no database activity here.

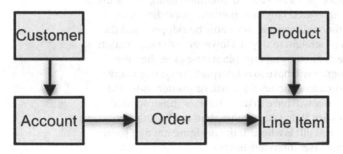

Figure 11-6. *Order management system*

The Add New Customer Account usage scenario contains only two database-related activities.

- Fetch Customer and Account occurrences where PHONE NUMBER matches the search argument.

- Add/Update Customer and Add Account occurrences for new customer.

To complete this usage scenario, a little more information is required to understand the properties of the scenario. First, each scenario should have a unique identifier and a unique name. Second, specify the scenario *processing type* as online or batch, and third specify the *frequency* of use. For an online scenario, the frequency might be 100 times an hour or 5,000 times a day. For batch jobs, the frequency might be that the program is run weekly, and each run involves an average of 20,000 evocations. Note, not every step is executed every time. If the steps have different frequencies, then that information should be included in the scenario.

To review, a usage scenario is a small document to tell the database designer how the application will use the database. The sources for the usage scenarios are the requirements definitions, process analysis, and process design documents, which could include interview notes, narratives, process models, and process specifications.

Putting a Usage Scenario Together

There are four steps for creating a usage scenario, although the first may be skipped if sufficiently detailed process specifications already exist.

1. Assemble all physical process documentation. Logical process documentation is a good thing to have, but if the analysts have done a good job documenting the physical characteristics of the system, then it can probably be ignored.

2. If the application processes are documented using one of the graphical or structured language methods for defining an application, then this step can probably be skipped, and the designer can go straight to step 3. However, if the application processes are defined using only plain language, then the database designer will have to reinterpret the system using a technique such as structured English or pseudocode. The database designer will have to use whatever (unstructured) information exists. Worst case (other than not having any documentation at all) is when all the designer has as a source are original end-user interview notes.

3. Strip out all non-database-related process specifications. Place the database requests in sequential order using appropriate database terminology (read, add, search argument, etc.).

4. Add the scenario properties of *unique identifier, name, processing type,* and *frequency.*

An Example

Do not underestimate the advantage of creating a usage scenario. It can be very helpful in removing extraneous information. For example, take the following case.

Step 1 is to gather whatever process documentation exists. In the example, the only information is the following plain English description of the application:

> *The system reads all product inventory records. Those falling below the reorder threshold are placed on a possible reorder list. For those on the possible reorder list if the sales of the product during the last 60 days was greater than 10 percent of the fully stocked number, then create a reorder record for x items where x is the difference between the items on hand and the fully stocked number. If the number of sales during the previous 60 days was less than 10 percent but greater than 5 percent, then reorder x items where x is 50 percent of the difference between the fully stocked number and the number on hand. If the number of sales during the past 60 days was less than 5 percent of the fully stocked number, then do not reorder the product.*

This is a plain-language usage narrative, so step 2 is to convert the plain-language description into structured English. It might look something like the following:

```
Read all Product records where INVENTORY COUNT is less that REORDER
THRESHOLD.

Read all Line Item records for each Product. If CURRENT DATE minus SALES
DATE <60 then add LINE ITEM QUANTITY to TEMP SALES COUNT.

If TEMP SALES COUNT > (FULLY STOCKED COUNT*0.10) then REORDER COUNT = FULLY
STOCKED COUNT - INVENTORY COUNT.

Else If TEMP SALES COUNT > (FULLY STOCKED COUNT*0.05) then REORDER COUNT =
(FULLY STOCKED COUNT - INVENTORY COUNT)/2.

Save the REORDER COUNT and the CURRENT DATE in the Inventory Reorder record.
```

Step 3 consists of two tasks. First, strip out all non-database-related process information. Second, use more database-like terminology and create a database sequence.

Here is the usage scenario:

(1) Enter at all Product occurrences where INVENTORY COUNT is less than REORDER THRESHOLD.

(2) For each Product occurrence, Find all related Line Item occurrences.

(3) Insert Inventory Reorder occurrence for each related Product occurrence.

In step 4, add the scenario properties.

Usage Scenario: 1 Name: Calculate Reorders   Processing type: batch Frequency: once per night.

(1) *Enter at all Product occurrences where INVENTORY COUNT is less than REORDER THRESHOLD (200 occurrences).*

(2) *For each Product occurrence, Find all related Line Item occurrences (approximately 1,200 occurrences).*

(3) *Insert Inventory Reorder occurrence for each related Product occurrence (50 occurrences).*

The result is a much simpler set of database service requests.

The designer should create one usage scenario for each process. For example, the order management system might have different usage scenarios for creating a new customer, generating an order, shipping, and processing returns. The collection of usage scenarios represents how the entire application adds, reads, updates, and deletes information from the database.

Activity 2.1.2: Map Usage Scenarios to the PDM

The usage scenarios can then be converted to a simple diagram, called a *usage map*, by drawing the actions of the usage scenario on the physical data model. Take the following usage scenario:

Usage Scenario: 2 Name: Produce Account Bills
Processing type: batch Frequency: 300 times per night.

2.1. *Enter database and Find Order occurrences where ORDER DATE equals CURRENT DATE (200 occurrences).*

2.2. *Find Line Item occurrences for associated Order record occurrence (average 2 occurrences).*

2.3. *Find Account occurrence for associated Order occurrence (average 1 occurrence).*

2.4. *Find Customer occurrence for associated Account occurrence (average 1 occurrence).*

2.5. *Update Order occurrence (1 occurrence) Comment: to update Order with billing date.*

Mark up the physical data model with the usage scenario steps using the following convention: x.y.z, where x is the scenario number, y is the step, and z is the database action (E for enter, F for fetch, I for insert, U for update, and D for delete).

Using usage scenario 2, you have "2.1E" for step 1, enter the database, written on the physical data model with a dashed arrow pointing at the Order record type (Figure 11-7). An arrow from Order to Line Item labeled "2.2F" says "Find Line Items records for that Order." Step 3 becomes "2.3F," step 4 is "2.4F," and step 5 is "2.5U," update the Order record with the billing information.

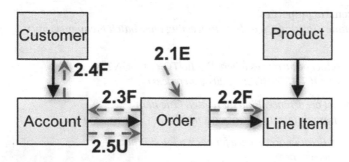

Figure 11-7. Usage map order entry system

A *usage map* is the result of applying one usage scenario to the physical data model.

The designer should create one usage scenario for each process and one usage map for each usage scenario. Start by printing out or photocopying as many copies of the physical data model as you have usage scenarios. Then, taking one usage scenario and one copy of the physical data model, draw the activities from the usage scenario on the physical data model.

A single-system *combined usage map* is created when all of the usage scenarios, placed on their individual copies of the physical data model, are collected onto a single physical data model page. The result might look something like Figure 11-8, which shows three usage scenarios (scenarios 4, 5, and 6) placed on a single combined usage map.

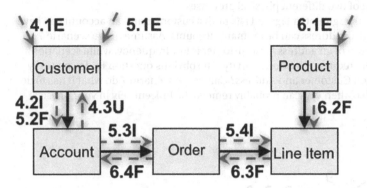

Figure 11-8. *Combined usage map order entry system*

The combined usage map is a graphical representation of how the entire application uses the database.

Task 2.2: Path Rationalization

Usage analysis can result in a crowded combined usage map. The task of Path Rationalization is to simplify the map without losing any important usage information.

Activity 2.2.1: Reduce to Simplest Paths

If you compare a logical data model with its actual database schema, one thing should be obvious. While the number of entities is roughly equal to the number of record types and the number of attributes is roughly equal to the number of fields, the number of relationships on the logical data model can be significantly greater than the number of linkages on the database schema. The reason? Not all of them are needed. Linkages on a data model are similar to roads on a street map. Some roads are heavily traveled, some are used only occasionally, and still others could easily not exist without significant hardship.

Roads and linkages have something else in common—they are expensive. Linkages take up space and consume processor cycles, so reducing their number can, in some cases, improve performance while driving down cost. Of course, as with roads, eliminating the wrong ones can create catastrophic problems. The art of the science is finding the right ones to eliminate.

227

If you examine the combined usage map in Figure 11-8, what should jump out at you is that many scenarios use the database in the same way. In this example, both scenario 4 and scenario 5 perform almost the same tasks. This should tell you two things. First, if you design the database to accommodate scenario 4, it should also be able to accommodate scenario 5. Second, the paths these two scenarios use are probably important because they are used as part of two different physical processes.

In the usage map fragment in Figure 11-9, both a customer and an account can have many addresses, and an address can be for many accounts. Assume usage scenario 7 indicates that the setup of an address for a customer is low frequency, while scenarios 8 and 9 process higher-frequency account activity. The obvious question is, do you really need the link between Customer and Address? Can usage scenario 7 do what it has to do without that link? If so, then you can probably remove the link entirely in your physical data model.

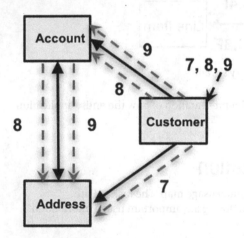

Figure 11-9. *Combined usage map fragment*

Excluding the Customer/Address link will simplify the physical data model. Even so, you should keep all the usage scenarios so you have the information available to undo this change if later it proves unwise.

Activity 2.2.2: Simplify Model

The designer can now pull it all together into a single rationalized physical data model with the final record types and all relevant keys, including necessary links between the record types while excluding unnecessary ones. The data dictionary entries created in step 1, Transformation, must be updated with any changes made in task 2.2, Path Rationalization.

The model no longer represents just the definition of the data but also how those data will be used. This is the final step and is the culmination of your physical model before making the necessary compromises imposed by the selected DBMS.

Utilization Notes

The only remaining step 2, Utilization, task is to complete the *Utilization notes.* As with Transformation, the database designer should document all the relevant issues and decisions made during Utilization.

As is the case with step 1, Transformation, the Utilization notes should illuminate all decisions made, not made, and unmade by answering the questions surrounding *why, where, when,* and *results.*

The other step 2 deliverables are important, but they are not enough. Future users, designers, and database administrators need to understand the thinking that went into this step. Without it, they are driving blind when it comes to updating the database with additional or modified functionality or a new DBMS product or version.

Deliverables

Step 2, Utilization, should produce the following deliverables:

2.1.   *Rationalized physical data model:* A graphical representation of the record types and links required for the application (Figure 11-10 in the next section)

2.2.   *Updated physical data model object definitions:* The same physical definitions created in step 1, Transformation, updated with any necessary changes made during step 2, Utilization

2.3.   *Usage scenarios:* Functional summaries describing how the database will be used by the application

2.4.   *Usage maps:* A mapping of the individual usage scenarios onto the physical data model showing how the application must navigate the database (Figure 11-7)

2.5.   *Combined usage map:* All of the individual usage map information on a single diagram (Figures 11-8 and 11-9)

2.6.   *Utilization notes:* A narrative or journal created by the database designer of the activities, issues, and decisions made during step 2, Utilization

Example of Deliverables

Figure 11-10 shows the Rationalized physical data model.

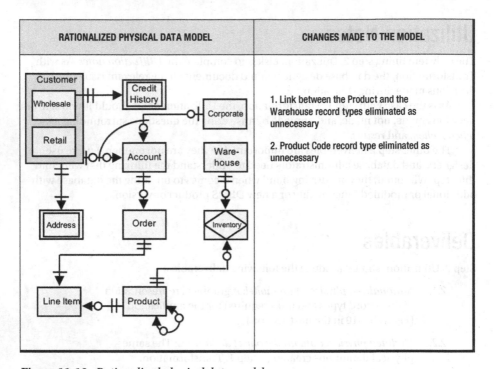

RATIONALIZED PHYSICAL DATA MODEL	CHANGES MADE TO THE MODEL
	1. Link between the Product and the Warehouse record types eliminated as unnecessary
	2. Product Code record type eliminated as unnecessary

Figure 11-10. *Rationalized physical data model*

Further Reading

A detailed look at a number of topics in the chapter is outside the scope of this book. Some of the following material should help those who want to investigate these subjects further.

Structured English

Gane, Chris and Trish Sarson, *Structured Systems Analysis: Tools and Techniques.* Englewood Cliffs, NJ: Prentice-Hall, 1978. This book focuses on data flow diagramming, but it has an excellent section on structured English. This book is out of print, but used copies are available.

Data Flow Diagramming

DeMarco, Tom, *Structured Analysis and Systems Specification*. Englewood Cliffs, NJ: Prentice-Hall, 1979. Closely linked with Ed Yourdon and Larry Constantine's structured approach, the book is currently out of print, but used copies are available.

Gane, Chris and Trish Sarson, *Structured Systems Analysis: Tools and Techniques*. Englewood Cliffs, NJ: Prentice-Hall, 1978. Also Yourdon alumni, their approach is almost identical to DeMarco's technique, although their diagramming conventions are easier to use.

Hathaway, Tom and Angela Hathaway. *Data Flow Diagramming by Example: Process Modeling Techniques for Requirements Elicitation*. Kindle Edition, 2015.

Flow Charts

IBM, *Flowcharting Techniques*, IBM Corporation, White Plains, NY, 1969. The granddaddy of them all, this manual can still be found online. More modern interpretations of flow charting appear in almost every system development textbook.

Pseudocode

Bailey, Therold and Kris Lundgaard, *Program Design with Pseudocode (Computer Program Language) Brooks*. Belmont CA: Cole Pub Co, 1989.

Farrell, Joyce, *Programming Logic and Design*. Boston, MA: Course Technology, 2013.

Structure Charts

Dennis, Alan and Barbara Haley Wixom, Robert M Roth. *Systems Analysis and Design 6th Edition*. New York: John Wiley & Sons Inc., 2014.

Martin, James and Carma McClure, *Diagramming Techniques for Analysts and Programmers*. Englewood Cliffs, NJ: Prentice-Hall Inc., 2000. This book deals with all the techniques presented in this chapter, so it is a good starting point for the novice, although sometimes at too high a level for the more experienced.

CHAPTER 12

■ ■ ■

Formalization: Creating a Schema

The schema is...a mere product of the imagination.

—Immanuel Kant

The first draft of anything is s*#t.

—Ernest Hemingway

Step 3, Formalization, is, unfortunately, the point at which database design starts for many designers (see Table 12-1). The first thing they do is dig out the vendor's DBMS manual and start coding. For the more enlightened, this is the third physical database design step—where the Rationalized physical data model meets the DBMS that will be used in its implementation.

Table 12-1. *Step 3: Formalization*

Step 3: Formalization		
Sources	**Procedures**	**Deliverables**
• 2.1: Rationalized physical data model (diagram)	• Task 3.1: Environment Designation: Identify/confirm the target information manager (architecture, product, version)	• 3.1: Functional database design (diagram)
• 2.2: Updated physical data model definitions (data dictionary)		• 3.2: Functional schema data definition language
• 2.3: Usage scenarios	• Task 3.2: Constraint Compliance	• 3.3: Functional subschema data definition language
• 2.4: Usage maps	• Activity 3.2.1: Map rationalized physical data model to the data architecture	• 3.4: Functional database object definitions (data dictionary)
• 2.5: Combined usage map		
• 1.3: Transformation notes		
• 2.6: Utilization notes		• 3.5: Formalization notes
• DBMS features and constraints	• Activity 3.2.2: Create a DBMS product/version-specific functional physical database design	

© George Tillmann 2017
G. Tillmann, *Usage-Driven Database Design*, DOI 10.1007/978-1-4842-2722-0_12

Formalization consists of two tasks. The first identifies or confirms the information manager (architecture, product, and version) that should/will be used to build the database. The second modifies the Rationalized physical data model to conform to the selected file manager or DBMS.

Task 3.1: Environment Designation

What database architecture is best for your application? This is the first question that needs to be answered, even if the choice of a database architecture is out of the database designer's hands.

Not so long ago, this task would involve DBMS shopping—figuring out the kind of DBMS the enterprise should acquire to build the desired applications. Nowadays, the enterprise probably already owns a DBMS, or even more than one, so the appetite to acquire another is minimal. In this case, the database designer will have to live with what the company has. Nonetheless, it makes sense to undertake this task anyway for two important reasons. First, after examining how the database is intended to be used (Chapter 11), the database designer might conclude that it is a major mistake to use the company's current DBMS. For example, if the organization has a relational DBMS but the new database application must store and retrieve video and music files, then the database designer might conclude that a DBMS based on a different architectural approach would be a wise purchase. The only way to find out is to compare the proposed usage with the features of the current DBMS.

The second reason to investigate the ideal architectural approach is to document what would work best for the application even if using the ideal database management system is not feasible. This will be particularly useful down the road if the current application/DBMS mix turns out to be a turkey.

It might be useful for the database designer to map the strengths and weaknesses of the various database architectures against the organization's information management needs in a chart similar to Table 12-2. Unlike Table 12-2 (which is a generic chart for illustrative purposes only), the left column in the database designer's chart should list the information manager characteristics most important to the application.

Table 12-2. Functional Comparison of Various Architectural Approaches

ILLUSTRATIVE								←----- NoSQL -----→		
Characteristic	Hierarchical	Network	Relational	Inverted File	Object	Multi-modal	Star	Key-value	Document	Graph
Atomicity	XXX	XXX	XXX	XXX	XXX	XXX		X	XXX	X
Consistency	XXX	XXX	XXX	XXX	XXX	XXX		XXX	XXX	
Isolation	XXX	XXX	XXX	XXX	XXX	XXX		XXX	XXX	
Durability	XXX	XXX	XXX	XXX	XXX	XXX		X	XXX	X
OLTP	XXX	XXX	X	X	X			XXX		
OLAP						X	XXX	XX		
Batch Processing	XXX	XXX						XXX		
High Availability	XXX	XX						XXX	XX	
Data Volume - Static	XXX	XX						XXX	XXX	
Throughput	XXX	XX				XXX		XXX	XXX	XXX
Complex data types					XXX	XXX	XXX		XX	XXX
Query			XXX	XXX		XXX		XX	XX	
Financial/Spreadsheet			XXX							
Structural Complexity		XXX			XX			XXX	XXX	
Data Warehouse			XX	XX			XXX		XXX	X

Note: XXX high, X Low -- Hierarchical Results for IBM's IMS, Network Results for CA Technologies' IDMS

As straightforward as this seems, there are some annoying wrinkles. First, two DBMS products sharing the same architectural approach do not necessarily have the same strengths and weaknesses. For example, because relational systems have been around for more than 40 years, their implementations can vary greatly, with some vendors stressing one feature, while others stress a totally different one.

Second, many of today's product offerings do not comply with a single architectural approach but rather with multiple approaches. This is particularly true as products age and new architectural approaches are developed. IDMS started out as a network DBMS but added relational features when the market shifted. The same is true for the inverted file products, which adopted many relational features in their later years. Oracle, the once quintessential relational system, now includes variations with object-oriented as well as NoSQL features.

Third, there are always new and expanded approaches, particularly in the NoSQL ranks. It can be difficult to keep up with what is happening in this rapidly changing field.

Do your chart in pencil. There will be many changes and updates as your knowledge of the various DBMS offerings increases and the functions the DBMS will need to support are better understood. Even with its drawbacks, a comparison chart is a good place to start the search for the ideal DBMS product for the current project.

Once the architecture is chosen, or more likely dictated by past purchases, the designer must modify the rationalized physical data model to meet the requirements of that approach. The good news is that some of this work might have already been done when the physical data model was modified for normalization. If not, then it needs to be done here.

There are few things you can say about *all* database management systems, but, fortunately, here is what you can say:

- *Many-to-many relationships*: Most DBMS products do not support them, and the few that do tend to be niche players and not (yet) suitable for prime time. A junction record will be needed to mimic an m:n relationship.

- *Recursive relationships*: The designer will be hard-pressed to find a DBMS supporting recursion. This is unfortunate because many programming languages do. Nonetheless, for at least the time being, a bill-of-material structure using a junction record will be needed instead.

- *Associative, attributive, and S-type record types*: The major DBMSs do not support associative, attributive, and S-type record types (although object-oriented systems support some of these features); rather, they need to be implemented as simple proper record types. Cardinality is supported, while modality is often not supported or supported only to a limited extent. Alternatives and workarounds, in the form of DDL or DML code, are sometimes available (for example, cascading delete).

Some missing features can be provided by triggers, procedural code, or application code written either by database staff and stored within the database or by application programmers as application code.

Hierarchical Systems

In this day and age, the term *hierarchical DBMS* usually refers to IMS or its Fast Path variations. IMS and particularly Fast Path have a number of restrictions and idiosyncrasies that involve a considerable amount of physical data model morphing to accommodate the DBMS architecture. Just getting the database language correct will require some work as records become segments and views become logical database descriptions.

The Rationalized physical data model must be restructured into hierarchical trees, and many-to-many structures must be morphed into the IMS logical database structure. The hierarchical characteristics also show up in the NoSQL ranks, particularly with XML-based products.

Network Systems

The network model, more than likely IDMS, also requires some language adjustment, but not as radical as for IMS. However, the network database structure can be easily derived from the physical data model, perhaps more so than any other architecture. Designing an IDMS database from a Rationalized physical data model is relatively easy. The additional ten IQ points to successfully navigate the network model (mentioned in Chapter 8) are needed by the application programmer and not the database designer.

Relational Systems

When it comes to a unique DBMS language, the relational model takes the prize. The good news is that most of the arcane words it uses have either already entered the database language sphere or have been dropped in favor of more common terminology and thus no longer cause the confusion they did a few decades ago.

Keys are a major issue with relational systems, and there are many keys in the relational model (primary, candidate, super, foreign, compound, alternate, natural, composite, simple, etc.). The key landscape varies by the relational product and sometimes, more insidiously, by the product version. Add to that how the keys are used, and the complexity explodes. (Not every RDBMS requires foreign keys or even primary keys. Some do not even support them.)

Keys aren't the only issue. Groups have to go (both multivalue and group data items). The good news is that most relational products support a few common groups, such as DATE. The bad news is that they rarely support them in the same way.

Nonstandard data types are the Achilles' heel of relational systems. The designer must examine the actual RDBMS selected, and its version, to learn how it handles documents, pictures, videos, and so on, if it does at all. Even text is not supported in any consistent way.

Object-Oriented

The original object-oriented systems were unique and proprietary in design and structure, but they have largely been supplanted by relational systems that morphed into object-relational hybrids. Some OODBMSs have hierarchical characteristics, mixed with inverted file characteristics, mixed with relational ones. The database designer needs to be aware that for the OODBMS that started out as a RDBMS, most features and constraints will be similar to those of its original data architecture rather than its adopted one.

NoSQL

Unfortunately, NoSQL is a grab bag of DBMS implementations. Many, in spite of their name, have relational-like syntax and follow relational-like rules, even if their internal structure is completely different. Others have an object type feel about them and can be mistaken for an OO database. A third group of NoSQL implementations follow a particular computer language and are structured as language extensions. Java is a common DBMS substrate. Lastly, some DBMSs, such as many key-value approaches, see the database as a set of key and nonkey pairs that function as pointers to data residing in a different part of the system.

The smartest way to think of NoSQL is to not think of it at all, but rather of its underlying structure, such as key-value or document.

DBMS Product and Version Selection

OK, now it has been decided or dictated which database architecture you will be using. However, there are still decisions concerning the DBMS product and version to use.

Vendors are clever. In their quest to attract and keep customers, they provide certain enticements, freebies, or enhancements with their products. The first "enhancement," and the one you wind up paying for whether you use it or not, is the embedded DBMS. If you buy certain applications or systems software, a DBMS comes as part of the system to manage the data. If you are an XYZ DBMS customer but purchase an application or some system software from ABC corporation, you still might have ABC's DBMS automatically installed.

Some IT shops have a formal "don't use the embedded DBMS" policy; others don't. Should you use it? Depends. ABC might offer a few features that are critical to the business, while XYZ, the product you are using, doesn't.

That brings us to the second vendor enticement: extensions. There is an old vendor saying, "Standards attract customer; extensions keep them." Vendors tout their ISO compliance to get new customers. No company wants to buy some unfamiliar product that the organization will be locked into for the foreseeable future. If you buy a standard version of COBOL or a standard version of a DBMS, you buy two benefits. First, to stay compliant, the vendor must update its product offering with new standards body approved features. Second, it makes it easier to move from one product to another. Don't like the ABC product? It's easier to move to the XYZ product if both comply with the same standard.

However, once a vendor attracts new customers by offering a standards-compliant product, the vendor wants to keep them. That's where extensions come in. Offer customers new goodies that are not in the standard, and if the customers uses them, then they are locked into the product—or at least it's considerably more expensive to leave.

Relational systems extensions include nonstandard data types, group items, storage considerations such as indices and clustering, and even keys.

Extensions can be double-edged swords for vendors as well as their customers. Many a vendor has offered an extension containing a new feature only to have a standards body subsequently develop that feature as a new standard with characteristics that are at odds with the vendor's implementation. The vendor is then forced to invest in creating a new feature that provides no new capability for its product and that makes it easier for its customers to leave.

You might have to select a DBMS or a DBMS version based on its nonstandard features. If you must, you must. But if you have a choice, be very wary of extensions. They sometimes have a heavy price down the road.

Once the database architecture is identified or confirmed, then the task is to select or confirm the target product. A good way to start is to go back to the Architectural Approach Comparison Chart and make it a Product/Version Comparison Chart by substituting a product and version under consideration for each column. Why version? In most cases, the current version will be the one used. However, your IT shop might not be working on the current version of the product or the vendor might have a beta version with features you need. In either case, create a column for each product version under consideration.

With a little bit of work and/or by simply following what is dictated for your organization, you now have the target environment consisting of the data architecture, product, and product version you will be using.

Task 3.2: Constraint Compliance

In the constraint compliance task, the designer creates the first-cut database schema. Some might think it rather strange to use the word *constraint* in the task title. The choice is intentional. Data modeling, both logical and physical, deals with specifying *what is wanted.* Schema design shows you *what you can realistically have.* The data model you built must now comply with the rules of the selected information manager.

Constraint compliance is divided into two activities. The first, Activity 3.2.1: Map rationalized physical data model to the data architecture, converts the Rationalized physical data model to a data architecture–specific, although otherwise generic, database schema. The second, Activity 3.2.2: Create a DBMS product/version-specific functional physical database design, transforms the generic schema into a vendor/product/version-specific schema.

Why two activities? Why first convert the rationalized physical data model into a generic schema? The same reason you created a logical data model before you created the physical data model: you need to ensure that when the vendor's DBMS product changes, and it will, you understand *what was wanted* in the first place rather than *what you had to settle for.*

Pseudocode...Again

When discussing process modeling, one of the techniques mentioned was pseudocode, which uses a mixture of English and phony computer code to describe what the system should do. Some designers and programmers find it very useful, others not so much. The same can be said for schema definition; a pseudocode or pseudo-DDL or pseudo-DML approach is sometimes useful for describing the database structure without getting into the restrictions and idiosyncrasies of a particular DBMS. Pseudocode can be useful when trying to make the description of what is wanted independent of product or version limitations.

For example, assume that your current DBMS has a 512-byte limit on the text field length and a 16-character limit on field names. This is in contrast to the Rationalized physical data model data item PRODUCT DESCRIPTION, which is a text field that can be 1,000 characters long. It is much more useful to pass the DBA the pseudocode, shown here:

```
PRODUCT DESCRIPTION    CHAR (1000)
```

than the more accurate but less descriptive example shown here:

```
PROD_DESCRIPT_1        CHAR (500)
PROD_DESCRIPT_2        CHAR (500)
```

A second advantage of pseudo-DDL is in version preparation. Imagine that the DBMS vendor comes out with a new version of the product that now supports a text field length of 1,024 bytes and 24-character field names. Without the pseudocode, how is the DBA to know that the original intention was to have a single product description field and not two separate fields? A significant advantage for the end user or the programmer could be lost because the DBA does not know the database designer's original intention.

A third benefit of pseudocode, although not ranking with the first two advantages, is nonetheless just as real. Some database designers are more experienced than some DBAs. It is not uncommon to see junior staff tasked with preparing a new DBMS version for installation. Their closeness to the new release gives them a front-row seat for understanding updates to the DDL, DML, and even application code supported by the new software.

Database designers, on the other hand, are often the more experienced employees who cut their teeth on earlier versions of the DBMS. Their DBMS knowledge might be deep, even if their familiarity with the syntax of the latest DBMS version is weak. Using pseudocode allows these more experienced designers to concentrate on what the systems needs to do using a pseudocode that might contain syntax from an earlier DBMS version. When the more senior designers have completed their tasks, the more junior staff can then focus on aligning their seniors' pseudocode with the new version's syntax.

While pseudocode is useful for designing a schema for any DBMS, it is even more critical and helpful for relational database management systems. As discussed earlier, there are dozens of RDBMSs, almost all of which use SQL and follow ISO standards but that are, nonetheless, different—sometimes significantly different. And the differences are not just from product to product but also from version to version.

For most new software products, there is a period of version frenzy right after product introduction that cools off over time. In the first 24 months after product introduction, three or four new versions may be provided to correct errors and to improve performance. The next 36 months see a flurry of new features. At about year 5, things start to slow down, with a new version coming out every 18 months or longer. The relational vendors were not so lucky.

RDBMS vendors have been under pressure from all sides to make changes to their product offerings. There is pressure to make their RDBMS more like the relational model (remember the 333 Codd rules); there is pressure to expand beyond the 333 rules, adding features to handle things such as group data items; there is pressure to make the DBMS more OO-like; and now there is pressure to add some NoSQL features. This version-driven code instability means that a more stable pseudocode can go a long way to better communicating designer intentions.

But what if the DBMS is changed and you created a SQL-like pseudo-schema when the company decided to use a non-SQL DBMS? There's no real problem because the pseudocode, even SQL like pseudocode, is sufficiently generic that most database designers and DBAs can convert it into any legitimate DBMS DDL. It just might require a bit more work on their part. However, the benefits of pseudocode outweigh any such possible disadvantage.

Activity 3.2.1: Map Rationalized Physical Data Model to the Data Architecture

In this activity, the Rationalized physical data modeling objects become data architecture–specific objects. It is the first time that the record type Customer or the link Owns is made to conform to a particular DBMS. The approach is to examine the rationalized physical data model, object by object, and make it conform to the features and constraints of the proposed DBMS.

Record Types

During step 1, Transformation, you created four kinds of record types: proper, associative, attributive, and S-type. Now you need to make these record types DBMS compliant.

Proper

Proper record types are supported by every DBMS. In fact, for most every DBMS, the definition of record type is a proper record type.

Associative

An associative record type is a link with its own data items. Take the example of two record types, Customer and Car, and the link Rents. Information about the rental, such as rental date and price, are properties of neither the Customer record nor of the Car record but rather of the rental agreement itself. You can test this by asking these questions: Can a customer rent more than one car? Can a car be rented by more than one customer? Is the rental agreement for a single customer and a single car? Because the answer to the three questions is yes, yes, and no, then the rental information is itself a record linked to the customer and car records. The database designer should create three record types, Customer, Car, and Rental Agreement, with the Rental Agreement at the many end of two one-to-many links.

Look at a second example. Keep the same Customer and Car records, but change the Rents link to Purchases. Because a customer can buy many cars and a car can be purchased by only one customer (at any one time), then the purchase information is linked one-to-many with Customer but in a one-to-one link with Car. The one-to-one linkage allows for the storage of the purchase information in the Car record, making the Purchases record not needed.

The way to integrate an associative record type into a DBMS that does not directly support associativity is to look at the relationships between the proper record types. Unless they are linked many-to-many, an associative record type's data items can often be merged with one of the proper records. If they are linked many-to-many, then the associative record type becomes a database "proper" record type in a mandatory relationship with its two partners.

Attributive

An attributive record's existence depends on another record. Take the example of two records, Customer and Customer Address. A Customer Address occurrence should exist only if it is linked to a Customer occurrence. If the Customer is deleted, then all associated Customer Address records should be deleted.

A number of DBMS products indirectly support attributive record types, although none use the term *attributive*. Rather than implementing attribution as a characteristic of the record type, they implement it as a characteristic of the link between the two records. In some relational systems there is the foreign key option ON DELETE CASCADE (sometimes called CASCADE ON DELETE), which tells the system that the child record cannot exist without its associated parent record.

```
CREATE TABLE ADDRESS (
    STREET      CHARACTER VARYING(20),
    TOWN        CHARACTER VARYING(20),
    CUST_NO     CHARACTER (10),
        FOREIGN KEY(CUST_NO)
        REFERENCES CUSTOMER (CUST_NUMB) ON DELETE CASCADE
);
```

Network-based systems have a similar feature implemented as part of the set-membership definition using the RETENTION (also called DISCONNECTION) option.

```
SET NAME IS CUST_ADDRESS
OWNER IS CUSTOMER
MEMBER IS CUSTOMER_ADDRSS
RETENTION IS FIXED
```

IMS has a simple solution to the problem. When a parent record (segment) is deleted, all its children records (dependent segments) are automatically deleted. In IMS, if you delete the root segment (the very top of the database tree), the system automatically deletes every bit of data in your database.

S-Type

An S-type (supertype/subtype also called *generalization* and *specialization*) is where a proper record type includes different roles containing different role-specific data and/or links. For example, take the record type Customer. A store might have two different types of customers, retail and wholesale. Both retail and wholesale customers have a number of data items in common (CUSTOMER NAME, CUSTOMER NUMBER, PHONE NUMBER, ADDRESS, etc.) and a number of data items unique to their role (DISCOUNT AGREEMENT, SHIPPING INSTRUCTIONS, CREDIT STATUS, INDUSTRY CODE, LOYALTY PROGRAM MEMBERSHIP NUMBER, etc.). The supertype contains the common data and links for both types of customers, while the subtype contains their unique role information.

Object-oriented database management systems support S-types. In fact, the supertype/subtype distinction is a fundamental feature of object technology—children objects inherit properties, including data and processes, from their parent.

Non-object-oriented systems usually do not support S-types, so the database designer must decide how to handle them. One solution is to create three proper record types with a one-to-many link between the common attributed parent and the two (or more) role-specific children.

A second solution is to have a single customer record type containing all the fields used by both types of customer. If the customer is a retail customer, then the wholesale data items are left blank. The same is true for a wholesale customer—any retail data items are blank. This approach assumes the designer does not have a problem with blank, or null, fields.

There is a simpler, third solution if the designer is comfortable that customers will never change roles, i.e., a wholesale customer will never become a retail customer or the reverse. If the type of customer is unchanging, then the designer can simply have two record types, one for wholesale customer and one for retail customer with the data item names adjusted to avoid confusion (not CUSTOMER NAME but WHOLESALE CUSTOMER NAME and RETAIL CUSTOMER NAME, etc.).

Links

Linkages become the stickiest part of Formalization because how they are implemented varies far more from DBMS to DBMS than record types or data items.

Membership Class: Cardinality

There are three types of cardinality: one-to-one, one-to many, and many-to-many.

One-to-One

The one-to-one linkage is rarely directly supported, but the workaround is both conceptually simple and easy. The first solution is to make the link one-to-many and simply ignore that there will never be more than one child per parent. The second solution is even simpler and easier and is the one used in 99 percent of the cases.

Combine all of the data items of the two record types in a single record type. The combined record type is more efficient (indexes, storage location, etc.) and easier for the programmer to deal with than the one-to-many approach.

One-to-Many

This is the garden-variety link supported by virtually every database management system. It is the direct descendent of the parent-child relationship of the punched card era. It is so fundamental that the network model is based on it. Because it is the default condition in most every DBMS, the database designer must do little to implement it.

Many-to-Many

Few DBMSs support native many-to-many linkages. The almost universal solution for handling this link is with two one-to-many links with two (or more) parents sharing a common child. The child record, called a *junction record*, allows the structure to mimic a many-to-many linkage.

For example, the relational model does not support many-to-many (m:n) relationships. Embedded foreign keys make many-to-many links impossible, so they must be "resolved."

If two record types are in a many-to-many relationship, you resolve the relationship by creating a third record type, traditionally called a *junction record*, that is at the "many" end of two one-to-many relationships between the two original record types. Figure 12-1 shows how the Employee-Department many-to-many relationship is resolved into the Employee-Employee/Department Junction-Department relationships.

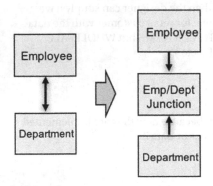

Figure 12-1. *"Resolving" a many-to-many link*

Membership Class: Modality

Modality indicates whether a record type must participate in a link.

Mandatory

Mandatory links are enforced in the DBMS using its DDL linkage constraints. Relational systems use foreign keys to enforce modality with the NOT NULL clause.

```
CREATE TABLE ADDRESS (
    STREET      CHARACTER VARYING (20),
    TOWN        CHARACTER VARYING (20),
    CUST_NO     CHARACTER (10),
        FOREIGN KEY NOT NULL (CUST_NO)
        REFERENCES CUSTOMER (CUST_NUMB)
);
```

This ensures that a child record cannot exist without its parent.

Network systems use their set membership construct, the insertion clause, to enforce a mandatory link, as follows:

```
SET NAME IS CUST_ADDRESS
OWNER IS CUSTOMER
MEMBER IS CUSTOMER_ADDRSS
INSERTION IS AUTOMATIC
```

Optional

Optional links are the easiest of all. For most database management systems, optional is the default. The designer does not have to do anything specific to create a modality of optional.

Degree

Degree indicates the number of record types that can participate in a single link.

Unary

A recursive or unary link exists when an occurrence of record type A is linked to other occurrences of record type A. Take the example of the record type Employee and the link Reports To. You can have Smith reporting to Jones, who reports to Williams, where Smith, Jones, and Williams are all Employee occurrences.

The approach taken by virtually every DBMS to support a unary or recursive relationship is through the bill-of-materials structure. As with many-to-many links, a junction record supplies the magic that makes this linkage work. In the example, in addition to the record type Employee, the designer creates the record type Employee BOM. Then two one-to-many links are created between Employee and Employee BOM (Figure 12-2). One link is Supervises, and the other is Supervised By. This allows the database to cruise from one occurrence of Employee to the next, going one level higher or one level lower with each new pass.

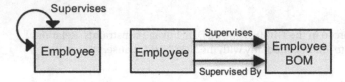

Figure 12-2. *"Resolving" a recursive link*

The bill-of-materials structure is a common way to handle recursion whether the DBMS is hierarchical, relational, object-oriented, network, or NoSQL.

Binary

Binary linkages are the staid and standard linkage between record types. They are supported by every DBMS and are often the only link supported by the DBMS.

N-ary

An n-ary link exists when one link connects three or more record types. Most database management systems do not handle n-ary linkages very well. The standard DBMS is designed to handle linkages that are binary, optional, and one-to-many. Any divergence requires a special workaround. For many-to-many links, there is the junction record, and for a bill-of-materials link, there is the bill-of-materials junction record. What do you think is going to happen with n-ary links?

Look at the n-ary relationship among Employee, Client, and Project, where an employee can work on one or more projects for one or more clients. The solution is a junction record that is at the many end and links to the three proper record types. In relational parlance, it looks like this:

```
CREATE TABLE EMPLOYEES (
     EMP_ID          CHAR(5),
     NAME            CHAR(20),
         PRIMARY KEY(EMP_ID)
);
CREATE TABLE PROJECTS (
     PROJECT_NAME    CHAR(12),
     BUDGET          DECIMAL(8,2),
         PRIMARY KEY(PROJECT_NAME)
);
CREATE TABLE CLIENT (
     CLIENT      NAME CHAR(20),
     ADDRESS     CHAR(40),
         PRIMARY KEY(CLIENT_NAME)
);
CREATE TABLE ASSIGNED_TO (
     EMP             CHAR(5),
```

```
    PROJ            CHAR(12),
    CLNT            CHAR(20),
      PRIMARY KEY(EMP,PROJ),
      FOREIGN KEY(EMP) REFERENCES EMPLOYEES(EMP_ID),
      FOREIGN KEY(PROJ) REFERENCES PROJECTS(PROJECT_NAME),
      FOREIGN KEY(CLNT) REFERENCES CLIENT (CLIENT _NAME)
);
```

Many NoSQL systems, particularly the column-based ones, store all information in an n-ary fashion as their default. In the example, everything about the employee, including the projects he worked on and the clients he worked for, are stored under his Employee record occurrence. Likewise, the Project instance includes all the employees working on the project as well as the clients for which it was done. NoSQL systems are not shy about duplication, and column-based systems not only allow duplication, but they count on it.

Constraints

Linkage constraints are the problematic area for DBMS implementation. No DBMS does a great job, some do an OK job, and many, unfortunately, fail completely.

Inclusion

The inclusion constraint exists if an occurrence of record type A can be linked to an occurrence of record type B, to an occurrence of record type C, or to both record types B and C. It is the standard condition between three record types (or more) and two links (or more). This is the default case; no special symbols or graphics are needed, and no special action is required by the database designer.

Exclusion

Exclusion is a little trickier than inclusion. It says that an occurrence of record type A can be linked to an occurrence of record type B *or* to record type C, but *not both* at the same time. Take the example of Customer, Dealer, and Car and the link Owns. A car can be owned by a dealer or it can be owned by a customer but not both—at least not at the same time. Owns is either-or, not both.

Conjunction

Conjunction says that if an occurrence of record A is linked to record B, then it must also be linked to an occurrence of record type C.

Both exclusion and conjunction are particularly problematic because they deal with not one but multiple links.

As mentioned in Chapter 3, there are two types of conjunction. *Simple conjunction* says that given three record types, A, B, and C, and two links, A to B and A to C, every occurrence of A must be linked to an occurrence of B and to an occurrence of C. Simple conjunction can be handled by making the modality of both links mandatory-mandatory.

Conditional conjunction states that given three record types, A, B, and C, and two links, one between A and B and one between A and C, if an occurrence of A is linked to an occurrence of B, then it must also be linked to an occurrence of C. Conditional conjunction cannot be implemented through membership class like simple conjunction can be.

Ideally, the DBMS should accommodate exclusion and conditional conjunction through its DDL although only a smattering of help is available here. The problem is that the average DDL can deal with only one link at a time. Handling multiple links simultaneously, when the status of one can affect the status of another, is beyond their scope. Uber-links, such as exclusion and conditional conjunction, defy most DBMS architectures and product offerings.

Failing a DDL accommodation, the DBMS should at least allow the designer a workaround using its DML, triggers, or stored procedures. Object-oriented DBMSs can accommodate exclusion and conjunction, to an extent, though even they fail to do a complete job. In too many cases, enforcement of exclusion and conjunction is, unfortunately, left to the application programmer if it is enforced at all.

Data Items

On the surface, data items are the easiest to formalize, but there are data architecture and DBMS-specific undercurrents that can make the task a challenge.

Domains

While both group and multivalue data items have a long IT history, domains do not. It was not until the late 1970s and early 1980s that domains were even included in, much less required by, some newer programming languages. DBMS vendors did not start incorporating them until a few years later. Even today, many DBMS implementations allow domain declarations but do not require them. However, domains are a useful way to help keep database data accurate and useful. Their use is encouraged. Database designers should include domain information if the DBMS allows.

Source: Primitive and Derived

As you should remember from logical data modeling, there are two types of data source: primitive and derived.

Primitive Data Items

As stated in logical data modeling, a primitive data item is a single or lowest-level fact about a record. Primitive data are the bread and butter of a database. The database designer need only ensure that all primitive data have a home in the database schema.

Derived Data Items

Derived data are data that can be calculated from one or more primitive or derived data items. For example, a database does not have to store the data item EMPLOYEE AGE if it can access CURRENT DATE and EMPLOYEE DATE OF BIRTH. Age can be calculated from the primitive data in the database.

Derived data should never be placed on an E-R diagram. Whether derived data should be in the database is a performance question and should probably be left to Chapter 13, which deals with database efficiency. In the meantime, derived data should be documented but not be part of the current database design.

Complexity: Simple and Group

Data item *complexity* is a term that refers to the intricacy of a data item. There are two types of data item complexity, simple and group.

A *simple data item,* also called an *atomic data item,* does not contain any other data items. For the database designer its place in the database design is as straightforward as it gets.

A *group data item,* also called an *aggregate data item,* contains a fixed number of other data items. An example would be the group data item ADDRESS, which contains the following simple data items: STREET NUMBER, STREET NAME, TOWN, STATE/ PROVINCE, POSTAL CODE, and COUNTRY.

ONE PERSON'S SIMPLE IS ANOTHER PERSON'S GROUP—IT'S ALL IN THE CONTEXT

The complexity of a data item can be context sensitive. For example, for most of us, COLOR is a simple or atomic data item because it cannot be broken down into constituent parts. However, for printers and graphic artists, COLOR might contain the data items MAGENTA, YELLOW, and CYAN, the three primary subtractive colors that make up all other colors in printing. As was true in logical data modeling, the designer needs to be sensitive to the context in which the data exists.

Most nonrelational DBMSs support some type of aggregation, virtually every programming language supports group data items, and most every relational product supports aggregation (for example DATE) to a limited extent. Unfortunately, how the DBMS supports groups is not always straightforward, requiring the database designer to delve into the DBMS product manuals.

Valuation: Single Value and Multivalue

Data item *valuation* describes how many values the data item can have. There are two types of valuation, single value and multivalue. A *single-value data item* can have only one value at a time. An example would be COLOR = "blue." If COLOR is "blue," then it cannot be "red," at least not at the same time.

A *multivalue data item* can contain a fixed or variable number of values. Examples include cases where the subject can contain more than one color (COLOR = "blue, red") or DAY OF THE WEEK contains seven values, "Mon, Tue, Wed, Thu, Fri, Sat, Sun."

This type of attribute has various other names such as repeating group and, unfortunately, group.

Most non-RDBMSs support multivalue data items. Even relational users can get around this constraint fairly easily. For them, it is more of a question of the IT shop standard than of programming difficulty.

Data item complexity and data item valuation are two sides of the same coin. Both have a history going back before database management systems existed; both are part of many, if not most, programming languages; and both are incredibly useful, which places pressure on the database designer to accommodate them. The only real difference is that the data item components in multivalue data items share a single data domain while those in a data item group need not.

A MILDLY USEFUL OBSERVATION

If your design is a *vanilla DBMS default structure*, meaning…

1. All records are proper record types.

2. All cardinality is one-to-many.

3. All modality is optional.

4. All links are binary.

5. All linkage constraints are inclusive.

6. All data items are primitive, simple, and single.

then go out and buy a lottery ticket. You are a very lucky designer.

Or you have missed some important features that need to be included in your database design. A review might be called for.

Vanilla DBMS default structure databases exist about 2 percent of the time in the business world and, unfortunately, about 70 percent of the time in IT shops, leading to a severe business/IT disconnect.

You should now have a preliminary database schema that is data architecture compatible, although not yet product or version specific. You have "resolved" the many-to-many linkages, created the necessary junction records, and have a pseudocode DDL. The next step is to make the design conform to the vendor's offerings.

The work product of Activity 3.2.1, Map rationalized physical data model to the data architecture, is a generic (although data architecture–specific) physical database design. The next activity will convert this generic design into a fully functional database design.

Activity 3.2.2: Create a DBMS Product/Version-Specific Functional Physical Database Design

Even though you have made your database design data architecture compliant, you still have only a pseudo-schema. One more activity gives you a workable (compliable) database schema and a design that complies with a DBMS product and version.

Regardless of promises of standards compliance, every vendor has proprietary features, legacies they need to support, and downright idiosyncrasies that often defy explanation. These constraints need to be incorporated into the schema.

Product and version constraints are of two types: structural and syntactical. To address structural constraints, the basic database objects (record types, links, data items, etc.) need to be modified to work with the DBMS. Ideally, you have already made most of these modifications in Activity 3.2.1, Map rationalized physical data model to the data architecture. Remaining structural changes usually relate to storage limitations, such as file or record type size.

Syntactical changes are more common and usually consist of vendor DDL and DML language accommodations. For example, the ISO SQL:2011 standard data type DECIMAL is not supported by Oracle, which uses NUMBER instead. Other syntactical changes might include name length and what to substitute for spaces.

Whereas structural compliance has to do with making sometimes major changes to database components, such as record type, links, etc., syntactical compliance deals more with the words used to describe the schema while leaving their meaning unchanged.

Table 12-3 illustrates the changes needed to make a generic SQL schema Oracle compliant.

Table 12-3. *Preliminary Design DDL Generic SQL Converted to Oracle*

Generic SQL	Changes Needed for ORACLE
CREATE TABLE PRODUCT (PRODUCT_NAME CHAR(30) NOT NULL, PRODUCT_NUMBER CHAR(8) NOT NULL PRIMARY KEY UNIQUE, -- primary key assumes unique but both make the message plain -- even if not a primary key, keep this field unique PRODUCT_DESCRIPTION VARCHAR(512), COST_BASIS DECIMAL(8,2) NOT NULL, LIST_PRICE DECIMAL(8,2) NOT NULL, CREATE INDEX PROD_NO_IDX ON PRODUCT (PRODUCT_NUMBER));	PRODUCT_NUMBER CHAR(8) NOT NULL PRIMARY KEY, /*can't use UNIQUE in PK statement */ PRODUCT_DESCRIPTION VARCHAR2(512), /*LONG was the standard but was dropped. VARCHAR being dropped in favor of VARCHAR2 */ COST_BASIS NUMBER(8,2) NOT NULL, /* substitute NUMBER for DECIMAL */ LIST_PRICE NUMBER(8,2) NOT NULL /* substitute NUMBER for DECIMAL */ /*Oracle automatically creates index on PRIMARY KEY columns */
CREATE TABLE MANUFACTURER (MANUF_NAME CHAR(30) NOT NULL, MANUF_ID CHAR(6) NOT NULL PRIMARY KEY UNIQUE, MANUF_CATEGORY INTEGER DEFAULT 1 CHECK(MANUF_CATEGORY IN (1, 2, 3)), MANUF_NOTES VARCHAR(512), ORDER_INSTRUCTIONS VARCHAR(512) CREATE INDEX MANUF_ID_IDX ON MANUFACTURER (MANUF_ID));	MANUF_ID CHAR(6) NOT NULL PRIMARY KEY, /* can't use UNIQUE in PK statement */ MANUF_CATEGORY NUMBER(1,0) NOT NULL DEFAULT 1 CHECK (MANUF_CATEGORY IN (1, 2, 3)), /* Oracle does not support the INTEGER data type, NUMBER used instead */ MANUF_NOTES VARCHAR2(512), /* VARCHAR2 replaces VARCHAR */ ORDER_INSTRUCTIONS VARCHAR2(512) /* Oracle automatically creates index on PRIMARY KEY columns */
CREATE TABLE PROD_MANUF_JCT (PRODUCT_NUMBER CHAR(8), MANUF_ID CHAR(6), PRIMARY KEY (PRODUCT_NUMBER,MANUF_ ID), FOREIGN KEY (PRODUCT_NUMBER) REFERENCES PRODUCT ON UPDATE CASCADE ON DELETE CASCADE, FOREIGN KEY (MANUF_ID) REFERENCES MANUFACTURER ON UPDATE CASCADE ON DELETE CASCADE);	FOREIGN KEY (PRODUCT_NUMBER) REFERENCES PRODUCT (PRODUCT_NUMBER) ON DELETE CASCADE, FOREIGN KEY (MANUF_ID) REFERENCES MANUFACTURER (MANUF_ID) ON DELETE CASCADE, /* Oracle does not support ON UPDATE CASCADE constraint - constraint with triggers */

Versions change far more frequently for newer products than for older ones. Even so, most database designers/DBAs must deal with three or four new DBMS versions during the life of the average database. Keeping the original database design as generic as possible will help the designer or DBA incorporate useful new version features. The generic database design will tell the DBA the difference between *what was wanted* and *what was settled for*. For example, earlier versions of Oracle did not support more than one column per table that was larger than 255 characters. Without proper documentation, the DBA would never know that the original desire was for 512-character MANUF_NOTES and MANUF_INSTRUCTIONS fields.

At this point, the database designer has a complete functional database schema. However, formalization is not yet complete. The application programmers will need subschemas, derived from the database schema, to do their work.

Subschema Creation

You now (ideally) have a working database schema. But more is needed. Remember all those usage scenarios? Well, they become the basis for the needed subschemas. In the relational model, subschemas are views and, for the most part, straightforward.

Subschemas came into their own with the network or CODASYL database model and were part of the original ANSI standard. Subschemas provide the application programmer with only the subset of the data (record types, data types, or sets) needed to do the job. Extraneous information, such as unneeded record types and links, are excluded. Subschemas can impose security by limiting what can be seen and what can be updated. Figure 12-3 is a diagram of a simple network schema and two subschemas.

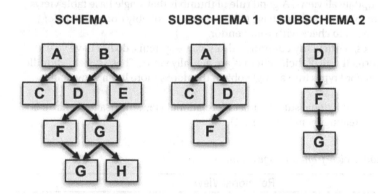

Figure 12-3. Schema and subschemas

Views are the relational version of a subschema but with considerable differences. A relational view is a single virtual table created from one or more base tables. Like the network subschema, a view can consist of a subset of the data items in a record type, but unlike a subschema, a view cannot contain links to other tables.

When the view includes more than one table, then the data items of the two tables are joined into a single flat virtual file or table. Figure 12-4 shows a relational database with two base tables and a view consisting of the data in the two tables.

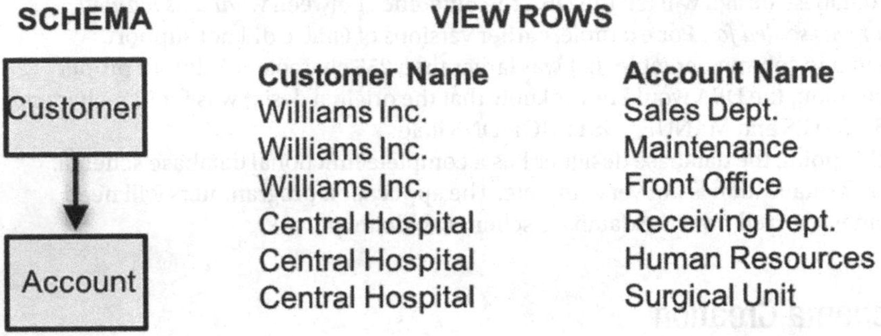

SCHEMA	VIEW ROWS	
	Customer Name	**Account Name**
Customer	Williams Inc.	Sales Dept.
	Williams Inc.	Maintenance
	Williams Inc.	Front Office
	Central Hospital	Receiving Dept.
Account	Central Hospital	Human Resources
	Central Hospital	Surgical Unit

Figure 12-4. *Relational view*

The virtual table is a flat file with the parent information replicated for each child. If the parent record occurrence "Smith" has four children record occurrences, then "Smith" will appear in the virtual table four times. Some designers use views to denormalize the database. Figure 12-4 gives an example of the un-normalized flat file nature of the relational view.

There is just one problem: not all views are updateable. The rules vary from product to product regarding whether a view is updateable. Some RDBMSs do not allow any view to be updated, while others allow some views to be modified. No RDBMS vendor has figured out how to update all views. A good rule of thumb is that single base table views are probably updateable, but multiple base table views are probably not updateable; however, you really need to check with your vendor.

NoSQL databases, particularly column and key-value systems, do not have views, or, perhaps more correctly, all of their schemas are actually views. These systems bundle data from multiple record types into a single object that looks more like a view than a relational base table.

Whether it's a non-relational subschema or a relational view, the usage scenario is the best resource for creating them (Table 12-4).

Table 12-4. *Relational View from a Usage Scenario*

Usage Scenario	Relational View

Usage Scenario: 21 Name: Customer Orders
(1) Enter Customer.
(2) Find Account occurrence for associated Customer occurrence.
(3) Find Order occurrences for associated Account occurrence.
	`CREATE VIEW CUSTOMER_ORDERS`
	`    (CUSTOMER_NAME, ACCOUNT NUMBER,`
	`        ORDER_NUMBER, DATE) AS`
	`SELECT (C.CUSTOMER_NAME, A.ACCOUNT_NO,`
	`        O.ORDER_NO,  O.ORDER_DATE,)`
	`    FROM CUSTOMER C. ACCOUNT A, ORDER O`
	`    WHERE (C.CUSTOMER _NO = A.CUSTOMER_NO)`
	`    AND (A.ACCOUNT_NO  =  O.ACCOUNT_NO)`
	`    ;`

In most cases, there will not be a one-to-one relationship between usage scenarios and subschemas/views. Rather, the database designer will find that a few well-defined subschemas will usually handle many usage scenarios.

The subschema sections of the vendor's manuals are usually chock-full of subschema do's and don'ts.

Formalization Notes

The last Step 3, Formalization, task is to complete the *Formalization notes*. As with the other steps, the database designer needs to record the issues and decisions made during Formalization (*why, where, when,* and *results*) so that future designers and DBAs can perform their jobs properly informed with what was done to the database design and why.

Deliverables

Step 3, Formalization, should produce the following deliverables:

3.1 *Functional database design diagram:* A database diagram showing the record types and links (Figure 12-5 in the next section).

3.2 *Functional schema DDL:* Two versions should be created.

- Generic DDL conforming to the database architecture

- Vendor product and version specific

3.3 *Functional subschemas DDL:* Two versions should be created.

- Generic DDL conforming to the database architecture

- Vendor product and version specific

3.4 *Functional database object definitions:* The same physical definitions created in step 1, Transformation, updated with any necessary changes made during step 2, Utilization, now need updating with step 3, Formalization, information.

3.5 *Formalization notes:* A narrative or journal created by the database designer of the activities, issues, and decisions made during step 3, Formalization.

Example of Deliverables

Figure 12-5 shows the functional database design.

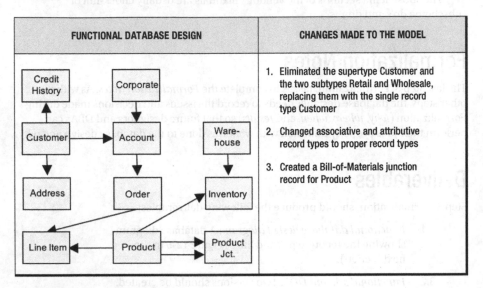

FUNCTIONAL DATABASE DESIGN	CHANGES MADE TO THE MODEL
	1. Eliminated the supertype Customer and the two subtypes Retail and Wholesale, replacing them with the single record type Customer
	2. Changed associative and attributive record types to proper record types
	3. Created a Bill-of-Materials junction record for Product

Figure 12-5. *Functional database design*

In Chapter 13, the DDL is modified to improve the performance of the database.

CHAPTER 13

■ ■ ■

Customization: Enhancing Performance

It is a bad plan that admits no modifications.

—Publilus Syrus

An expert is a person who has made all the mistakes that can be made in a very narrow field.

—Niels Bohr

For a number of crucial reasons, enhancing the performance of the database design is done last. First, any performance considerations need to wait until the database design is well understood. This ensures that critical functional components are completely identified, included, and documented before any changes are made to the database design. If you start modifying the design before properly documenting it, you risk losing critical functional information. To avoid this confusion, do not mix functional database design requirements with database performance considerations—this is the reason U3D separates steps 3 and 4.

The second reason to separate functional and performance considerations is that vendors change the database design syntax far more frequently for performance reasons than for functional ones. Most DBMS software maintenance releases contain at least some performance enhancements but might not contain any functional ones at all. Keeping the more volatile performance enhancements separate from the more stable functional ones improves the chances of providing performance improvements without destroying functional necessities. See Table 13-1.

© George Tillmann 2017

G. Tillmann, *Usage-Driven Database Design*, DOI 10.1007/978-1-4842-2722-0_13

Table 13-1. *Step 4: Customization*

Sources	Procedures	Deliverables
• 3.1: Functional database design (diagram)	• Task 4.1: Resource analysis	• 4.1: Enhanced database design (diagram)
• 3.2: Functional schema DDL	• Task 4.2: Performance enhancement	
• 3.3: Functional subschemas DDL	• Activity 4.2.1: Customize hardware	• 4.2: Enhanced schema DDL
• 3.4: Functional database object definitions (data dictionary)	• Activity 4.2.2: Customize software	• 4.3: Enhanced subschema DDL
• 2.3: Usage scenarios		• 4.4: Enhanced database object definitions (data dictionary)
• 2.4: Usage maps		
• 2.5: Combined usage map		• 4.5: Customization notes
• 1.3: Transformation notes		
• 2.6: Utilization notes		
• 3.5: Formalization notes		
• DB: DBMS features and constraints		

In step 4, Customization, the designer has the option to use design techniques or tools (vendor, third-party, or homegrown) to improve database performance while keeping all functional components intact. This step is divided into two tasks. The first task applies some analytical rigor to the database usage information, followed in the second task by the actual performance-enhancing changes to the database.

Task 4.1: Resource Analysis

Because you now have a working DBMS schema, you could stop here, and if demands on your database are minimal (few transactions and a small amount of data), you are probably done. However, for many databases, performance is a significant driver of good service. Without special performance-enhancing features, most of which are provided by DBMS vendors, many transactions or queries could take minutes, or even hours, to return results. An enhancement as simple as adding an index, often requiring fewer than a dozen lines of code, can improve performance by one, two, or even three orders of magnitude. The trick is understanding the trade-offs and knowing where to place the performance-enhancing components.

Step 3, Formalization, focused on the language to translate the physical design specifications into something the DBMS software can understand. The skills the designer needs are concept and software related. For example, the database designer needs to know both the functional requirements of the application and the vendor-specific DDL and DML for creating and using a database.

Performance tuning, on the other hand, requires all the database designer Formalization skills and, in addition, knowledge of how computer systems work—the hardware and system software the database lives under, as well as any DBMS functionality, needs to be understood. This is because, by far, the most significant issue associated with database tuning is efficiently getting information to and from auxiliary storage devices. The reason? Fetching a record from main memory can be 1,000 times faster than fetching the same record from disk. If two records are needed and they are stored on two separate database pages, then two physical I/Os might be required. However, if they are stored on the same page on disk, then the second record can be fetched up to 1,000 times faster than the first.

The Trade-Off Triangle

How do you know when you're done? The only way to really know the answer is to examine your database to see whether the off-the-rack implementation will work satisfactorily. If, on the other hand, performance enhancements are needed, the designer can dip into the DBMS tool kit and improve the database design.

There are no free rides in the DBMS world. For everything you gain, there is something you lose. Everything (almost) is possible; however, everything (almost) has a cost. It all comes down to trade-offs.

Just listen to medication ads on TV. "Wonder drug Nonosedripz gets rid of your runny nose; however, side effects can include brain damage, anal leakage, and growing extra toes." The consumer has to analyze the trade-offs and decide whether nose relief is worth the risk.

Trade-offs are everywhere, including database design. A good DBMS schema involves trade-offs related to three competing performance dimensions—flexibility, throughput, and volume.

- *Flexibility* is the ability of the database system to support a broad range of known and unknown services and to easily adapt to business and technology changes.

- *Throughput* is how quickly the database system can perform its function either in terms of response time for online applications or runtime for batch programs.

- *Volume* is the number of objects/actions the database system can accommodate, such as the number of record types, or occurrences, it can support or the number of concurrent online transactions it can handle.

These three dimensions can be easily represented as a triangle (Figure 13-1).

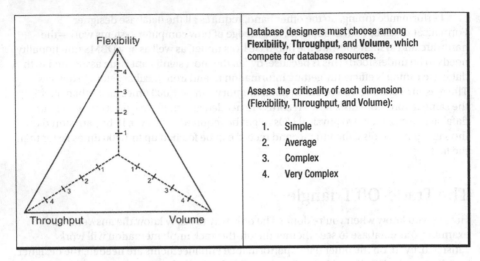

Figure 13-1. Trade-off triangle

Trade-off decisions come at a cost. For example, design the database for flexibility and you might have to sacrifice some of the database's ability to handle large volumes or perform functions quickly.

In many cases, the hardware, system software, and DBMS can accommodate all three dimensions. However, in cases where demands are high, or extreme, the system might be able to accommodate only one or two dimensions comfortably (Figure 13-2).

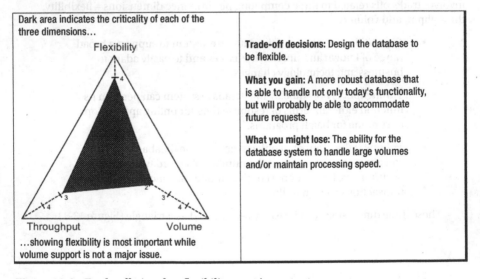

Figure 13-2. Trade-off triangle—flexibility most important

Understanding the trade-offs helps in making decisions about design options and tool usage (Figure 13-3). Most of all, the trade-off triangle provides a design-trade-off perspective (Table 13-2).

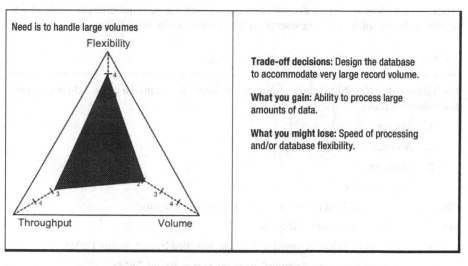

Need is to handle large volumes

Trade-off decisions: Design the database to accommodate very large record volume.

What you gain: Ability to process large amounts of data.

What you might lose: Speed of processing and/or database flexibility.

Figure 13-3. Trade-off triangle—volume most important

Table 13-2. Critical Dimensions

Two Most Critical Dimensions	Design Options to Consider	Tools to Consider
Throughput and volume	• Fewer larger record types, read-only • Use of specialized storage (SSD, cache, main memory, large buffers, read-only, multiple disks, etc.) • Use of partitioning, clustering, and hashing	• NoSQL • DBMS middleware • IMS/Fast Path
Throughput and flexibility	• Distribute across multiple disks • Use of indexing, clustering, and hashing • Robust use of links	• In-memory DBMS (no/limited update capability) • T/P monitors
Flexibility and volume	• Use of many record types and relationships • Partitioning • Strong use of indices	• Parallel DBMS processing • Distributed DBMS • DBMS middleware

The trade-off triangle is a simple visual way to demonstrate, and gain buy-in for, the database design. It is not a decision tool but rather a communications tool for illuminating the decisions that need to be made. The trade-off triangle can, and should, be customized to an organization's situation—reflecting local data and transaction volumes as well as functional flexibility and processing speed requirements. Table 13-3 is an example of a *trade-off triangle serviceability index* tool for one IT shop.

Table 13-3. *Trade-Off Triangle Serviceability Index*

Each dimension (flexibility, throughput, and volume) is assigned a value 1 through 4 on the following scale:

1. Simple
2. Average
3. Complex
4. Very complex

The values are then added together to give the *serviceability index.*

Here's a sample of the serviceability index:

- An index less than or equal to 3 can be handled by almost any DBMS.
- 4 to 6 requires a good general-purpose server-based DBMS.
- 7 to 8 requires trade-offs in the design and/or implementation of the database.
- 9 to 10 requires a special-situation DBMS (specialized DBMS (OO, NoSQL, IMS Fast Path), and/or special hardware, and/or special database design).
- No database should have a serviceability index greater than 10.

Although it is certainly not scientific and could be criticized on multiple fronts, nonetheless the trade-off triangle serviceability index gives the database designer a framework for structuring potential challenges as well as managing expectations when meeting with other technical staff and end users.

Task 4.2: Performance Enhancements

If you created a trade-off triangle for your database and it came out 1, 1, 1 (flexibility = 1, throughput = 1, and volume = 1), then you are done. There is little this chapter can add to your database design. If your database is 2, 2, 2, you are also probably done, although reading the chapter might show you some small performance tweak that should be applied to make your system more efficient. However, if you scored a 3 in any category, then keep reading—there will be some tidbits here that you can use.

Activity 4.2.1: Customize Hardware

A simple, although not inexpensive, way to improve database performance is through hardware. Faster processors and/or more memory can improve the performance of most databases and overcome a multitude of poor database design sins. But first...

A Few Words About Secondary Storage

Before going further, you need to understand a few things about secondary storage, both rotating and stolid-state drive (SSD).

Currency is an interesting word. If you use a search engine to wander through the Internet, you discover that nuclear weapons are *the currency of* power, attention is *the currency of* leadership, secrets are *the currency of* intimacy, personal information is *the currency of* the 21st century, and so on, and so on. The word *currency* is used to denote how you measure something important. If you have nuclear weapons, then you have power; more nuclear weapons = more power.

One can safely say that inputs and outputs (I/Os) are the currency of databases. The efficiency of a database application, batch or online, can be improved—sometimes by orders of magnitude—simply by changing how it performs its database I/O. No fairy tales—systems that were deemed turkeys by users have become champs after changing a dozen lines of DDL. It should be no surprise that the number-one place DBAs look to improve database performance is I/O.

Take a simple example. Imagine a program that reads a customer file. Assume that there are 100,000 customer records on disk, each 1 KB long. Starting with the first customer, it takes 100,000 trips to the disk to read the complete file. If the average disk can read a record and ship it to the computer in 8 milliseconds, then it will take almost 14 minutes to read the file. The same file in main memory would take less than 1 second to read on a fast computer. That's an amazing difference.

The reality is that disk is slow while main memory is fast. A second reality is that disk is cheap while main memory is expensive (at least in the quantities needed to compete with disk). The moral is that if you have a very small database, put it in main memory. Your users will love you. If you have a big database, you're stuck with disk...but there are a few things you can do to speed things up.

Look at the typical disk. It consists of a motor rotating a magnetic oxide–covered aluminum or some other nonmagnetic substrate. There could be a single platter or multiple platters, and there might be one read/write head per platter or two (one above and one below). The disk can have a diameter as small as less than 2 inches or as large as 12 inches. It also has one or more arms, part of the actuator, which moves the read/write heads across the platters. Modern disks spin at from 4,000 RPM to greater than 15,000 RPM.

Each platter is divided into concentric tracks. Each track is divided into multiple sectors. If there is more than one platter, then the platters are stacked, one on top of each other, sort of like pancakes, except there is space between each platter for an actuator arm. All of the vertically aligned tracks are called a cylinder.

Reading the data from disk requires a series of steps. First, the request is sent to a controller, which determines the exact location of the desired data. Second, the actuator arm is positioned over/under the correct track. The time it takes to position the arm is called *seek time*. Third, the system goes into a wait state until the correct sector rotates under/over the read/write head. This is called *rotational latency* or *rotational delay*. When the correct sector is in position, the data are read from the disk and transferred to the host.

All of these steps take time. Table 13-4 gives the times for a typical database disk.

Table 13-4. *Disk Data Transfer Speeds, in Milliseconds*

	1 KB Data	2 KB Data	10 KB Data	100 KB Data
Controller	0.01	0.01	0.01	0.01
Seek Time	4.0	4.4*	8.0*	44.0*
Rotational Latency	4.0	4.4**	8.0**	44.0**
Data Transfer	0.01	0.02	0.1	1
Buffer to CPU	0.0003	0.0006	0.003	0.03
Total Time (ms)	8.0	8.8	16.1	89.0

Notes: *Assumes the actuator arm needs repositioning 10 percent of the time.
**Assumes the desired sectors are contiguous 90 percent of the time.

As Table 13-4 shows, the problem is the seek time and the rotational latency (the dreaded disk duo)—both mechanical activities. If you could eliminate both mechanical functions, then the speeds would be considerably faster.

An SSD appears to the system as a rotating disk, but the data are stored in nonvolatile flash memory. Table 13-5 gives typical speeds for an SSD and main memory.

Table 13-5. *Nonrotating Disk Data Transfer Speeds, in Milliseconds*

	1 KB Data	2 KB Data	10 KB Data	100 KB Data
Solid-State Drive (SSD)	0.030	0.042	0.133	1.150
Main Memory	0.00013	0.00026	0.0013	0.013

SSD not fast enough for you? Then keep your data in the computer's main memory where speeds are even faster.

There is just one problem—the faster memory access is, the more expensive it is. SSDs are much faster than rotating disks, but the per-megabyte cost is considerably higher and even more so for main memory. However, the message is not "don't use nonrotating memory." Rather, the message is "use your head." Putting the customer file in main memory might not make sense, but putting the price list there just might.

In most cases, until SSD prices come closer to those of rotating disk, rotating disk will be where the majority of the database's data is stored. The goal for the designer must be to anticipate, as much as possible, the application's data needs and fetch a large amount of desired data from disk with each read. If 10 customer records can be fetched with each trip to the disk, then the amount of time spent doing physical I/O is substantially reduced. To the application program, there were 10 (logical) reads, but for the operating system, only a single (physical) read took place. The objective of the database designer is to maximize the amount of required data fetched with each physical I/O. And that is the goal for this chapter. Examine the size of the data and the number of times data is accessed and then decide where and how the data should be stored and accessed. If the database designer understands the real cost (currency) of database performance, then they are in a position to make informed hardware choices.

Add Disk

Imagine a rather small online transaction processing database for a multiuser application. When the system was new, users complained about slow response time, but as time went on the performance improved. The only difference? More data. In a stranger-than-fiction situation, as the database got bigger, the online performance improved. Why? As the database got larger, it outgrew its single disk. As additional disks were added, along with their additional read/write heads, the contention caused by multiple users repositioning the disk heads decreased. The bigger database is actually faster than the smaller one.

Multiple users or multiple applications requesting the service of a single disk can require the constant repositioning of the read/write head as each user or application gets its turn. The disk head can wind up "thrashing" between the requested cylinders. Adding physical disks increases the number of read/write heads, which, in turn, reduces the very expensive seek time and rotational delay caused by the contention.

Few organizations have only one database supporting one application. Rather than putting five databases on five separate disks, mixing them (spreading all five databases over the five disks) can (based on time of use, etc.) sometimes reduce disk contention, speeding up access for all five.

Faster Disk

There was a time when a disk was a disk—they all ran at approximately the same speed (2,400 to 3,600 RPM), and the disk platters were all about the same size (about 12 inches in diameter). Not true today. Disk RPM can vary from as low as 4,000 up to 15,000 RPM, and smaller disk platter size means that the read/write head travels shorter distances. SSDs can be orders of magnitude faster than rotating disks.

Routinely fetched information, such as product or price tables, can be kept on the smaller, more expensive, but faster disks, while less routinely accessed information can stay on more lumbering media.

Main Memory

Nothing beats main memory for speed, but at a cost. However, if the application is reading data in a predictable way (such as sequentially), then large buffers in main memory can be a godsend. IBM allows disk sectors as large as 50 KB, and most DBMSs use a database page that can be many times the size of the disk sector. Pulling large amounts of information into a buffer in main memory can significantly reduce the number of required physical I/Os. If there is sufficient memory, tables (such as tax and price tables) can be read once and then kept in main memory to be shared by multiple users and applications.

Of course, big buffers are useful only if you want all the information in the buffer. Large buffers and large database pages are not only useless but can be an impediment if the application wants only 50 of the 5,000 bytes returned from storage.

The main memory sticking point is that it works best for read-only data. Journaling and backup and recovery activities require nonvolatile memory such as disk.

Once again, to make an informed choice, the database designer must know how the application will use the data.

Activity 4.2.2: Customize Software

There are a number of ways software can be used to customize a DBMS.

Indices (B-Tree, Hash, Bitmap)

Indices were discussed in Chapter 8, so a repeat is not needed here. Most of the emphasis on indices has been on retrieval, which is where they shine. Which fields you index is driven by two criteria: (1) which fields you want to search the database for and (2) which fields the DBMS uses to access record occurrences.

With relational systems, to add indices you need to simply add a statement to the DDL, as follows:

```
CREATE TABLE PRODUCT (
                PRODUCT_NAME          CHAR(30) NOT NULL,
                PRODUCT_NUMBER        CHAR(8) NOT NULL PRIMARY KEY,
PRODUCT_DESCRIPTION      VARCHAR(512),
                COST_BASIS            DECIMAL(8,2) NOT NULL,
                LIST_PRICE            DECIMAL(8,2) NOT NULL,
CREATE UNIQUE INDEX PRODUCT_NUMBER_IDX ON PRODUCT (PRODUCT_NUMBER)
);
```

Unfortunately, indices are rather poor performers when it comes to index updates. Inserting, modifying, or deleting an index entry can be I/O expensive.

Clustering

Clustering is placing one record occurrence on the same database page as another record occurrence so that the physical I/O to access one occurrence will also access the other occurrence. A common clustering strategy involves the parent-child binary relationship where the child record type occurrences are placed physically near the parent record type occurrence. This increases the chance that the physical I/O to access the parent will also access its children. (The term *clustering* is also used for index storage and distributed databases. The use here is for the storage of content data within the database.)

For effective clustering, the database designer needs to identify the record types that are functionally associated with other record types. On a grand scale, it is as simple as saying that Customer is more closely associated with Account than with Manufacturer, while Manufacturer is more closely associated with Distributor than with Customer.

Look at this manual example. Assume that manufacturer paperwork is stored in the company warehouse and customer paperwork is stored in the sales office. Where should distributor and account paperwork be stored? If, when you need distributor information, you also usually need manufacturer information but you almost never need customer information, then it makes sense to store the distributor information in the warehouse and not the sales office. In addition, although you infrequently need manufacturer paperwork and account paperwork at the same time, you often need customer and account paperwork at the same time. Therefore, it makes sense to store the account information with the customer information in the sales office. Using clustering terminology, it makes sense to cluster Customer and Account information and to cluster Distributer and Manufacturer information.

However, with an automated system and usage maps, you can go further. Which do you typically access first, Manufacturer or Distributor? If you typically access the Manufacturer occurrence first followed by the Distributor occurrence, then the Distributor occurrence should be clustered around the Manufacturer occurrence; but if you typically access Distributor data first, then Manufacturer should be clustered around Distributor. The combined usage map tells you this. Follow the usage arrows and see which is more common—accessing Manufacturer first or Distributor first (Figure 13-4). If the arrows show that you typically move from Distributor to Manufacturer, then cluster Manufacturer with Distributor. This means all Manufacturer occurrences for a specific Distributor occurrence are stored with their Distributor occurrence, ideally on the same database page. Typically, the cluster is named after the parent record.

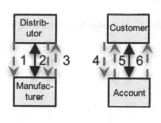

Given these six Usage Scenarios, it makes sense to:

1. Cluster Manufacturer around a Distributor.

2. Cluster Customer around Account.

Figure 13-4. *Clustering example*

Consolidation can be of two types. The first stores the child records on the same physical page as the parent, so by accessing the parent, the child records can be read without an additional physical I/O (assuming there is room on the page for all the children). The second type of clustering stores the parent and children on different database pages, but all the children for a given parent are stored on the same physical page. For example, record X might be stored in database file 1, page 10; while all of X's children are stored in file 2, page 86. All of X's children can be fetched with a single physical I/O (assuming there is room on the page), but not the same physical I/O used to fetch the parent X.

Consider the order management system in Figure 13-5. If the Line Item record occurrences are stored on the same database page as their parent Order record occurrence, then when the Order record is read, all (or most all) of the Line Item occurrences are fetched with the same physical I/O.

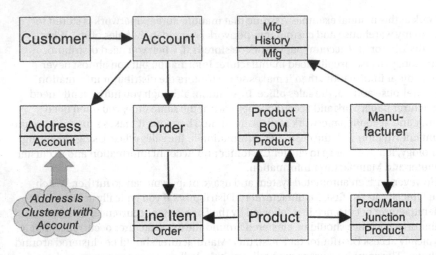

Figure 13-5. *Order management system physical database design*

The downside of clustering is that records can be clustered only one way. Line Item could be clustered around Order or Product, but not both. Clustering Line Item around Order means that when the Order record is accessed, the Order's Line Items are probably also there. However, accessing Line Item from Product means that every Line Item access probably requires a physical I/O. The database designer must understand the trade-offs to make the best all-around decision.

Creating a cluster is quite easy with most database systems. The following is a simple SQL clustering example:

```
CREATE TABLE ORDER    (
    ORDER_NO          CHAR (5) NOT NULL,
    ORDER_TYPE        CHARACTER(1),
    ACCNT_NO          CHARACTER(8),
    ONUMB             NUMBER(4) NOT NULL,
    OAMT              NUMBER(6,2),
    CLUSTER           ACCOUNT(ACCT_NO)
);
```
Note: Some SQL-based systems do not allow a table called Order, a reserved word, while others will.

You can graphically indicate clustering on the database diagram by placing the clustering record type name at the bottom of the record type box.

Figure 13-5 shows a database design fragment including the clustering information at the bottom of each record type box.

Example Using Indices and Clusters

Usage scenarios can help the database designer make the correct clustering choices. If you go back to the trade-off example in Chapter 9, you can now add some additional usage scenario–driven vigor to the solution.

Take the simple database design fragment of the three record types (Figure 13-6) consisting of 200 Product occurrences and 1,000 Order occurrences, each linked to an average of 10 Line Items occurrences per Order occurrence.

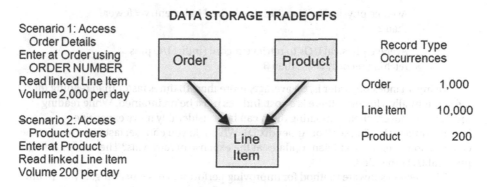

DATA STORAGE TRADEOFFS

Scenario 1: Access
 Order Details
Enter at Order using
 ORDER NUMBER
Read linked Line Item
Volume 2,000 per day

Scenario 2: Access
 Product Orders
Enter at Product
Read linked Line Item
Volume 200 per day

Record Type	Occurrences
Order	1,000
Line Item	10,000
Product	200

Figure 13-6. Physical database design trade-offs

Two software options can improve performance: (1) *indices* placed on certain fields and (2) *clustering* of multiple occurrences of linked but different record types on the same physical database page. In the example, Line Item occurrences could be stored either on the same physical page as their related Order occurrence or on the same physical page as their related Product occurrence, but not both.

Examining scenario 1, the first scenario task is to enter the database at a specified Order occurrence. Because there are 1,000 Order occurrences, a sequential search for the desired Order takes, on average, 500 logical I/Os to find the right record. Assume that, on average, 10 Order occurrences fit on a physical database page, then a sequential search for the desired Order instance requires, on average, 50 physical I/Os.

You can reduce the number of physical I/Os by creating an index on ORDER_NUMBER. Of course, indices are not free. They also require storage on disk and a number of I/Os to fetch their information. Luckily, there are simple formulas (see Appendix D) to calculate the number of physical I/Os required to fetch the occurrence location from the index. Using formula (5) introduced in Chapter 8, the average number of physical I/Os needed to fetch a particular Order record averages 3 (2 for the index and 1 to fetch the record instance), as illustrated here:

If:

N = Number of index entries to search

C = Average number of compares to find desired entry

m = Blocking factor of index

Then:

$$C = Log\ N/Log\ m \qquad\qquad (5)$$

If you assume:

> Number of occurrences (N): 1,000
>
> Number of entries per index page (m): 50

Then using formula (5):

> Average physical I/Os to find the desired index entry = fewer than 2
>
> Average physical I/Os to retrieve record (index I/O plus fetching record) = less than 3

Using an index on Order is, on average, more than 16 times faster than reading the file sequentially. However, there is a cost. Indices must be maintained. While reading indices is relatively cheap, updating them can be considerably more expensive (see formula (7) in Chapter 8 or Appendix D). Which do you choose: faster retrieval at the cost of updates or more efficient updates at the expense of retrievals? The answer is in the physical I/O expended.

The second software method for improving performance is clustering. If you assume you have the desired Order occurrence, sequentially fetching its related 10 Line Item occurrences requires an additional average 5,000 logical I/Os. Assuming you can place 50 Line Item occurrences on a physical database page, fetching now requires, on average, 100 physical I/Os.

Adding an index is better. Using formula (5), you can fetch a Line Item occurrence in approximately 4 I/Os—but that is per Order occurrence. The average of 10 occurrences per Order would translate into (allowing for some occurrences being on the same database page) between 30 and 40 physical I/Os per Order.

You can do better. You can cluster (store) all of Order X's related Line Item occurrences on a single database page or on the same physical database page that Order X is on. Then, when you fetch Order X, you also have all of Order X's Line Items with the same physical I/O or all clustered together on their own database page (assuming that they could all fit on one database page).

Scenario 2 is similar to scenario 1, except you enter the database at Product and then traverse to Line Item. You can place an index on a Product data item to reduce the number of physical I/Os to fetch a given Product occurrence from 2 (assuming the same blocking factor of 50 Product occurrences per physical database page) to 2 or 3—no savings and a potential deficit.

You can also cluster Line Item around Product. If you assume an average of 50 Line Item instances per Product instance (10,000 divided by 200), you should be able to fetch all of a Product's Line Item occurrences with the same physical I/O.

However, while both Order and Product can be indexed, Line Item occurrences can be stored around only one record. The designer must choose to cluster Line Item around Order or around Product—clustering around both is not possible. Which do you choose?

These are the five critical questions:

1. Should Order be indexed?
2. Should Product be indexed?
3. Should Line Item be indexed?
4. Should Line Item be clustered?
5. If so, clustered around Order or Product?

To answer these questions, you need to collect all the facts and assumptions.

Number of Order occurrences: 1,000

Order occurrence size (bytes): 200

Number of Product occurrences: 200

Product occurrence size (bytes): 400

Number of Line Item occurrences: 10,000

Line Item occurrence size (bytes): 100

Database page size of 5,000 bytes

Number of scenario 1 transactions (executions) per day: 2,000

Number of scenario 2 transactions (executions) per day: 200

Question 1: Should Order Be Indexed?

Twenty-five Order records can fit on a database page (ignoring database page overhead), which translates into 40 database pages. (This assumes that the page is dedicated to storing Order records and that page free-space and expansion space are ignored.) Therefore, it takes, on average, 20 physical I/Os to sequentially fetch the desired Order record.

Formula (5) says that it takes, on average, 2.15 physical I/Os to fetch the desired record address from an index (assuming that the index page is the same size as the database page). Adding an additional I/O to fetch the actual (content) record totals 3.15 physical I/Os.

Therefore, other things being equal, it is more efficient (3.15 versus 20 physical I/Os) to fetch an Order using an index.

Question 2: Should Product Be Indexed?

Twelve Product records can fit on a database page (the caveats are the same as for the Order case), meaning that all the Product records can fit on 17 database pages. Fetching a Product record sequentially requires, on average, 9 physical I/Os.

Formula (5) says that fetching the Product index entry requires, on average, 2.13 physical I/Os. Adding one physical I/O to read the content results in an average of 3.13 physical I/Os per fetch. Three plus physical I/Os is certainly better than 9, but the benefit is minimal.

Question 3: Should Line Item Be Indexed?

Fifty Line Item records fit on a database page, taking up a total of 200 database pages. A sequential read of the database to find a specific Line Item record requires, on average, 100 physical I/Os.

An index on Line Item requires 2.35 index physical I/Os to fetch the record address and one additional I/O for content, totaling 3.35 physical I/Os per Line Item record. It makes sense to index Line Item.

Question 4: Should Line Item Be Clustered?

This is a nonmathematical question whose answer is dictated by the structure of the database and the usage scenarios. Because both scenarios move from fetching a parent to the Line Item child, it would seem that there could be significant benefit from clustering.

Question 5: Should Line Item Be Clustered Around Order or Product?

To answer this question, you need to examine two alternatives.

For alternative 1, you need to calculate the total daily physical I/Os consumed by scenario 1 and scenario 2 if Line Item is clustered around Order.

Alternative 2 calculates the total physical I/Os consumed by each scenario in a day if Line Item is clustered around Product.

Alternative 1: Line Item Clustered Around Order

Scenario 1 says fetch 1 Order record and then, on average, 10 Line Item records and do this entire process 2,000 times a day.

The physical I/O to fetch the Order record is 3.15 (from question 1).

The physical I/O to fetch the Line Items depends on the DBMS and how you chose to store/access them. If you stored Line Items in their own file and on their own pages and used an index to access them, then you could fetch all 10 Line Items with an additional 3.35 physical I/Os. Because all 10 records are on the same page, you need to read the Line Item index only once to fetch all 10.

The *total scenario 1 daily physical I/O count* is 6.5 physical I/Os per transaction times 2,000 transactions per day, equaling 13,000 physical I/Os.

Scenario 2 says fetch one Product record and then, on average, 50 Line Item records and do this entire process 200 times a day.

If Line Item is clustered around Order, then it cannot be clustered around Product. Physical I/Os to fetch one Product record are 3.13. Total physical I/Os to fetch 50 Line Items (3.35 times 50) are 167.5.

The *total scenario 2 daily physical I/O count* equals 170.63 times 200, which is 34,126 physical I/Os.

The total alternative 1 daily physical I/O count is 47,126.

Alternative Two: Line Item Clustered Around Product

Scenario 1 says fetch 1 Order record and then, on average, 10 Line Item records and do this entire process 2,000 times a day.

The physical I/O to fetch the Order record is 3.15 (from question 1).

If Line Item is clustered around Product, then it cannot be clustered around Order. From question 3, you know that it takes, on average, 3.35 physical I/Os to fetch 1 Line Item record or 33.5 physical I/Os to fetch 10.

The *total scenario 1 daily physical I/O count* is 36.5 physical I/Os per transaction times 2,000 transactions per day, equaling 73,300 physical I/Os.

Scenario 2 says fetch 1 Product record and then, on average, 50 Line Item records, and do this entire process 200 times a day.

The physical I/Os to fetch 1 Product record are 3.13.

Each Product record has an average cluster size of 50 Line Item records. The total physical I/Os to fetch 1 Line Item is 3.35 for a transaction (execution) total of 6.48 physical I/Os.

The total scenario 2 daily physical I/O count at 200 times a day times 6.48 is 1,296 physical I/Os.

The total alternative 2 daily physical I/O count is 74,596.

Comparing the two alternatives, clustering Line Item around Order saves more than 27,000 physical I/Os a day—a reduction of almost 40 percent.

IT DOESN'T HAVE TO BE ACCURATE, IT JUST HAS TO BE DIRECTIONALLY CORRECT

Any approach to calculating physical I/Os will run into difficulties. Many a DBA has been surprised when the DBMS statistics-gathering function reports that a record fetch took 5 physical I/Os while the operating systems indicated that there were 25. What's happening?

Any effort to accurately calculate physical I/Os is problematic. The statistics gathered by the DBA probably will not agree with those gathered by the operating system support staff, which will probably disagree with any given by the secondary storage subunit, which will almost certainly be greater than those predicted by the database designer. The problem is that the various components needed to perform an application-driven I/O need to do their own I/O as well to support the application. Many of these additional I/Os are under-reported or not reported at all to the DBMS. The CPU, which once managed all disk activity, now hands the task over to a secondary storage subsystem that does something the CPU is unaware of but that often involves the subsystem's own I/O. The DBMS gets some information from the operating system; however, the operating system always seems to have a few tasks of its own that require I/O. And then there are the statistics-gathering systems. The operating system has them, the DBMS has them, the secondary storage systems have them, the transaction processing monitor has them—all that data gathering involves I/Os—lots of them.

So, where does that leave the database designer and the DBA? Why perform these physical I/O-counting exercises when the number could be off by an order of magnitude or more? The answer is, although the designer-generated number might under-report the actual I/O count, it is almost always directionally correct. Given two situations, with two different predictions, the higher count forecast will almost always require more I/Os than the lower one. The actual number might be low, but the direction the forecast indicates (greater or lesser) will almost always be correct. The database designer might get the actual count wrong, but the conclusions drawn from the analysis, and the associated decisions made based on that information, are almost always correct.

The takeaway from all of this: *it doesn't have to be accurate; it just has to be directionally correct!*

The previous example examined only a single approach to storing and clustering records in a database. Had the DBMS stored different record types on the same page (a default with most systems), then the counts would have been different. A single record type would have been spread across more database pages than predicted, increasing the cost of a sequential read.

On the other hand, multiple record type page storage allows the Line Item records to be stored on the same physical page as their parent (Order or Product), reducing I/O, but this approach also increases the chance of page overflow resulting in not all clusters fitting on a single page.

The calculations are not different, although there might be a few more of them. The principle, however, remains unchanged.

Partitioning

Partitioning is deciding where to locate database files on disk to reduce disk contention. For example, database inserts, updates, and deletes require writing to the database journals and log files. If there are sufficient updates, the journals or log files can become bottlenecks. A simple solution is to place the journals and log files on separate disks from the database content files. This allows the different disk seek and rotational delay times to overlap.

Database content can also be partitioned. By looking at the use of the database, the designer can locate different record types in different files or even the same record type spread across multiple files partitioned by a data item value.

Partitioning can also be used in conjunction with clustering. The database designer can cluster Line Item around Order while storing each in a different partition. Partition 1 might contain all Orders while Partition 2 all Line Items. The trick is that all the Line Items for a particular Order are stored together, ideally on a single database page, in Partition 2.

For most systems, partitions are a DDL matter and not a DML one, making them totally transparent to the application program. Partitioning works particularly well when customizing hardware. The database designer can create a partition on an SSD for the most frequently accessed record occurrences while less frequently accessed occurrences are on slower media. Partitions also are useful when the database is spread across multiple servers, allowing each server to support its own backup and recovery. Independent backup and recovery is particularly useful when the volume of data is quite large.

Both partitioning and clustering information can be displayed on the physical database design diagram (Figure 13-7).

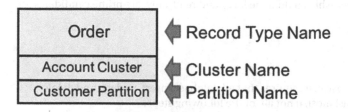

Figure 13-7. *Clustering and partitioning information on the enhanced database diagram*

Derived and Duplicate Data

In logical data modeling, only primitive data are modeled. Derived data are excluded because they are the result of one or more processes acting on primitive data. For example, there is no need to model the total number of courses a student has taken if you have all the courses the student has taken in the database. The application can simply count them.

However, you might want to include a TOTAL COURSES TAKEN data item in the Student record if (1) it would require excessive physical I/Os to calculate the number of courses or (2) the calculated data are often required. The database designer could decide that, for performance reasons, it makes sense to store this derived data.

There might be similar reasons to store duplicate data. Adding a few redundant data items into different record types can reduce physical I/Os and speed up processing.

WORD SOUP

Some authors make a distinction between data duplication and data redundancy. Duplicate data are always a no-no, while redundant data are permissible duplicate data. Other authors think it's a case of toMAto-TOmato.

The argument against duplicate data is the mess that can occur if not all copies of the data are updated simultaneously. However, duplication is perfect for read-only databases. Duplicate data are a favorite of many NoSQL systems, which sprinkle popular data items around the database to reduce physical I/O.

Denormalization

Denormalization is another favorite of NoSQL database systems, which like to cram a lot of data into a single record occurrence. They also like to add group data and repeating groups back into the parent record. If few customers have more than one address, then it might make sense to place the primary address in the customer record.

The purpose of normalization is to protect the database from ill-conceived inserts, updates, and deletes. However, if the database is read-only, then normalization is not needed. Data warehouses, which tend to be large and read-only, are prime candidates for denormalization.

Get Rid of ACID

ACID (Chapter 8) is expensive. It requires that all database insert, update, and delete transactions follow at least most, if not all, of the following steps:

1. The data to be changed (and sometimes even the data stored around it on the same database page or file) must be locked so that others cannot access them while the change is occurring.

2. An image of the existing data (before image) is written (involving one or more disk writes) to a journal file before the data are changed, and another image of the data (after image) is saved (one or more disk writes) to a journal file after the change.

3. All the transaction steps taken are recorded to a separate log file (one or more disk writes).

4. All the writes are *flushed* to ensure that all the changes are physically on the disk and not stored in some buffer awaiting transfer to disk.

Updating a single database record occurrence could involve more than a dozen physical disk writes (not logical writes) before the actual record occurrence update is completed. In terms of resource utilization, a database update could require 10 or more times the resources of a simple database read.

Eliminating or reducing one or more of these steps can significantly speed up a database transaction and, if all goes well, nothing is lost. This is how many of the NoSQL systems obtain their speed. By not getting into locking, journaling, and logging the update, the speed of a transaction can be increased tenfold.

If you can live with the proclivities and vagaries of the non-ACID world, then you can, if your DBMS allows, turn off the ACID functions to improve performance at the cost of guaranteed data integrity.

Figure 13-8 is a completed Enhanced database design diagram showing clustering and partitioning.

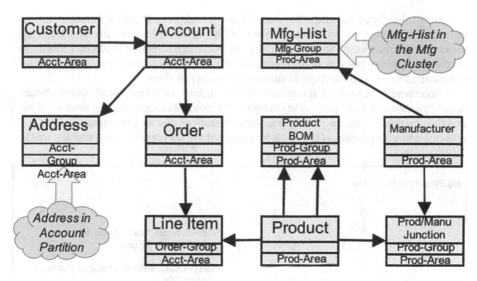

Figure 13-8. *Physical database design diagram showing clusters and partition information*

Ideally, applying the techniques presented in this chapter should allow your general-purpose DBMS (SQL Server, IMS, Oracle, MySQL, etc.) to accommodate your productivity requirements. Unfortunately, there are times when the standard DBMS, no matter how you configure it, cannot handle the required load. For example, Big Data, the reams of information generated by automated systems, are often more than the traditional DBMS can handle. How big is big? There are no specific or even agreed-upon answers, but a useful rule of thumb is that the delineator between traditional data and Big Data is the practical storage and processing limits for traditional information managers. For Big Data, you might have to use a specialty or niche DBMS, such as one of the NoSQL products.

Big Data, Big Problems, Big Solution

Big Data is one of the latest technologies to unsettle IT. Organization after organization is in a quandary, trying to figure out what to do about the large volumes of data streaming in from a myriad sources. For example, a supermarket or chain store might record every customer transaction, resulting in a database that could grow to petabytes in size.

How big is Big Data? Nobody knows—or everybody knows but nobody agrees. Does "big" refer to the number of records in a database or to the number of data items in a record or to the number of bytes that need to be stored? Perhaps it refers to the amount of data that must be processed in a certain period of time or the number of users that need to access it? If you read the literature, you discover that the answer is, yes—which, in a entanglement of twisted logic, is also the same as saying no. For convenience, if nothing else, Big Data is usually classified by the number of bytes that need to be stored *and* accessed.

How many bytes constitute Big Data? Gigabytes might be Big Data. Petabytes are most assuredly Big Data, and exabytes are very big Big Data. However, the label is not only inexact, it is unnecessary. Storing such large amounts of data is easy if you can afford the hardware—you can place as many records in a flat file as you want although the file might consume miles of magnetic tape or span hundreds of disk drives.

Accessing the data to use it is another matter entirely. Most traditional DBMSs should handle gigabytes of data, they might struggle to the point of collapse with terabytes of data, and they might drop dead on the floor faced with exabytes of data. Processing Big Data presents some big problems (Figure 13-9). Luckily, there is a big solution available: NoSQL.

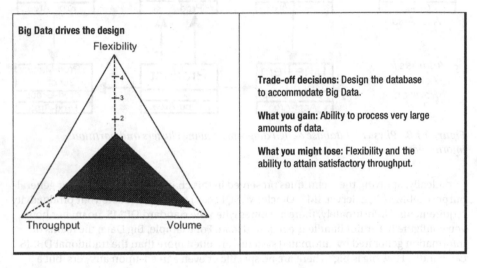

Figure 13-9. Trade-off triangle—accommodating Big Data

To Plunge or Not to Plunge

Before diving into a Big Data solution, the IT organization needs to be comfortable that the plunge is necessary. Big Data can sometimes be handled by traditional data managers such as Oracle and DB2. If not, then there are number of nontraditional solutions that specifically target Big Data. However, choosing to use these tools is a big decision that should not be taken lightly. Table 13-6 presents a good guideline to follow: *use a nontraditional solution only if you absolutely have to.*

Table 13-6. Technology Escalation Rules

---

1.   If the application can be adequately managed by a traditional data manager (e.g., RDBMS), then use a traditional data manager.

2.   If, and only if, a traditional data manager cannot adequately manage the application's throughput or volume requirements, then look to nontraditional solutions (e.g., NoSQL).

278

Why choose a traditional system over a nontraditional one? Reasons include

- The pool of staff experienced with traditional DBMSs is considerably larger than the pool of staff experienced with nontraditional DBMSs.

- The availability of traditional DBMS training, documentation, consulting help, and support tools greatly exceeds that for the nontraditional DBMSs.

- Most IT organizations that support a nontraditional DBMS also support at least one traditional DBMS, often requiring duplicate staff expertise, procedures, training, development, test, and maintenance environments.

- Nontraditional DBMSs—being newer than traditional DBMSs— will likely undergo a greater rate of change (features, syntax, maintenance fixes, etc.) than traditional systems, resulting in greater instability and support costs.

However, circumstances often dictate the direction you must take, and a nontraditional DBMS, such as NoSQL, might be the only practical solution to an application problem.

NoSQL

NoSQL is not so much data architecture as a collection of data architectures tuned to solve a single problem, or at most just a few.

NoSQL products are categorized by some authors as schema-less, meaning that there is no formal schema like you might find with a traditional DBMS. Although the statement is technically not true, it does capture an important characteristic of NoSQL systems. You could describe NOSQL as a series of stand-alone subschemas. This observation is driven by two common NoSQL features—its usage-driven nature and its single record type structure.

First, NoSQL systems place significantly more emphasis on data usage than traditional data management systems. In fact, usage is the primary driver of database design. Data structures, such as records, attributes, clusters, and partitions, are primarily determined by how data is accessed rather than its definition.

Second, a goal of a NoSQL database design is to have each usage scenario supported by a single NoSQL record type. Denormalization, specifically cramming all the user-required data into a single NoSQL record, is what gives NoSQL its speed and traditional DBA weltschmerz. A single NoSQL record might contain multiple occurrences of multiple entities. The resulting NoSQL *fat record* can then be accessed with a single I/O.

Cassandra is an open source NoSQL DBMS originally developed by Facebook and now maintained by the Apache Software Foundation. Some authors refer to Cassandra as a key-value architecture, others as a wide-column architecture, and still others as a partitioned-row store. Actually it is all of these. As with many NoSQL products, it is an assemblage of numerous, sometimes diverse, features. For example, key-value is how Cassandra stores data fields, while wide-column architecture describes how records are constructed.

Cassandra's essential features include

- *Clustering*: The Cassandra partition is a multiple-record type, multiple-record occurrence, basic unit of storage, allowing the retrieval of multiple record types and occurrences with the same physical I/O (the NoSQL fat record).

- *Hashing*: All Cassandra partitions are automatically stored based on a hash of all or part of the partition's primary key, providing fast storage and retrieval, ideally with a single physical I/O.

- *Aggregation*: Both group and multivalue attributes are supported and heavily used.

In the previous section it was mentioned that when using a traditional DBMS, the designer can improve performance by turning off ACID features. Well, Cassandra does that for you. Cassandra adds to its lightning speed by not having to lock records and journal activity.

While Cassandra is not ACID compliant (though it does optionally support some ACID features), it does, like a number of NoSQL products, go half the distance. Cassandra is BASE compliant (Chapter 8), which means it may provide these steps but not in real time. They might write to a journal file but not before the transaction is declared complete. If the system goes down a minute of two after the transaction is "complete," then you are probably safe. If it goes down a half-second after the transaction is declared complete, well, who knows. Cassandra even calls it "eventual consistency," reflecting its policy of "we'll get there when we get there."

Modeling Big Data U3D Style

In Cassandra, the basic unit of storage is called a *partition*, or a *column family*. (Cassandra, it seems, has at least two names for everything.) The partition is stored by hashing the partition key, which makes up all or part of the primary key. All access to the partition is by the hash value derived from its partition key—no indices needed. Within the partition there can be multiple rows that can be stored in a particular order according to a clustering column or clustering key (the second part of the primary key).

Take the following usage scenario:

> *Usage Scenario: 7 Name: Produce Active Employee Roster by Department*
>
> *Processing type: Query Frequency: Upon Request*
>
> *7.1 Enter Department, for all occurrences (75 occurrences)*
>
> *7.2 Find Employee occurrences where Employee STATUS = "Active"*
>
> *(2,000 occurrences)*

Cassandra has a stated goal of maintaining only one table per query (usage scenario). Figure 13-10 shows how the two traditional record types supporting Usage Scenario 7, Produce Active Employee Roster by Department, are stored as a single Cassandra partition.

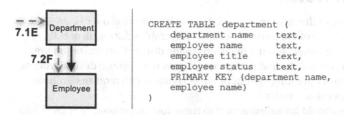

```
CREATE TABLE department (
    department name     text,
    employee name       text,
    employee title      text,
    employee status     text,
    PRIMARY KEY (department name,
    employee name)
)
```

Figure 13-10. Creating a Cassandra petition

The DDL code in Figure 13-10 sets up a partition called department with the partitioning (hashing) key department_name. Within the partition, rows of employee information are sorted by the cluster key or cluster column, employee_name, in employee_name order (giving Cassandra its wide-column designation). Think of a parent-child relationship with the partition as the parent and the rows as its children.

Cassandra also supports aggregation (Table 13-7), which is used to store a limited number repeating items.

Table 13-7. Cassandra-Supported Aggregation

Group Attribute	Multivalue Attribute

CREATE TYPE address (
    // a user defined data type
   street   text,
   town   text,
   state_province text,
   postal_code   int
 );
	CREATE TABLE customers (
	   customer_id int PRIMARY KEY,
	   first_name text,
	   last_name text,
	   phone_number set <text>
	   /* repeating group for
	     multiple phone numbers */
	);

The only way NoSQL can support each usage scenario with a single partition is with large amounts of data duplication and denormalization. (A note on Cassandra replication and duplication terminology: Replication is storing a partition in more than one node [server]. The database designer has the option to store each partition on one, two, or up to all servers in the server cluster. Duplication is storing the same data items multiple times within a partition or across multiple partitions.)

By capitalizing on the partition/row architecture, its use of aggregation and hashing, fueled by a liberal use of data duplication and denormalization, Cassandra could conceivably retrieve an account, all of its orders, and all of their line items (the unceremonious NoSQL *fat record*), with one physical I/O.

The features found in Cassandra are not unique to Cassandra. Other NoSQL systems support similar concepts providing similar results.

Customization Notes

Customization notes is one of the most important deliverables coming out of step 4, Customization. In fact, it's one of the most important deliverables during all of U3D. The reason is that the issues raised and the decisions made during Customization are some of the most volatile, debatable, and controversial ones of the entire design process. Hardware changes, or a new operating system or DBMS release, can require significant database updates on rather short notice.

Customization notes should include answers to these four questions:

- *Why?* If an index was added, or removed, it is important to document it. Equally important are the reasons for decisions surrounding changes that were discussed but not made and why they were not made.

- *Where?* The notes should reflect exactly where in the database design any new concepts were introduced or existing ones changed.

- *When?* Design changes and test results do not always align. Comparing test results with an incorrect state of the design can prove disastrous.

- *Results?* Document all results: the good, the bad, and the ugly. There are times when the bad and the ugly are more useful to future designers and DBAs than the successes. A report of a misapplied index or partition can save a successor from making the same mistake.

The designer or DBA will be well served with a robust set of customization notes.

Deliverables

Step 4, Customization, should produce the following deliverables:

4.1: Enhanced database design diagram: The final physical database design diagram (Figure 13-11 in the next sections shows an EPDDD for a traditional data manager)

4.2: Enhanced schema (DDL): Performance enhanced version of the schema created in step, 3 Formalization

4.3: Enhanced Subschemas (DDL): Performance-enhanced version of the schemas created in step 3, Formalization

4.4: Enhanced database object definitions: Update of all database object definitions to reflect step 4, Customization, changes (Figures 13-12, 13-13, and 13-14)

4.5: Customization notes: A narrative or journal created by the database designer of the activities, issues, and decisions made during step 4, Customization

Examples of Deliverables

Figure 13-11 shows the Enhanced database design diagram.

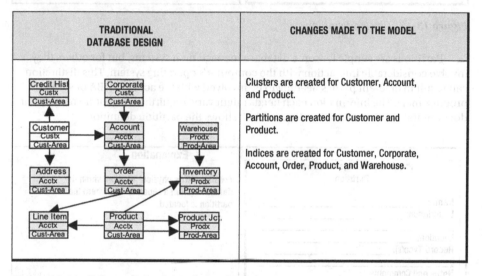

Figure 13-11. Enhanced database design diagram

All clusters need to be documented, including the reasoning for having them. Figure 13-12 shows the cluster definition.

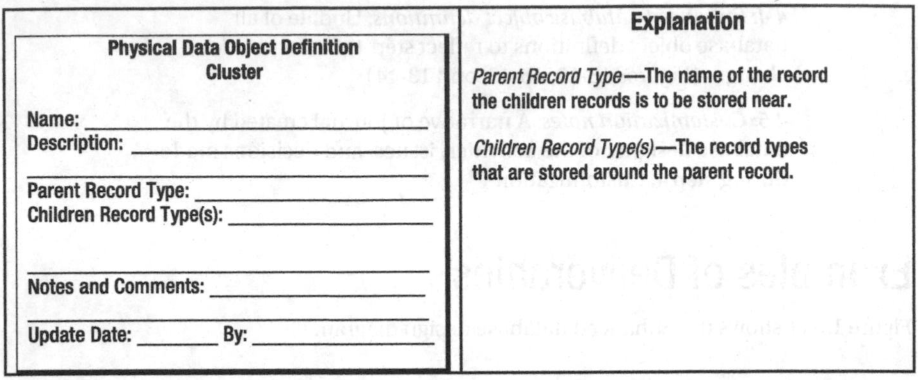

Physical Data Object Definition Cluster	Explanation
Name: _____ Description: _____ _____ Parent Record Type: _____ Children Record Type(s): _____ Notes and Comments: _____ _____ Update Date: _____ By: _____	*Parent Record Type*—The name of the record the children records is to be stored near. *Children Record Type(s)*—The record types that are stored around the parent record.

Figure 13-12. *Cluster definition*

Partitions are simple for some database management systems, but for others they involve considerable interaction with the computer's operating system. This distinction can result in different parties needing to be involved with the activity (DBA or system programmer). The information each needs might vary, requiring the capture of different documentation for partitioning. Figure 13-13 shows the partition definition.

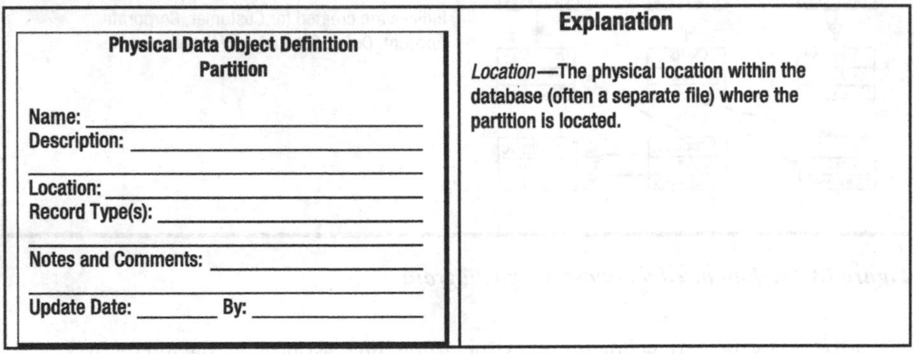

Physical Data Object Definition Partition	Explanation
Name: _____ Description: _____ _____ Location: _____ Record Type(s): _____ _____ Notes and Comments: _____ _____ Update Date: _____ By: _____	*Location*—The physical location within the database (often a separate file) where the partition is located.

Figure 13-13. *Partition definition*

Most databases contain a considerable number of indices, with the index count easily eclipsing the number of record types, even more so for relational databases. Having accurate information about each index is critical for good database maintenance. Figure 13-14 shows the index definition.

Index Data Object Definition	Explanation
Index Data Object Definition **Index** Name: _____ Description: _____ _____ Type: (ISAM, B-tree, Hash, Bitmap, etc.) _____ Data Item(s) (in proper order): _____ Record Type: _____ Location: _____ Notes and Comments: _____ _____ Update Date: _____ By: _____	**Explanation** *Type*—The index variety. Note, some database management systems classify hashing as an index. *Data Items*—If the index consists of more than one data item, then the data items need to be listed in the same order as in the database. *Location*—The physical location within the database (often aseparate file) where indices are located.

Figure 13-14. Index definition

*   *   *   *   *

"No battle plan survives contact with the enemy," said Prussian Chief of Staff General Helmuth von Moltke. A more modern version of his quote might be that the best battle plan is useless once the first shot is fired. A database design is questionable as soon as the database is put into production unless it is monitored and tuned starting on day 1. Considerable time and expense goes into database design; however, the cost of keeping a live, breathing database functioning to specification is often an undervalued, underfunded, and underperformed task. However, both the database and its documentation need to be monitored and kept up to date if the database is to be successful. If the database designer follows the steps laid out in U3D, then the difficult task of maintenance should be easier and, more important, the efficacy of the database that much greater.

CHAPTER 14

■ ■ ■

The Data Warehouse

*The fewer data needed, the better the information. And an overload of
information...leads to information blackout.*

—Peter F. Drucker

*It is not the facts that we can put our fingers on that concern us but the
sum of these facts; it is not the data we want but the essence of the data.*

—John Cheever

Over its nearly 50-year history, the decision support system (DSS) has assumed various
names encapsulating sometimes identical, sometimes unique, components and features;
however, the fundamentals remain essentially the same. The basic DSS includes (1) a
user interface or front end, often bristling with analytical and mathematical capabilities,
and (2) a storage system, or back end, to house the data the user interface analyzes
(Table 14-1).

Table 14-1. *The Basic Decision Support System*

Front-End Analytical User Interface	Back-End Database
Business intelligence (BI)	Data warehouse
Predictive analytics	Data mart
Business analytics	Knowledge base
Dashboard	Information base
Online analytical processing (OLAP)	Multidimensional database
Data mining	Data cube
	Information repository

Regardless of the fancy charts and graphics it produces and the clever gimmicks it
embraces, a DSS is a system that provides management and certain subject experts with
the capability to dig deep into the voluminous data created by the operational systems to
uncover the trends and patterns they, not so obviously, contain. The job of the database
designer is to create the storage system, most commonly called a *data warehouse*, to
support these varied analytical-user interfaces. This chapter focuses on the design and
construction of the data warehouse.

© George Tillmann 2017
G. Tillmann, *Usage-Driven Database Design*, DOI 10.1007/978-1-4842-2722-0_14

The Data Warehouse

Early database designers had a problem. Their major success—transaction processing—allowed the database to be *the* record-keeper of business events, documenting each and every important business interaction. Reports of those transactions provided line supervisors with timely and accurate detailed information about enterprise activity for that day, week, month, or year.

Senior management staff now wanted to get in on it, but the information they wanted was often not what the transaction systems provided. There were two fundamental problems. First, transaction-based applications provide line managers with standard, predefined reports at predetermined times. Senior management was looking for...well, they didn't know what they were looking for—that was the problem. Rather, they wanted to interrogate the system with questions that might have been formulated just moments before and were based on the answers to previous questions.

Second, query-based software made management requests possible but not necessarily practical. Remember those old-time movies of the state prison the night of an electrocution? Everybody was looking at the clock as it approached midnight when suddenly the lights dimmed and all knew that the switch was thrown on the condemned inmate. Well, the same thing happened when management started querying the production database. The lights might not have dimmed, but transaction processing response time tanked.

In spite of what you might have read, the first impetus to create a separate database for management information was not some intellectual *coup de maître* or epochal academic paper, but rather the complaints of frontline managers who saw their transaction systems grind to a halt. The solution was to dedicate a separate database, ideally on a separate machine, to house I/O-hungry DSS queries. The moaning of transaction supervisors was fortuitous because it provided the opportunity not only to copy the production database but to change its design to better support this new mission.

The modern data warehouse is a repository of information for the purpose of answering unstructured and unscheduled queries (Table 14-2). These DSS queries can require sifting through hundreds, thousands, or even millions of records, and summarizing a result that is, sometimes, a one-line answer. Think of the iPhone's Siri answering the question, "Where is the closest Italian restaurant?" The phone might have to sift through dozens and dozens of records to find the answer, which is then delivered in ten words or fewer.

Table 14-2. *Difference Between Transaction Processing and Decision Support Systems*

	Transaction Processing System	Decision Support System
Mission	Recordkeeping, documenting business activity	Support management decision making
Type	Single event	Multiple related events
Purpose	Record an event	Uncover a trend
User	Clerk, line supervisor	Senior management, subject specialist
Reporting	Standardized at fixed moments in time	Variable over different time periods
DBMS	Process focused	Subject focused
DBMS Output	90% detail, 10% summary	10% detail, 90% summary

The data warehouse cartel took off like a Texan at a handgun convention. Suddenly there were specialized databases, specialized software, specialized consultants, and specialized academic departments. All of these resources were dedicated to stuffing all those arcane management and statistical formulas, which had been sitting unused on college shelves for decades, into a new IT endeavor. Business was good even if success was chimeral.

The threat to the data warehouse's success was the data—often millions of records that DBAs had no idea what to do with. The solution: summarization. Early data warehouse designers spent considerable time on summarization and consolidation, trying to pare the data mountain down to a manageable molehill. The problem was, exactly how do you do that? How do you consolidate a million nit-level transactions into the couple thousand proxies your computer, database, and query language could handle without misrepresenting the detail?

Consolidation can unintentionally skew the answer to those heady management questions. It would help if designers knew the questions that were going to be asked, but that was difficult because *ad hoc* queries have a nasty tendency to be, well, *ad hoc*. Database designers had little to go on in determining how exactly to summarize the data. The details of summarizing became a central issue of data warehouse design.

CONSOLIDATION VERSUS MISREPRESENTATION?

Consolidation (summarization) assigns a record to a summary bin where certain detail fields are counted or aggregated. The problem is that unless its eventual use is known, the designer has no idea how many bins there should be or how detail data should be assigned to them. For example, if there are one million Line Items, should there be five bins for cost (less than $10, $10 to $39.99, $40 to $99.99, $100 or greater) or a thousand bins each representing a $1 increment?

The fewer bins there are, the better the performance but at an increased risk of biasing query results. Too many bins and performance suffers. Assign detail to the wrong bin and the results are questionable.

Technology came to the rescue just in time for *Big Data*. New cheap hardware made much of the worry about summarization superfluous because why summarize? The warehouse could now handle the terabytes or petabytes or, heaven forbid, exabytes of data that production systems could spew out. This does not mean that rigorous consolidation is not useful and cost effective, just that there is now a hardware backstop in case accurate summarization is not possible.

Now that the volume problem could be *corralled*, if not necessarily tamed, database designers could move on to the next problem: how do you design a database for a data warehouse? Luckily, there is no shortage of answers; unluckily, most of them are questionable. The best way to design a database for a data warehouse is to do the same thing you do to design a database for any other application—use U3D.

Start at the beginning. Your garden-variety database is designed to support one or more mega-processes. A payroll database supports the mega-process payroll (which might include dozens of normal-sized processes), an order entry database supports the order entry mega-process, and an inventory database supports the inventory uber-process. The common word here is *process*. As was presented in Chapter 11, as much as you might like to think that databases are independent of applications, they are, in fact, still tied to them.

Data warehouses, on the other hand, are not usually designed to support a process but rather a subject. The subject might be products, or it might be customers, or even distributors. The typical application supports one mega-process (e.g., payroll), while the subject data it uses (employee, project, etc.) might be spread across multiple databases (supporting other applications). The data warehouse inverts this structure. The warehouse contains all the data on a particular subject (employee) that might be used by multiple applications (payroll, project planning, benefits, general ledger).

Data Warehouse Architecture

If you look at successful decision support systems (there are a few), you will notice that the data warehouse database design looks nothing like its operational cousin. The most common data architecture is the star schema—a single fact record surrounded by multiple dimension records forming a star pattern (Figure 14-1). The fact record type sits in the middle of the schema at the many end of a number of one-to-many relationships. The dimension records are used to query the fact record.

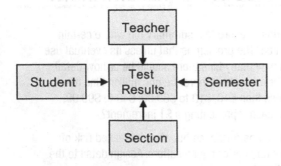

Figure 14-1. Star schema

For example, using Figure 14-1, if you want to know exam results by teacher, you would enter the database at Teacher, find the Teacher occurrence(s) you want, and then follow the link to all the Test Results occurrences for that Teacher. It is a two-step process: (1) select the dimension record for the search criteria and then (2) follow the links to the fact records where the desired data are stored.

If the dimensions are linked to record types other than the fact record, the structure is then called a *snowflake schema*. Although a bit more complicated, it works using the same two-step process as with the star schema.

The challenge for the designer is to identify the fact record. A common immediate reaction is to think that the fact record is the subject record type (Product, Employee, Student, etc.), but, as in the example, that is often not the case. If one were forced to pick the most likely candidate for a fact record in an operational database, it would most likely be the record type with the most occurrences and/or the record type at the many end of the most one-to-many links.

In reality, this is not always true either. The best fact record is often constructed from multiple record types, often denormalizing what was normalized when creating the operational database.

Using U3D to Develop a Data Warehouse

The steps to create a data warehouse are no different from those to create an operational database. U3D works for all database design, regardless of use. The following demonstrates how the same four U3D steps can help the database designer create a successful data warehouse design.

Step 1: Transformation

As with any database, the first step in creating a data warehouse is converting, or transforming, any subject-related logical data models into a physical data model. Figure 14-2 consists of two logical data model fragments showing the Product entity and its entity neighbors.

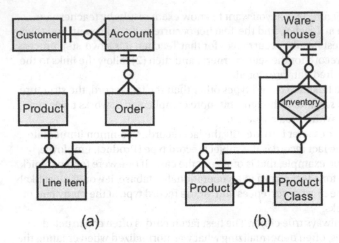

Figure 14-2. *Order management system and warehouse system logical data model fragments*

The only aspects of step 1 unique to developing a warehouse are finding all the logical data models for all the applications that deal with the data warehouse subject. If the designers want to create a product data warehouse, then they should look for all the logical data models for any application that involves products. Put them all together, and you have a physical data model for the warehouse subject.

Step 2: Utilization

In step 2, Utilization, the major differences between operational and warehouse databases first show up. The way the data were used in the order entry system and all the other applications will not be the way they will be used in the data warehouse. The database designer needs to rethink the usage by developing new data warehouse–specific usage scenarios.

Although it is a fundamental part of the data warehouse catechism that users do not know how they will use the warehouse, it is, in fact, not entirely true. If business executives did not have some idea of what they would do with the data warehouse, they would never have come up the money to pay for one. Data warehouses start at $100,000, and many add one or two zeroes before they are done. No business will fund a data warehouse unless it has a good idea of what it will use it for even if specifics are elusive. The designer should talk to the managers who will be using or feel they will be benefitting from the warehouse to get some idea of what they have planned. Often a decision support or business intelligence vendor is standing somewhere behind the user (contract in hand) that can help the designer understand how others have used similar systems. In any event, the data warehouse designer should develop several likely scenarios describing how the warehouse will be used, at least initially.

ONE QUESTION PER WAREHOUSE?

I once met a successful and well-known DSS designer for a major international bank. He believed that every DSS and data warehouse was designed to answer only one question. Any other uses were either serendipitous or erroneous.

While it is doubtful he was correct, nonetheless that 25-year-old exchange is remembered for a reason. Experience has shown that behind every DSS is one, two, or a few important questions its owners want answered. The data warehouse designer just has to uncover them.

The product warehouse might include the following scenarios:

Usage Scenario 101: What is the average size of an order?

101.1 Enter Order

101.2 Find Line Item

Usage Scenario 102: Which customers, consumer or wholesale, generate most of the business?

102.1 Enter Customer

102.2 Find Account

102.3 Find Order

102.4 Find Line Item

Usage Scenario 103: Which products are the best sellers?

103.1 Enter Product

103.2 Find Line Item

Usage Scenario 104: Who is the most important manufacturer?

104.1 Enter Manufacturer

104.2 Find Line Item

A few things should become obvious. First, each scenario ends with the Line Item record. Second, other records are accessed at the beginning of the scenario and are used to select a subset of Line Items.

This is the basic structure of a warehouse. The center is a single (often voluminous) record type called a *fact record*, and the other record types, used to group the Line Items into desirable cohorts, are called *dimensions*. A data warehouse consists of a (usually) single *fact record type* surrounded by numerous *dimensional record types*. In most cases, each dimension is attached to a fact record in a one-to-many linkage (one dimension to many facts). It is, in most cases, the only link tied to a dimension. The fact record type, on the other hand, looks like a pincushion, with links to multiple dimensions.

The Rationalized physical data model in Figure 14-3 is not a star but a snowflake (because the Customer and Account records are linked to the Order dimension), although "spiderweb" would be a more accurate though less majestic name.

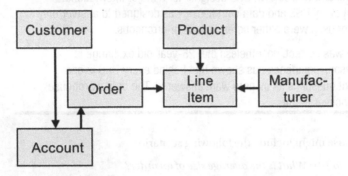

Figure 14-3. *Rationalized physical data model*

The snowflake moniker is used to reflect more complex structures than the simpler star. However, many designers work to reduce the snowflake to a star, allowing an easier link between fact and dimension. If the warehouse uses a relational DBMS, a star would require only a simple join to answer queries.

Key to data warehouse success is figuring out which record type is the fact record and which are the dimensions. These are a few simple rules of thumb to help:

- The most populace or detailed record type is a good candidate for the fact record.

- The fact record is often, although not always, an attributive or associative record.

- The fact record is often the one with the most links to other record types, usually one-to-many, with the "many" end attached to the fact record.

The Time Dimension

Almost every dimension should come from the physical data model, with a few exceptions. Virtually every data warehouse requires a time dimension—a way to provide a time slice of the information in the fact record.

The database designer needs to consult with the warehouse users and business analysts to determine exactly what time slices are needed and their granularity. For example, a retail organization needs to know not only date but the day of the week, holidays, and more. If is often more important for a retail organization to compare sales figures for the first Monday of June this year with the first Monday of June last year, regardless of the date of each Monday. Comparing June 4 this year with June 4 last year is useless if this year it's a Monday but last year it was a Sunday.

Also important is granularity. The time dimension needs a record occurrence for each time slice. If the time granularity (lowest level) of data for a warehouse is monthly, then storing 10 years of data requires only 120 time records. Weekly granularity requires approximately 520 time records, daily 3,650 time records (ignoring leap years), and hourly (assuming a 24-hour window) 87,600 records.

Step 3: Formalization

Formalization is no different for a data warehouse than for any operational database. The only variation might be the choice of DBMS. A number of data management products on the market specialize in supporting decision support systems. About half of the NoSQL vendors say that their products are perfect for a warehouse. However, the majority of data warehouses are developed using a standard RDBMS.

Step 4: Customization

The data warehouse designer has a number of options to ensure that warehouse performance is acceptable.

Streamlining

If the warehouse is designed correctly and the business uses it appropriately (not as a substitute transaction processor), then it is most likely read-only. This means that ACID compliance is not needed, freeing the DBMS from record locking, journaling, logging, and backup and recovery overhead. If you are using a general-purpose DBMS, you might have to do some system software work to stop the DBMS from creating and maintaining these support functions and files.

Duplication

Read-only databases are excellent candidates for a liberal use of duplicate data. The designer should feel free to use duplicate data when and where they can improve performance.

Denormalization

Normalization was created to avoid insertion, update, and deletion anomalies. As with duplication, denormalization can be ignored if the database does not do any insertions, updates, or deletes—at least not at the transaction level. The most frequent use of denormalization is the reintroduction of groups (aggregate and multivalue).

Indices and Hashing

Indices on the dimensions allow quick access. In some cases, the dimension might contain only a primary key. There are times, with some DBMSs, when the dimension record type can be eliminated and an index placed on the "phantom" foreign key in the fact record. That's the good news. The bad news is that indices might consume more than half of a warehouse's disk storage. Adding new records and their associated indices to the warehouse can be a process that takes many hours. More than one IT shop schedules its warehouse updates for over the weekend because of the time required.

Hashing is a useful warehouse tool if (and only if) the database is sufficiently stable not to require expansion beyond its design. If the database must be constantly made larger to accommodate new data, then the hashing algorithm might need to be modified and all of the hashing keys recalculated...a very long process.

Bitmaps

Bitmaps were described in Chapter 8. These are technically index files in which a bit represents a binary data value within a record occurrence. Two outstanding features define bitmaps. First, the bitmap file is a sequential string with one bit for every record occurrence. The sequence of bits in the string is identical to the sequence of the record occurrences in the file. For example, the first bit in the string stands for the first record occurrence in a file, the 10th bit in the string stands for the 10th record in the file, and so on.

Second, the value of the bit represents the binary value for one data field in that record occurrence. For example, assume the Employee file includes the data item GENDER, which can have the value "M" or "F." If the first record occurrence in the file is for Peter Yarrow with GENDER = "M," the second record occurrence in the file is for Paul Stookey with GENDER = "M," and the third record occurrence is for Mary Travers with GENDER = "F," and if the bitmap stores a 1 for "M" and a 0 for "F," then the first three bits of the Gender bitmap will be "110."

The beauty of bitmaps is that you can apply logical operations (i.e., and, or, not) to them. Imagine the Employee file with the two data items GENDER and VESTED. As in the previous example, the only data values for GENDER are either "M" or "F." A bitmap index is created on GENDER (bitmap file 1 in Table 14-3) storing a 1 if GENDER's data value = "M" and a 0 if the value is "F." The data item VESTED indicates whether the employee is vested in the company retirement plan. VESTED also has only two data values, "Yes" and "No." Bitmap file 2, the VESTED bitmap, stores a 1 if the value of VESTED is "Yes" and 0 if the value is "No."

Table 14-3. *Applying Logical Operators to Bitmaps*

Record Type Employee Name	Gender	Vested	Bitmap File 1 Gender	Bitmap File 2 Vested	Bitmap File 3 And
Rudolf Carnap	Male	Yes	1	1	0
Alonzo Church	Male	No	1	0	0
Priscilla Dance	Female	Yes	0	1	1
Emily Jones	Female	No	0	0	1
Willard Quine	Male	No	1	0	0
Christine Ladd-Franklin	Female	Yes	0	1	0
Ada Lovelace	Female	No	0	0	1
Alfred Tarski	Male	Yes	1	1	0
Ludwig Wittgenstein	Male	Yes	1	1	0

If the company wants to know how many female employees are not vested, they could construct a query using bitmap files 1 and 2. If the first bit of the Gender bitmap is a 0 and the first bit of the Vested bitmap is a 0, then the system sets the first bit of the Result bitmap (bitmap file 3) to a 1, else the first bit of bitmap 3 is a 0. The same operation is applied to all of the Gender and Vested bits. The Result bitmap shows that three female employees are not vested. The system did not have to touch the content data to report its results; it just had to add up the 1 bits in the Result file.

If a query is issued to report the names of all female employees who are not vested, the system knows to go to the 3rd, 4th, and 7th records to return the names Dance, Jones, and Lovelace.

Well-constructed and intelligently used bitmaps can turn an overnight query into a few-second exercise.

Bulk Loading

Online transactional systems add and modify data, often one record at a time, all day long. Index maintenance is carried out in real time before the (ACID compliant) transaction is declared complete. Data warehouses are updated on a schedule, often only once a week or once a month. Updating indexes on each record as it is added would make the process slower than a Christmas holiday at your in-laws.

The solution is to bulk load the data, dumping all the data in the database and then building an index from scratch. This allows the DBMS to fill one database page at a time, significantly reducing physical I/O.

Clustering

Clustering is useful for the dimensions but less so for the fact record type. If the designer knows in advance that one particular dimension will dominate all others, then clustering it with the fact record can be helpful.

Partitioning

Partitioning can become the data warehouse designer's best friend. Partitions can be used for initial data loads, placing each month's data in a separate file with separate indices. This not only speeds up data insertion but also leaves other parts of the warehouse undisturbed. The value of this advantage becomes obvious if you have to rebuild a warehouse-wide index.

Partitions can also be used for the fact record type and for the different dimensions. Having each dimension in its own file can speed up not just single dimensional but also multidimensional processing.

Distributed Processing

Distributed database managements systems (DDBMSs) were once the future of data management. In the 1980s, considerable buzz and gallons of ink were devoted to this technology. The hope was to create a network of databases on multiple computers in the same room or across the globe that were all part of the same system. Any, and all, transactions, wherever they were initiated, would propagate to any relevant machine in real time. If any machine failed, anywhere in the world, before the transaction was complete, it would be rolled back in every machine everywhere. The magic that would keep this system ACID compliant was the two-phased commit, an amalgam of signals sent back and forth from machine to machine to ensure that all were synchronized.

Unfortunately, although the two-phased commit reduced the window of vulnerability, it did not remove it, so the updateable DDBMS went the way of Ford's Edsel and Sony's Betamax.[1] Then a miracle happened—the data warehouse. It didn't need the disappointing two-phased commit because there was nothing to commit. The read-only warehouse gave the DDBMS a new lease on life and created the option of a global warehouse.

Distributing data can spread the workload across multiple servers, improving everyone's performance. Distributed servers can provide hot backup in the event of a server or network disruption. They can also resolve some regulatory concerns. For example, some countries restrict where certain data such as employee health records, can be stored. Having a distributed system allows sensitive information to remain "in country," while summary-level data can be shared across multiple sovereignties.

All Together Now...

Note that a few options work best when they work together. Indexing, hashing, bulk loading, and distributed processing are at their best in a partitioned database. The partition allows new data to be added to the warehouse without disturbing existing data, index nodes do not have to be split, hash-keyed data do not have to be unloaded and reloaded, bulk loading can be an offline process, and distributed databases can...well... they can exist.

Figure 14-4 is the product data warehouse database design. Note the following:

- The fact record is Line Item even though the system is called a product data warehouse.

- Given anticipated usage and performance reasons, the Customer and Account records became dimension records, turning an otherwise snowflake schema into a star schema.

- A Time dimension was added.

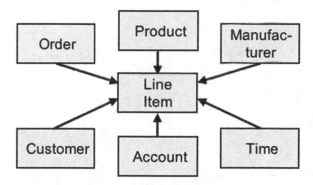

Figure 14-4. *The product data warehouse*

A hopefully obvious question was not—but should have been—asked by the database designers. If the usage is as suggested in the usage scenarios, and there is no downside to denormalizing, then why have the Customer, Account, Order, Manufacturer, and Product records at all? Why not make Customer, Order, etc., just indices on fields in the Line Item record? That's a good question and one that needs serious consideration.

Oops...

If you have done everything recommended here—created a distributed, bulk-loaded, read-only database that is not ACID compliant, that uses data duplication and denormalization, and that makes liberal use of hashing, indices, clustering, and partitioning—then congratulations, you have created a NoSQL database.

It might not be in the advertising literature, but the original purpose for many NoSQL implementations—their bread and butter as it were—was the data warehouse.

Customization Notes

The *Customization notes,* described in Chapter 13, are even more important now since future DBAs will need to know exactly why certain decisions were made regarding such things as the fact and dimension records, the data warehouse structure, usage scenarios, and so on.

Note

1. George Tillmann. "The Trouble with Two-Phase Commit." *Database Programming & Design.* Volume 3 Number 9, September 1990, pp. 64–70.

CHAPTER 15

■ ■ ■

The Big Data Decision Support System

The purpose of computing is insight, not numbers.

—R. W. Hamming

I have always wished that my computer would be as easy to use as my telephone. My wish has come true. I no longer know how to use my telephone.

—Bjarne Stroustrup (originator of C++ programming language)

The traditional decision support system/data warehouse (DSS/DW) approach works well with large databases and structured data. However, decision-making often involves more than structured data. It also uses very large databases consisting of considerable amounts of unstructured data—Big Data.

ANYBODY SEEN MY MACE?

For those who missed the database religious wars of the 1980s, a mini-version is going on right now. Is Big Data stored in a data warehouse or something entirely different? Some very vocal authors say that the Big Data repository cannot be a data warehouse because a data warehouse stores only structured data. They prefer to call it a *data lake*, reflecting Big Data's unstructured data (apparently they never came across a structured lake). Still others simply call the Big Data repository "Big Data," indicating, it would seem, that Big Data doesn't need a house—it is the house.

Others say, just as loudly, some modern version of "poppycock." If it is a subject-oriented, time-dependent database for a decision support system, then it is a data warehouse.

© George Tillmann 2017

G. Tillmann, *Usage-Driven Database Design*, DOI 10.1007/978-1-4842-2722-0_15

It's a silly argument.

As you will see, using U3D, you look at the problem from the data definition and functionality perspectives, decide what the systems should do (the *what* from Chapter 1), and then, and only then, pick the architecture, product, and version that best does the job (the *how* from Chapter 1). Is the answer Oracle? Maybe. Hadoop? Maybe. Or just maybe, it's a flat file on a PC. The answer is in the data, not some IT pseudo-religious text.

To placate the annoying, this book could have called an unstructured Big Data repository a NoDW, or maybe a Data Swamp; however, the decision is to just call it an unstructured Big Data warehouse.

As described in Chapter 13, Big Data refers to the terabytes and petabytes of data collected for trend analysis, among other uses. What is not mentioned in Chapter 13 is that Big Data is almost always unstructured data. Although Big Data and unstructured data are not the same, the two share a considerable overlap in the literature as well as the real world.

Structured, Unstructured, and Semistructured Data—Another Small Digression

What is structured data? That's an easy question. Go back to Chapter 8 and the punched-card era of data processing. A card (record) might reserve the first 10 columns (positions) for CUSTOMER FIRST NAME, the next 25 positions for CUSTOMER LAST NAME, and the next 8 for ACCOUNT NUMBER. Further, the program or the DBMS might indicate that CUSTOMER FIRST NAME and CUSTOMER LAST NAME are text fields, while ACCOUNT NUMBER is an integer. The system knows each field's name, its length, its data type, and, if it is in a data dictionary, its definition. This is structured data—the bread and butter of computer processing.

If its structure is known, then systems can easily display it, modify it, and use it in any way its definition allows. It is ideal for application programs as well as information managers. The RDBMS is the poster child for structured data—if it is stored and used in an RDBMS, then it is probably structured.

PUB TRIVIA

During a coffee break at an ANSI SPARC (database standards) meeting in the late 1970s, a committee member shared a problem he was having with an experimental relational database management system his team was developing. He asked, "How do you do a relational join on a large text field?" And, if the notion of unstructured data was not born then, it was at least seen in an entirely new light—the RDBMS killer.

Unstructured data do not have the well-defined pedigree of structured data. There might not be any distinction between record and field, and the length might be unknown as well as its data type. In addition, unstructured data are also often sparse data, meaning that much of their significance, even their existence, is tenuous. The archetype for unstructured data is text; but pictures, videos, and anything not easily classifiable are often labeled unstructured. Popular belief is that 80 percent of all data are unstructured.

Text is an interesting example of unstructured data because while the values "Y" and "N," for yes and no, are text, they are easily supported by RDBMS operators. So is CUSTOMER LAST NAME, which can be easily used as a secondary key or in a secondary index. On the other hand, the *Bhagavad Gita* is not easily supported by a RDBMS and is usually considered unstructured and relegated to BLOB status (a cinematic way, after the movie *The Blob*, of saying it doesn't really belong in a DBMS but we will put it here anyway). Where is the line between structured and unstructured? Nobody knows. Then again, maybe it is unimportant, because the previous neat, simple, and clean definition of unstructured is totally wrong.

SPARSE DATA

There are two different definitions for sparse data, although, surprisingly, both apply to Big Data. The older definition of sparse describes data fields, or even records, that are all (or mostly) blank, zero, or null—or whatever concept you use for digital nothingness. This definition is important for Big Data because it raises the possibility of significant storage reduction through data compression.

More recently, sparse has been used to refer to tidbits of information that, although individually insignificant, contain significant meaning when part of a group. For example, one warm day is not an indicator of global warming, but hundreds or thousands of warm day readings prove very significant. In practice, much of Big Data can be described by this second definition. For example, although the list of all the products a single supermarket customer buys might be individually insignificant, knowing whether many customers buy certain products together might be very significant.

The newest member of the structured-unstructured trio is semistructured data. Only it isn't new. Computers entered the newspaper industry in the mid-1960s—more than a decade before that ANSI coffee break conundrum mentioned in the previous sidebar. Printing instructions (i.e., style, size, bold, etc.) were conveyed to the typesetter using a set of markup codes or tags embedded in the text. The tags tell the typesetter where to start new paragraphs, break a line, add italics, bold a name, or underline a word. Tags can also be used to indicate proper names, numerical values, and dates. Is such a document structured or unstructured? The answer is, both.

These structure distinctions took on additional importance with the advent of NoSQL and similar systems. While traditional DBMSs work with structured data, some NoSQL systems were specifically designed, according to their vendors, to store unstructured data. Other NoSQL products are advertised as working with semistructured data. Adding to the confusion, a review of technical magazines, blogs, and advertising literature indicate that there is widespread disagreement about whether a particular product handles unstructured or semistructured data.

The fly in the whole structured-unstructured ointment is semistructured data. If one understands that, then the whole structured-unstructured problem disappears.

Data are semistructured if

- They are not structured, meaning that they do not fit the punched card/RDBMS mold.

- They are not raw data, where raw means there is no way to look inside the data and discern some meaningful information.

How much raw data is there? If you think about it, you will probably conclude not much. Almost any data item contains some embedded information that can be extracted with a little effort.

An example of semistructured data can be found in the data collected by many supermarket chains. They want to better understand what their customers buy, when and where they buy it, what else they buy, and how often they visit the store. In essence, the chain wants to know *who, what, where, when,* and *how much.* All but *who* is captured by most electronic cash registers—they just don't all catch it in the same way. The data coming in might be a hodge-podge of *who, what, where, when, how much* data, varying in size, delimiter, and order, and with missing information scattered about. These data are semistructured because they are not structured, but they do contain analyzable information.

If the pundits are correct and only 20 percent of data are structured and little more than 0 percent are raw, then almost 80 percent of the data are semistructured.

How real is this? There are now companies that market products whose sole purpose is extracting meaningful (structured) information from "unstructured" data.

What should one conclude from all this? Well, there are four possible conclusions.

1. Structured data exist. An example is customer name. A good name for this is *structured data.*

2. There is data that are not structurable. An example consists of the babblings of an infant. A good name for this is *nonstructured data,* meaning they cannot be structured. Luckily there is not a lot of this kind of data.

3. There are data that are not yet structured. An example is cash register transaction information. A good name for this is *unstructured data,* indicating that the data is not structured now but could be sometime in the future after processing.

4. Finally, there are data that, by their very nature, seem unstructured but, nonetheless, contain structurable components. An example is the CEO's annual report, which contains, in the text of the introductory statement, annual sales figures, products that will be introduced during the coming year, and new retail outlets. A good name for this is *semistructured data*.

Conclusion 1 is something IT has been dealing with for more than 100 years. IT understands *structured data*.

Conclusion 2 is accurate, but given the number of cases of *nonstructured data* that actually exist, it's rather useless for database design purposes.

Conclusions 3 and 4, while accurate, present a distinction without much difference. *Unstructured* and *semistructured data* are sufficiently similar, particularly from a functional perspective, to be used interchangeably.

Like the words *flammable* and *inflammable*, unstructured and semistructured are, from a practical perspective, interchangeable, and either can be used.

DSS and Big Data

Table 14-2 in Chapter 14 showcases some of the differences between transaction processing systems and DSSs. Those distinctions can now be expanded (Table 15-1) to include Big Data.

Table 15-1. *Difference Between Transaction Processing System (TPS) and Decision Support System (DSS)*

	Transaction Processing System (TPS)	Decision Support System (DSS)
Structured Data/ Reasonable Volume	Traditional DBMS - High level of structure - Single processor/cluster - Data: Structured - Example: RDBMS - Common database Classification: production or operational	Traditional DBMS - High level of structure - Single processor/ cluster - Data: Structured - Example: RDBMS - Common database Classification: Data warehouse
Unstructured Big Data	Nontraditional DBMS - Distributed processing - Data: Semistructured - Example: NoSQL, ex. Cassandra - Common database Classification: Production or operational	?

The traditional DBMS, be it SQL Server or Oracle, is most commonly used for transaction processing systems supporting structured data and reasonable volumes, where a reasonable definition of reasonable data is data that can be supported by a single machine or simple cluster (as represented in the top-left quadrant [quadrant 1] of Table 15-1). The TPS repository is usually referred to as the *production* or *operational* database.

The traditional DSS database is designed to support user queries and can store and process a reasonable amount of data (Table 15-1, quadrant 2, top-right). Decision support systems with structured data and reasonable volumes tend to use traditional DBMSs, such as DB2 and Sybase (the same as quadrant 1). The most common and appropriate name for the DSS repository is data warehouse.

Big Data transaction processing systems often require specialized (nontraditional) data managers such as those offered by NoSQL vendors (quadrant 3, bottom-left). These systems tend to use distributed processing to support their high transaction volumes (data and process). However, even here, the repository is usually regarded as a production or operational database.

However, Table 15-1 raises the question about the DSS/Big Data quadrant (quadrant 4). NoSQL systems, such as Cassandra, are designed for rapid access of *fat records* (consisting of multiple occurrences of multiple entities that can be accessed with a single I/O)—a TPS approach—meaning that Cassandra-like systems are not ideal candidates to support a Big Data DSS.

It doesn't take a doctorate from Trump University to conclude that none of the solutions for the three quadrants will work for the unstructured Big Data DSS quadrant.

Using U3D to Develop a Big Data Decision Support System

If you are building a DSS for an organization that has petabytes of data, then you will probably need a rather unique storage solution. Not immune to the influence of trade journal articles, you might be thinking of products such as Hadoop as a possibility. Good thinking. However, it is still important to go through the four U3D steps for deciding on a technology dictated by the definition and use of the data—and nothing else. Remember the technology escalation rule presented in Chapter 13: use a nontraditional solution only if you absolutely have to.

The steps to create an unstructured Big Data data warehouse are no different than those to create an operational database or a structured data warehouse. U3D works for all database design, regardless of use. Abiding by the U3D steps helps keep the designer's mind focused on completely understanding the problem before moving on to a solution. In addition, a structured design approach provides proper documentation for those who will have to support your decision. The following sections demonstrate how the same, now familiar, four U3D steps can help the database designer create a database to support an unstructured Big Data warehouse.

Step 1: Transformation

As with any database, the first step in creating an unstructured Big Data warehouse is converting, or transforming, any subject-related logical data models into a physical data model. To build a Big Data employee DSS, the designer needs to scour the data dictionary for any data models incorporating employee-related entities. Figure 15-1 consists of two logical data model fragments showing the Employee entity and its entity neighbors.

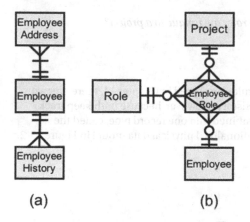

(a)   (b)

Figure 15-1. *Employee system and project system logical data model fragments*

Not all employee information will be part of existing data models. A look at application programs might turn up some important unmodeled information. Put all of the collected data together and you have a physical data model for the Big Data subject.

Step 2: Utililization

For Big Data, step 2, Utilization, is carried out significantly differently than for an operational database—however, it is identical to the way a designer builds a data warehouse. As described in Chapter 14, the designer should talk to the managers who will be using or feel they will be benefitting from the Big Data DSS to get an idea of what they have planned. The designer should then develop several likely usage scenarios describing how the Big Data will, at least initially, be used. The result should be a set of usage scenarios similar to those created in Chapter 14.

The employee DSS might include the following scenarios:

> *Usage Scenario 201: What is the average employee salary?*
>
> *201.1 Enter Employee*
>
> *201.2 Find Employee History*
>
> *Usage Scenario 202: What is the average employee tenure?*
>
> *202.1 Enter Employee*

202.2 Find Employee History

Usage Scenario 203: How many projects does the average employee work in a calendar year?

203.1 Enter Employee

203.2 Find Employee Role

203.3 Find Project

Usage Scenario 204: How many roles are unique to a project?

204.1 Enter Role

204.2 Find Employee Role

What is the fact record? Following the rules presented in Chapter 14, there are two candidates, Employee Role and Employee History. However, because both keep track of an employee's history, the two can be combined into one record type, called the Employee Detail record type, yielding the rationalized physical data model in Figure 15-2.

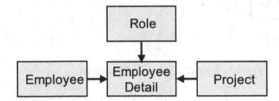

Figure 15-2. *Rationalized physical data model*

The result is a perfect star, but this is largely because of the simplicity of the example. In most real-world cases, the resulting PDM will look more like a snowflake than a star. The Employee Detail record (a combination of Employee History and Employee Role) is the fact record (or fact table), and the Role, Project, and Employee records are the dimensions.

Step 3: Formalization

Formalization is no different for a Big Data DSS than for any operational or traditional DSS database. The designer should develop a database design to support the DSS. It just might be the case that a traditional DSS/DW approach can support the application. However, given Big Data's volume and structure, most cases will require a quick trip to step 4, Customization.

Figure 15-3 is the employee data warehouse database design. Note the following:

1. The fact record is Employee Detail, which is a denormalized combination of the Employee History and Employee Role record types.

2. A Time dimension is added.

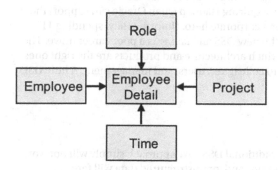

Figure 15-3. *The employee Big Data data warehouse*

The database design in Figure 15-3 should work with most traditional DBMSs.

One issue might preclude use of some traditional systems. The Employee History and Employee Role record types were combined to form the Employee Detail because both meet a number of fact record requirements. Both are associative or attribute record types, both are at the many end of multiple one-to-many links, and both are the most populace record types in their respective systems. Both also store similar (although not identical) information. However, combining them will mean that the composite record type could have some empty (blank or null) data fields, and in certain situations, one or more of these fields could be part of the primary key. The DBMS for this DSS will need to support sparse and probably semistructured data.

If it is obvious that a traditional system will not handle the required volumes or types of data, then why should the designer go through step 3? Why not skip Formalization and go directly from step 2, Utilization, to step 4, Customization?

The answer is simple. The choice of a nonstandard solution needs to be a conclusion and not a premise. The whole purpose of U3D is to make all decisions demonstrable and justifiably through proper documentation. The designer needs to prove that a standard solution will not work.

An example is useful. Assume that the proposed employee DSS will house multiple terabytes of structured (i.e., name, employee number, etc.) and unstructured data (i.e., annual performance reviews, examples of reports produced by the employee, articles in which the employee is mentioned, photos, etc.). The most economical solution is a traditional data warehouse (one or more of which the organization might already have) if it will support the proposed system. Purchasing a nontraditional system, even one that is open source, can involve hundreds of thousands of dollars in software, hardware, additional staff, and training costs. Not acquiring Hadoop when Oracle can support the proposed DSS could make the designer a corporate hero. Unfortunately, spending 11 months trying to make Oracle handle the new DSS and failing is a poor career move. The designer needs to know—not guess—which architecture and products are the right ones and to be able to defend that decision to colleagues, users, and management. A little U3D effort could be a good career strategy.

Step 4: Customization

It might very well be the case that the traditional DSS/DW approach simply will not work for the proposed system. High data volumes and/or unstructured data will force the designer to look elsewhere for a solution. One possible solution is an architecture similar to that of Hadoop.

A Little About Hadoop

Hadoop is not a product but rather a family of products. The core of Hadoop, both figuratively and literally, is two products, Hadoop Distributed File System (HDFS) and MapReduce. HDFS allows data to be stored in a large number of nodes, collectively called a *cluster*. A single file might be distributed and replicated across multiple nodes within the cluster. The distribution—one file broken into multiple parts (called *blocks*)—allows parallel processing of a single file, while replication—storing multiple copies of the same data (blocks) in multiple locations—provides high availability and backup. With HDFS and a sufficient number of inexpensive servers (could be hundreds or even thousands of machines), terabyte files are not only possible but in use today.

MapReduce is the application framework that oversees how files are processed by assigning application programs to various nodes. MapReduce copies and sends computer code to servers where there are data waiting to be processed.

To really understand Hadoop, it pays to look at how conventional data processing—particularly distributed data processing—works. Imagine a distributed environment as a pyramid. At the top of the pyramid is the application program. As the job executes, the data manager finds the data required by the application, copies them to the server where the program is running, and returns them (if there were modifications) to their original location.

Hadoop inverts the pyramid or, perhaps more accurately, places the data at the top of the pyramid. If you look at the typical Big Data job, the size of the application (in bytes) is dwarfed by the size of the data. So why do systems move the data (the larger component) to the application (the smaller-sized component)? Would it not be more efficient to move the smaller application to the larger data? That is what MapReduce does—it moves applications to the nodes where data need to be processed.

Immediately, two advantages are evident. The first, as mentioned earlier, is there is less traffic between nodes. Shipping data between nodes is incredibly expensive. HDFS's philosophy is that data are stored once and almost never move. The second advantage is that it makes distributed processing more efficient.

For decades, parallel computing has been the great hope and the great disappointment of IT. Being able to process the same data sets on multiple machines simultaneously is an efficient and inexpensive way to improve computing performance. Unfortunately, accomplishing this goal has often required complicated and convoluted code. Getting the right data into the right CPU at the right time is difficult, requiring coordination between the program components running on different machines (what do you do if two machines want to update the same data?). If data are updatable, then cross-machine locking and journaling mechanisms are needed. A simpler, though more disappointing solution, is to have the different nodes do entirely different though related tasks, thus reducing, if not eliminating, the need for process coordination.

The Holy Grail of distributed processing is to have a one-to-one (1:1) relationship between hardware and throughput. Ideally, doubling the hardware doubles the throughput, tripling hardware triples throughput, and so on. Traditional distributed processing is far from attaining the ideal 1:1 relationship. Worse, as hardware is added, the ratio degrades, and as more and more hardware is added, the drop can become precipitous.

Hadoop's MapReduce comes closer to the sought-after 1:1 ratio than traditional distributed processing, making it a desirable platform for very large data files.

However, there is a case where the MapReduce/HDFS model does not work well—Small Data. Considerable work and execution time is required to set up a MapReduce/HDFS cluster-wide process. This effort makes sense if the data file is very large. It makes no sense if the data file is small. Have a database with 2,000 records? Excel will fetch the desired record faster than Hadoop. Where is the cutoff point—the point where it makes sense to consider Hadoop? Opinions differ, but most agree that if your database fits on four or fewer servers (CPU and disk), then skip Hadoop.

Many IT professionals compare Hadoop to products such as Cassandra, MongoDB, and other NoSQL DBMSs. However, as explained previously, Hadoop is not a DBMS but a family of products, best described as data management *middleware*, which includes a DBMS. Hadoop's DBMS, named HBase, shares many similarities with its cousin Cassandra (both are supported by the Apache Software Foundation). If you are a Cassandra expert or an HBase expert, then you are likely convinced that Cassandra and HBase have little in common. For the rest of us, they are very similar. Both are key-value column-family data stores. Both use SQL-like terminology to describe their components (table, column, row, etc.). Both use fat records consisting of multiple occurrences of multiple entities stored contiguously to achieve single I/O retrieval. And the list goes on.

HBase is a viable substitute for Cassandra in the Big Data transaction processing space. However, along with its strong points, HBase shares many of Cassandra's shortcomings. Neither Cassandra nor HBase is a great candidate for DSSs. Their internals are designed for one I/O retrieval of fat records. Supporting a query by reading thousands or millions of records will require a database scan that could take eons to complete. Both products disdain indices—a DSS mainstay—as expensive substitutes for hashing.

Fortunately, the Hadoop family also includes another product—Hive. Hive is a SQL-like product that can front-end both MapReduce and HDFS. Hive can also create its own relational-like database stored in its own workspace. The Hive users think they are querying a relational database, but the data they are using might be in HDFS, in a native Hive file, or in some third-party database.

Of course, there are some prices to pay for this access. First, because Hive data are often HDFS data, they do not have a normal schema. In fact, they do not have a schema at all until runtime.

Traditional DBMSs bind data to the schema when the data are written to the database. This is called *schema on write*. As the data are read into the database, the DBMS reads the schema and confirms that the data are as defined (size, data type, etc.). Conforming data are stored in the database while nonconforming data initiate an error procedure.

Hive uses a different technology. The bind takes place when the data are accessed. This approach is called *schema on read*. Any and all data are entered into HDFS willy-nilly. When the data are accessed, the DBMS compares the data in HDFS with the schema. If the data are acceptable to the schema, they are passed on to the user. If the data are unacceptable, an error routine is initiated.

Schema on read is used for systems in which the DBMS has full control of the data in the database. For example, to insert data into an Oracle database, the application must go through Oracle software that keeps track of all data-related activity.

Hive, on the other hand, has control over only data stored in its own workspace. Data stored in HDFS can be accessed and changed by any application running through HDFS. To accurately reflect what is out there, Hive must review all the data in the HDFS file just before processing them. This runtime bind guarantees that the most recent data, in their most recent state, will be part of the query response. However, binding the data to the schema every time it is accessed requires time and resources that the schema-on-write DBMS need only expend once.

Table 15-2 completes the database 4x4 diagram.

Table 15-2. Difference Between Traditional and Big Data TPS and DSS

	Transaction Processing System (TPS)	Decision Support System (DSS)
Structured Data/ Reasonable Volume	Traditional DBMS - High level of structure - Single processor/cluster - Data: Structured - Example: RDBMS - Common database Classification: Production or operational	Traditional DBMS - High level of structure - Single processor/cluster - Data: Structured - Example: RDBMS - Common database Classification: Data warehouse
Unstructured Big Data	Nontraditional DBMS - Distributed processing - Data: Semistructured - Example: NoSQL, ex. Cassandra - Common database Classification: Production or operational	Nontraditional DBMS - Distributed processing - Data: Semistructured - Example: Hadoop - Common Database Classification: Data warehouse

Using Hadoop, the DSS user can interact with the database in a SQL-like environment that supports terabytes or petabytes of unstructured data.

Putting It All Together

Using products such as Hadoop, the database designer can create an HDFS file storing Cassandra-like fat records but using Hive's SQL-like commands. The combined structures allow the application or end user to work with a rather traditional DSS star schema. In fact, to the end user or application, the resulting database design can look similar if not identical to the one created in step 3, Formalization (Figure 15-3).

Done correctly, the convoluted machinations needed to assemble this complex structure can be almost transparent to the end user, who sees a structure and processes similar to the more traditional DSS/data warehouse.

Deliverables

The deliverables for a Big Data DSS are the same as those listed in Chapter 14. The only difference is that the Customization notes are even more important now because future DBAs need to know exactly why certain decisions were made regarding such things as the fact and dimension records, the data warehouse structure, usage scenarios, and so on.

As with all other U3D *notes*, those for a Big Data DSS should include the answers to these four questions:

- *Why?* This would seem obvious. However, why a decision was made the way it was is often an area of confusion for future system maintainers. If an index was added, or removed, it is important to specify why this was done. If Oracle was rejected for the data warehouse, the reasons should be clearly stated.

- *Where?* The notes should reflect exactly where in the database design new concepts were introduced or existing ones changed.

- *When?* Design changes and test results do not always line up. It is important to document exactly when a change was made to a system so its impact can be properly assessed.

- *Results?* There is a tendency for designers to document successes only. Sometimes documenting "fascinating results" (a Spock-ism to avoid saying failures) is more important than successes. Knowing that an index added little to database performance can save valuable time by avoiding reinventing the wheel months or years later. Knowing that a test using SQL Server for the DSS failed is vital information that needs to be shared.

The answers to these four questions are even more important when dealing with performance issues and nontraditional systems. For example, implementing Hadoop can be quite complex, requiring a team of experts with skills in using HDFS, Hive, and MapReduce. The Customization notes should include input from all of these experts (whether in-house or external consultants) and not just the database designer.

PART IV

Where from Here?

CHAPTER 16

■ ■ ■

A Look Ahead

I really didn't foresee the Internet. But then, neither did the computer industry. Not that that tells us very much of course—the computer industry didn't even foresee that the century was going to end.

—Douglas Adams

The most likely way for the world to be destroyed, most expert agree, is by accident. That's where we come in; we're computer professionals. We cause accidents.

—Nathaniel Borenstein

IT's track record for prognostication is miserable.

"There is a world market for maybe five computers," is a quote attributed to Thomas J. Watson Sr., founder and president of IBM. Whether he said it or not (there is some controversy about the origin of the quote), it reflects a position held by many in the 1940s. IBM proved Watson (or whoever) wrong in the 1960s by dominating the lucrative mainframe market. By the 1970s, there were dozens of minicomputers companies and, although IBM was an early manufacturer of minis, it failed to see the market shifting to those machines. It believed all *real* data processing would take place on mainframes.

The minicomputer market was dominated by Digital Equipment Company (DEC), which grew to become the second largest computer company in the world. DEC's founder and CEO, Ken Olsen, when confronted with the personal computer, is reported to have said, "There is no reason for any individual to have a computer in his home."

DEC's failure to see the rise of the microcomputer would lead to the company's eventual sale to, of all things, Compaq Computer Corporation, a PC manufacturer. (Interestingly, Compaq was not able to weather the shift to servers and was sold to HP.)

Poor prognostication seems to extend to the Internet—it was more than 20 years old before anyone knew it was there, much less saw it coming. The same is true of the World Wide Web, and who predicted that phones would play music and spend a lot of their time being a camera?

I wrote an article in the early 1980s predicting that the DBMS would become a data-architecture-neutral back-end engine, fronted by a network (relational, hierarchal, or whatever) user interface.[1] Wrong...although, come to think of it, Oracle has its OO and NoSQL versions....

© George Tillmann 2017

G. Tillmann, *Usage-Driven Database Design*, DOI 10.1007/978-1-4842-2722-0_16

So no predictions. But a wish list? Maybe. A semi-educated wish list, based on a few observations from years of slugging it out in the DBMS trenches, might make sense.

The following are four DBMS issues I, and many of the database designers and DBAs I interviewed, would like to see addressed.

We Need to Ask the Awkward Questions

Some questions seem too awkward to ask. Maybe they are politically incorrect, or maybe they will hurt someone's feelings. However, maybe they just need to be asked. The data management questions that have never been raised, much less answered, are about the value of a theoretical foundation.

Database management systems have traditionally been categorized by architecture, such as network, relational, and (although it is not properly an architecture but rather a grab bag of sundry architectures) NoSQL. There is, however, another way to categorize DBMSs—functional versus theoretical. Functional systems, such as IMS, IDMS, and NoSQL, grew out of need. Their utility expanded as problems arose and solutions became apparent. Consequently, their structure tends to be a bit ad hoc, with new features bolted on to existing ones. The result can look like a Picasso portrait where the eyes were put... er...wherever they fit.

Theoretical systems, such as the relational model, have a mathematical foundation. If fact, Codd's aim was to get the DBMS out of the realm of the functional, which he considered "troublesome...confusing...and...mistaken," and into the realm of the "cleaner...sound...and...superior."[2] [3]

How successful was the shift from functional to theoretical? Well, the academics took to it like politicians to a junket. As Peter Chen, the creator of the entity-relationship model, stated, academics were comfortable with the mathematical language of the relational model and published, published, and published about it.[4] A cursory look at Google Scholar turned up more academic references to the relational model than to all other architectures combined.

However, since the publication of the first Codd paper on the relational model almost 50 years ago, there have been no other theoretically based DBMS architectures, models, or products—at least none that have seen the light of day. The relational model is the one and only theoretically based system I could find in production today. All DBMS implementations since the relational model have been functionally oriented. Even many of the relational products have abandoned some of the theoretical roots for functional features.

What does this say about the importance of DBMS theoretical foundations? How important is a theoretical foundation if no other DBMS creator has followed in Codd's footsteps? Why should data management practitioners care about the theoretical foundation of their DBMS? The commercial community seems to be saying that it is not important to them and that they are more concerned with performance, ease of use, and getting the job done than mathematical purity.

This is not a philosophical question but rather one that asks where the attention of some of our best information technology-oriented minds should focus. Do we really need another normal form or would the world be better served with a more efficient way of updating distributed data? Can academics put aside those delusions of relevance and focus on something more useful, such as helping the guy trying to get his database to work?

There are also publishing implications. Visit any bookstore. While you will find a few subject-related books on object-oriented and NoSQL databases from practitioners, virtually every college textbook assumes that the database will be relational. They are so relationally driven that relational concepts, such as foreign keys and the ban on repeating groups, are baked into their interpretation of logical data modeling. If you look up the definition of Data Definition Language (DDL) in most textbooks, it will refer only to relational objects such as tables and rows.

The relational model is a great achievement and an important part of the information management landscape. However, it is only part of that landscape. There are other fascinating ideas out there that should be part of every database designer's and DBA's experience.

We need a Don't Assume movement that works to ensure that no authors or teachers assume that the RDBMS is the one and only tool for managing data.

There is another consideration to take into account: the Multiple Experience Concept. You have probably never heard of the Multiple Experience Concept because I just made it up. However, it goes like this.

Imagine that you are the programming manager for a company that needs a system written in an obscure assembler language (call it OAL). You have no OAL-trained staff and cannot find any qualified OLA programmers to hire. You will have to train some existing staff in OLA. What criteria do you use to select OLA training candidates?

1. Someone who does not know any assembler language

2. Someone who knows one assembler language

3. Someone who knows two or more assembler languages

The obvious answer is 3. Knowing one assembler language is good and is certainly better than not knowing any at all, but certainly not as good as knowing several. Knowing one assembler language means knowing the syntax of one assembler language. However, knowing two or more languages means that the programmer not only knows the syntax of multiple languages but also understands at least some of the essence of what it means to be an assembler language. They understand concepts that are not just part of a particular language's structure but also the fundamentals that all assemblers have in common. Understanding the foundation behind a language makes it easier to learn and use a new language.

The same holds true for high-level languages. Need to teach someone C? Rather than picking the COBOL programmer or the FORTRAN programmer, pick the programmer who knows both. And there is an interesting side effect. Teach the COBOL programmer C, and you wind up with not just a new C programmer but also a better COBOL programmer.

The same is true for data management. Knowing one data architecture is good, but knowing two or more is better because then the database designer, DBA, or application programmer understands more of what is going on underneath the hood, not just what appears on the surface.

Tools Need to Take Usage into Account

The late 1980s and early 1990s were the era of the software development or Computer Aided Software Engineering (CASE) tool. You could not swing a dead cat without hitting a CASE tool startup. These products came in various flavors. There were the code generator holdovers from the 1970s, the process modeling tools that turned flow charts and DFDs into programs, the data modeling tools that turned your E-R diagram into a DBMS schema, and the tool that did it all, soup to nuts, idea to code.

As with most everything else in IT, these tools were oversold. A productivity improvement of 5 percent would have cost justified the tool; however, many vendors promised a 50 percent (or greater) improvement that was both unachievable and ultimately disappointing. (It's amazing how IT jumps from panacea to panacea, seemingly learning nothing from continuous disappointment while blithely looking for the next catholicon.) The hype pushed these tools to near extinction.

The frenzy is now over, and the advantages of these tools are more realistically understood. A few CASE products have survived and are benefiting a number of IT shops. However, many of these tools exhibit one or more very disappointing characteristics.

First, they rely on a logical model that is impregnated with physical design (almost always RDBMS) concepts. They assume that the DBMS is a relational one. Based on this assumption, their logical data models establish relationships using foreign keys and do not allow group or multivalue data items, among other truly annoying disappointments. The value of these tools with nonrelational databases is minimal and, because of their rejection of a DBMS-independent logical data model, misleading even for relational designers.

Second, they tend to disregard how the data are used. The extent of this flaw ranges from not considering some usage aspects, such as volume or path traffic, to the most prevalent failure—not taking usage into account at all.

In an odd twist, the tools that erroneously inject physical database considerations into logical data modeling totally omit from physical database design how the database will be used.

Tool designers need to do a better job of separating the logical from the physical (Principles 1 and 2 of the database design principles from Chapter 1) and a better job of incorporating usage into their physical database design (Principle 3 from Chapter 1).

The One and Only DBMS

Before the database management system, data in files were considered characteristics or properties of a program. The program opened the file, interpreted the data (see the "Data or Information?" sidebar), and closed the file when the program was finished, placing the data in the cyber-equivalent of a coma, until they were needed again. It was not uncommon for multiple files to contain the same data items used by different programs for different purposes. Synchronization problems were so common, but solutions so elusive, that they were essentially ignored. If the customer name in the customer file agreed with the spelling of the customer name in the account, billing, and credit files, then it was often luck rather than craft.

DATA OR INFORMATION?

Many information technologists make a distinction between data and information. Data are strings of characters, while information is data with *interpretation*. For example, take the following string:

5553426978ROBERTABODE

What information is in this data string? Back in the era of flat files, the interpretation of the data was stored in the program. If the program, call it Program A, said that the first seven characters were PHONE NUMBER, the next six characters were FIRST NAME, and the last five were LAST NAME, then you would know the following:

```
PHONE NUMBER = "555-342-6978"
FIRST NAME = "ROBERT"
LAST NAME = "ABODE"
```

However, suppose that Program B said that the first four characters were BRANCH NUMBER, the next six were ACCOUNT NUMBER, the next seven were FIRST NAME, and the last four were LAST NAME. Then you would have this:

```
BRANCH NUMBER = "5553"
ACCOUNT NUMBER = "426978"
FIRST NAME = "ROBERTA"
LAST NAME = "BODE"
```

That's a very different interpretation.

Associative array systems placed the interpretation in the record. Their key-value structure preceded every data value with a key containing at least part (the attribute's name) of its interpretation. Consequently, every program would know the following:

```
STREET NUMBER = "55534"
POSTAL CODE = "26978"
FIRST NAME = "ROB"
MIDDLE INITIAL = "E"
LAST NAME = "RTABODE"
```

Most traditional DBMSs go one step further. They move the interpretation of the data from the program (or the record) into the DBMS's data dictionary.

The DBMS changed everything. A data item, such as CUSTOMER NAME, would be stored only once in the DBMS along with its interpretation. At last, the data existed all the time, whether a program had a file open or not. The single occurrence of a data item along with its single interpretation meant that synchronization problems were a thing of the past. The DBMS became the Swiss Army knife of information management, incorporating all the features an enterprise needed (Table 16-1). However, it didn't last forever.

Table 16-1. *General-Purpose DBMS Features*

- *Full lifecycle*: Oversees the full lifecycle management of the data (creation, access, update, deletion)
- *Multiuser*: Provides multiuser support (simultaneous database access for multiple end users and programs, whether batch or online)
- *Full interpretation*: Ensures a single, complete, and continuous interpretation of all database data
- *Data independence*: Assures that data exist independent of any users or programs
- *Consistency and integrity*: Enforces both system and user-defined consistency, integrity, and edit rules
- *Reliability*: Guarantees reliability (ACID compliant)
- *Synchronized redundancy*: Guards against uncontrolled data duplication (allows selective fully synchronized redundant, but not duplicate, data)
- *Security*: Protects data from unauthorized access or use
- *Single source*: Is capable of safeguarding the official and only reliable instance of enterprise data

---

The world changed when *big* was invented—Big Data, big computers, big companies, big ideas, and, unfortunately, big problems.

The DBMS that solved the "files everywhere problem"—guaranteeing that there existed one and only one instance of a data item, guaranteeing that synchronization problems were a thing of the past, guaranteeing that the single data instance had only a single interpretation, guaranteeing that there was one and only one official repository of enterprise data—exists no more. The dreaded multiple data files have been replaced with multiple DBMSs managing multiple databases. Need to guarantee the integrity of the data? Store them in a general-purpose ACID-compliant database. Need varied data types? There is a specialty DBMS for that. Need super-fast retrieval? There is a specialty DBMS for that. As a result, after some really fine work solving some real-world problems, we are, in many ways, back where we stated.

The poster child for the specialty DBMS is NoSQL, although other systems share this category. Although NoSQL DBMSs are good products, providing necessary services, they represent a disturbing trend. Rather than adding new features to accomplish these new tasks, they shed expensive existing ones. For example, the DBMS that was ACID compliant is now *user beware*—the fully interpreted data item is now a bucket or folder to store unformatted data. Rather than storing the interpretation in the DBMS, these systems need to be "interpreted by the application." The basic tenets of what it is to be a DBMS—maintaining data integrity or transforming data into information—can be lost. The average commercial organization now faces the uncomfortable emergence of a two-tiered information structure. One tier is the generic all-purpose DBMS, with all of its associated guarantees, and a second tier of specialty or niche data managers, each catering to a different need while offering fewer assurances.

Table 16-2 lists the fundamental features that almost every general-purpose DBMS supports and grades a representative sample of NoSQL systems on their ability to support these features.

Table 16-2. *Comparing General-Purpose and NoSQL DBMSs*

DBMS Feature	Description	NoSQL Grade (A to F)
Full lifecycle	Oversees the full lifecycle management of the data (creation, access, update, deletion)	B
Multiuser	Provides multiuser support (simultaneous database access for multiple end users and programs, whether batch or online)	B
Full interpretation	Ensures a single, complete, and continuous interpretation of all database data	B
Data independence	Assures that data exist independent of any users or programs	D
Consistency and integrity	Enforces both system and user-defined consistency, integrity, and edit rules	B
Reliability	Guarantees reliability (ACID compliant)	C
Synchronized redundancy	Guards against uncontrolled data duplication (allows selective, fully synchronized redundant, but not duplicate, data)	F
Security	Protects data from unauthorized access or use	A
Single source	Is capable of safeguarding the official and only reliable instance of enterprise data	F

The majority of general-purpose DBMSs do a good job supporting all nine features. How do NoSQL systems do? Not so well. Arguably the most damaging of the missed features is single source. By admitting that it cannot function as the enterprise's official information repository, the NoSQL database relegates itself to a secondary role.

Almost 100 years ago, the economist Joseph Schumpeter wrote that the market leaders (the status quo) who provide the market with an "infrastructure" were disrupted by entrepreneurs who often, through innovation and change, put what they replaced out of business. He called this "creative destruction" (and became the source of nearly a dozen books of the same name, even if not entirely the same subject). However, if the cycle Schumpeter described is to continue, and the market to thrive, then these new disrupters must provide the new infrastructure.[5]

Creators of products such as NoSQL have been the entrepreneurs that attacked the entrenched status quo infrastructure, and although they have not yet made a significant monetary impact on the market, they might just be Schumpeter's disrupting force. If so, then it is time for them to start assuming the role of infrastructure provider, meaning that their products must move out of the niche realm and into the data management mainstream to become the new Swiss Army knives.

IT needs choices, but they need to be choices that compete for the same place in the center of the organization, not ones that reside in its corners. The NoSQL vendors have done some amazing stuff; however, their accomplishments center on either jettisoning some current features (ACID, interpretation, etc.) or digging up some old ideas (hierarchal and network features). Their retrograde change was a needed temporary fix, but now it is time for a more permanent prograde solution. It's time for the new crop of DBMS designers to shake up the data management world by coming up with some new ideas that build on the past rather than tearing it down.

We need the specialty capabilities NoSQL and similar products provide, but we also need the general-purpose DBMS features we had. The breakthrough product—the killer app of data management—just might be the general-purpose DBMS with web-browser-like plug-in features provided by the specialty DBMS vendors. The ability to plug key-value, document management, or multidimensional capabilities into the enterprise's official general-purpose DBMS—whether the feature is database-wide or restricted to one or more partitions—could be a best-of-all-possible-worlds solution. It will be interesting to see who the winners will be.

Better Training

Looking back at Chapter 1, Database Design Principle 1 called for an impenetrable wall between logical design and physical design. Principle 2 of the database design principles called for distinguishing logical data modeling from logical process modeling. The word *separate* is considerably harsher than the more intellectual *distinction*. This is intentional. The very nature of good design calls for the separation of logical and physical (the *what* from the *how*), while the distinction between data and process is more of an observation and realization of the real world of system development. In short, data and process are approached separately because that is how people work.

Object technology started as object-oriented programming, a code development approach that dealt with objects. Objects consist of data and processes. Object-oriented programming led to object-oriented design, object-oriented databases, object-oriented analysis, and object-oriented modeling. The hallmark of object-oriented modeling (OOM) is that the model (graphics and documentation) deals with both data and process.

OOM techniques, such as the Unified Modeling Language (UML), require the modeler to document the system's data and how those data are used, all in one single model, all in one single step.

It would seem that ideally, OOM would make Principle 2 unnecessary. Unfortunately, the critical word is *ideally*—in practice, there have been some problems.

OO OR UH, OH

I visited an IT organization of a major financial institution that was "committed to object technology." They had OO analysis tools, OO design tools, OO programming tools, and, of course, an OODBMS.

An analyst was demonstrating how a process he was working on was entered into a very expensive OOM tool. As he ran through the various operations, I asked him about some of the data on the model. His response was that I would have to talk to the data team about that. Sooo, so close.

Unfortunately, this was not an isolated incident. In the majority of the few IT shops that reported they used OO techniques, either the OO models were just fancy data flow diagrams or, if there was a real effort to use OO techniques, the data and process tasks were performed by two separate teams or one team composed of two separate sets of experts.

Any success in unifying data and process will come from neither the technology nor the tools, but from the people. And so far that is missing.

UML is criticized for being bureaucratic, cumbersome, and ineffective. It is certainly true that the commercial IT world has not embraced it. However, the problem with UML is not the clumsiness of the language, but the psychology of the people in IT.

As was mentioned in Chapter 1, until analysts and designers see the equal importance of understanding both data and process, not much will happen. As long as IT still has process people and data people, schools and vendors still train the two separately, and IT management is concerned with one more than the other, the problems will continue—and books like this one will still be necessary. Only when the data teams and the process teams are merged into the analysis team, not just organizationally but intellectually, can we even consider replacing Principle 2. And the one prediction I am willing to make is that this change will take a very long time.

Notes

1. George Tillmann, "The Impact of Relational Systems on Future Database Management Systems." *TeleSystems Journal.* Volume IX, No. 2, March–April 1982.

2. Edgar F. Codd, "A Relational Model of Data for Large Shared Data Banks." *Communications of the ACM.* 13.6 (1970) p. 377.

3. Edgar F. Codd, *Deliverability, Redundancy, and Consistency of Relations Stored in Large Data Banks.* San Jose, IBM Research Report RJ599 (1969) p. 1.

4. Peter Chen, "Entity-Relationship Modeling: Historical Events, Future Trends, and Lessons Learned," pp. 296-310 in Manfred Broy and Ernst Denert (Editors), *Software Pioneers: Contributions to Software Engineering.* Springer Science & Business Media, 2002.

5. Schumpeter, Joseph. *Capitalism, Socialism, and Democracy.* London: Allen & Unwin, 1943.

PART V

■ ■ ■

Appendixes

Appendixes

APPENDIX A

■ ■ ■

Glossary

0NF   See Zero Normal Form (0NF).
1NF   See First Normal Form (1NF).
2NF   See Second Normal Form (2NF).
3NF   See Third Normal Form (3NF).
Abstraction   A representation of a subject that excludes unnecessary detail while focusing on important features.
ACID   An acronym for atomicity, consistency, isolation, and durability.
Action Diagram   Generic term for a graphical representation of the movement of data in a system.
Actuator   A mechanical arm consisting of a read head and/or a write head that can extend over or under a disk platter.
Aggregate Data Item   See Group Data Item.
Alternate Key   In the relational model, a candidate key that was not selected to be the primary key.
Analysis   See Logical Design.
Analyze Information   The second step in the Logical Data Modeling phase and the activity in which the logical data modeling principles and techniques are applied to the information gathered in the *Gather Information and Review* step.
Anomaly   A data integrity problem that occurs in a database when an object that is inserted, updated, or deleted causes an unintended change in another object or objects.
Architectural Approach   The underlying physical structure of a DBMS. Examples include hierarchal, network, and relational.
Architecture   See Architectural Approach.
Association   In object technology, the relationships between objects.
Associative Array   A table of pairs of keys and their values. The key is used to find its associated value.
Associative Entity   A relationship that has its own relationships or attributes.
Associative Record Type   A link that has its own links or data items.
Asymmetrical Relationship   A recursive modality constraint. A unidirectional unary relationship that represents a sequence or hierarchy that must have a beginning and end. In an asymmetrical relationship, each entity occurrence plays a different role. For example, take the relationship Supervises. One role is "Supervisor," and the other role is "Is supervised."
Atomic Attribute   See Simple Attribute.
Atomic Data Item   See Simple Data Item.

© George Tillmann 2017
G. Tillmann, *Usage-Driven Database Design*, DOI 10.1007/978-1-4842-2722-0_17

Atomicity   An ACID component. Atomicity requires every part of a transaction to be executed before the transaction can be considered complete.

Attribute   A property of an entity such as COLOR, NAME, EMPLOYMENT DATE, or SOCIAL SECURITY NUMBER.

Attribute Complexity   Refers to the intricacy of an attribute. There are two types of attribute complexity: simple and group.

Attribute Domain   The set of possible values of an attribute. There are three types of attribute domains. Data types are broad categories of data values, such as text, integers, and dates. Ranges are values between end points, such as years between 1900 and 2020. Acceptable values are a list of allowed values, as in the abbreviations USA, EU, and UK.

Attribute Occurrence   See Attribute Value.

Attribute Source   The origin of an attribute. There are two sources: primitive and derived.

Attribute Valuation   Defines how many values the attribute can have at any one time. There are two types of valuation: single value and multivalue.

Attribute Value   The property of an attribute.

Attributive Entity   An entity whose existence depends on another entity.

Attributive Record Type   A record type whose existence depends on another record type.

B-tree   An inverted tree index consisting of layers of nodes. Each node contains one or more entries consisting of a search key and a database address.

Bachman Diagram   See Data Structure Diagram.

Best Practices   An experienced-based collection of rules, advice, and insight regarding the correct, most effective, and/or productive application of one or more techniques.

Big Data   A generic name for large but nonspecific amounts of data.

Bill of Materials   1. The problem of representing an n-level hierarchy where n is unknown. For example, a parts model where a part can be composed of other parts. 2. A solution to the bill of materials problem using recursion to represent the various levels. An example is the entity or record PART related or linked recursively to other PART occurrences.

Binary Link   A link between two, and only two, records.

Binary Relationship   A relationship between two, and only two, entities.

Binary Search   A search technique that divides a sorted file into two equal parts. If the desired record is in one part, then the other part is discarded, and the remaining part is divided into two equal parts. The process repeats until the desired record is found.

Bitmap   A subject index in which each bit aligns with the displacement of a record in a file or database (i.e., bit 1 represents the first record in the file/database, bit 2 the second record, etc.). The subject must be testable as a binary condition—either true or false, yes or no, on or off, and so on. If the condition is met (true, yes, etc.), the bit is set to 1. If the condition is not met, then the bit is set to 0. For example, if the subject COLOR is defined as "blue," then if the COLOR data item in the first record is blue, the first bit in the bitmap is set to 1. If COLOR in the first record is not blue, then the first bit is set to 0. Bitmaps are especially efficient for Boolean searches.

Blob   Originally an informal or whimsical term for large records or data fields that defied structural classification. It was later formalized to mean Binary Large OBject.

Blocking Factor   The ratio derived by dividing the database page size by the (average) size of the records stored on that page. A blocking factor of five means that (on average) five records can be stored on a database page.

Branch Node   In an inverted tree-structured file, the records that are neither root nodes nor leaf nodes.

Business Key   See Natural Key.

Candidate Key   In the relational model, a data item that uniquely identifies a record occurrence or row. A record can have multiple candidate keys.

Cardinality   1. In the Logical Data Modeling phase, the maximum number of occurrences of one entity type that can be related to an occurrence of another entity type. There are four cases of cardinality: one-to-one (1:1), one-to-many (1:N), many-to-many (M:N), and many-to-one (M:1). 2. In the Physical Schema Definition phase, the maximum number of occurrences of one record type that can be linked to an occurrence of another record type. There are four cases of cardinality: one-to-one (1:1), one-to-many (1:N), many-to-many (M:N), and many-to-one (M:1).

CASE   See Computer-Assisted Software Engineering.

Class   See Object Class.

Clustering   Placing one record occurrence on the same database page as another record occurrence so that the physical I/O to access one occurrence will also access the other occurrence. A common clustering strategy involves the parent-child binary relationship; the child record type occurrences are placed physically near the parent record type occurrence so that there is a significant chance that the physical I/O to access the parent will also access the child.

CODASYL   See Conference/Committee on Data Systems Languages.

Column   In the relational model, a data item.

Combined Usage Map   Deliverable PSD.2.3; multiple individual usage maps are combined into a single diagram.

Composite Key   See Compound Key.

Compound Key   A key consisting of more than one data item.

Compound Unique Identifier   Two or more attributes used by the business to uniquely identify an entity occurrence.

Computer-Assisted Software Engineering (CASE)   A product consisting of one or more tools to automate all or part of the system development process.

Concatenated Unique Identifier   See Compound Unique Identifier.

Conditional Conjunction   1. In the Logical Data Modeling phase, a type of conjunction that states that, given three (or more) entities A, B, and C and two (or more) relationships, one between A and B and one between A and C, if an occurrence of A is related to an occurrence of B, then it must also be related to an occurrence of C. 2. In the Physical Schema Definition phase, a type of conjunction that states that, given three (or more) records A, B, and C and two (or more) links, one between A and B, and one between A and C, if an occurrence of A is linked to an occurrence of B, then it must also be linked to an occurrence of C.

Conference/Committee on Data Systems Languages (CODASYL)   A volunteer standards group that gave us, among other things, standardized COBOL.

Conjunction   A relationship and linkage constraint. 1. In the Logical Data Modeling phase, if an occurrence of entity A is related to an occurrence of entity B, then it must also be related to an occurrence of entity C. There are two types of conjunction: simple conjunction and conditional conjunction. 2. In the Physical Schema Definition phase, if an occurrence of record A is linked to an occurrence of record B, then it must also be linked to an occurrence of record C. There are two types of conjunction: simple conjunction and conditional conjunction.

Consistency   An ACID component. Any change to the database must be consistent with all validation rules.

Constraint Compliance   A Physical Schema Definition step 3, Formalization, task. The rules of the particular vendor's DBMS product are applied to the rationalized physical data model.

Construct Model   The third step in the Logical Data Modeling phase and the activity in which the logical data model is created using the information collected in *Gather Information and Review* and analyzed in *Analyze Information*.

Convergence Principle   The third database design principle, Merge Physical Process Modeling with Physical Data Modeling. During physical design, data and process should converge into a single usage-driven physical database design.

Currency   1. A cursor's position within a database. 2. The record, link, or data item most recently accessed.

Customization   The fourth step of the Physical Schema Definition phase. It focuses on improving the performance and enhancing the usability of the database, resulting in an enhanced physical database design.

Customization Notes   Deliverable PSD.4.5; a narrative or journal created by the database designer describing the activities, issues, and decisions made during step 4, Customization.

Data Aggregate   See Group Attribute.

Data Architecture   See Architectural Approach.

Data Base Task Group (DBTG)   A committee of the voluntary standards organization CODASYL that, when working to standardize the network model, introduced the first Data Manipulation Language (DML) and Data Definition Language (DDL).

Data Definition Language (DDL)   A language or sublanguage that is used by the database administrator to create, modify, and delete database schemas and subschemas.

Data Dictionary   A repository of detailed documentation and other useful information about logical and physical data objects. The dictionary can be as simple as a loose-leaf binder or as sophisticated as an automated library system.

Data Field   See Data Item.

Data Flow Diagram (DFD)   A graphical representation of the logical or conceptual movement of data within an existing or planned system.

Data Independence   The isolation of data from the use of the data such that a change to one does not affect the other.

Data Item   A characteristic or descriptor of a record. If the record type is Employee, then typical data items are EMPLOYEE NAME, EMPLOYEE START DATE, and EMPLOYEE SALARY. Using the type/occurrence distinction, data item is the type, while data value or just value is the occurrence.

Data Item Complexity   Refers to the intricacy of a data item. There are two types of data item complexity: simple and group.

Data Item Domain   The set of possible values of a data item. There are three types of domains. Data types are broad categories of data values, such as text, integers, and dates. Ranges are values between end points, such as years between 1900 and 2020. Acceptable values are a list of allowed values, as in the abbreviations USA, EU, and UK.

Data Item Occurrence   See Data Value.

Data Item Type   See Data Item.

Data Item Valuation   Describes how many values a data item can have. There are two types of valuation: single value and multivalue.

Data Lake   A data repository for unstructured data.

Data Manipulation Language (DML)   A sublanguage that is used to define how database information is accessed, created, and destroyed by the programmer or end user.

Data Mart   A subset of a data warehouse.

Data Model   1. A representation, using text and/or graphics, of the definition, characterization, and relationships of data in a given environment. 2. No longer used, the DBMS architecture (hierarchical, network, relational, etc.).

Data Modeling Objects   The building blocks of a data model. The three basic logical objects are entities, attributes, and relationships. The three basic physical objects are records, data items, and linkages.

Data Modeling   The process of identifying and representing the definition, usage, and/or storage of data.

Data Repository   See Data Dictionary.

Data Structure Diagram (DSD)   Also called a Bachman diagram. This was the first graphic data modeling technique, created by Charles Backman in 1969, which depicts entities or record types as rectangles and relationships as arrows.

Data Value   The characteristics of a single data item. For example in COLOR = "blue," COLOR is a data item and blue is its data value. Using the type/occurrence distinction, data item is the type, while data value or just value is the occurrence.

Data Warehouse   The storage system to support decision support system data.

Database Administrator (DBA)   The IT person responsible for planning, designing, operating, and maintaining enterprise databases.

Database Design   See Physical Database Design.

Database Design Missing Link   The missing component that merges the static definition of data (the data model) with the more dynamic use of those data (the process models), resulting in a structurally resilient, functionally rich, effective, and efficient database design.

Database Design Principles   The postulates or axioms guiding the Usage-Driven Database Design (U3D) approach. There are four principles: (1) Separation Principle, which is to separate logical design from physical design; (2) Distinction Principle, which is to distinguish logical data modeling from logical process modeling; (3) Convergence Principle, which is to merge physical process modeling with physical data modeling; and (4) Minimal Regression Principle, which is to design a database so that business and technology changes minimize database redesign.

Database Designer   The IT person responsible for converting the logical data and process models into a physical database schema and subschemas.

Database Key   A key that tells the information system where a record occurrence is located.

Database Management System (DBMS)   A software system to manage the storage, access, and update of information for one or many users.

Database Page   An allotment of secondary storage usually consisting of multiple contiguous sectors that are read or written as a block by the DBMS.

DBA   See Database Administrator.

DBMS   See Database Management System.

DBTG   See Data Base Task Group.

DDBMS   See Distributed Database Management System.

DDL   See Data Definition Language.

Decision Support System (DSS)   A system that provides management and certain subject experts with the capability to dig deep into the voluminous data created by the operational systems, to uncover the trends and patterns they contain. The basic DSS includes (1) a user interface or front end, often containing analytical and mathematical capabilities, and (2) a storage system to house the data the user interface analyzes.

Declarative Programming Language   A programming language that the programmer or user uses to instruct the system on what has to be done, not how it is done. Declarative programming is usually contrasted with procedural programming.

Degree   An indicator of the number of entity types that are allowed in a relationship. There are three degree cases: unary or recursive, binary, and n-ary.

Denormalization   Reintroduction into a normalized database design features that were removed to meet normalization requirements, such as repeating groups, aggregate data items, and data duplication. Denormalization most often occurs for performance reasons.

Derived Attribute   An attribute that is the result of a calculation or algorithm applied to one or more other attributes (primitive or derived). For example, the derived attribute TOTAL AMOUNT is the sum of individual AMOUNT attributes.

Derived Data Item   A data item that is the result of a calculation or algorithm applied to one or more other data items (primitive or derived). For example, the derived data item TOTAL AMOUNT is the sum of individual AMOUNT data items.

Descriptor Attribute   A not necessarily unique characteristic or property of an entity or relationship.

Descriptor Data Item   A data item that describes or gives the characteristics of a record.

Design   See Physical Design.

DFD   See Data Flow Diagram.

Dimension   The searchable characteristics of a data warehouse.

Dimension Record   In a data warehouse, the record used to search and select the desired fact records. Dimension records are usually in a one-to-many relationship with the fact records.

Disk Contention   Competition for disk access. Contention can result in thrashing, which is the movement of the actuator arm rapidly back and forth across the disk to accommodate competing requests for service.

Distinction Principle   The second database design principle. Distinguish logical data modeling from logical process modeling. All data definitions, characteristics, and relationships need to be analyzed, designed, and documented separately from all process definitions, characteristics, and uses.

Distributed Database Management System (DDBMS)   A DBMS that can fully support a database that resides on more than one computer, whether the computers are in the same room or across the globe.

DML   See Data Manipulation Language.

Document Management   A DBMS, usually of a key-value structure, that stores, accesses, and deletes documents and document components such as graphics, pictures, tables, and so on.

DSD   See Data Structure Diagram.

Duplicate Data   Two or more attributes or data items with the same definition.

Durability An ACID component. Once a transaction is committed, it stays committed. Failures from a loss of power to a computer, communications disruptions, or crashes of any type will not affect a completed transaction.

Embedded Attribute An attribute hidden in another attribute.

Encapsulation An object technology concept that allows an object to hide internal data and procedures from other objects. What goes on in an object stays in an object.

End Users Those who commission the building of an information system, representing those who commission the system or will use the commissioned system. They are usually nontechnical staff (unless the system is designed to serve technical staff, e.g., an application tracking system).

Enhanced Database Object Definitions Deliverable PSD.4.4; an update of all database object definitions to reflect changes made in step 4, Customization.

Enhanced Physical Database Design Diagram Deliverable PSD.4.1; the final physical database design diagram.

Enhanced Schema DDL Deliverable PSD.4.2; the performance-enhanced version of the schema created in step 3, Formalization.

Enhanced Subschema DDL Deliverable PSD.4.3; a performance-enhanced version of the subschema created in step 3, Formalization.

Entity A person, place, or thing about which an organization wants to save information.

Entity Fragment A view or portion of the data model that characterizes a specific process. Entity fragments are useful for logical process modelers who want to understand the data used in a particular function or to elicit process information from end users.

Entity-Relationship Approach Also called entity-relationship model; an approach to logical data modeling, introduced by Peter Chen in 1976, that focuses on the nontechnical "business" data objects, entities, attributes, and relationships rather than on files, records, and databases.

Entity-Relationship Diagram (ERD) The logical data modeling diagram created using the E-R approach.

Entity-Relationship Model See Entity-Relationship Approach.

Environment Designation A task of step 3, Formalization, of the Physical Schema Definition phase; analysis and selection of the physical information manager (architecture, product, and version).

ERD See Entity-Relationship Diagram.

Exclusion A relationship and linkage constraint. 1. In the Logical Data Modeling phase, an occurrence of entity type A can be related to an occurrence of entity type B or to an occurrence of entity type C, but not both at the same time. 2. In the Physical Schema Definition phase, an occurrence of record type A can be linked to an occurrence of record type B or to an occurrence of record type C, but not both at the same time.

Expansion A task of step 1, Transformation, of the Physical Schema Definition phase; augmentation of the record type in its transformation from logical to physical information management.

Fact Record Type In a data warehouse, stores facts about the data warehouse subject. Fact records are linked to dimension records in a many-to-one relationship.

Fat Record Informal; the result of contiguously storing multiple occurrences of multiple entities as a single database record in order to allow single I/O retrieval.

File A collection of related records.

First Normal Form (1NF)   In normalization, a record is in 1NF if (1) the record is in zero normal form and (2) all multivalue data items (Codd calls them repeating groups) have been removed from the record.

Flexibility   A trade-off triangle component; the ability of the database system to support a broad range of known and unknown services and to easily adapt to business and technology changes.

Foreign Key   In the relational model, one or more fields in one table that have the same definitions and domains as the primary key in another table. Foreign keys are used for linking related tables together.

Formalization   The third Physical Schema Definition step; modifies the rationalized physical data model to comply with the rules/features of the DBMS (or file manager) being used, creating a functional physical database design.

Formalization Notes   Deliverable PSD.3.5; a narrative or journal created by the database designer describing the activities, issues, and decisions made during step 3, Formalization.

Framework   A structured guide for developing a system encompassing a common set of steps, definitions, techniques, and deliverables.

Full Functional Dependence   In normalization, a state in which a data item is functionally dependent on a compound key but is not functionally dependent of a subset of that compound key.

Functional Dependence   In normalization, a state that exists when one data item uniquely determines another data item. For example, given two record occurrences with the data items EMPLOYEE NAME and the unique EMPLOYEE NUMBER, if the data values of both occurrences of EMPLOYEE NAME are "Smith" and if EMPLOYEE NUMBER will always point to the correct "Smith," then EMPLOYEE NAME is functionally dependent on EMPLOYEE NUMBER.

Functional Physical Database Design Diagram   Deliverable PSD.3.1; a database diagram showing the record types and links.

Functional Physical Object Definitions   Deliverable PSD.3.4; the same physical definitions created in step 1, Transformation, updated with any necessary changes made during step 2, Utilization, which now need updating with step 3, Formalization, information.

Functional Schema DDL   Deliverable PSD.3.2; two versions should be created: (1) generic DDL conforming to the database architecture and (2) vendor product and version specific.

Functional Subschema DDL   Deliverable PSD.3.3; two versions should be created: (1) generic DDL conforming to the database architecture and (2) vendor product and version specific.

Fundamental Entity   See Proper Entity.

Gather Information and Review   The first step of the U3D Logical Data Modeling phase; the activity in which the data modeler assembles all available documentation about the subject area, interviews subject-matter experts, and then reviews the results with both experts and management.

Generalization/Specialization   See Subtypes/Supertype.

Group Attribute   An attribute that contains a fixed number of other attributes. An example would be the group attribute CUSTOMER ADDRESS, which contains the five simple attributes CUSTOMER STREET NUMBER, CUSTOMER STREET NAME, CUSTOMER CITY, CUSTOMER STATE/PROVINCE, and CUSTOMER POSTAL CODE.

Group Data Item   Also called an aggregate data item; contains a fixed number of other data items. An example would be the group data item CUSTOMER ADDRESS, which contains the five simple data items CUSTOMER STREET NUMBER, CUSTOMER STREET NAME, CUSTOMER CITY, CUSTOMER STATE/PROVINCE, and CUSTOMER POSTAL CODE.

Hash Algorithm   A formula applied to a search key to determine its physical storage location.

Hash Key   A result of applying a hash algorithm to a search key.

Hashing   The application of an algorithm to a search key to derive a physical storage location.

Hierarchical Data Model   See Hierarchical Model.

Hierarchical Model   A DBMS architecture where record types are organized into a one-to-many inverted tree structure consisting of one or more parent-child layers.

I/O   See Input/Output (I/O).

Identifier   1. An attribute(s) that can pick out or identify one or more entity occurrences. 2. A short, although technically incorrect, name for a unique identifier.

Inclusion   A relationship and linkage constraint. 1. In the Logical Data Modeling phase, an occurrence of entity type A can be related to an occurrence of entity type B or to an occurrence of entity type C or to both. 2. In the Physical Schema Definition phase, an occurrence of record type A can be linked to an occurrence of record type B or to an occurrence of record type C or to both.

Index   A file that stores the search key and the location of each record with that key.

Inheritance   1. The transference of the properties of one data object to another data object. For example, in logical data modeling, subtypes can inherit attributes and relationships from the supertype. 2. In object technology, a concept that allows a child object to inherit data and/or procedures from its parent.

Input/Output (I/O)   Accessing data from (input) or writing data to (output) a secondary storage device, such as a disk or tape.

Instance   See Occurrence.

Intelligent Key   A data item, fabricated, in whole or in part, from one or more business-relevant data items, usually for the purposes of making the data item unique.

Interpretation   The metadata (name, size, data type, etc.) associated with a data item.

Inverted File   A sequential file of search keys and file or database pointers or locations, sorted by search key. Each search key corresponds to a content data item in a database (or file), which, if sorted, is usually sorted on a different key.

Inverted Index   See Inverted File.

Isolation   An ACID component. Every transaction must be completed as though it were the only transaction, regardless of how many transactions there are and in what sequence they are executed. Isolation deals with the notion of currency control.

IUD Anomaly   See Anomaly.

Junction Entity   In the Logical Data Modeling phase, the inappropriate and misapplied "resolving" of a many-to-many relationship by inserting between the two original (m:n) entities a third "junction" entity with a many-to-one relationship to each of the original entities. Resolving many-to-many relationships is a physical database design issue inappropriate in logical data modeling.

Junction Record   The result of an activity in the Physical Schema Definition phase to remove a many-to-many link between record types for database management systems that cannot support them. The database designer creates a junction record type between the two original record types. The single many-to-many relationship is replaced with two one-to-many relationships with the junction record at the "many" end of both.

Key   One or more data items used to identify a record occurrence.

Key-Value   A storage and retrieval technique. Key refers to the access key to fetch the pair, and the value is the data item content. For example, the key value pair STUDENT NUMBER:STUDENT NAME (a colon separates the key from the value) is stored as a single data item. Fetching STUDENT NUMBER returns the value of STUDENT NAME. In most cases, there is one occurrence of a key for each occurrence of value.

Latency   The time it takes for the desired disk sector to rotate under/over the read/write head.

Leaf Node   In an inverted tree-structured file, the records at the lowest level of the tree.

Linkage Constraint   A restriction on how records can link to each other. There are three linkage constraints: exclusion, inclusion, and conjunction.

Linked List   A sequential storage and retrieval technique in which a record occurrence in a list (file) includes the pointer to the next record occurrence in the list (file).

Logical Data Model   1. A text and/or graphical representation of the information used in an organization from an end-user perspective, without regard to its functional or physical aspects. 2. Logical Data Modeling deliverable LDM.1 (E-R diagram), which is the diagram showing all entities and relationships.

Logical Data Model Object Definitions   Data dictionary; Logical Data Modeling deliverable LDM.2, which consists of the detailed documentation for each entity, attribute, relationship, and domain.

Logical Data Modeling   1. A collection, verification, and communication technique to fully document data requirements to aid in the development of accurate, efficient, and flexible information platforms (database or file) 2. The first Usage-Driven Database Design phase (U3D:LDM). An iterative approach focused on identifying business entities and then determining the attributes and relationships supporting those entities.

Logical Data Modeling Notes   Deliverable LDM.3; any comments, advice, difficulties, questions, suggestions, warnings, or other information the logical data modeler wants to communicate to physical designers.

Logical Database Description   An IMS view or subschema.

Logical Design   The phase in the system development lifecycle in which the user's view of the application is documented in terms of *what* the user wants, not *how* it will be delivered. The logical design becomes the input to the physical design phase.

Logical I/O   A request to access a secondary storage device.

Logical Process Model   A text and/or graphic representation of the existing or planned functional capabilities of an application.

Mandatory-Mandatory (M:M)   A modality case. 1. In the Logical Data Modeling phase, every occurrence of entity type A must be related to at least one occurrence of entity type B, and every occurrence of entity type B must be related to at least one occurrence of entity type A. For example, an Order must be related to at least one Line Item, and a Line Item must be related to an Order. 2. In the Physical Schema Definition phase, every occurrence of record type A must be linked to at least one occurrence of record type B, and every occurrence of record type B must be linked to at least one occurrence of record type A. For example, an Order must be linked to at least one Line Item, and a Line Item must be linked to an Order.

Mandatory-Optional (M:O)   A modality case. 1. In the Logical Data Modeling phase, every occurrence of entity type A must be related to at least one occurrence of entity type B, but an occurrence of entity type B need not be related to an occurrence of entity type A. For example, an Account need not be related to any Orders (it might have been just set up), but an Order must be related to an Account. 2. In the Physical Schema Definition phase, every occurrence of record type A must be linked to at least one occurrence of record type B, but an occurrence of record type B need not be linked to an occurrence of record type A. For example, an Account need not be linked to any Orders (it might have been just set up), but an Order must be linked to an Account.

Many-to-Many (M:N)   A cardinality case. 1. In the Logical Data Modeling phase, an occurrence of entity type A can relate to many occurrences of entity type B, while an occurrence of entity type B can relate to many occurrences of entity type A. For example, an uncle can have many nephews while a nephew can have many uncles. 2. In the Physical Schema Definition phase, an occurrence of record type A can be linked to many occurrences of record type B, while an occurrence of record type B can be linked to many occurrences of record type A. For example, an uncle can have many nephews while a nephew can have many uncles.

Many-to-One (M:1)   A cardinality case. Because both Logical Data Modeling relationships and Physical Schema Definition linkages are bidirectional, a many-to-one relationship is the inverse of a one-to-many relationship.

Membership Class   1. In the Logical Data Modeling phase, the number of instances of one entity type that can be related to another entity type. There are two types of membership class: cardinality and modality. 2. In the Physical Schema Definition phase, the number of instances of one record type that can be linked to another record type. There are two types of membership class: cardinality and modality.

Method   A detailed approach to applying one or more techniques that usually includes the sequence of steps to be performed, deliverables to be produced, discipline to be followed, and project management steps to be executed.

Methodology   See Method.

Middleware   Software that is used as an intermediary between other software components, often between the operating system and other system software.

Minimal Regression Principle   The fourth database design principle. Design a database so that business and technology changes minimize database redesign. Changes to any database design step should not require going back to the beginning and starting the design process over again.

Modality   1. In the Logical Data Modeling phase, expresses whether an entity's involvement in a relationship is mandatory or optional. There are four cases of modality: mandatory-mandatory (M:M), mandatory-optional (M:O), optional-optional (O:O), and optional-mandatory (O:M). 2. In the Physical Schema Definition phase, expresses whether a record's involvement in a linkage is mandatory or optional. There are four cases of modality: mandatory-mandatory (M:M), mandatory-optional (M:O), optional-optional (O:O), and optional-mandatory (O:M).

Model   An abstract representation of a subject that looks and/or behaves like all or part of the original.

Modeling   The process of creating the abstract representation of a subject so that it can be studied more cheaply (a scale model of an airplane in a wind tunnel), at a particular moment in time (weather forecasting), or manipulated, modified, and altered without disrupting the original (economic model).

Multivalue Attribute   An attribute that can have any number of values at the same time. An example would be the Employee entity and its attribute EMPLOYEE DEGREES. Smith might have only one degree, a "BS," while Jones has three degrees, "BS," "MA," and "PhD."

Multivalue Data Item   A data item that can have any number of values at the same time. An example, the Employee record and its data items EMPLOYEE DEGREES. Smith might have only one degree, a "BS," while Jones has three degrees, "BS," "MA," and "PhD."

N-ary Link   A single link between three or more record types.

N-ary Relationship   A single relationship between three or more entities.

Natural Key   A logical data modeling business-relevant identifier.

Navigation   A network model term to describe the programmer or end user controlled movement about the database.

Neighborhood Diagram   A diagram containing a single entity, its relationships, and the entities that are directly tied to those relationships.

Network Data Model   See Network Model.

Network Model   A DBMS architecture where record types are organized in a many-to-many structure consisting of multiple parent-child sets.

Node   The records in an inverted tree-structured file.

Normalization   A Physical Schema Definition phase physical database design technique involving the application of a set of mathematical rules to the physical data model to identify, eliminate, or reduce insertion, update, and deletion (IUD) anomalies.

NoSQL   Any of a class of database management systems that reject the limitations and drawbacks dictated by, or associated with, the relational model. NoSQL products tend to specialize in a single or limited number of areas, such as high-performance processing, big data (giga-record systems), diverse data types (video, pictures, mathematical models), documents, and so on. Their specialized focus often requires deemphasizing other areas such as data consistency and backup and recovery.

Object   In object technology, a data construct (logical or physical) whose properties include both data and the operations or procedures that create, access, modify, or delete that data.

Object Class   In object technology, the type or set of objects that share a distinguishing factor.

Object Technology   A model and development approach in which a system is composed of objects that contain both data and procedures (computer code). Two object technology trademarks are encapsulation and inheritance.

Object-Oriented Database Management System (OODBMS)   A database management systems based on object technology.

Occurrence   A particular member or participant of a type, such as the Bob (the occurrence) of (the type) Employee.

OLTP   See Online Transaction Processing.

One-of-a-Kind   Also known as an OOAK (rhymes with "nuke"); an entity type containing only a single occurrence.

One-to-Many (1:N)   A *cardinality* case. 1. In the Logical Data Modeling phase, one occurrence of entity type A can relate to many occurrences of entity type B, but an occurrence of entity type B can relate to only one occurrence of entity type A. For example, a mother can have many children, but a child can have only one mother. 2. In the Physical Schema Definition phase, one occurrence of record type A can be linked to many occurrences of record type B, but an occurrence of record type B can be linked to only once occurrence of record type A. For example, a mother can have many children, but a child can have only one mother.

One-to-One (1:1)   A cardinality case. 1. In the Logical Data Modeling phase, an occurrence of entity type A can relate to at most one occurrence of entity type B, and an occurrence of entity type B can relate to at most one occurrence of entity type A. For example, a husband can have only one wife, and a wife only one husband. 2. In the Physical Schema Definition phase, an occurrence of record type A can be linked to at most one occurrence of record type B, and an occurrence of record type B can linked to at most one occurrence of record type A. For example, a husband can have only one wife, and a wife only one husband.

Online Transaction Processing (OLTP)   An application-based computer activity corresponding to a business activity that wholly or partially occurs in real time.

OOAK record   A concept from the network model, a one-of-a-kind record type with a single record occurrence. It is used primarily to store application housekeeping information, such as next order number or billing closing dates.

OODBMS   See Object-Oriented Database Management System.

Operation   In object technology, a process or procedure that acts on an object.

Optional-Mandatory (O:M)   A modality case. Because both Logical Data Modeling relationships and Physical Schema Definition links are bidirectional, an optional-mandatory relationship is the inverse of a mandatory-optional relationship.

Optional-Optional (O:O)   A modality case. 1. In the Logical Data Modeling phase, an occurrence of entity type A need not be related to any occurrence of entity type B, and an occurrence of entity type B need not be related to any occurrence of entity type A. For example, in Banks Finance Cars, a Bank might, but need not, Finance any Cars, and a Car might, or might not, be Financed by a Bank. 2. In the Physical Schema Definition phase, an occurrence of record type A need not be linked to any occurrence of record type B, and an occurrence of record type B need not be linked to any occurrence of record type A. For example, in Banks Finance Cars, a Bank might, but need not, Finance any Cars, and a Car might, or might not, be Financed by a Bank.

Optionality   See Modality.

Parent-Child Link   Two record types organized with a single parent record occurrence linked to one or more child record occurrences. An example would be a single parent Order record occurrence linked to one or more Line Item record occurrences.

Parent-Child Relationship   Two entity types organized with a single parent entity occurrence related to one or more child entity occurrences. An example would be a single parent Order entity occurrence related to one or more Line Item entity occurrences.

Partial Dependency   See Partial Functional Dependency.

Partial Functional Dependency   In normalization, a state in which a data item is functionally dependent on a subset of a compound primary key.

Participation   See Modality.

Partition   A region, area, or subset of a file.

Partitioned-Row Store   The result of storing multiple (usually related) rows as a single partition.

Path Rationalization   A task of step 2, Utilization, of the Physical Schema Definition phase; reduces the complexity of the physical data model to only what is needed to perform its assigned functions.

Performance Enhancement   A task of step 4, Customization, of the Physical Schema Definition phase; the application of software and/or hardware techniques and tools to improve the performance of the database.

Physical Data Model   Deliverable PSD.1.1; the physical representation of the logical data model.

Physical Database Design   1. A data model configured to reflect the usage of data for a particular physical environment. 2. The DBMS or language-dependent specifications of what the information base should look like and how it should function. 3. A process for identifying and evaluating trade-offs and calculating the best solution to balance performance and cost for the current and near-term needs of the end user.

Physical Design   The phase in the system development lifecycle in which the user's view of the application is converted into technical design specifications—the core theme is *how* to deliver *what* the user wants.

Physical I/O   The actual (physical) accessing of information from a secondary storage device.

Physical Object Definitions   Data dictionary; deliverable PSD.1.2, which is the detailed documentation for each record type, data item, link, and domain.

Physical Process Model   A text and/or graphical representation of a system (hardware and software), focusing on what the system does or how it should perform the functions identified in a logical process model.

Physical Schema Definition   U3D:PSD, the second phase of Usage-Driven Database Design, that is divided into four steps: (1) *Transformation* turns the logical data model into a physical data model, (2) *Utilization* merges the deliverables defined in Logical Process Modeling and Physical Process Definition phases into the rationalized physical data model, (3) *Formalization* creates a working DBMS functional physical database design, and (4) *Customization* improves the performance of the database schema resulting in an enhanced physical database design.

Pointer   A data field containing either the actual or symbolic address of a database record.

Presentation Data   Copies of legitimate modeled attributes (primitive and derived) used in reports or on computer screens but not included on the data model.

Primary Key   A Physical Schema Definition data item or group of data items that uniquely identify a record occurrence.

Primitive Attribute   An attribute that cannot be derived from other attributes.

Primitive Data Item   A data item that cannot be derived from other data items.

Procedural Programming Language   A programming language with which the programmer or user instructs the system exactly what steps to perform and in what order to perform them. Procedural programming is usually contrasted with declarative programming.

Process Model   A representation, using text and/or graphics, of the definition of processes and procedures in a given environment.

Proper Entity   A simple or fundamental entity that can exist independent of other entities of relationships.

Proper Record Type   A simple or fundamental record type that can exist independent of other records of links.

Pseudocode   An imaginary computer language, mimicking formal computer language structure and detail, to document how a system does, or should, work.

Rationalized Physical Data Model   Deliverable PSD.2.4; a physical data model derivative that reflects how the user or application will use database.

RDBMS   See Relational Database Management System.

Real World Corollary   Corollary to Principle 1 of the database design principles. The purpose of logical design is to document the real world, which is the business world. There are two parts to Corollary 1: (1) a logical design is valid if, and only if, it reflects the real (business) world, and (2) a logical design is invalid if it contains nonreal (business) world objects or concepts. Invalid objects and concepts include items belonging in physical design such as foreign keys, pointers, and disk drives.

Record   The basic unit of stored data.

Recursive Relationship   See Unary Relationship.

Recursive Modality Constraint   Determines how entity occurrences in a recursive relationship relate to each other. There are two recursive modality constraint cases: symmetrical and asymmetrical.

Redundant Data   A term used by some data modelers to indicate intentional and justifiable duplicate data.

Relation   In the relational model, a record type.

Relational Database Management System (RDBMS)   A database management system based on the relational model.

Relational Model   A database architecture created by Edgar (Ted) Codd in 1969. The model is the first, and likely the only, architecture based on a formal foundation of predicate calculus and set theory. Data are represented as tuples (rhymes with couples) in relations.

Relational Theory   A popular, but technically incorrect, name for the relational model.

Relationship   A natural connection between two or more entities.

Relationship Constraint   A restriction on how entities can relate to each other. There are three relationship constraints: exclusion, inclusion, and conjunction.

Relationship-Entity Pair   A sentence construct (entity-relationship-entity) that represents a binary relationship.

Repeating Group   See Multivalue Attribute.

Repository   See Data Dictionary.

Resource Analysis   A task in step 4, Customization, of the Physical Schema Definition phase; examines the database to understand the demands that are placed on it and the impediments to meeting those demands.

Result Set   The record(s) meeting the condition(s) set by a query.

Role   1. The different parts subtypes play in a supertype. 2. In a recursive modality constraint, the type of relationship (symmetrical or asymmetrical) that exists between the two occurrences of a single entity in a recursive relationship. All occurrences play the same role in a symmetrical relationship but different roles in asymmetrical relationships.

Root Node   In an inverted tree-structured file, the records at the highest level of the tree.

Rotational Delay   See Latency.

Rotational Latency   See Latency.

S-type   See Supertype/Subtype.

Schema   A physical machine-readable detailed description of a database.

Schema On Read   A process ensuring that data conform to the schema (size, data type, etc.) when they are read from the database. Schema on read is less efficient for retrieval than schema on write and is used only when the DBMS does not have exclusive database write authority.

Schema On Write   A process ensuring that data conform to the schema (size, data type, etc.) when they are to be written to the database. Schema on write, the most popular DBMS storage technique, ensures that only schema-correct data are stored in the database.

SDLC   See Systems Development Life Cycle.

Search Argument   A character string used to search a file or index to locate one or more record occurrences.

Search Key   A data item or group of data items used to search a file or index to locate one or more record occurrences in a file or database.

Second Normal Form (2NF)   In normalization, a record is in 2NF if (1) the record is in First Normal Form, and (2) every non-key data item is fully functionally dependent on the primary key.

Secondary Key   A key that needs not be unique and is most commonly used to locate one or more related record occurrences.

Seek   To physically position a disk actuator to read or write a disk sector.

Seek Time   The time it takes to correctly position the disk actuator arm.

Segment   An IMS term for record.

Semantic Key   A key consisting of one or more (usually visible) user-meaningful data items.

Semistructured Data   See Unstructured Data.

Separation Principle   Principle 1 of the first database design principle. Separate logical design from physical design. The principle is to identify, analyze, and exhaust everything knowable about the logical definition of data before considering any physical design concepts.

Set   A network model term to describe a parent-child relationship. The parent is called the set owner and the child the set member.

Simple Attribute   An attribute that does not contain other attributes. A simple attribute is also called an atomic attribute.

Simple Conjunction   A conjunction constraint. 1. In the Logical Data Modeling phase, given three (or more) entities A, B, and C and two (or more) relationships, one between A and B and one between A and C; every A occurrence must be related to an occurrence of B *and* related to an occurrence of C. 2. In the Physical Schema Definition phase, given three (or more) record types A, B, and C and two (or more) links, one between A and B and one between A and C, every A occurrence must be related to an occurrence of B *and* related to an occurrence of C.

Simple Data Item   Also called an *atomic data item*. A data item that does not contain any other data items.

Single-Value Attribute   An attribute that can have only one value at a time. An example would be COLOR = "blue." If COLOR is "blue," then it cannot be "red," at least not at the same time.

Single-Value Data Item   A data item that can have only one value at a time. An example would be COLOR = "blue." If COLOR is "blue," then it cannot be "red," at least not at the same time.

Smart Key   See Intelligent Key.

344

Snowflake Schema   A data warehouse star schema in which a dimensional record type is linked to one or more nonfact record types.

Solid-State Drive   A completely electronic (no mechanical or moving parts) nonvolatile flash memory that appears to the system as a traditional rotating disk.

Sparse Data   1. A record containing one or more data fields that are blank, zero, or null. 2. Data fields that are individually insignificant but can be significant when taken as a group.

SQL   Originally a declarative query language created to front-end a relational database management system. It includes both an RDBMS DML and DDL. SQL grew to include an embedded procedural sublanguage. More recently, versions of SQL have been adapted for nonrelational database management systems as well.

Star Schema   A data warehouse design, consisting of a single fact record at the "many" end of a one-to-many link with multiple dimension records.

Structure Chart   A diagrammatic physical process modeling technique that represents the process as an inverted tree. The top of the tree is the root system or program level. Subsequent levels are modules representing greater process granularity. The very bottom levels usually represent program modules performing a single task.

Structured Data   A data field of a definable data type, usually of a specified size or range, that can be easily processed by a computer.

Structured English   A modified version of the English language used to communicate concepts with more exactness, simplicity, and rigor than common in everyday use.

Subject Area   A subset of a data model that contains the entities, relationships, and attributes that share certain common business characteristics and that facilitates the creation and development of, and communication about, the complete logical data model.

Subschema   A subset of a schema.

Substitution Data   Data stored in an abbreviation or conversion table that allows the storage of smaller codes (such as POSTAL CODE) in large occurrence record types (such as Customer). When the record is accessed, a table is read to fetch the name of the town relating to the postal code.

Supertype/Subtype   Sometimes abbreviated S-type, also called generalization and specialization. 1. In the Logical Data Modeling phase, an entity (the supertype) that contains more than one role (the subtypes). For example, the supertype Customer can include the subtypes Retail Customer and Wholesale Customer. The subtypes inherit the attributes and relationships of the supertype but can also have their own attributes and relationships. 2. In the Physical Schema Definition phase, a record (the supertype) that contains more than one role (the subtypes). For example, the supertype Customer can include the subtypes Retail Customer and Wholesale Customer. The subtypes inherit the data items and links of the supertype but can also have their own data items and links.

Surrogate Key   A user transparent key whose value is assigned either randomly or by a non-semantic-driven process such as the next integer in a series.

Symbolic Key   1. A user-recognizable character string for searching a file (a search argument). 2. Used by some computer languages to link related record types together, such as parent-child.

Symmetrical Relationship   A recursive modality constraint. A bidirectional unary relationship that represents a sequence or hierarchy that does not have a beginning or end. In a symmetrical relationship, all entity occurrences play the same role. For example, in the relationship Dances With, if A Dances With B, then B must Dance With A.

System Development Life Cycle (SDLC)   A formal process for the planning, analyzing, designing, developing, testing, and implementing of a computer-based system.

System-Generated Key   See Surrogate Key.

Technical Users   The system designers who use the output of other system designers.

Technique   A series of steps applied to a subject to change its representation. Data modeling, processing modeling, and prototyping are all techniques.

Third Normal Form (3NF)   In normalization, a record is in 3NF if (1) the record is in Second Normal Form and (2) there are no transitive functional dependencies.

Thrashing   The rapid repetitive movement of a disk actuator arm to accommodate service requests. Thrashing is often the result of competition for database resources.

Throughput   A trade-off triangle component. How quickly the database system can perform its function either in terms of response time for online applications or in terms of runtime of batch programs.

Tool   A physical or conceptual product that aids in applying techniques. CASE products and flow-charting templates are tools.

Trade-Off Triangle   A simple visual way to demonstrate, and gain buy-in to, database design trade-offs.

Trade-Off Triangle Serviceability Index   A tool that gives the database designer a framework for structuring potential challenges as well as a managing performance expectation when meeting with other technical staff and end users.

Transformation   The first Physical Schema Definition step; turns the logical data model into a physical data model by converting the logical objects entity, attribute, and relationship into the physical database objects record, data field, and linkage.

Transformation Notes   Deliverable PSD.1.3; a narrative or journal created by the database designer of the activities, issues, and decisions made during step 1, Transformation.

Transient Data   Temporary, duplicate, or process-related data that is usually not kept by the system or included on the logical data model.

Transitive Dependency   See Transitive Functional Dependency.

Transitive Functional Dependency   Functional dependency of a data item on another data item that is not part of the primary key.

Translation   A task of step 1, Transformation, of the Physical Schema Definition phase. The conversion in name and definition of logical data object into physical data objects.

Tuple   In the relational model, a row or record occurrence.

Two-Phase Commit   A protocol for synchronizing the creation, update, or deletion of a multirecord transaction where the transaction records reside, or will reside, on physically distinct computers. The protocol was an attempt to make distributed database management systems ACID compliant.

Type   A class or set of objects that share a distinguishing factor.

Type-Occurrence Distinction   Also type-instance distinction. The difference between a class of objects, the type, and a particular occurrence or instance of that type. For example, Employee is a type, while the particular employee, Bob, is an occurrence or instance of that type.

UML   See Unified Modeling Language.

Unary Link   A link between two or more occurrences of the same record type.

Unary Relationship   A relationship between two or more occurrences of the same entity type.

Unified Modeling Language (UML)   An ISO standard object-oriented modeling technique that focuses on both data and process within the same model (graphics and documentation).

Unique Identifier   A unique attribute that is used by the enterprise to point out a specific entity occurrence. Examples are SOCIAL SECURITY NUMBER = "123-45-6789" and CUSTOMER NUMBER = "123456."

Updated Physical Object Definitions   Deliverable PSD.2.5; the same physical definitions created in step 1, Transformation, updated with any necessary changes made during step 2, Utilization.

Usage Analysis   A task of step 2, Utilization, of the Physical Schema Definition phase; understanding exactly how the database will be used (data creation, access, update, and deletion) by users and applications.

Usage-Driven Database Design (U3D)   A database design principles–compliant, end-to-end approach for designing databases that encompasses the entire database development lifecycle, from logical data modeling through database schema definition.

Usage Map   Deliverable PSD.2.2; the graphical application of the individual usage scenarios onto the physical data model showing how the application must navigate the database.

Usage Scenario   Deliverable PSD.2.1; functional summaries describing how the database will be used by the application.

Unstructured Data   A data field that is not definable by definition, data type, or size but either contains structured components or can be at least semistructured through processing.

Utilization   The second Physical Schema Definition step; takes the deliverables defined in logical process modeling and physical process modeling and merges them with the physical data model. The step deliverable is a modified or rationalized physical data model that represents how the applications will use the database.

Utilization Notes   Deliverable PSD.2.6; a narrative or journal created by the database designer of the activities, issues, and decisions made during step 2, Utilization.

Value   1. In the Logical Data Modeling phase, an attribute instance or occurrence of an attribute type. 2. In the Physical Schema Definition phase, a data item instance or occurrence of a data item type.

Volume   A trade-off triangle component; the number of objects/actions the database system can accommodate, such as the number of record types or occurrences it can support or the number of concurrent online transactions it can handle.

Weak Entity   See Attributive Entity.

Weak Record Type   See Attributive Record Type.

Wide Column   A NoSQL variant of a key-value store in which each key can be linked to multiple columns, with each column containing multiple rows.

Zero Normal Form (0NF)   A concept created for this book that alters a physical data model to allow normalization. It does this by ensuring that every record has a primary key.

APPENDIX B

■ ■ ■

Logical Data Modeling Definitions

Software tools for data modeling, database design, and documentation, as well as corporate data dictionaries and the database management system, will all have their own documentation standards. This appendix gives examples of the minimum information about data that needs to be available for database designers, DBAs, database maintenance staff, and application designers and programmers.

Entity

- Entity name

- Entity description

- Entity type (proper, associative, attributive, S-type)

- Name of supertype (if any)

- Name of subtypes (if any)

- Synonyms or aliases (other names for this object)

- Attributes in the entity

- Unique identifier(s)

- Relationships the entity participates in

- Number of occurrences

- Growth rate (can include multiple answers, for example, 700 occurrences per day or 100 during peak hours)

- Insertion, update, deletion rules

- Notes, constraints, other rules, and comments

- History of updates, modifications, and changes to the object by date

© George Tillmann 2017
G. Tillmann, *Usage-Driven Database Design*, DOI 10.1007/978-1-4842-2722-0_18

- Version number
- Entity ID number*

Relationship

- Relationship name
- Relationship description
- Relationship type (unary, binary, n-ary)
- Synonyms or aliases (other names for this object)
- For each entity participant specify the entity name, cardinality, modality (for example, *Buys* in Customer Buys Car from Dealer)

Entity	Cardinality	Modality
Customer	Many	Zero
Car	Many	Zero
Dealer	Many	Zero

- Other constraints
- Notes, rules, and comments
- History of updates, modifications, and changes to the object by date
- Version number
- Relationship ID number*

Attribute

- Attribute name
- Attribute description
- Attribute uniqueness (descriptor, identifier)
- Attribute source (primitive, derived—if derived, what algorithm and other attributes)
- Attribute complexity (simple, group—if group, list attributes in group)

- Attribute valuation (single value, multivalue)

- Synonyms or aliases (other names for this object)

- Size

- Whether attribute is required or optional

- In entity (if more than one, name all)

- Domain

- Edit mask

- Notes, constraints, rules, values, and comments

- History of updates, modifications, and changes to the object by date

- Version number

- Attribute ID number*

Domain

- Domain name

- Domain description

- Data type

- Range

- Acceptable values

- Part of domain (for example, the domain Dates Between December 7, 1941, and September 2, 1945, can be part of the domain Dates)

- Contains domain(s) (covered earlier)

- Synonyms or aliases (other names for this domain)

- Notes, constraints, other rules, and comments

- History of updates, modifications, and changes to the domain

- Version number

- Domain ID number*

*Note: Good form is to assign a unique number to each data object. This number will be useful if two object have the same name (though different contexts), or similar names, or if an object name changes over time.

APPENDIX C

■ ■ ■

Physical Schema Definition Object Definitions

Software tools for data modeling, database design, and documentation, as well as corporate data dictionaries and the database management system, will all have their own documentation standards. This appendix gives examples of the minimum information about data that needs to be available for database designers, DBAs, database maintenance staff, and application designers and programmers.

Record

- Record name
- Record description
- Logical data model name
- Type (proper, associative, attributive, S-type)
- Name of supertype (if any)
- Name of subtype (if any)
- Synonyms or aliases (other names for this object)
- Data items in the record
- Key(s) and type (primary, secondary, etc.)
- Links the record participates in
- Number of occurrences
- Growth rate (can include multiple answers, for example, 700 occurrences per day or 100 during peak hours)
- Cluster
- Partition
- Location (database or file name)

© George Tillmann 2017
G. Tillmann, *Usage-Driven Database Design*, DOI 10.1007/978-1-4842-2722-0_19

- Constraints
- Insertion, update, deletion rules
- Notes, constraints, other rules, and comments
- History of updates, modifications, and changes to the object by date
- Version number
- Record ID number*

Linkage

- Linkage name
- Linkage description
- Linkage type (unary, binary, n-ary)
- Logical data model name
- Synonyms or aliases (other names for this object)
- For each record participant specify the record name, cardinality, modality (for example, *Buys* in Customer Buys Car from Dealer)

Record	Cardinality	Modality
Customer	Many	Zero
Car	Many	Zero
Deale	Many	Zero

- Other constraints
- Notes, rules, and comments
- History of updates, modifications, and changes to the object by date
- Version number
- Link ID number*

Data Item

- Data item name
- Data item description
- Data item uniqueness (descriptor, identifier)
- Key type (if any)
- Data item source (primitive, derived—if derived, what algorithm and other data items)
- Data item complexity (simple, group—if group, list data items in group)
- Data item valuation (single value, multivalue)
- Synonyms or aliases (other names for this object)
- Size
- Whether attribute if required or optional
- Edit mask
- In index(s)
- In record (if more than one, name all)
- Domain
- Notes, constraints, rules, values, and comments
- History of updates, modifications, and changes to the object by date
- Version number
- Data item ID number*

Domain

- Domain name
- Domain description
- Data type
- Range
- Acceptable values
- Part of domain (for example, the domain Dates Between December 7, 1941, and September 2, 1945, can be part of the domain Dates)

- Contains domain(s) (covered earlier)
- Synonyms or aliases (other names for this domain)
- Notes, constraints, other rules, and comments
- History of updates, modifications, and changes to the domain by date
- Version number
- Domain ID number*

Cluster

- Cluster name
- Cluster description
- Parent record type
- Parent cluster key
- Child record type(s)
- Child cluster key
- Synonyms or aliases (other names for this cluster)
- Notes, constraints, other rules, and comments
- History of updates, modifications, and changes to the cluster by date
- Version number
- Cluster ID number*

Partition

- Partition name
- Partition description
- Partition location
- Record types(s)
- Synonyms or aliases (other names for this partition)
- Notes, constraints, other rules, and comments
- History of updates, modifications, and changes to the partition by date

- Version number
- Partition ID number*

Index

- Index name
- Index description
- Data items in key (in proper order)
- On record type
- Index type (ISAM, VSAM, B-tree, Hash, Bitmap, etc.)
- Synonyms or aliases (other names for this index)
- Notes, constraints, other rules, and comments
- History of updates, modifications, and changes to the index by date
- Version number
- Index ID number*

*Note: Good form is to assign a unique number to each data object. This number will be useful if two object have the same name (though different contexts), or similar names, or if an object name changes over time.

APPENDIX D

■ ■ ■

Formulas Used in This Book

Formula Number	Formula	In Chapter	Source
1	$C = \log 2\,(N)\text{-}1$	8	James Martin, *Computer Data-Base Organization*. Prentice Hall, 1977, p. 655.
2	$=(\text{LOG}(N,2))\text{-}1$	8	Excel formula derived from (1).
3	$W = \lfloor \log 2\,(N) \rfloor +1$	8	James Martin, *Computer Data-Base Organization*. Prentice Hall, 1977, p. 654.
4	$=\text{FLOOR}(\text{LOG}(N,2),1)+1$	8	Excel formula derived from (3).
5	$C=\text{Log } N/\text{Log } m$	8 13	Donald E. Knuth, *The Art of Computer Programming: Volume 3 Sorting and Searching*. Addison-Wesley, 1998, Sect. 6.3.
6	$=\text{LOG}(N)/\text{LOG}(m)$	8 13	Excel formula derived from (5).
7	$\text{Percent Split} = 1/(\lceil m/2 \rceil \text{-}1$	8 13	Donald E. Knuth, *The Art of Computer Programming: Volume 3 Sorting and Searching*. Addison-Wesley, 1998, Sect. 6.2.4.
8	$=1/((\text{CEILING}(m,1)/2)\text{-}1$	8 13	Excel formula derived from (7).

© George Tillmann 2017
G. Tillmann, *Usage-Driven Database Design*, DOI 10.1007/978-1-4842-2722-0_20

Where:

- N = Number of (index) entries to search
- C = Average number of compares to find desired entry
- W = Worst-case number of compares
- m = Blocking factor of index
- Percent split = Probability that the index node will have to be split

APPENDIX E

■ ■ ■

List of U3D Deliverables

Logical Data Modeling		
Deliverable	**Definition**	**Examples**
LDM.1: Logical data model (E-R diagram)	The diagram showing all entities and relationships	Figure 4-12
LDM.2: Logical data model object definitions (data dictionary)	Detailed documentation for each entity, attribute, relationship, and domain	Figures 4-13 through 4-16 Appendix B
LDM.3: Logical data modeling notes	Any comments, advice, difficulties, questions, suggestions, warnings, or other information the logical data modeler wants to communicate to physical designers	

Physical Schema Definition—Step 1: Transformation		
Deliverable	**Definition**	**Examples**
PSD.1.1: Physical data model	The physical representation of the logical data model	Figure 10-6
PSD.1.2: Physical data model object definitions (data dictionary)	Record types, data elements, linkages, keys, formats, and so on	Figures 10-7 through 10-10 Appendix C
PSD.1.3: Transformation notes	A narrative or journal created by the database designer of the activities, issues, and decisions made during step 1, Transformation	

© George Tillmann 2017
G. Tillmann, *Usage-Driven Database Design*, DOI 10.1007/978-1-4842-2722-0_21

Physical Schema Definition—Step 2, Utilization

Deliverable	Definition	Examples
PSD.2.1: Rationalized physical data model	A subset of the physical data model that reflects exactly how the user or application will use database	Figure 11-10
PSD.2.2: Updated physical data model object definitions	The same physical definitions created in step 1, Transformation, updated with any necessary changes made during step 2, Utilization	Appendix C
PSD.2.3: Usage scenarios	Functional summaries describing how the database will be used by the application	
PSD.2.4: Usage maps	A mapping of the individual usage scenarios onto the physical data model showing how the application must navigate the database	Figure 11-7
PSD.2.5: Combined usage map	All the individual usage map information on a single diagram	Figure 11-8 Figure 11-9
PSD.2.6: Utilization notes	A narrative or journal created by the database designer of the activities, issues, and decisions made during step 2, Utilization	

Physical Schema Definition—Step 3, Formalization

Deliverable	Definition	Examples
PSD.3.1: Functional physical database design diagram	A database diagram showing the record types and links	Figure 12-5
PSD.3.2: Functional schema DDL	Two versions should be created: (1) generic DDL conforming to the database architecture and (2) vendor product and version specific	
PSD.3.3: Functional subschema DDL	Two versions should be created: (1) generic DDL conforming to the database architecture and (2) vendor product and version specific	
PSD.3.4: Functional physical object definitions	The same physical definitions created in step 1, Transformation, updated with any necessary changes made during step 2, Utilization, updated with step 3, Formalization, information	Appendix C
PSD.3.5: Formalization notes	A narrative or journal created by the database designer of the activities, issues, and decisions made during step 3, Formalization	

Physical Schema Definition—Step 4, Customization

Deliverable	Definition	Examples
PSD.4.1: Enhanced database design diagram	The final physical database design diagram	Figure 13-11
PSD.4.2: Enhanced schema (DDL)	Update of the schema DDL created in step 3, Formalization	
PSD.4.3: Enhanced subschemas (DDL)	Update of all subschema DDL created in step 3, Formalization	
PSD.4.4: Enhanced database object definitions	Update of all database object definitions to reflect step 4, Customization changes	Figures 13-12, 13-13, and 13-14 Appendix C
PSD.4.5: Customization notes	A narrative or journal created by the database designer of the activities, issues, and decisions made during step 4, Customization	

Index

© George Tillmann 2017
G. Tillmann, *Usage-Driven Database Design*, DOI 10.1007/978-1-4842-2722-0

■ U

■ V

■ W, X, Y

■ Z

Get the eBook for only $5!

Why limit yourself?

With most of our titles available in both PDF and ePUB format, you can access your content wherever and however you wish—on your PC, phone, tablet, or reader.

Since you've purchased this print book, we are happy to offer you the eBook for just $5.

To learn more, go to http://www.apress.com/companion or contact support@apress.com.

Apress®

Printed in the United States
By Bookmasters

Printed in the United States
By Bookmasters